WBI DEVELOPMENT STUDIES

MW01104256

Leadership and Innovation in Subnational Government

Case Studies from Latin America

Edited by

Tim Campbell
Harald Fuhr

The World Bank
Washington, D.C.

Library of Congress Cataloging-in-Publication Data

Leadership and innovation in subnational government / Tim Campbell, Harald Fuhr.
    p.   cm. — (WBI development studies)
    Includes bibliographical references.
    ISBN 0-8213-5707-7
    1. Decentralization in government—Latin America. 2. Decentralization in
government—Latin America—Case studies. I. Campbell, Tim. II. Fuhr, Harald.
III. Series.

JL959.5.D42L43 2004
352.2'83—dc22
                                                            2004040701

Contents

Foreword

Cities face many new challenges in meeting the demands of decentralized governance, including adapting to the global business environment, decentralizing governance, and achieving democratic choice making. With decentralization, democratization, and globalization, cities now have more decisions to make, more money to spend, and a vastly more open political and economic system in which to operate. These conditions shift the focus of policy attention in nations and cities. To achieve sustainable cities and improve public sector management, both national and local authorities must address the capacity of cities to reform and to innovate.

This book takes stock of promising innovations that began to appear in local government across the region of Latin America during the 1990s. The purpose of this work—in contrast to many reports that document best practice—is to deepen our understanding of the genesis and evolution of change as local leaders cope with the challenges of governing in decentralized democracies. One of the most striking features of change in the region is that local authorities often are creating change without help from outside donors. The authors, Tim Campbell and Harald Fuhr, call such enterprising risk takers an "engine of change." Specific cases of innovation have been documented in this book covering the core business areas of cities: finance, popular participation, service delivery, privatization, and personnel management. The book aims to show ways, both in policy and practice, to increase and sustain the velocity of this engine of change.

One of the central messages of this book is that donors, by supporting creation and adoption of best practice, can have a cost-effective impact on the next stages of reform in the region. But to do so, the World Bank and other donors must focus on the policies at the local level as well as engage in issues of urban management and systemic reform that occur when political reform takes place. The Bank can continue to build on the foundation of participation in public choice and work more actively to help local actors learn from each other.

We are especially pleased to acknowledge the support of the German Technical Cooperation (better known as the GTZ), the Swedish International Development Agency, and the U.S. Agency for International Development in the production of this book and the study on which the book is based.

The publication of this book contributes to a stream of learning activities and materials in urban development, fiscal decentralization, and public participation and empowerment already flowing through the World Bank Institute in an ongoing exchange with its partners and clients.

Frannie A. Léautier
Vice President
World Bank Institute

Acknowledgments

The authors wish to acknowledge the important contributions and assistance provided by many people during the course of this project. Our thanks go first to team members Florence Eid, Travis Katz, and Daniel Taillant, who made contributions at every stage of the Innovations Study. Taillant compiled an exceptionally comprehensive bibliography on decentralization and helped organize and coordinate the case work. Eid and Katz helped to arrange workshops and review materials and contributed in many other ways. They also conducted field work and authored cases. We are also grateful to all the authors of cases. In addition to accepting the framework for field work, the authors provided valuable insight and ideas into the several regional seminars organized to discuss case study findings. We also recognize our institutional partners for their patience and good, especially of Per Froberg and Goren Tannerfeld of the Swedish International Development Authority, Albrecht Stockmayer of Gesellschaft fûr Technische Zusammenarbeit, and Mark Schneider of the U.S. Agency for International Development. Thanks also to Dianne Ferguson for her editorial work and to Marion Hoermann for reviewing early drafts. Finally, many thanks to Bob Ebel and Mila Freire for recommending the book for the series on decentralization and development, to John Didier of the World Bank Institute for his patience and cooperative spirit, and to Alice Faintich for her tireless editorial work managing the initial editing and preparation of the final product.

Contributors

Tim Campbell directs the urban management program at the World Bank Institute. He holds a bachelor's degree in political science, a master's degree in city and regional planning from the University of California, Berkeley, and a Ph.D. in urban studies and planning from the Massachusetts Institute of Technology. (tcampbell@worldbank.org)

Rafael de la Cruz is a senior urban economist in the Inter-American Development Bank, Washington, D.C. He holds a Ph.D. in economics and a master's degree in political sociology from the Paris University in France. (rafaelcr@iadb.org)

Florence Eid is an assistant professor of finance and economics at the School of Business, the American University of Beirut, Lebanon. She holds a Ph.D. in organization economics from the Massachusetts Institute of Technology and has worked with the World Economic Forum, the World Bank, the United Nations Development Programme, and the Ford Foundation. (feid@alum.mit.edu)

Harald Fuhr is professor and chair of international politics at the Economics and Social Science Department, University of Potsdam, Germany. He holds a Diploma (MA) in political science from the University of Marburg, and a Ph.D. in social sciences as well as a habilitation in political and administrative sciences from the University of Konstanz. (hfuhr@rz.uni-potsdam.de)

Travis Katz is a strategy consultant for McKinsey & Company in San Francisco. He holds an AB in public policy from Stanford University and an MBA from the Wharton School of Business, University of Pennsylvania. (Traviskatz@yahoo.com)

Arianna Legovini is a senior economist at the Inter-American Development Bank. She completed her coursework and exams for a doctorate in economics at the University of Maryland at College Park. (arianal@iadb.org)

Josef Leitmann is a senior urban planner with the World Bank. He holds a Ph.D. in city and regional planning from the University of California, Berkeley, and an MPP from the Kennedy School of Government at Harvard University. (jleitmann@worldbank.org)

Alberto Maldonado is a senior analyst in the public sector unit of the Departmento Nacional de Planeacion in Bogota, Colombia. He completed a master's degree in Urban Studies and Planning at the Massachusetts Institute of Technology and holds an AB from the Univesidad de los Andes in Bogota, Colombia. (amaldona@supercabletv.net.co)

Zander Navarro is professor and researcher in the postgraduate program in rural sociology at the Federal University of Rio Grande do Sul, in Porto Alegre, Brazil. He holds a BA in Agronomy and a master's degree in rural sociology from the Federal University of Rio Grande do Sul and a Ph.D. from the University of Sussex in England. (mnavarro@portoweb.com.br)

Fernando Rojas is sector leader in the public sector in the Latin American region of the World Bank. He holds a law degree from the Universidad de los Andes and a master's degree in public administration from the Kennedy School of Government at Harvard University. (frojas@worldbank.org)

Roberto Dimas Vasconcellos del Santoro is executive director for operations at PARANACIDADE in Curitiba, Brazil. Mr. Santoro, who has a bachelor's degree in civil engineering, holds a master's in urban management from the Compiegne University of Technology in France. (santoro@pr.gov.br)

Mark L. Schneider was formerly director of the Peace Corps in Latin America and assistant administrator for Latin America and the Caribbean for the U.S. Agency for International Development. He is currently senior vice president of the International Crisis Group, based in Washington, D.C. He holds an honorary doctor of law from American University and a master's in political science from San Jose State University. (icgwashington@ crisisweb.org)

Alfredo Stein was formerly a consultant to the PRODEL project in Nicaragua and is currently affiliated with the Swedish International Development Agency in Central America. (alfredo.stein@foreign.ministry.se)

Albrecht Stockmayer is the head of the Governance and Gender Team of the German Technical Cooperation (GTZ), Eschborn, Germany. Prior to this appointment he headed the Governance Outreach office at the Organization for Economic Co-operation and Development. Dr. Stockmayer was educated as a lawyer and business administrator, and he holds a Ph.D. from Johann Wolfgang Goethe University, Frankfurt am Main, Germany, and a master's degree (LL.M.) from the University of Michigan Law School. (Albrecht.stockmayer@gtz.de)

Daniel Taillant heads the Responsible Business Programs at the Center for Human Rights and Development in Cordoba, Argentina. He holds an AB in political science from the University of California, Berkeley, and a master's in political economics and Latin American studies from Georgetown University. (Daniel@cedha.org.ar)

Part 1

Background and Scope

1

Introduction and Preview

Tim Campbell, World Bank
Harald Fuhr, University of Potsdam

Highly centralized government has been the norm in many parts of the world until very recently, and state, provincial, and local governments have usually been the weak partners in the governing relationship. These arrangements are changing rapidly as nations decentralize and leaders in many cities take up the challenge of inventing and implementing better local government (see Campbell 2003). This book reports the findings of a multicountry research project that explored processes of reform at the local level, particularly innovations in decentralized democracies of Latin America in the mid 1990s (Campbell, Fuhr, and Eid 1995). The aim of the Innovations Study was to draw insight from the experiences of innovative reform in order to understand the dynamics of progressive change and to be able to better formulate policies of decentralization and reform.

Many governments around the globe are, in one way or another, moving toward greater decentralization to local authorities, along with increased democratization and stronger market orientation (Bennett 1990). Subnational governments are on the move toward change as well.[1] The

---

1. The term "subnational" will be used throughout the text to describe *all* levels below the national level—local and municipal, regional and intermediate, and meso. The terms "local" and "municipal" are used interchangeably, and the terms "intermediate," "meso," "regional," and "provincial" are used interchangeably, unless otherwise noted.

world could have as many as 10,000 cities with populations of 100,000 or more by 2025, including more than 800 cities with a half-million people or more. Most of the world's 35 megacities—cities with populations of 10 million and more—will be located in the developing world by that year. These cities will, for the most part, be affected by decentralization of the public sector. Better urban management is high on the agenda of many governments in Africa, Asia, and Latin America. During the 1990s some 70 countries, of all sizes and governance systems, embarked on a strategy of decentralization, expecting from it everything from improvements in allocating, managing, and mobilizing resources to better quality services for citizens, more accountability, and, eventually, more balanced economic and social development.

Interestingly, the processes of globalization and decentralization seem to go hand-in-hand and influence each other.[2] Faster and cheaper international communication has allowed local experiences to "go global," meaning that global perspectives and experiences from different regions have become increasingly available to local arenas. Citizens around the world are communicating better than ever before, sharing experiences about their governments and feeling encouraged to articulate their interests. Such interlinked processes have influenced local decisionmakers to consider alternatives to the way they do business. They have also provided decisionmakers with new incentives to make practical use of international experiences by learning lessons, forging creative imitations, and even leapfrogging, or bypassing, pitfalls of reform. Mayors and governors around the world are increasingly interested in sharing ideas about better local governance and learning from each other, particularly about how to establish new relationships with their staff, their citizens, and private sectors, and how to encourage new linkages between their jurisdictions and the global environment (Tendler 1997).

Demand for knowledge about decentralization—and innovative ways to achieve reform—is thus increasing rapidly, and Latin America is perhaps the most experienced region in reforming state and local governments (see Burki, Perry, and Dillinger 1999; Cabrero Mendoza 1995; Campbell 2003; de la Cruz 1998; and Rojas 1995). But viable and capable local government in the region is based on a complex blend of historical and contemporary social, economic, and political factors. Only some of these factors are fully under the control of present-day governments. In many contexts,

---

2. See Jun and Wright (1996, pp. 2–3), for a discussion within industrial countries.

the decentralization process is highly fluid, and many problem areas complicate the pathway of reform once policymakers embark on redesigning intergovernmental arrangements.[3]

The purpose of this book is not to provide another exhaustive review of the pros and cons of decentralization in the Latin American context. Nor is it to gauge the merits of specific innovations. Rather, the objective is to explore the mechanisms that lead to invention at the local level and to understand better how decentralization helps to foster innovation and how, in turn, it benefits from innovation. Like other areas of the public sector that have begun with, or became objects of, institutional change, decentralization can lead to many of the desired outcomes only under certain conditions. Otherwise, as some authors have argued, decentralization policies run the risk of doing more harm than good, and overall public sector efficiency and effectiveness may suffer considerably (Prud'homme 1994). Indeed, knowing more about pitfalls is key for policymakers. Yet, although there is an emerging consensus on a set of preconditions that need to be met at the central level, little is known about the necessary conditions for success at lower levels, and what subnational governments can do to make decentralization work.

This book is about inventing successes and good practices of governments that are "closer to the people." Numerous examples throughout Latin America indicate—often despite macroeconomic instability, high inflation, and strong top-down regulation—that subnational actors have repeatedly achieved what their central counterparts preached: sound policymaking, better administration, better services, more participation, and sustained economic development. But what makes some governments change course and move toward innovation? What triggers experimentation and, eventually, turns ordinary practice into good practice?

The book answers some of these questions. It goes beyond a mere documentation of good and best practice, which is increasingly provided through international networks and Internet sites.[4] Instead, it seeks a better

---

3. Compare the discussions in Burki, Perry, and Dillinger (1999); Tanzi (1996); and World Bank (1997, chapter 7), which all reiterate the need for sound overall macroeconomic management and well-performing central-level institutions in order to make decentralization work effectively.

4. For both developing and industrial countries see, for example, Ayudaurbana, Red Inter-Municipal: http://www.ayudaurbana.com; Cities Alliance: http://www.citiesalliance.org/citiesalliancehomepage.nsf; Cities-of-Tomorrow: http://www.cities-of-tomorrow.net; City Development Strategies Initiative: http://www.citydev.

understanding of the origins and fates of such successes at the micro level. The case studies and analytical chapters seek to explain:

- How good practice is born at the local level
- Where innovative ideas come from
- How such ideas are introduced in a new context, successfully implemented, and propagated locally and beyond
- What donors can do to effectively assist processes of self-induced and bottom-up change.

The volume is based on research known as the Innovations Study, which was carried out by the World Bank's Latin America and the Caribbean Technical Department from 1995 to 1997 under the management of the editors. The Innovations Study followed in the footsteps of Perlman (1987, 1990, 1993), Hopkins (1995), and Clark (1994). It documented 21 cases of successful innovations at the local and regional levels. About half of these cases are presented here. Others are mentioned to illustrate points or add dimension to the analysis. All case studies were based on a common framework that consisted of a set of questions guiding research in different contexts.

The cases produced a wide range of insights and suggestions:

- Visionary leaders innovate—and though natural leaders cannot be cloned, outside agencies can help to stimulate leadership and encourage prospective risk takers. Because leaders learn from each other, outside agencies have substantial scope to facilitate the learning process through such steps as gathering good ideas, financing basic informational and managerial tools, offsetting risks

---

org/intro.html; European Good Practice Information Service: http://www3.iclei. org/egpis; European Local Government: http://www.elgo.co.uk; GTZ-Network for Decentralization and Municipal Development (Urbanet): http://www.gtz.de/ urbanet; Harvard University, Institute for Government Innovation: http://www. innovations.harvard.edu; Local Economic Forums (Scotland): http://www. scotland.gov.uk/enterprise/localeconomicforums/bestpractice.asp; Local Government Association: http://www.lga.gov.uk; National Office of Local Government (Australia): http://www.nolg.gov.au; *Premio Gobierno y Gestión Local*, Mexico: http://www.premiomunicipal.org.mx/site2002/index.php; U.S. Conference of Mayors Best Practices of City Governments http://www.usmayors.org/uscm/best_practices; U.N.-Habitat Best Practices Database: http://www.bestpractices.org and http://www.sustainabledevelopment.org; and UN-Habitat Best Practice and Local Leadership Programme: http://www.iclei.org/iclei/bpsearch.htm.

of innovation, incubating promising ventures, and disseminating success stories.

- The counterparts of leaders are grassroots organizations. Successful innovators engage local groups extensively to sound out needs and get feedback. Leaders also have broken new ground in communicating to the public and mobilizing local groups to help implement small-scale projects.
- Innovators often restore the severed ties between voters and their governments. Decades of centralized governance have broken this linkage. Restoring it is fundamental to mobilizing finance, recovering costs, instilling legitimacy, and ensuring sustainability in decentralized democracies.
- The arena for reform has shifted to the local level in Latin America, and many lessons for the next steps for reform can be drawn from the experiences of risk-taking leaders who have innovated on their own, often without the help of outside agencies.
- The experiences in Latin America have structural and practical similarities to countries in many other regions undergoing decentralization. This suggests that Latin America's experience can be helpful to leaders in other parts of the world.
- Virtually all of the cases studied are idiosyncratic in terms of conditions and the circumstances of their creation. But they also share features, or at least a family resemblance, in three specific phases of Hopkins' cycle of innovations—origins, launch, and dissemination (1995). Many findings and insights in these three areas are drawn from the case materials appearing in this volume.
- The overarching message arising from this work has ineluctable policy consequences for governments and assistance agencies at all levels. Leaders and innovators at the local level are a central part not only of the decentralization process, but also of the reform mechanisms needed to implement democratic governance itself. This message assumes greater significance in the contemporary circumstances of progressive globalization of the economy, trade, learning, and reform.

Sustaining Innovation and Reform

These and many other changes—for instance the incorporation of civil society and the private sector into local public life—have transformed the nature and style of local government in many cities. More important, a wave of reforms sampled in this book creates new opportunities for self-sustained growth. However, the policy dialogue between governments and international assistance organizations has lagged somewhat behind the dynamic of change at the subnational levels. The policy dialogue is usually focused, appropriately, on sustaining fiscal balance and redressing the mismatch between local functions and financial resources. But the translation of this focus into operations—for example, in assistance in public sector modernization and state reform—often fails to address municipal levels and ignores the growing cultural and business matrix emerging in cities and regions. Several countries exhibit robust horizontal linkages being forged by business interests and actors in civic affairs. These alliances underpin local and regional economic activity in industrial countries, but they are not well accommodated in strategies to implement decentralization by contemporary development assistance agencies.

Still another feature of the new era of governance is that local governments are claiming a more prominent place in national and local growth (for example, see Campbell 2003; World Bank 1997, 1999a, 1999b). Unless central governments and international agencies buttress the mechanisms that produce innovative change at the local level, such as civil society engagement and nongovernmental organization initiatives, policies of decentralization and reform stand a smaller chance of being sustained despite the creative energies at the local level. Newly emerging regional interests and proactive local governments, taken together, constitute fertile ground for development assistance agencies. Donor agencies can leverage assistance by taking advantage of, and building on, the new dynamic already underway in Latin America. A key step in moving toward self-sustaining change is to understand the process of innovation.

For agencies like the World Bank and other donors, perhaps the most important finding of this study is the many opportunities to foster and deepen reform, especially at the local level. Though many innovations trace their roots to national reforms and to a new environment for innovative leadership, actions for reform at the local level are also needed. Innovators are driven by a desire to meet public needs, and leaders are ready for new ideas. They show a growing self-interest in controlling their own destinies by taking advantage of trade pacts, competing for investments, and generating local jobs. Donors can help in many ways. They can shape the institutional environment to encourage change, incubate promising ventures, and evaluate and disseminate results. The strategic aim should be to turn spontaneous change into sustained reform.

Roadmap to the Book

This book is divided into three parts. Part 1 (chapters 1–4) surveys the broad political and institutional context of reform, particularly the underlying incentives that have induced reform in Latin America. It also discusses the method for studying innovation in this context. Chapter 2 helps to locate our case studies within this framework; chapters 3 and 4 provide material on the background study, particularly research questions, methodology, and strategy. Part 2 (chapters 5–9) presents individual case studies arranged according to the type of reform and innovation implemented. Five areas are explored: fiscal management and resource mobilization (chapter 5), administrative performance and management (chapter 6), participation in local and regional decisionmaking (chapter 7), public service provision (chapter 8), and public-private collaboration (chapter 9). Part 3 (chapters 10 and 11) widens the focus by turning to the implications of these findings. Chapter 10 looks at challenges to national and subnational government in the region and chapter 11 discusses policy lessons for decisionmakers, both in subnational government and in agencies that assist governments undergoing decentralization in Latin America.

References

Bennett, Robert J., ed. 1990. *Decentralization, Local Governments, and Markets: Toward a Post-Welfare Agenda.* New York: Oxford University Press.

Burki, Shahid Javed, Guillermo Perry, and William Dillinger. 1999. *Beyond the Center. Decentralizing the State.* Washington, D.C.: World Bank.

Cabrero Mendoza, Enrique, ed. 1995. *La nueva gestión municipal en México. Analisis de experiencias innovadoras en gobiernos locales.* Mexico, D.F.: Center for Economic Research and Training.

Campbell, Tim. 2003. *The Quiet Revolution.* Pittsburgh, Pa.: The University of Pittsburgh Press.

Campbell, Tim, Harald Fuhr, and Florence Eid. 1995. "Decentralization in LAC: Best Practices and Policy Lessons." Initiating memorandum for a regional study. World Bank, Washington, D.C.

Clark, Terry N., ed. 1994. *Urban Innovation: Creative Strategies for Turbulent Times.* London: Sage Publications.

de la Cruz, Rafael, ed. 1998. *Descentralizacion en perspectiva.* Caracas, República Bolivariana de Venezuela: Instituto de Estudios Superiores de Administración.

Hopkins, Elwood. 1995. "The Life Cycle of Urban Innovations," vol I. Urban Management Program Working Paper Series. World Bank, Washington, D.C.

Jun, Jong S., and Deil S. Wright. 1996. "Globalization and Decentralization: An Overview." In Jong S. Jun and Deil S. Wright, *Globalization and Decentralization: Institutional Contexts, Policy Issues, and Intergovernmental Relations in Japan and the United States.* Washington, D.C.: Georgetown University Press.

Perlman, Janice. 1987. "Mega Cities and Innovative Technologies." *International Quarterly of Urban Policy* 4(2): 128–86.

———. 1990. "A Dual Strategy for Deliberate Social Change in Cities." Guest Editor, *CITIES, International Journal of Urban Policy Planning* (special issue on Urban Innovation for the 21st Century 7(1): 3–15).

———. 1993. "Mega-Cities: Global Urbanization and Innovation." In Shabbir Cheema, ed., *Urban Management: Policies and Innovations in Developing Countries.* Westport, Conn.: Greenwood/Praeger Press.

Prud'homme, Remy. 1994. "The Danger of Decentralization." *The World Bank Research Observer* 10(2): 201–20.

Rojas, Fernando. 1995. "The Political, Economic and Institutional Dimensions of Fiscal Decentralization in Latin America." Unpublished manuscript, U.N. Development Programme, New York.

Tanzi, Vitor. 1996. "Fiscal Federalism and Decentralization: A Review of Some Efficiency and Macroeconomic Aspects." In M. Bruno and B. Pleskovic, eds., *Annual World Bank Conference on Development Economics, 1995.* Washington, D.C.: World Bank.

Tendler, Judith. 1997. *Good Government in the Tropics.* Baltimore, Md.: Johns Hopkins University Press.

World Bank. 1997. *World Development Report 1997: The State in a Changing World.* Oxford, U.K.: Oxford University Press.

———. 1999a. *Annual World Bank Conference on Development in Latin America and the Caribbean 1999. Decentralization and Accountability of the Public Sector.* Proceedings of a Conference held in Valdivia, Chile, June 20–22, 1999. Washington, D.C.: World Bank.

———. 1999b. *Cities in Transition. Bank Strategy on Urban Development and Local Governance.* Washington, D.C.

2

Context of Change: Decentralization and State Reform in Latin America

Tim Campbell, World Bank
Harald Fuhr, University of Potsdam

The decentralization of governance—defined as the shift in decisionmaking and spending power from central to regional and local governments—began in much of Latin America well before the 1980s. In the early years of decentralization, many governments followed a similar, and rapid, succession of steps that handed municipalities resources and decisionmaking power far beyond anything local officials had imagined in the previous decades. Campbell (2003) calls this rapid change a "quiet revolution," and argues that the rapidity and wholesale nature of change in very many cities created a new model of governance characterized by fresh leadership, widespread participation, and a new willingness to mobilize revenues. These changes, in turn, contributed to the dynamic that triggered innovation in the region.

Organizational inefficiency and low institutional performance in many local governments were part of the justification that sustained state-directed development. Weak local governments fit logically into a "traditional" system of financing municipal development and making corresponding arrangements between officials in local governments and those in the larger public sector. Particularly in the oil-exporting countries, macroeconomic policies and strong top-down financing arrangements for subnational governments provided strong incentives for rapid expenditure and deepened nonmarket interactions, such as rent seeking. Both national and local decisionmakers tended to engage in bargaining processes and populist and clientelist rent allocation to acquire and maintain political support.

Mayors and city council members depended traditionally on the central political parties for advancing their political careers, and local options for electing mayors and governors were quite limited throughout the region until well into the 1980s. Added to these political factors was the severe constraint on local fiscal autonomy. All in all, local policymakers had few incentives to make long-term policy commitments. As long as the center had resources to spend and allocate, policymakers had to maintain vertical, and politicized, relationships within the public sector. Bargaining and spending patterns were rational for decisionmakers at the central and local levels. In a nutshell, and paradoxically, the more resources the center had available, the weaker were the incentives to improve public sector performance.

Beginning in the early 1980s, state-led and rent-financed development in Latin America became increasingly nonviable in economic, financial, and political terms. In addition, factors around the world helped trigger a change. Campbell (2003) suggests that many seeds of decentralization were sown in the 1980s. Decentralization in Spain, the collapse of the Soviet Union, and subsequent events such as the Velvet Revolution in Czechoslovakia and the much publicized demonstrations in China's Tienamen Square, all served to heighten the already growing regional tensions inside many Latin American countries.

Accordingly, a new interest in public sector reform and decentralization emerged progressively both at the center and at subnational levels. Local officials found new incentives to foster participation. Compared with other regions, demand in Latin America for decentralization—that is, the clamor for power sharing and autonomy in decisionmaking—was strong at the subnational level. Another factor, unique to Latin America, bolstered this movement: clusters of "civil organizations" had flourished at the local level under national authoritarian governments or military dictatorships, successfully ensuring citizen participation. This maintenance of civil and democratic resistance helped lead to a significant reemergence of local level politics.[1] In Latin America, decentralization thus has been accompanied from the very beginning by a strong demand for democratization at all levels of government.

---

1. Such traditions, however, have also led to some unintended consequences. For example, they contributed to a strong political demand for increasing subnational autonomy in Brazil, which was eventually expressed in the Brazilian constitution of 1988 (see de Souza 1997). Strong state and local government autonomy has not yet, however, been accompanied by credible rules guiding intergovernmental relationships, creating checks and balances, and restraining arbitrary action at subnational levels effectively (see World Bank 1995, 1997, chapter 7).

Emerging Model of Governance

The pace of decentralization in the 1980s and 1990s was intermittent and marked by dramatic financial rearrangements and stunning political reforms. Although governments moved at different paces, and the centralist instincts of some national policymakers slowed or reversed reforms, nearly all governments took actions in three areas: fiscal relations, democratization, and local governance. The combined effect of these changes led to the creation of a new model of governance.

Political and Fiscal Reform

In the rush to share power, many governments promulgated decentralization without fully thinking through how national objectives—for instance in health, education, and welfare—could be reconciled with decentralized powers of decisionmaking and spending by subnational governments. Thus, for the first few years of decentralization, transferred monies in large quantities could be caricatured as "finances chasing functions." (Although in some cases local governments were saddled with new responsibilities without transferred revenue). Most local governments were left with a good deal of discretion and uncertainty about service responsibilities. This ambiguity, plus continued spending by national governments on local matters, left excess funds at the local level, at least during the initial years of decentralization. Local governments from Guatemala to Argentina began to handle between 10 and 40 percent of total public spending, amounting to significant fractions of GDP (see table 2.1).

But even though some state governments sank into debt—Sao Paulo and Cordoba were two outstanding examples—municipal governments by and large avoided precipitous spending, at least in the initial years of decentralization. They did not create destabilizing pressures as many observers had feared. This book looks at some of the most progressive subnational governments, such as the municipalities of Manizales and Valledupar and the province of Mendoza, thereby showing how decentralization was successfully implemented.

Democratization

The transition to democracy represented another trend sweeping the region, and it bolstered the fiscal nature of reform in Latin America. In the mid 1980s, countries began selecting not only national leaders democratically, but also virtually all of the 14,000 executive and legislative officeholders on the state

Table 2.1. *Changes in Subnational Finance, Selected Latin American Countries, 1974–94*
(percentage of expenditures or revenues for all levels of government)

Country	Subnational expenditures			Subnational revenues		
	1974	1994	Trend	1974	1994	Trend
Argentina	25	45	↗	25	37	↗
Brazil	30	38	↗	23	25	?
Chile	2	9	↗	2	5	?
Colombia	25	33	↗	16	18	?
Mexico	19	29	↗	9	17	↗

? Trend is not clear.
Note: Data for all levels of government other than central government. Data include transfers from central government to subnational governments. Arrows indicated changes of 5 percentage points or more. Where data for 1974 or 1994 were unavailable (indicated by italics), data for the closest available year were used. Data for Mexico for 1974 were estimated.
Source: International Monetary Fund (various years).

and local levels. Moreover, many countries promulgated such electoral reforms as switching to uninominal elections and requiring candidates to publish intended spending programs during their campaigns. Along with making electoral choices, voters in many countries also participated in planning and spending decisions and implementing public works projects.

Internal Governance

The additional power and revenues fueled democratization at the local level, creating new energy. Many in the new generation of leaders, fresh with mandates and ideas for reform, began to rejuvenate municipal institutions. Internal changes complemented the ongoing national reforms. A new governance model emerged, which was characterized by (a) a new leadership style, (b) more professional staffing in executive agencies, (c) tax and revenue increases, and (d) much stronger participation in public decisionmaking.

Perhaps the most startling change was that more qualified persons began seeking local public office. Surveys of officeholders elected in the mid 1990s in Central America, Paraguay, and Colombia revealed that the number of professionals jumped from around 11 percent in the early 1980s to more than 46 percent in the 1990s. In addition, the new officeholders brought in more professional staff. A sample of 16 municipalities in Colombia, for which detailed data were gathered, showed that the ratio of total staff to professionals dropped from 12:1 to 4:1 over a 10-year period. Mayors reported that these changes were aimed at improving services.

Local tax reform provided more evidence of a new model of governance. Contrary to some predictions, many local governments were able to increase levies on their populations because, to paraphrase many local executives, "when taxpayers see they are getting new services, they are willing to pay" (see table 2.2). In Colombia's municipalities, which number more than 1,000, the rate of property tax increases doubled, on average, from 7. 5 percent in the late 1980s to 15 percent in the early 1990s. The Colombian increases were partly due to requirements for revenue sharing, and partly because, in certain cities, mayors sought to link levies, like gasoline surcharges and betterment taxes, to specific improvements in service. In some cases, mayors simplified cadastres or land ownership records (La Paz), introduced self-assessments (Bogota), or did both (Quito). Mayors of other cities (Puerto Alegre, Tijuana) simply raised property tax collections.

Mayors also stepped up participatory consultations, using a large variety of communications and consultative techniques to sound out their constituents' preferences. This participatory process unleashed a new level of expectations in many cities, making it difficult to ignore the voices of voters and taxpayers in successive rounds of programs and elections.

The new leadership, increased citizen participation, higher taxes, and stronger administrations all pointed to a new model of governance. With the departure of a rent-financed economy, central authorities could no longer afford paternalistic and clientelist practices. Democratization began to strengthen civil society and buttress civic movements. The power arrangements that emerged created incentives for horizontal connections at the

Table 2.2. *Own-Source Revenue Increases, Selected Cities and Years*

City	Years	Increase (%)
Puerto Alegre	1991–95	22
Tijuana	1989–94	58
Manizales	1988–94	165
La Paz	1990–95	218
Valledupar	1988–94	246
Villanueva (HO)	1991–93	373

Source: Authors.

local level and for vertical, or intergovernmental, arrangements characterized by a demand for more autonomy from the central government and a sharing of revenue and power. The sum effect, in macroeconomic terms, was the emergence of a new and different conception of the state, with local governments playing a more pronounced role and attracting professional players. Public and private sector actors began to see new opportunities and to feel pressure to invent better ways to conduct their business.

Policy Environment of Decentralization

Ironically, a number of policy weaknesses in the decentralization process may have set back reform efforts even as they inadvertently fostered innovation at the local level. Reviews of World Bank operations, analytical work (for instance, Lopez Murphy 1994; Peterson 1997), and the record of policy dialogue within Latin America concur on a number of weak points about decentralized arrangements.

REVENUES. Revenue sharing raced ahead of expenditure needs for balanced decentralization, as well as ahead of efforts to discipline spending by subnational governments. In addition, evidence indicates that financing arrangements often *preceded*—although, in theory, they should *follow*—functional assignments of spending.[2] When expenditure assignments precede finances , decentralization can be a short-term method of "pushing down the deficit" to subnational levels of government, especially during macroeconomic adjustment. Although this problem was practically universal, the prescribed procedure would involve a sector-by-sector, level-by-level analysis of service need, delivery capacity, and benefits. In any case, reformed intergovernmental relationships must be tailored within a framework that ensures overall macroeconomic stability and fiscal discipline, and that encourages performance at *all* governmental levels. Virtually none of the governments in Latin America conducted this sector-by-sector analysis in any detail before intergovernmental revenue sharing began to flow to local governments. As a consequence, newly elected mayors suddenly, in the first phases of decentralization, had greatly increased revenues. Their spending decisions had new force and new meaning, and these conditions opened opportunities to try new arrangements.

---

2. For the complex issue of balancing, and progressively defining, revenue and expenditure assignments for subnational governments, see Bahl and Linn (1992); Bird (1994); Shah (1998); Winkler (1994); and World Bank (1997, chapter 7).

FISCAL CHOICE MODEL. Many governments, buttressed by donor agencies, perhaps gave excessive emphasis to a fiscal choice model of local governance. They placed the focus of decisionmaking and spending on the options and choices that were shaped by local governments and, increasingly through the 1990s, made by local citizens. Governments and donors may also have been too narrowly focused on property taxes as the chief target for local resource mobilization, and this may have suggested too narrow a focus for new mayors on sources of finance. More analysis is needed in the areas of devising alternative means of raising and managing local revenues and improving voter-taxpayer communication with government ("voice and choice").

MESO LEVEL. Most decentralization policies in Latin America focused excessively on the municipal level of government as the main unit of analysis and addressed its relationship only with the center. This approach tends to omit or underestimate the relevance of the intermediate (meso) level of government, which often plays a pivotal role in decentralized systems. Omission of the meso level in policy design and analysis, such as in Colombia and Bolivia, has been found to limit options and preclude potential synergy and economies of scale that result from both continuity and efficient exchange of information on intergovernmental relations.

FISCAL AND ADMINSTRATIVE COOPERATION. More mechanisms were needed concerning intergovernmental fiscal and, particularly, administrative cooperation. The expansion in the role of intermediate governments and the occasional fiscal indebtedness in federated republics (for instance in Brazilian states) suggest that more attention should have been given to vertical cooperation and control. In addition, numerous subnational regions—Valle in Colombia and Santa Cruz in Bolivia, among many others— were able to accelerate horizontal linkages and fill in the developmental matrix with new actors and innovative alliances. These largely private innovations, together with the need for cooperation and control in the public sector, suggest a high return on efforts aimed at understanding the role of civil society and the state at both the intermediate and municipal levels.

BLOATED LOCAL GOVERNMENTS. The professional base is the hidden key to success in local government. But decentralization offered too little help in addressing the problems of bloated local governments. Local professional cadres were, in the words of a senior government official, "a floating, moonlighting mass." In addition to merit schemes of employment and promotion, some cities adopted ways to separate political from technical functions in city management. Although some innovators achieved remarkable success in paring down the size of municipal personnel, insufficient attention was paid to this during the decentralization process.

ORGANIZATIONAL AND INSTITUTIONAL REFORM. Many national and international projects that sought to address decentralization fell short of making the important distinction between organizational and institutional reform. Consequently, projects frequently overemphasized tool-oriented approaches, such as training and informational modernization, while omitting the crucial issue of encouraging the development of new rules and setting new incentives that would guide the behavior of decentralized agencies and actors and help sustain reforms.

Concepts and Perspectives for Bank Assistance

The rapidly changing context of decentralization in Latin America made management of policies and projects more difficult. Many new actors and clients came to have a stake in the development process. While we prepared our research, task managers in the World Bank and other assistance agencies expressed deep concern with the complexity and overwhelming scope of managing development projects in decentralized arrangements.[3] Oversight, supervision, and procurement were problematic when projects and subprojects embraced a variety of local and subnational governments. Above all, managing assistance projects across different levels of government—with multiple actors and interests involved—proved a daunting task.[4]

Furthermore, to meet the challenges presented by these changing circumstances, we felt that the prevailing conceptual approaches to decentralization

---

3. William Dillinger's work on Brazil indicates that severe problems may indeed result from highly federalized systems when underlying incentive structures and respective institutional settings remain untouched (see World Bank 1995).

4. Such multilevel policy assessments—and options for policy advice—in a decentralized setting were part of an investigation in a policy research project managed by the German Technical Cooperation (Deutsche Gesellschaft für Technische Zusammenarbeit, or GTZ) and the University of Potsdam, Germany (the Potsdam team included Harald Fuhr, Christoph Reichard, Frank König, Astrid Harnisch, Heiko Nitzschke, Heike Scherff, and Kristin Vorpahl). For a more general discussion see Gage and Mandell (1990, Part 1), and World Bank (1997, chapter 7), on the respective institutional incentives among different levels of government needing revision and readjustment during decentralization policies.

were too narrow and incomplete. A review of the actual experiences and of published and unpublished literature, together with our empirical evidence in the field, suggested that further refinements in concepts and perspectives were necessary to understand fully the problems and potential outcomes of decentralized systems in government, both in public service delivery as well as in private sector development. Accordingly, we sought to introduce key concepts in our approach to the case material and in this book's conclusions in chapters 10 and 11:

- **Political economy of decentralization.** Due to historically strong state intervention, decentralization, in practice, is a difficult and complex economic and political process, involving numerous social and political actors. Various types of interest groups and anomalous relationships between the private and the public sectors have formed in Latin America since as far back as the 1920s. Rent seeking and skewed redistributive systems, administrative resistance, and reluctance to change in such inherited settings are pervasive and, from the point of view of established arrangements, rational reactions. A political economy paradigm can bring to light the less obvious dynamics underlying the reluctance of decisionmakers to embark on new governmental arrangements and the difficulties of transition to decentralized government.
- **New institutional economics and decentralization.** Established organizations operate according to specific rules of the game, particularly according to a set of incentives that influence the behavior of public and private decisionmakers. The analysis of decentralization policies must account for the dynamics that alter institutions and reorder incentives or develop new ones. While market orientation may, to a large extent, prevail at the national level, subnational settings are often still characterized by a mix of traditional and market incentives. Existing local institutions reflect such layers of often contradictory incentives, which ultimately result in high transaction costs for the local private sector. New perspectives on institutional economics have encouraged analysis in this area.
- **Neocorporatism and decentralization.** In addition to the conventional categories of decentralization (deconcentration, delegation, devolution, and privatization), implementation experience in the region and elsewhere has demonstrated the importance of delving more deeply into politico-institutional dimensions of decentralization. These include options for, and experiences in, reform of intergovernmental

cooperation, local organizations and institutions, and elections and other modes of popular participation. These dimensions have not been fully covered in assistance agencies' customary frameworks covering sectoral dimensions (particularly in education, health, and infrastructure management) and financial and fiscal dimensions (revision of revenue-sharing systems, fiscal federalism, and financial management).

These concerns formed part of the contextual backdrop for the Innovations Study. Our aim was to draw insights from the problem-solving skills of natural leaders elected at the local level and to translate those insights into operational conclusions. Such conclusions might hold lessons that could improve, and simplify, the design of technical assistance programs.

References

Bahl, Roy, and Johannes Linn. 1992. *Urban Public Finance in Developing Countries.* New York: Oxford University Press.

Bird, Richard. 1994. *Decentralizing Infrastructure: For Good or for Ill?* Washington, D.C.: World Bank.

Campbell, Tim. 2003. *The Quiet Revolution.* Pittsburgh, Pa.: The University of Pittsburgh Press.

de Souza, Celina. 1997. *Constitutional Engineering in Brazil: The Politics of Federalism and Decentralization.* New York: St. Martin's Press.

Gage, Robert W., and Myrna P. Mandell, eds. 1990. *Strategies for Managing Intergovernmental Policies and Networks.* New York: Praeger.

International Monetary Fund. Various Years. *Government Finance Statistics.* Washington, D.C.

Lopez Murphy, Ricardo. 1994. *"La descentralizacion in America Latina: Problemas y perspectivas."* Working paper 188. Inter-American Development Bank, Washington, D.C.

Peterson, George. 1997. *Decentralization Experience in Latin America: Learning Through Experience.* Washington, D.C.: World Bank and Latin American Technical Department.

Shah, Anwar. 1998. *Balance, Accountability, and Responsiveness, Lessons about Decentralization.* Policy Research Working Paper 2021. World Bank, Washington, D.C.

Winkler, Donald. 1994. *The Design and Administration of Intergovernmental Transfers.* Washington, D.C.: World Bank and Latin American Technical Department.

World Bank. 1995. *Brazil. State Debt: Crisis and Reform.* Washington, D.C.: World Bank.

————. 1997. *World Development Report 1997. The State in a Changing World.* New York: Oxford University Press.

3

Research Questions: Inventing Decentralized Government

Tim Campbell, World Bank
Harald Fuhr, University of Potsdam

We saw in the last chapter how the context of decentralization set up a new dynamic in the creation of working arrangements between and among institutions at the local and national levels. The evidence suggests that these new arrangements provided a fresh incentive structure for public and private actors at the local level to engage in long-term goals of economic and social development. The Innovations Study attempted to explore what we might call "successful" decentralization by observing the processes and dynamics of innovators.

The specific objectives of the Innovations Study were to:

- Identify decentralization achievements in specific countries and sectors. This included studying local civil service and management reforms and the development of subnational alliances among civic groups, and documenting the process of introducing, promulgating, and disseminating innovation. The study noted many innovative changes in relation to participation, management, and other aspects of governance that emerged during the process of decentralization. It sought to explore the conditions and precipitating factors for such change.
- Analyze success stories and underscore their relevance or application elsewhere in the region. Special attention was given to the underlying politico-institutional structures of selected cases, with a view to

broadening the options open to governments and assistance agencies when designing institutional strengthening and organizational reforms at subnational levels.
• Disseminate best practices in Latin America. The goal was to enhance the exchange of information among both policymakers in subnational governments and task managers in assistance agencies involved in subnational institutional reform through a series of policy briefs, workshops, seminars, and conferences.

Although the purpose of the Innovation Study was to deepen the understanding of decentralization policy and practice by examining successful innovations, the study also aimed at providing some inputs in two other areas (see Bardach 1994). One was to develop specific responses to operational needs of the World Bank's Latin America and Caribbean Region, such as designing appropriate institutional strengthening components into urban and municipal projects, an area common to all country departments in the region. The other aim was to assist in the formulation of new policies in areas of emerging interest, such as improving subnational government performance and fostering private sector development through decentralized institutional arrangements.

To prepare for the study on which this book is based, our team conducted an extensive review of published and unpublished literature, including academic literature and documents by agencies such as the World Bank. We discussed ongoing assistance projects with World Bank staff and reviewed demand for further operational and conceptual work. We have, consequently, tried to incorporate links to emerging issues such as subnational institutional development (with a focus on public sector modernization), private sector finance for subnational governments, and strengthening intermediate levels of government. Given a similar debate in other donor agencies, we based much of our research and dissemination on extensive collaboration with staff in these agencies. Carrying out case studies effectively made such collaborative efforts indispensable.

Reviewing the Record

In the mid 1990s most of the World Bank's approaches to decentralization had a strong bias toward municipal finance and basic social infrastructure (for example, see World Bank sector work on municipal development in World Bank 1989, 1990, 1991, 1992). Supporting decentralization in Latin America (as in other regions) meant, in essence, supporting urban development. One of the most important inputs at that time was an out-side review of economic sector work and lending concerning decentralization in urban and sector issues (Peterson 1997). As the decade drew to a close, the Bank's body of literature began to stress decentralization issues increasingly within a broader framework (for example, Burki, Perry, and Dillinger 1999; Peterson 1997; World Bank 1999a). The key starting point was a strong focus on fiscal issues and the management of structural adjustment policies, with a careful eye on containing subnational debt. Economic and sector work began to emphasize the political underpinnings needed to support decentralization and subnational development. Our study reflects the emerging debate over institutional and political factors that appeared in the latter part of the 1990s, for instance, with two World Development Reports (World Bank 1997, 1999b).

The Innovations Study addressed another need created by the structure of the Bank's organization. Bank employees working on decentralization issues were spread across different departments. For example, experts in finance had, over the years, focused mainly or exclusively on urban finance, while experts in infrastructure projects specialized in basic (poverty-oriented) urban infrastructure. In the same way, staffers in education and health were pressed to meet a swiftly growing demand for information about subnational management of these issues. Rural development experts became aware also of the importance of the institutional strengthening of local rural governments. In key sectors and in rural and urban areas alike, staffers were often insufficiently aware of the fact that the constraints they were facing in their own project environment were partly dealt with by their coworkers (or by other bilateral or multilateral development agencies) working on related problems. Before the formation of clusters and networks during the late 1990s, the Bank had created neither sufficient incentives to bring these experts together for joint development policy formulation nor appropriate mechanisms to deal effectively with other donor agencies working in the same area.

Collaborating with Other Donors

Given the variety of studies the donor community produced on decentralization issues (such as Aghón 1996; Blair 2000; UNDP-BMZ 2000), the study team established extensive contacts with other bilateral and multilateral donors; namely, the Inter-American Development Bank, the U.N. Economic Commission for Latin America, the Swedish International Development Cooperation Agency, and the German Technical Cooperation (Deutsche

Gesellschaft für Technische Zusammenarbeit, or GTZ). Moreover, a system of conceptual collaboration and research results interchange was established with the Massachusetts Institute of Technology, the John F. Kennedy School of Government at Harvard University, the Social Science Research Council in New York, and the Institute of Development Studies at the University of Sussex. Such arrangements helped to enrich the conceptual approach, incorporate and adjust theoretical ideas, and avoid unnecessary overlap. The collaborative approach also helped in terms of operational practices at the country level.

Why Innovations at Local Levels?

As national authorities and international assistance agencies became aware of the need to strengthen local capacity—in professional skills, finances, and the incorporation of the private sector—they observed puzzling, if anecdotal, evidence of self-induced reform at the local level. For example, each of the World Bank's studies mentioned earlier (concerning Argentina, Brazil, and Chile) found growing evidence of innovation by newly established local governments in such areas as community consultations (Chile), financing local public works (Argentina), and local budgeting (Brazil). Researchers also saw other examples—for instance, new planning arrangements and private industry in República Bolivariana de Venezuela and an expansion of collaborative planning in Mexico. Other cases began to surface in conferences and seminars, such as the First Inter-American Conference of Mayors, organized by the World Bank and other development assistance agencies in Washington, D.C., in 1991. Many cases consisted of innovative reforms undertaken usually, but not always, without much outside help. Why should local authorities begin to undertake reform on their own? Empirical evidence was beginning to pile up suggesting that some largely unexplained factors were at work that fostered risk taking and change by local authorities.

Shaping an Approach for the Innovations Study

Various approaches were found in the literature to explain these emerging self-help efforts. Academic work focused on such concepts as accountability (Moutritzen 1992), new reference groups for change (Geddes 1994; Grindle and Thomas 1991), fiscal stress (Clark 1994), political incentives (Collins 1988; Ostrom, Schroeder, and Wynne 1994), and leadership (Hopkins 1994).

Based on the literature and on previous empirical work gathered in the course of development institutions, we formulated an approach to the idea of successful decentralization. Both at the intermediate and local levels, successful decentralization appeared to depend on many essential organizational and institutional requisites—such as leadership, communication at the community level, and the process of forming coalitions at the local and "horizontal" levels. Few, if any of these, had been the focus (or were even in the scope) of most work by development agencies, and relatively little work had been devoted in the literature to an empirical test of these ideas. Further, as we suggested in the previous chapter, even conceptual categories were undeveloped (particularly in the area of political economy), at least in assistance agencies like the World Bank. This may explain why most attempts at instituting sweeping decentralization have not yielded impressive results in Latin America, while narrow and discrete efforts have resulted in dramatic improvements. Some cities and regions have demonstrated impressive capacities to break local bottlenecks in resource mobilization and growth and to sustain organizational and institutional performance.

The central proposition in this Innovations Study was that the sea change in Latin America—from strongly regulated, interventionist economies and societies to decentralized, more market-oriented ones—induced gradual and progressive changes in the incentive system at the subnational level. Although different in speed and depth than at the central government level, the evolving local institutional environment—as manifested in new laws, new mandates, democratization, and increases in discretionary finance—induced in turn a fundamentally new contract between voters and government. These new relationships created the political and institutional space for innovative experimentation.

Incorporating Links to New Issues

Both the written record and oral responses received during preparatory phases indicated gaps in two distinct but related areas. One gap was revealed by the very strongly articulated concern for solutions to such problems as designing municipal-strengthening projects. In this regard, our review showed that institutional strengthening under decentralized systems had tended to follow a somewhat obsolete pattern of technical assistance and training designed originally to assist local governments in better implementing projects still commanded from the center. De facto innovations, quite often introduced by local governments without donor assistance, however, had not been analyzed sufficiently to draw further operational conclusions. One outstanding exception was a thorough empirical study on Colombian municipalities' institutional performance (World Bank 1995).

A second and related concern involved intermediate levels of government. Previous work called for intermediate levels of government to play a stronger role (in countries such as Argentina, Brazil, Chile, Colombia, and Mexico) to buttress strengthening efforts at the local levels. The conceptions of such a role still appear somewhat narrow. Yet, interestingly, political practice (particularly in Colombia) clearly indicated a strong demand for advice and applicable instruments in this area. Looking back, most decisionmakers in Colombia would agree that decentralizing health and education services during the early 1990s all the way down to the municipal level was a mistake. Capacity limitations at the local level made management of such services effectively unfeasible. More important, efficiency and oversight considerations suggest—as in many other countries—that it is wise, at least initially, to shift such competencies up to an intermediate level of government, such as the *departamento* (department) level in Colombia. *Departamentos* were neglected in the early stages of Colombia's decentralization policies.[1]

Despite such concerns, research on intermediate levels of government and operational attention in Latin America remained low. One reason that the focus remained instead on macrostability was the severe debt problems that had occurred at this level in Brazil and Argentina during the 1980s when provinces and states took a free ride on government indebtedness.[2] With states and provinces then regarded mostly as problems, rather than as places that provided a potential solution to decentralization issues, the Bank neglected comprehensive strengthening of middle-tier government for quite some time, despite its heavy lending for infrastructure and education.

Research Questions and State of Knowledge

In order to address both the policy and practical questions of innovation and decentralization, the researchers conducting the Innovations Study

---

1. For a similar debate in World Bank assistance policies in transition countries, see Bird, Ebel, and Wallich (1995, pp. 15–19).

2. Similar problems of intermediate-level indebtedness had occurred during the early to mid 1990s in the Republic of South Africa, China, and Russia, which seriously jeopardized efforts toward macroeconomic stability at the national level (World Bank 1997, chapter 7).

sought to focus their inquiry on key areas of concern in the local public sector. They consulted with collaborating institutions and the World Bank to produce a consensus. Five areas of concern to policymakers and development assistance agencies became the central scope of the study:

- **Administrative performance.** Increase in professional capacity, administrative reorganization and strengthening, expansion of training programs, and other administrative improvements.
- **Fiscal management and resource mobilization.** Efficient and transparent intergovernmental transfer systems and creative mechanisms to mobilize and manage local financial resources.
- **Public service provision.** Improved efficiency in delivery; more effective coordination among levels of government; and new options for service delivery, such as contracting out and privatization.
- **Enhancing private sector development.** Arrangements that foster local private investment, activate private sector participation in policy and services at the local level, and improve public responsiveness to private sector needs.
- **Participation in local and regional decisionmaking.** Expansion of options for local voice, participatory planning, and consultative mechanisms, among other initiatives.

These areas of course are not intended to be exhaustive, nor are they intended to comprise the minimum scope of issues and policy areas needed to understand innovation in decentralized settings. Many other areas of public and private sector could be explored, and many other dynamics in the innovation process have been the subject of research and inquiry (for instance, Clark 1994 on fiscal stress). Our purpose was not to define the minimum conditions for decentralization, but rather to explore cases of innovation in decentralized settings in each of the five specific areas of concern.

Each of the five areas selected for focus in the study has been the subject of extensive policy analysis, academic research, and operational experimentation, but not necessarily of empirical inquiry at the subnational level and not of innovation. This section presents a review of the core concepts in the literature and practice, which will set the stage for discussing the specific approach to the cases.

Area 1: Incorporating Professionalism in Municipal Management

In many countries decentralization efforts are seriously hampered by low managerial capacities at the respective levels of government (see, for example,

Campbell, Peterson, and Brakarz 1991; Cheema 1993; Fuhr 1994a; Hoffman-Martinot 1992; Nickson 1995). Unless properly addressed, the delegation of new functions toward lower levels of government runs many risks. Low institutional performance at subnational, particularly municipal, levels may increase public spending and thus harm macroeconomic stability or cause severe interruptions in, and diminished quality of, service delivery. To offset these risks, institutional and organizational strengthening strategies have long been seen as indispensable in any decentralization effort. Such strategies formed the cornerstone for the strengthening of local development.[3] Professionalization in municipal management typically encompassed several strategies, including hiring professionals or introducing city manager models, increasing salaries for selected key positions, improving overall management of human resources through extensive education and training, and selectively reducing redundant municipal employees (see Cabrero Mendoza 1995; Cheema 1993).

THE REASONS FOR INNOVATIONS AT THE LOCAL LEVEL. As discussed previously, the new organizational and institutional arrangements with decentralization created an impetus for stronger horizontal coordination between mayors and decisionmakers and their citizens. Under traditional, largely rent-seeking arrangements, it was still rational for local authorities *not* to seek coordination with other local actors. Instead local authorities found it more beneficial to enter excessive bargaining and seek the favor of central authorities. In the period following import substitution reform, the evolution of more local accountability structures not only increased the benefits of coordination among local agencies, but made coordination necessary for survival.

Combined with increased pressures toward political participation and liberalization, such new directions of accountability created opportunities for the formation of political nuclei for change, or "change groups" (Fox 1994; Grindle and Thomas 1991). Local leadership in public office tended to bring increased awareness of accountability and, along with it, new rules

---

3. The renewed focus on local-level institutional performance is consistent with the findings in other developing countries. East Asian experiences underline the importance of a highly performing civil service because of competitive salaries, well-trained managers, leadership efficiency, and financial management (Leipziger and Thomas 1994, p. 24). These aspects also seem to hold for local levels of government (Akizuki 1993; Kitayama 1993).

of the game and new incentive structures that led to innovative ways of managing local affairs.

One main branch of literature on innovation points to fiscal strain as the main impetus behind the search for new ways of managing cities and subnational governments (Clark 1994; Mouritzen 1992). The extent to which fiscal strain leads to innovation in management, especially when political office is contestable and renewable, however, was thought to depend on whether and how the new local leadership reacts to new rules and incentives emerging from such change. When decentralization has come about as a top-down response to fiscal stress, what types of strategies have local administrators used? One strategy is to try to cut expenditures and increase revenues. Another is using reduced resources in an innovative way.

As noted previously, the success of local innovations depends more on reliable leadership and high-level staff encouragement than on the presence of affluent residents or a large revenue base. High-level staff encouragement can come either in the form of a new mayor or governor or as a result of enhanced professionalization of middle and upper civil service managers. Public information campaigns, conceived and managed by high-level staff, have been known to play a key role in the encouragement and dissemination of innovations in public service delivery.

MECHANISMS FOR IMPROVING THE PERFORMANCE OF LOCAL PUBLIC EM-PLOYEES. Municipal and subnational employees tend to be little studied and inadequately understood actors, partly due to their low rank in the national civil service hierarchy. In reality, local employees often play very significant roles in subnational policymaking, and increasingly so under decentralization. These new roles come in various forms, such as new ways of articulating their interests and preferences and incorporating themselves into local policymaking—for example, as work committees or special purpose teams (Hoffman-Martinot 1992).

Perhaps the most important factors for increasing municipal and subnational institutional performance are a sustained change in the employment and salary regimes of local civil servants and the revamping of the organization and functioning of municipal administrations.

In terms of the employment and salary regimes, reforms in most countries seem to be severely hampered by national civil service legislation, which allows for little change at the local levels. The inflexibility of labor contracts and the procedures of hiring and firing of staff are particularly problematic. Salary increases are usually easier to achieve, but in most cases they need to be combined with strategies for reducing costs in other areas.

Better salaries, according to qualifications and merit, as well as clear-cut (transparent) rules for hiring and firing are likely to be basic preconditions for gradually reducing clientelism in public administration and upgrading overall service provision.

The second factor, effective reorganization, may yield significant efficiency gains once a definition of critical posts has taken place, and new professional staff, with better salaries, enters local public administration. Like consultation mechanisms with citizens, improvement in the morale of employees through extensive training and employee participation are additional mechanisms to monitor progress and overall performance and to sustain management innovations.

Municipal employees can also form organized pressure groups as members of public sector unions. In most countries, unionization is substantially higher in the public than in the private sector, where it is now in decline. Local unions can play an important role in either promoting or obstructing public sector reform policies like decentralization (Hoffman-Martinot 1992). The set of questions to pose in this regard is related to the specific innovations in local management as a necessary response to polices of decentralization. Do such policies, eventually, help increase competitiveness in the local public sector by trimming it and forcing it to compete with the private sector? Or do they further marginalize the local public sector by reducing its responsibilities? It should be noted that shifting local service provision to the private sector is seen by local personnel as "dismantling the public sector." The Innovations Study sought to explore responses in this area.

THE CITY MANAGER MODE. Hiring a city manager is another option that has been noted in a few local governments in Latin America. Such municipalities are often overseen by skillful mayors who face a daunting managerial task. The mayors must reach political objectives and, at the same time, achieve efficient performance in governance. Intrinsic conflicts of this sort are reminiscent of the good government reform movement in the United States that began in the late 19th century. The solution in the United States, as in many European countries, was to separate the political from the managerial role of local government, which led to the invention of the city manager position (adopted in about half of all U.S. cities). In the Latin American context, the city manager would enjoy an extra margin of insulation from the mayor and the electorate (Katz 1994). One outcome was enhanced professionalism in public sector management. This degree of autonomy facilitated the enactment of politically unpopular measures such as staff layoffs and budget cuts, and it allowed for priorities to be set along more objective, technical lines. Several cities in the region—Riberalta, Bolivia; Tegucigalpa, Honduras; and Cali and Baranquilla, Colombia, to name a few—have taken similar steps to modernize local administration.

Two cases chosen in this study—Mendoza and Conchali, Chile—illustrate several of these motivating factors and some of the options. Argentina as a whole, and Mendoza Province in particular, showed acute attention to the problems of fiscal stress. The governor's budgetary reforms were prompted entirely by fiscal pressure. Conchali, by contrast, suggests that a stronger part of the motivation arose from wholesale political change in the transition from dictatorship to democracy. The corresponding drive toward more direct contact with citizens produced, in turn, an impact on administrative personnel who grew more sensitive to local needs. Neither case reflects internal union organizing nor private sector pressures per se, but rather the overriding importance of determined leaders to respond to closer contact with the public and to deliver services more effectively. Both cases start with strong measures to improve performance following an abrupt change in political regimes. These initial conditions provide much of the reasons for change. But the consequences of cultural change in the local government organization offer some of the most promising outcomes— as well as the most difficult to sustain.

Area 2: Innovations in Mobilizing and Managing Local and Regional Resources

Local resource mobilization and management remain weak in most countries in Latin America, and a disconnect persists in the minds of voter-taxpayers between tax payments on the one hand and the creation or improvement of public goods on the other hand. This observation flows from numerous sector reviews as well as from repeated frustration in operational efforts to reform property taxes. Although property taxes tend to be the main source of local government revenue, conventional wisdom holds that they are not the best revenue-raising instruments because they are difficult to administer, can have undesirable land use effects, and are unpopular with taxpayers (Bahl and Linn 1992). Property tax reforms have been launched under decentralized, democratic administrations, but their impact has been diluted either by taxpayer resistance or residual centralist traditions that undermine the effort, for instance, by keeping control over the valuation of property or the setting of rates out of the hands of the municipality.

In general, the fiscal base of local governments in Latin America remains small for various reasons. These include insufficient local capacity for revenue generation, restricted revenue bases, excessive central control over bases and rates, and excessive reliance on central government transfers. Although no systematic study on fiscal correspondence (the share of own-source revenue out of total local and regional government revenue) had been carried out for the region, some evidence suggests that that central revenue sharing has substituted for own-source revenue generation. Studies on República Bolivariana de Venezuela, Bolivia, Chile, Ecuador, Colombia, and Guatemala show evidence of substitution in the short run despite increases in local taxing authority (IDB 1994; Peterson 1997). Innovative strategies in resource mobilization would be expected to either improve the efficient use of a local government's current base or expand the fiscal base of subnational government.[4]

EFFICIENCY IMPROVEMENTS. Innovations in the mobilization of local resources can be achieved through improvements in the efficiency of the system in place without necessarily altering its broad organizational structure. Dillinger (1992) refers to these as "procedural reforms." Innovations may include:

- Boosting revenue collection by improving the system's capacity to identify and monitor delinquents or by using tax clearances to enforce payment
- Increasing compliance by establishing or enforcing penalties or through more positive measures like information campaigns
- Improving coverage through more effective identification of tax sources by employing, for example, tax maps for identifying property and cross-referencing to update data on the characteristics and ownership of property
- Imposing surcharges (Davey 1993)
- Improving the management of tax administration through new incentive structures (as discussed in the earlier section on professionalism).

Where there are problems of concurrent powers, lack of clarity in the division of responsibility for service provision, or externalities and scale economies associated with the public good, there often will be insufficient

---

4. For an overview, see Bahl, Miner, and Schroeder (1984).

local resource allocation for certain types of services. Brazil and Chile are notable examples (Campbell, Peterson, and Brakarz 1991; Lordello de Mello 1993) where various types of environmental services have been neglected as a result. More proactive subnational governments can innovate to overcome these organizational and institutional shortcomings. Finally, subnational governments can innovate by redeploying the resources available to them. Examples are improvements in productivity through labor-saving and new management techniques, reductions in administrative expenses, cutting the least efficient departments, and reducing overtime.[5]

CREATING NEW SYSTEMS. Government can also achieve innovations in resource mobilization by expanding the fiscal base or taking advantage of other options open to them. One popular option, often appearing in the literature, policy studies, and some local governments, is the imposition of betterment levies. These levies are perhaps the most interesting such innovations being carried out in Latin America (for example, in Tijuana and Monterrey, Mexico), and are among the revenue sources most suited for local infrastructure improvement because they are tied to specific, identifiable benefits and limited to those taxpayers considered to be direct beneficiaries (Bahl and Linn 1992). Therefore, in addition to their practical benefits, betterment levies are a means of remedying the disconnect in accountability by redefining the fiscal contract between the citizen and the state.

Other options are to create new fees, such as user charges through cost recovery or a broadened tax base, and to increase local capacity for borrowing (given constitutional and statutory provisions for doing so). Campbell, Peterson, and Brakarz (1991) concluded that there has been "much less action to grant new revenue-raising authority to local governments than there has been to increase centrally financed resource transfers" (p. 13).

IMPROVED FINANCIAL MANAGEMENT. Effective financial management is central to improving accountability to higher authorities in government and to citizens. Experience in financial management and auditing in Latin

---

5. The U.S. Fiscal Austerity and Urban Innovation Project surveyed 517 cities and concluded that decreased spending on supplies, improved productivity through new management techniques, and increased user fees were among the 5 most common strategies (out of 33) resorted to under fiscal strain. See Clark (1994).

America is only slightly less troublesome than the experience in local resource mobilization. Many Bank projects have included efforts to improve financial management by strengthening information, planning, and budgeting capacities. Although successes can be shown, sustainability remains a problem. Most recent efforts in this area have focused on developing integrated financial management (IFM) systems that encompass a number of areas: tax administration, budgeting, cash management, public debt management, accounting and financial reporting (internal and external), internal control, information management structures, compliance and performance auditing, and human resource training.

According to the principles of IFM, timely and accessible information on all levels of government is central to sound financial management and oversight. Local IFM reforms can improve the management of subnational administrations by linking them to central level information and decisionmaking processes.

Some cities, including the three selected to illustrate finance in this book—Valledupar and Manizales in Colombia and Tijuana in Mexico—have achieved remarkably robust systems on their own, without external assistance or at least without external prodding. These cases do not support the position that local action cannot improve the scope and rates of property taxes. They also show the underlying institutional preconditions, the organizational strategies, and, most of all, the risky political approaches (in the case of Tijuana) that were taken to achieve innovation in financial management.

Area 3: Decentralization and Innovations in Public Service Delivery

The decentralization of public services creates two checks, or "circuit breakers," ensuring that service providers are sensitive to public needs. One breaker is between consumers (taxpayers) and producers (bureaucrats). Consumers can, in theory, opt to move to a different producer by changing locations, or they can at least speak out for better government. A second breaker is between producers and the state. Decentralized producers have no legitimate excuses for not producing competitively. These circuit breakers remedy two problems commonly noted in the literature. One problem is the tendency to overproduce services; a second is that producers are unresponsive to specific consumer demands. Decentralized public services are effectively "sold" to the public in the form of discrete bundles provided to individual customers, rather than being distributed in the form of diffuse benefits available in varying degrees to large classes of people.

Decentralization has shifted the border between state and society by pushing the state out into society and subjecting state agencies and subnational governments more strongly to market discipline. The decentralization of public service provision could shift conflicts over declining resources out of the central state into local governments. Schwartz (1994) suggested that the pressures placed on subnational governments as a result of this process could result in innovative strategies for service delivery.

IDENTIFYING INNOVATIONS IN LOCAL PUBLIC SERVICE DELIVERY. Innovations in public service delivery can be defined in terms of new services provided or new ways of delivering services.[6] Anecdotal evidence also suggests that new financing mechanisms and new relationships with clients are important dimensions of innovations in service delivery. Accordingly, our work sought examples in one or more of these categories.

INNOVATIONS IN PUBLIC SERVICE DELIVERY AND LEVELS OF SOCIO-ECONOMIC DEVELOPMENT. In both industrial and developing countries, the relationship between innovation and level of development tends to be weak (Clark 1994; Clark, Hellstern, and Martinotti 1985). First, less affluent public administrations tend to be as capable of innovation as others because many innovations come at little or no cost. Although the effects of innovations can cause significant improvements in public service delivery, the innovations themselves can amount to nothing more than minor variations in, or addition to, the way services are normally delivered.[7] Second, for innovations to come about, encouragement of staff at the top is far more important than having affluent residents or a large revenue base. Top staff encouragement can come in the form of a new mayor or governor, or it can result from the enhanced professionalization of middle and upper management in the local or regional civil service. Public information campaigns,

---

6. See Dillinger (1994) for an overview. By "public service" we mean health (both urban and rural), education (mostly at the primary level), garbage collection, and the construction and maintenance of local utility delivery facilities and rural roads.

7. For example, the village of Lombard, Illinois, carried out the following innovation at no cost: the village water bureau noted that staff from a private utility might save them money by reading both the village's water meters and the utility's gas meters simultaneously. The savings were immediate and dramatic and could be generalized to other locales (Clark 1994, p. 223).

conceived and managed by top staff, have been known to play a key role in the encouragement and dissemination of innovations in public service delivery. This has been well illustrated in the case of the state of Ceara, Brazil, where the enthusiasm of top-level state workers for improved infant health service resulted in a broad information campaign that turned the local population into monitors of the quality of the services delivered by grassroots health agents of the health ministry (Tendler and Amorim 1996).

THE EMERGENCE AND UNFOLDING OF INNOVATIONS. As in most developing areas, especially those that underwent a protracted period of reform, public service delivery in Latin America has long been considered public domain. Under import substitution policies, the state was unquestionably the dominant actor in both the economy and society. The design and provision of services under this system were based largely on top-down decisionmaking—on central government estimates of what was "needed" on the local level and rarely sufficiently informed by what was "demanded" by local residents. Services, particularly in the social sectors, were provided (and expected to be produced) and financed in a top-down regime as well.

The mismatch between supply and demand of services was fully exposed once the exigencies of the debt crisis and structural adjustment placed heavy constraints on the public purse, and centralized financing of services came under severe constraints. Yet a constructive instability seemed to have resulted from the breakdown of such regimes and the paternalism of import substitution industrialization, creating options and providing the incentives for local decisionmakers to experiment with alternative and innovative ways of doing things.

As mentioned in the earlier section on professionalization, the new organizational and institutional arrangements that emerged after the shift away from import substitution industrialization created a broad impetus for horizontal coordination between state actors and agencies. This was particularly true under structural adjustment, when unconditioned and sometimes generous (though unpredictable) transfers of central government and strongly centralized financing of public services were either significantly curtailed or provided under new rules (such as more transparent, equitable, and competitive revenue-sharing systems). When this happened, new incentives developed to use local resources more economically, effectively, and efficiently.

Some literature on innovation points strongly to fiscal strain as the main impetus behind the search for new ways of delivering services (Clark 1994; Mouritzen 1992). The extent to which fiscal strain leads to innovations in service delivery, especially where political office is contestable and renewable, depends on whether, and to what degree, the new local leadership questions or reacts to the new rules and incentives emerging from such change. Several scenarios could be taken into account here in order to understand why leaders, acting under such constraints and within a competitive political framework, eventually embark on new strategies to provide local services.

Innovations in service delivery can come about as a result of factors outside the realm of subnational administrations and politics. Natural disaster, drought, famine, disease, and civil war are some examples of external pressures that can precipitate a creative response in the reorganization of a service delivery system. This has been the case with natural disasters in Peru and El Salvador and civil strife in Colombia.

There are also cases in which the local public sector engages in a "takeover" of service innovations that are developed in the local community or nongovernmental organization (NGO) sector. Often, because a governmental agency or local administration is undeveloped or understaffed, a voluntary agency may play a vanguard role and develop a way of delivering services that the government does not provide (Carroll 1992; Lipsky 1980). Having watched its success, the local public sector will then take over delivery of services, sometimes in a predatory manner, but often with the noble intention of ensuring the continuity of service delivery and increasing the funds available for it. A more complex set of factors is likely to be needed to explain cases of noncash arrangements in the provision (or maintenance) of public services, with the involvement of community groups and largely traditional labor arrangements.

A move toward decentralization can create a strong demand for innovation by making local governments more visible and forcing them to innovate under tight budgetary conditions. By subjecting state agencies and local governments to market discipline, the decentralization of public service provision shifts conflicts over declining resources out of the central state into local governments (Schwartz 1994). The pressures such conflicts create can provide the impetus for innovative strategies on the local level for responding to demand. Pressures from local constituencies—the private sector networks that identify with the new leadership, the poor who manage to organize, NGOs, and civic associations—can force local authorities to reconsider the way they conduct business.

Until recently, political careers in places like República Bolivariana de Venezuela were determined at the center, and local officials were generally insulated from user pressure (Vallmitjana 1993). As mentioned previously, once such clientelist relationships break up due to external financial constraints and increased options for local participation, new accountability structures evolve. Once users and civil actors have an effective voice (see the section on local participation later in this chapter) or increased options to "exit" (through alternatives provided by the market), local decisionmakers have to react accordingly. They will be held accountable for what they do with delivery of local services and how they provide them. Most likely, their own political careers or their parties' election showings will depend on effective policymaking and better services for their citizens.

In Chile, for example, the establishment of the elected regional council in 1991 was aimed at increasing regional government responsiveness to local demand. This move has invited increased public scrutiny of the regional government's investment decisions related to the Fondo Nacional de Desarrollo Regional (National Fund for Regional Development).[8] In other cases, neighborhood associations, local partisan groups, *clubes de madres* (mothers clubs) and other user groups have pressured local authorities to provide public infrastructure for new services, such as marketplaces, soup kitchens, and new transportation facilities. Both as a result of domestic reforms and rapid information exchange about public sector troubles throughout the developing world, change has also taken place outside large urban areas where people are increasingly aware of their prerogative to demand better services. The provision of educational services in Minas Gerais (Guedes and others 1995, p. 14) and El Salvador's Escuelas de Disempeño Communal (community-managed schools) program seem to be particularly striking cases in this respect.[9]

---

8. In Colombia and Peru, innovative policymaking throughout the 1980s was based on the necessity to react more properly to local demands—particularly to guerilla-related instability.

9. The EDUCO project in El Salvador is one interesting example of the effect of local pressures on improving the quality of primary education delivery in rural areas, where it is common for teachers to absent themselves from their teaching responsibilities (Government of El Salvador 1997). One of the innovations EDUCO brought about was a system of "elections" of local schoolteachers through community groups. This new system effectively handed over the control of primary education delivery to community groups, which in turn imposed accountability from their elected teachers. While the central government continues to be responsible for teacher salaries, selection and employment decisions regarding teachers has been transferred to the local level where the quality of their work can be monitored (Prawda 1992).

Despite many successful and innovative cases of decentralizing and providing services at local levels, however, numerous constraints impede the
sustainability of the new institutional arrangements that follow such new
ways of service delivery. As cases of decentralized education, health, and
transportation services seem to indicate, there are increasing needs to maintain progress achieved by involving new supportive actors. Particularly
once quality and equity as well as efficiency (economies of scale) concerns
are raised, some types of decentralized service delivery may run into serious deficiencies, especially if they remain overly centralized (see Bird 1994;
Ostrom, Schroeder, and Wynne 1994 for infrastructure policies). To overcome such constraints, innovative service provision most likely needs much
stronger support, either through intermunicipal cooperation and coordination or through reinforced links with intermediate levels of government.

Many of these factors—leadership, structures of accountability, takeover
of services, and fiscal pressures, among others—were involved in the innovation for better public service in two cases selected for review in this study.
In Brazil, Cruitiba's transport system reflected a response to oil price changes
in 1973 in addition to many other factors. In Bolivia, Santa Cruz innovated
its public services as a matter of local autonomy and civic culture. Both
cases are illustrative of the many considerations reviewed in the preceding
paragraphs. The cases also reflect a long-term perspective in conceiving
and refining innovative reforms in public services.

Area 4: Decentralization and Innovation in Mobilizing Private Sector Development

In many countries it has become obvious that decentralization has mobilized greater private sector interaction, but not always with lasting or effective results. Often, relations between the private and the public sector are
adversarial at the local levels, or function along clientelist and patronage
lines with a tendency to distort incentives and impose restrictions on market entry.

Yet in Latin America there are several notable cases in which symbiotic,
mutually reinforcing relationships evolved between the public and private
sector. Some cases exhibit successful takeover of key responsibilities for
public service provision. But several others go beyond this point, resulting
in innovative approaches in local public administration. Various mechanisms come into play, including the provision of incentives that support
and foster entrepreneurial activities or the creation of formal and informal
links to civil society (a "vibrant associational life" as defined by Putnam,

Leonardi, and Nanetti 1993). These and other experiences lead to further progress: the building of trust among local public and private sector actors.

INNOVATIONS IN PRIVATE SECTOR PARTICIPATION AND DEVELOPMENT. In the area of private sector development, local innovative policies have been defined as leading to new institutional arrangements. These arrangements may produce such results as an increase in the number of formal registered enterprises or in a rich and active network of secondary associations, such as local labor and public sector unions, with significant levels of membership and involvement in mediating public-private relations (Locke 1994; Putnam, Leonardi, and Nanetti 1993).

Informal enterprises might be important players in the local economy, but they are more difficult to track. Registered enterprises allow for a rough measure of relations between the local public and private sectors, whereas the predominance of informal economic activity could be an indication of lack of cooperation between them. Information on the longevity and rate of failure of firms, where available, would also be useful, although these variables are likely to be affected by macroeconomic conditions as well as local ones.

Evidence from the literature also suggests that successful organizations or public agencies at the local level perform at least three types of functions. First, they provide support services for the local private sector, especially small firms. For instance, the local government may support some sort of commerce agency that provides services for small businesses. Second, local governments maintain a public procurement policy that favors local manufacturers and producers (Tendler and Amorim 1996). Third, the local public sector follows a consistent policy of contracting out the provision of services to the local private sector (see cases in Cointreau-Levine 1994).

The manner in which local businesses and elites are represented in subnational government has proven to be an important source of innovation as well (Tendler 1997). For example, there have been cases of self-made entrepreneurs seeking political office and enhancing local public sector efficiency through business skills and a developmental vision for their regions.

LOCAL INNOVATIONS IN PRIVATE SECTOR PARTICIPATION AND DEVELOPMENT. The causes of such innovative developments vary and are linked to different international and domestic conditions of competition, both central and subnational. In response to changes in domestic and international demand and technological innovation—away from rigid manufacturing and industrial relations and toward more frequent product innovations—industrial restructuring and flexible production processes become imperative (Sable 1994). Some common features of private sector growth are increased specialization and vertical integration between clusters of small and medium enterprises (Pyke and Sengenberger 1992; Schmitz 1993) as well as between local interest groups, like organized interest groups and secondary associations, more professional civil servants, and reformist local policymakers (Locke 1994). Small- and medium-firm clustering around restructured larger enterprises is not uncommon. From a sociological perspective, such cases of local economic development tend to be based on effective networking between members of the local middle class.

It is assumed that once such collaboration occurs at local levels, mutually beneficial arrangements between public and private sectors develop over time and gradually reduce transaction costs (North 1991). Local public sector performance can be enhanced by increased private sector involvement and its embeddedness in circuits of local decisionmaking. An improved entrepreneurial environment can stimulate public sector entities to behave differently. Fuhr (1994a,b) discusses several forms of changed behavior. In one, a more active middle class tends to build up and gain significant economic and political veto power that serves to articulate and represent private sector interests. This in turn serves as a counterbalance to, and check on, the public sector, and has an influence on budgetary processes and the setting of policy priorities as well. Another outcome is that a broader market orientation is formed, and this has spillover effects like increased contracting out of public service provision. By virtue of increasing public-private transactions, this new orientation serves to increase private access to the public sector. This is most significant for the poor, who otherwise have minimal access to government services. Local alternatives to public service delivery provided by private actors—for instance, water vendors and private school providers—increase exit options for consumers as well as pressure for improved performance.

Moreover the development history of many of today's industrial economies illustrates that dynamic local entrepreneurial environments, in addition to contributing to economic growth as such, eventually constitute the social and political actors and interest groups of a civil society.[10] These

---

10. Moore (1966) writes extensively on this aspect. See also the famous Nassau Charter written in 1806 by Freiherr vom Stein to introduce Prussian municipal institutional reforms and to encourage the business sector's participation in local policymaking and administration (Stein 1959).

groups, in turn, ensure private economic growth independently of (and often in opposition to) strong state control. Over time, local economic activity involves larger numbers of interest groups and secondary associations, like labor unions and NGOs. For such actors, local horizontal networking (for local corporatism, see Locke 1994; Oi 1992) becomes a viable alternative to traditional vertical bargaining with the central government and a means of improving distorted political and economic conditions at the macrolevel through auto-regulatory arrangements and bottom-up pressures (Amin and Thrift 1994).

Historically, several types of incentives induce local actors to become involved in economic clustering and networking. It is not always clear why these changes occur. At times they are reactions to domestic macroeconomic conditions like trade liberalization, whereas at other times they are reactions to economic and political changes that are purely local in nature, like a change in the hold of the local elite on economic activity. In addition, such evolution in local private sector growth can be either market-driven or government-driven. At times the changes evolve due to specific local natural resource endowments or local transport facilities (ports, roads, and rivers). Clusters of industrial and manufacturing interests have evolved and were successful at maintaining their ability to counterbalance the power of the central government, exploiting geographic distance to escape some political and economic decisionmaking and control. The eschewal of central control gains particular importance during periods of fiscal restraint or macroeconomic and political instability.

Industrial policies that promote competition and exert pressures on local producers have had similar effects. Under what are perceived as adverse commercial conditions, some local economic actors have clustered and worked clandestinely in informal ("shadow") arrangements or in open competition with the central government and the more privileged classes of larger cities. In addition cases exist in which the central and regional governments play a more proactive role in promoting local economic activity (Barzelay 1991, Cabieses and others 1980, Kitayama 1993).

The cases covered in this study—the privatization of ports and mines in República Bolivariana de Venezuela, the creation of private-public partnerships in Cali, and the forging of working relationships between banks, municipalities, and the poor in Nicaragua—all owe their origin to increased autonomy at the local level. Also, with the exception of Cali, decentralization in legal and administrative matters played an important role. Private participation in public affairs in Cali went back half a decade. Other cities spearheading such efforts can be found in the literature (Cabieses and others

1980 for Arequipa; Carlos and Diaz 1987 for Santa Cruz). The cases included in this book provide some insight into the institutional underpinnings of more effective, catalytic, and proactive roles for subnational governments. The wide range of experiences throw some light on issues of industrial policy and practice—for instance, on state-owned enterprises in República Bolivariana de Venezuela, the embeddedness of working entrepreneurial partnerships in management in Cali, and the blending of local governments with local banks to support the move of informal economic activity into formalized settings for some óf the poorest urban residents in Nicaragua.

Area 5: Innovations in Local Participation, Electoral Reform, and Public Policy

Many formal instruments of local democracy, like those that channel communication between residents and elected officials, have fallen into disuse or were never fully developed at subnational levels in Latin America. This neglect was largely due to protracted periods of authoritarian rule under which all elections were suspended and local political and associational life was regarded as a threat to domestic security. The state viewed the elimination of local politics as its mandate. However several informal channels of contact (between grassroots groups and local officials, for example) are commonly found in the region. In fact, largely because of their pariah status, these mechanisms thrived under authoritarian rule and, during the period of redemocratization, have played a key role in representing the interests of the poor. Many countries in the region exhibit a vibrant local associational life that has helped articulate the voice of the poor and carry their interests to the forefront of national social policy dialogue with the resumption of democracy (see Loveman 1994, 1995 on Chile).

OPTIONS FOR INNOVATION IN LOCAL PARTICIPATION. Despite the reestablishment of democratic rule in most of the region, few countries have paid systematic attention to the institutionalization and broadening of options for voice and participation at subnational levels. These options are important for at least three reasons. First, in respect to political representation, the literature has examined participation, voice, consultation, and other mechanisms of political articulation as ways to help mend the disconnect that persists between the demand for public goods and the recognition of the duty to pay for them (as seen in the earlier discussion on resource mobilization). A residual from the paternalistic import substitution period, when the citizen expected the state to provide, the Latin American mindset is a significant obstacle to improving cost recovery and increasing local resource mobilization in general. This disconnect has also resulted from the incapacity of the political system to accurately read and appropriately respond to citizen-taxpayer demand for local investments and services. Both aspects of the problem must be addressed by encouraging the citizen to voice preferences on local as well as national matters. Perhaps the most interesting case of broad electoral reform comes from Bolivia, where the 1994 Participation Law transferred a wide range of new responsibilities to local government and mandated local involvement in public sector policy formulation and execution. *Cabildos abiertos,* or open town hall meetings, are another common example of opening channels to citizen input. These two examples represent a paradigm of subnational government that stresses the proactive, accountable, transparent, nondependent, and managerial roles of local officials, as distinguished from the Napoleonic paradigm that understands local governments as extensions and executing agents of the central government (Davey 1994).[11]

Broadening options for public voice is also important for economic development. The acute exposure of subnational governments to public scrutiny under decentralization has focused more attention on their role in the management of public-private partnerships in investments in social and physical infrastructure. As discussed in the earlier section on public-private relations, subnational government is expected to play an increasingly vital role in representing local economic actors and facilitating their transactions. In Latin America, the literature reflects much enthusiasm and high expectations for bolstering the role of regional and local government in providing various types of support services to promote small- and medium-enterprise development (Boisier 1994; Fuhr 1993; Levy 1993; Schmitz 1990).

Civic representation and social development is a third area of importance for participation and voice. NGOs, professional associations and clubs, and other actors in civil society shape local policy, often regardless of official representative channels. However, the literature shows no consensus about the role such actors play when they work in collaboration with the public sector and are represented by it (Carroll 1992; Castaneda 1990). Some argue against such collaboration because it undercuts their reason for being or dulls the competitive edge of these groups as "outsiders" (Lipsky 1980). Others argue for various permutations of the Weberian state corporatist model, which incorporates local associationalism with political

---

11. See the discussion in Campbell and Frankenhoff (1994).

representation and economic governance (Putnam, Leonardi, and Nanetti 1993). For example, local social and economic development in some countries is fostered in close consultation with boards or committees that include representatives of the private sector, labor unions, and local government.[12] A project to reinforce decentralized government in Chile sought to create similar arrangements between the state and civil society on the regional level.

INSTRUMENTS FOR INNOVATIONS. The instruments of participatory inputs into public choice fall into at least two broad areas: consultation and electoral choice. (In theory, judicial instruments could also be considered, but the primitive development of law and legal institutions does not yet make this area very productive.) The state of knowledge of these areas is greatly weighted toward consultation. A large literature base has concentrated primarily on consultative participation by citizen groups (see Campbell 2003; Carroll 1992; Reilly 1994). Carroll and Reilly suggest that decentralization reinvigorated local public life and made participation much more accepted, more widespread, and even necessary in the first decade of decentralization. Consultation by community and grassroots groups can be subdivided according to the degree of effort and formality. Thus, at one end of a spectrum, passive neighborhood residents can be consulted on an occasional basis through surveys, opinion polls, or hearings by outsiders with little or no initiating effort on the part of residents. Groups that get themselves mobilized would represent a point of greater activity and effort. For instance, dedicated resources, often in the form of a community or social affairs secretary with staff in the municipal government, are needed for grassroots, community-based activists (Carroll 1992). Even greater commitment of resources is needed for such things as beneficiary contributions of cash or labor in local projects and for such actions as citizen-initiated contact—for instance, to publish the results of local government performance (UNICEF 1993).

ELECTORAL AND VOTING SYSTEMS. Participation has also been extended to the electoral domain, both in the selection of local leaders at the ballot

---

12. The northern European states are some of the most interesting recent examples of this model. Oi (1992) has developed the concept of "local state corporatism" to describe similar arrangements between state and society in China. The local and state governments in Germany are further examples that have generated much interest.

box as well as in the use of voting mechanisms to make public choices (Shugart 1996). But little policy literature has focused on municipal elections as a participatory choice mechanism (Burki, Perry, and Dillinger 1999; Rojas 1999). One exception is Molina and Hernandez (1995). Some countries has simplified the electoral process and made choices easier and more transparent for voters.

Two cases in this book—Porto Alegre and Tijuana—illustrate active participatory input from citizens. In both cases, input was organized by the city. One widely publicized case is that of participatory budgeting in Porto Alegre, where tens of thousands of citizens take part in thousands of meetings to express preferences and rank priorities for local government investments and services. Mendoza is another case that illustrates the incorporation of neighborhood groups into the planning, implementation, and financing of public works. The study paid special attention to the dynamics of new settings to determine whether they had truly created new options or, instead, built new mechanisms of fostering clientelism and exclusionary political institutions.[13]

Conclusion

This chapter has attempted to reflect the state of the literature and policy questions about each of the five main areas of innovation in local public sector at the time the field research was being launched. Some changes and advances in the field have been registered since that time (1995), but many, if not most, of the key policy questions remain valid. A second set of questions is: "why and how to innovate?" Literature and policy issues help to some degree to frame the question of motivation and process. But the cases will show a distinct divergence between the framing of policy questions on the one hand and, on the other hand, the points of departure from which local leaders set about solving problems in decentralized administrations.

It is useful to reiterate that the scope of research was never intended to address all the rich complexity of issues surveyed in this chapter. Rather, our intention was to explore the mechanisms, dynamics, and outcomes of a few innovations in each of the fields in order to gain insight into achieving reform in a more sustainable manner in decentralized systems of government.

---

13. As such, the research in this book will begin with the assumption that creating the mechanisms for voice and choice is desirable, but it will also examine whether the outcomes of innovations do indeed promote participation.

References

Aghón, Gabriel. 1996. *Descentralización fiscal en América Latina: balance y principales desafíos.* Santiago, Chile: U.N. Economic Commission for Latin America and the Caribbean/German Technical Cooperation.

Akizuki, Kengo. 1993. *Institutionalizing the Local System. The Ministry of Home Affairs and Intergovernmental Relations in Japan.* Washington, D.C.: World Bank.

Amin, Ash, and Nigel Thrift, eds. 1994. *Globalization, Institutions, and Regional Development in Europe.* Oxford, U.K.: Oxford University Press.

Bahl, Roy, and Johannes Linn. 1992. *Urban Public Finance in Developing Countries.* Oxford, U.K.: Oxford University Press.

Bahl, Roy, Jerry Miner, and Larry Schroeder. 1984. "Mobilizing Local Resources in Developing Countries." *Public Administration and Development* 4(3): 215–30.

Bardach, Eugene. 1994. "Comment: The Problem of 'Best Practice Research.'" *Journal of Policy Analysis and Management* 13(2): 260–68.

Barzelay, Michael. 1991. "Managing Local Development: Lessons From Spain." *Policy Sciences* 24 (August): 271–90.

Bird, Richard. 1994. *Decentralizing Infrastructure. For Good or for Ill?* Washington, D.C.: World Bank.

Bird, Richard M., Robert D. Ebel, and Christine Wallich. 1995. "Fiscal Decentralization: From Command to the Market." In Richard M. Bird, Robert D. Ebel, and Christine Wallich, eds., *Decentralization of the Socialist State.* Washington, D.C.: World Bank.

Blair, Harry. 2000. "Participation and Accountability at the Periphery. Democratic Local Governance in Six Countries." *World Development* 28(1): 21–39.

Boisier, Sergio. 1994. "Crisis y alternativas en los procesos de regionalización." *Revista de la CEPAL* 52: 179–90.

Burki, Shahid Javed, Guillermo Perry, and William Dillinger. 1999. *Beyond the Center. Decentralizing the State.* Washington, D.C.: World Bank.

Cabieses, Hugo, Dirk Kruijt, Raúl Lizarraga, and Menno Vellingo. 1980. *Industrialización y desarrollo regional en el Perú.* Lima: Ediciones Economía, Política y Desarrollo.

Cabrero Mendoza, Enrique, ed. 1995. *La nueva gestión municipal en México. Analisis de experiencias innovadoras en gobiernos locales.* Mexico, D.F.: Centro de Investigación y Docencia Económicas.

Campbell, Tim. 2003. *The Quiet Revolution.* Pittsburgh, Pa.: The University of Pittsburgh Press.

Campbell, Tim, and John Frankenhoff. 1994. "Institutional Development and Decentralized Governance. Looking Back on Lending, Looking Ahead to a Contestability Model of Institutional Development in LAC." Latin American Technical Department Dissemination Note, World Bank, Washington, D.C.

Campbell, Tim, George Peterson, and José Brakarz. 1991. *Decentralization to Local Government in LAC National Strategies and Local Response in Planning, Spending and Management.* Washington, D.C.: World Bank.

Carlos, Juan, and Urenda Diaz. 1987. *Autonomías departamentales. La alternativa al centralismo boliviano.* La Paz: Los Amigos del Libro.

Carroll, T. F. 1992. *Intermediary NGOs: The Supporting Link in Grassroots Development.* West Hartford, Conn: Kumarian Press.

Castaneda, T. 1990. *Para Combatir la Pobreza: Politica Social y Descentralizacion en Chile Durante los 80s.* Santiago, Chile: Centro de Estudios Públicos.

Cheema, G. S., ed. 1993. *Urban Management: Policies and Innovations in Developing Countries.* London: Praeger.

Clark, Terry N., ed. 1994. *Urban Innovation: Creative Strategies for Turbulent Times.* London: Sage Publications.

Clark, Terry N., Gerd-Michael Hellstern, and Guido Martinotti, eds. 1985. *Urban Innovations as a Response to Urban Fiscal Strain.* Berlin: Verlag Europäische Perspektiven.

Collins, Charles D. 1988. "Local Government and Urban Protest in Colombia." *Public Administration and Development* 8(4): 421–36.

Cointreau-Levine, Sandra. 1994. *Private Sector Participation in Municipal Solid Waste Services in Developing Countries,* vol. 1: *The Formal Sector.* Washington, D.C.: World Bank.

Davey, Kenneth. 1993. *Elements of Urban Management.* Washington, D.C.: U.N. Development Programme, World Bank, and U.N. Centre for Human Settlements.

———. 1994. "Institutional Development and Decentralized Governance, an Outsider's View." Latin American Technical Department Dissemination Note, World Bank, Washington, D.C.

Dillinger, William. 1992. *Urban Property Tax Reform, Guidelines and Recommendations.* Washington, D.C.: U.N. Development Programme, World Bank, and U.N. Centre for Human Settlements.

———. 1994. *Decentralization and Its Implications for Urban Service Delivery.* Washington, D.C.: World Bank.

Fox, Jonathan. 1994. "Latin America's Emerging Local Politics." *Journal of Democracy* 5(2): 105–16.

Fuhr, Harald. 1993. "Mobilizing Local Resources in Latin America: Decentralization, Institutional Reforms and Small-Scale Enterprises." In Brigitte Späth, ed., *Small Firms and Development in Latin America: The Role of the Institutional Environment, Human Resources and Industrial Relations.* Geneva: International Labor Organization/International Institute of Labor Studies.

———. 1994a. "Municipal Institutional Strengthening and Donor Coordination: Experiences from Ecuador." In Paul Collins and Peter Blunt, eds., *Institution*

Building in Developing Countries. Special Issue, *Public Administration and Development* 14(2).

————. 1994b. "The Missing Link in Structural Adjustment Policies: The Politico-Institutional Dimension. Some Lessons from Latin America for Eastern European Transitions." In Heinz Bongartz and R. B. Jain, eds., *Structural Adjustment, Public Policy and Bureaucracy in Developing Societies.* New Delhi: Har-Anand Publications.

Geddes, Barbara. 1994. *Politician's Dilemma: Building State Capacity in Latin America.* Berkeley, Calif.: University of California Press.

Government of El Salvador. 1997. *EDUCO. A Learning and Teaching Experiment.* San Salvador: Ministry of Education.

Grindle, Merilee, and Charles Thomas. 1991. *Public Choices and Policy Change: The Political Economy of Reform in Developing Countries.* Baltimore, Md.: The Johns Hopkins University Press.

Guedes, Andréa, Theresa Lobo, Robert Walker, and Ana Lucia Amaral. 1995. *Descentralización educativa, organización y manejo de las escuelas al nivel local: el caso de Minas Gerais, Brazil.* LAC Human and Social Development Group Paper Series 11. World Bank, Washington, D.C.

Hoffman-Martinot, Vincent. 1992. "Municipal Employees and Personnel Policies: A Comparison of Seven Countries." In Poul Erik Moutritzen, ed., *Managing Cities in Austerity: Urban Fiscal Stress in Ten Western Countries.* London: Sage Publications.

Hopkins, Elwood. 1994. *The Life Cycle of Urban Innovations,* vol. 1: *Urban Management Program.* Working Paper Series, World Bank, Washington, D.C.

IDB (Inter-American Development Bank). 1994. *Economic and Social Progress in Latin America. 1994 Report.* Washington, D.C.

Katz, Travis. 1994. *The City Manager Experience in the US.* Washington, D.C.: World Bank.

Kitayama, Toshiya. 1993. *Local Governments and Small and Medium-Sized Enterprises.* Washington, D.C.: World Bank.

Leipziger, Danny M., and Vinod Thomas. 1994. *The Lessons of East Asia. An Overview of Country Experience.* Washington, D.C.: World Bank.

Levy, Brian. 1993. "Obstacles to Developing Indigenous Small and Medium Enterprises: An Empirical Assessment." *World Bank Economic Review* 7(1): 65–83.

Lipsky, Michael. 1980. *Street Level Bureaucracy: Dilemmas of the Individual in Public Services.* New York: Russell Sage Foundation.

Locke, Richard M. 1994. *The Composite Economy: Local Politics and Industrial Change in Contemporary Italy.* Cambridge, Mass.: MIT-Sloan School of Management.

Lordello de Mello, Diogo. 1993. "Resource Mobilization Strategies for Urban Development in Brazil." In G. Shabbir Cheema, ed., *Urban Management: Policies and Innovations in Developing Countries.* London: Praeger.

Loveman, Brian. 1994. *"Las ONG chilenas: Su papel en la transición a la democracia."* In Charles A. Reilly, ed., *Nuevas políticas urbanas: Las ONG y los gobiernos municipales en la democratización latinoamericana.* Arlington, Va.: Inter-American Foundation.

———. 1995. "The Transition to Civilian Government in Chile, 1990–1994." In Paul W. Drake and Iván Jaksic, eds., *The Struggle for Democracy in Chile, 1982–1990.* Lincoln, Nebr.: University of Nebraska Press.

Molina, José, and Janeth Hernandez. 1995. *"Sistemas Electorales subnacionels en America Latina." Lateinamerikaforschung. Arbeitspapier 20. Universitat Heidelberg, Institute fur Politische Wissenschaft.*

Moore, Barrington. 1966. *Social Origins of Dictatorship and Democracy: Lord and Peasant in the Making of the Modern World.* London: Allen Lane.

Mouritzen, Poul E., ed. 1992. *Managing Cities in Austerity. Urban Fiscal Stress in Ten Western Countries.* London: Sage.

Nickson, Andrew. 1995. *Local Government in Latin America.* Boulder, Colo.: Lynn Reiner Publishers.

North, Douglass. 1991. *Institutions, Institutional Change, and Economic Performance.* New York: Cambridge University Press.

Oi, Jean C. 1992. "Fiscal Reform and the Economic Foundations of Local State Corporatism in China." *World Politics* (45)1: 99–126.

Ostrom, Elinor, Larry Schroeder, and Susan Wynne. 1994. *Institutional Incentives and Sustainable Development. Infrastructure Policies in Perspective.* Boulder, Colo.: Westview Press.

Peterson, George. 1997. *Decentralization in Latin America: Learning through Experience.* Washington, D.C.: World Bank.

Prawda, Juan. 1992. *Educational Decentralization in Latin America: Lessons Learned.* Washington, D.C.: World Bank.

Putnam, Robert D., Robert Leonardi, and Raffaella Y. Nanetti. 1993. *Making Democracy Work. Civic Traditions in Modern Italy.* Princeton, N.J.: Princeton University Press.

Pyke, Frank, and Werner Sengenberger, eds. 1992. *Industrial Districts and Local Economic Regeneration.* Geneva: International Institute for Labor Studies.

Reilly, Charles A. 1994. *Nuevas Politicas Urbanas. Las ONG y los gobiernos municipales en la democratización latinoamericana.* Washington, D.C.: Inter-American Foundation.

Rojas, Fernando. 1999. "The Political Context of Decentralization in Latin America." In *Annual World Bank Conference on Development in Latin America and the Caribbean 1999. Decentralization and Accountability of the Public Sector.* Proceedings of a Conference held in Valdivia, Chile, June 20–22, 1999. Washington, D.C.: World Bank.

Sable, Charles. 1994. "Bootstrapping Reform: Rebuilding Firms, the Welfare State and Unions." Unpublished paper, Massachusetts Institute of Technology, Cambridge, Mass.

Schmitz, Hubert. 1990. "Small Firms and Flexible Specialization in Developing Countries." *Labour and Society* 15(3): 257–85.

———. 1993. *Small Shoemakers and Fordist Giants: Tale of a Supercluster.* Sussex, U.K.: Institute for Development Studies.

Schwartz, Herman. 1994. "Small States in Big Trouble." *World Politics* 46(4): 527–55.

Shugart, Matthew Soberg. 1996. *Checks and Balances in Latin America in an Age of Globalization.* Working Paper Series, Inter-American Development Bank, Washington D.C.

Stein, Freiherr vom. 1959. "Über die zweckmäßige Bildung der obersten und der Provinzial-, Finanz- und Polizei-Behörden in der preußischen Monarchie. Nassauer Denkschrift." In Walther Hubatsch, ed., *Freiherr vom Stein: Briefe und amtliche Schriften.* Stuttgart, Germany: Kohlhammer.

Tendler, Judith. 1997. *Good Government in the Tropics.* Baltimore, Md.: The Johns Hopkins Press.

Tendler, Judith, and Mónica Alves Amorim. 1996. "Small Firms and Their Helpers: Lessons on Demand." *World Development* 24(1): 407–26.

UNICEF (U.N. Childrens Fund). 1993. *Focussing Information to Focus Political Responsibility—Case Study of Advocacy and Social Mobilization for Children Linked to Decentralization and Elections in Colombia.* Bogota.

UNDP-BMZ. 2000. *The UNDP Role in Decentralization and Local Government. A Joint UNDP—Government of Germany Evaluation.* New York: United Nations Development Programme and German Federal Ministry for Economic Cooperation and Development.

Vallmitjana, Marta, ed. 1993. *Caracas: nuevos escenarios para el poder local.* Caracas: U.N. Development Programme and Nueva Sociedad.

World Bank. 1989. *Brazil: Municipal Development Project in the State of Rio Grande do Sul. Staff Appraisal Report.* 7714-BR. Latin American Region, Washington, D.C.

———. 1990. *Argentina: Provincial Government Finance.* Latin American Region, Washington, D.C.

———. 1991. *Mexico: Decentralization and Urban Development.* Report 8924-ME. Latin American Region, Washington, D.C.

———. 1992. *Chile: Subnational Government Finance.* Report 10580-CH. Latin American Region, Washington, D.C.

———. 1995. *Colombia Local Government Capacity: Beyond Technical Assistance.* Washington, D.C.

————. 1997. *World Development Report 1997: The State in a Changing World.* New York: Oxford University Press.

————. 1999a. *Annual World Bank Conference on Development in Latin America and the Caribbean 1999. Decentralization and Accountability of the Public Sector.* Proceedings of a conference held in Valdivia, Chile, June 20–22, 1999. Washington, D.C.: World Bank.

————. 1999b. *Entering the 21st Century. World Development Report 1999/2000.* Washington, D.C.: World Bank and Oxford University Press.

4

Selection of Cases and Methods

Tim Campbell, World Bank
Harald Fuhr, University of Potsdam

Earlier chapters have set the stage by describing the context of decentralization, speculating on how this regionwide trend triggered an emerging model of governance, and how this model in turn began to frame new incentives for local actors. The previous chapter posed key research questions based on a review of the literature, and it explored many of the most important policy issues in five areas of local development. This chapter describes the methods used to select to document the innovations in these areas.

Research Method and Case Selection: Describing the New Generation of Innovators

The case material for this book has been selected from 21 examples of innovation that were documented in the Innovations Study carried out in the former technical department of the World Bank's Latin America and the Caribbean Region from 1994 to 1997. This chapter reviews the methods that were used in organizing and implementing the Innovations Study and that underpin the cases appearing in Part 2 of this book.[1] The singular feature setting this study apart from others about best practices was the focus on contextual conditions and origins of innovation. Each of the cases takes account of historical, political, economic, and cultural factors that might help not only to explain the genesis of innovation, but also to gain insight

---

1. The "Regional Study 'Decentralization in LAC. Best Practices and Policy Lessons'" was jointly managed by Tim Campbell and Harald Fuhr, with assistance from Florence Eid, Travis Katz, and Daniel Taillant.

into its incorporation into the prevailing system of government and to explore the conditions for replication.

Criteria for Selection of Cases

Cases reflecting change in the five areas were selected mainly on the basis of reputation among professional practitioners. A first-cut list of over 30 cases was compiled from various sources, most important from analysts familiar with the field who worked for the World Bank, the Inter-American Development Bank, and the Economic Commission for Latin America, as well as for bilateral donors (U.S. Agency for International Development, German Technical Cooperation, Swedish International Development Cooperation Agency, Canadian International Development Agency) and universities. After the formation of the team for the Innovations Study, including a peer review panel, nominations were solicited from analysts and practitioners in the field based on empirical observation or systematic review of data gathered in the course of professional work. For example, the Colombian cases were spotted during the course of economic and sector work that was underway there in 1995 (World Bank 1995). Many of the cases were common knowledge (such as Curitiba), widely recognized as innovative. Other cases (such as Tijuana) were put forward as relative newcomers in published studies (Guillen 1995) or, in the case of Mendoza, in unpublished reports. A large number of cases emerged in professional conferences and seminars. For example, the first two Inter-American Conference of Mayors produced a half-dozen nominations (Campbell, Fuhr, and Eid 1995).

An effort was made also to include relatively new innovation cases, as well as older ones, that have spawned secondary changes at the local level and beyond. In this respect, the study sought to take into account conditions before decentralization by registering experiences that could be compared on contextual grounds with "later comers." In hindsight, it is possible to see that not all of the innovations were completely successful, but in the beginning all appeared to be moving toward an improved standard of practice. The selection criteria also included a longevity measure. All but one case had survived more than one political administration.[2] In addition,

---

2. It should be noted that a deliberate decision was made to not study failures, on the following methodological grounds: (a) practitioners and professionals are relatively more familiar with many of the common impediments and pitfalls that defeat innovations, and (b) success stories of a representative cross-section often will have overcome the problems that typically lead to failures (Bardach 1994).

geographical and sectoral criteria were applied to achieve a broad cross-section of experiences in Latin America and the Caribbean.

Classification by Area of Impact

From the first cut, the study team selected 21 cases. Table 4.1 maps out each of the cases studied and indicates the primary (as well as secondary and tertiary) impacts in each of the five focal areas affected by the innovation.

Many of the cases cross our categorical boundaries. "Participation," for instance, is found everywhere, and this made it impractical to follow a clean classification by category in the following chapters. Often the cases impacted several major areas. The Tijuana case, for instance, is about participation, fiscal reform, and infrastructure services. It would be undesirable and counterproductive to maintain a rigorous separation of these aspects.

Classification by Age and Complexity

It is helpful to consider the cases in four broad (and somewhat overlapping) categories: simple versus complex, and first generation versus mature. A "simple" case refers to an innovation of a tool, technique, or process familiar and central to the everyday flow of municipal business, like training

Table 4.1. *Cases by Area of Impact*

Case	Admin- istration	Fiscal	Service	Private sector	Partici- pation
Cali			++	+++	+
Conchali	+++		++		++
Curitiba	+		+++	++	
Manizales/Valledupar	++	+++	+		
Santa Cruz			+++	++	+
Mendoza (budget)	+++	+++			
Mendoza (infrastructure)	+	++	+++	+	+++
Porto Alegre budget	+	++			+++
Tijuana		+++	+		++
Nicaragua			++	+++	++
Venezuela			+++		

Note: +++ Primary. ++ Secondary. + Tertiary. Empty cells represent either no impact or not applicable.

Source: Campbell, Fuhr, and Eid (1995).

municipal officials, budgeting, city planning, management and finance, and the like. In reality, these projects are hardly simple, but their distinguishing feature is they do not involve extensive contact with large segments of the public. More than half the cases selected in this study fall into the simple category. The remaining cases, classified as "complex," are more elaborate and complicated. They involve extensive participation of the public, such as neighborhood groups, volunteer organizations, and the voters at large. For instance, some cases involve the convening of many hundreds of meetings to determine city spending priorities or to work out neighborhood indebtedness arrangements.

Simple and complex cases can be either initial innovations in the city or part of a sequence of several or more. Manizales, for instance, set up a training institute, reformed its finances, started new health care service, and launched an innovative waste service. These innovations took place mostly under one political administration, making Manizales a "first-generation" case. Curitiba, on the other hand, launched a long series of innovations branching out from land use to transport to solid waste and management of commercial vendors, all over a period of 30 years. The lengthy, sustained sequence of innovations makes Curitiba a "mature" case (see table 4.2).

Both complex and mature cases build sequentially on past innovations, allowing for some broadening of the scope of inquiry. By examining an innovation that has been preceded by others, it is possible to look for clues about the conditions for sustained change, often under the assumption that preceding innovations enrich the environment for change and that management of the innovation process becomes a new level of endeavor. In all cases, we focused on the breakthrough of the initial innovation. These aspects of complexity and age, together with more detail about the scope of innovations, are also indicated in table 4.2.

Methodology and Work Program

The field research was carried out in close consultation and cooperation with World Bank task managers in the region. Existing lending projects and economic and sector work had already provided valuable inputs for the design and preselection of case studies. The conjoint nature of the project (involving staff from other Bank departments, as well as country officials and consultants) helped leverage resources and provided important education and training, ultimately promoting the interregional perspective and approach embodied in the study.

Table 4.2. *Age, Context, and Scope of Cases*

City or country	Innovation	Scope	Complexity	Generation and launch date
Cali	Private role in public life	Planning, finance, and management of public business by private sector	Simple	Multiple 1920s
Curitiba	Transportation	Integrated urban transport system building on sequence of innovations	Complex	Multiple 1960s
Manizales and Valledupar	Financial reform	Tax reform and major improvements in financial management	Simple	First 1990
Mendoza	Social censure to guarantee credit	Infrastructure finance in low-income households	Complex	First 1991
Santa Cruz	Public-private collaboration in services	Incorporation of private sector role in cooperative delivery of key services	Complex	Multiple 1980s
Conchali	Neighborhood improvements	Combined municipal service delivery with organized community inputs	Complex	First 1990
Mendoza	Administrative reform	Reform of budgeting process	Simple	Multiple 1990
Porto Alegre	Participatory budgeting	Incorporation of community inputs in all phases of capital budgeting	Complex	Multiple 1985
Venezuela	Privatization of ports and mines	Methods and techniques of transferring public enterprises to private sector	Simple	Multiple 1989
Nicaragua	Neighborhood improvements	Coordination of municipalities, banks, and the poor in shelter and infrastructure improvements	Complex	First 1985
Tijuana	Capital improvements	Use of betterment levy backed by referendum to mobilize political and financial support for city investments	Complex	Multiple 1992

Source: Authors.

Research Methodology

Consistent with the case study approach outlined in chapter 3, the study team used a qualitative analysis research methodology. The case study approach facilitated a very detailed sectoral analysis of prominent institutional issues in decentralization. Because most of the casework consisted of gathering information about the genesis and dynamics of local institutional change over time, reviewing documents and conducting interviews comprised an important part of the research methodology.

The original fieldwork was based on five research framework papers that discussed some relevant background material and literature and that included research questions (terms of reference) as guidelines for research on good and best practice in different subnational environments. The key sections of these papers are incorporated into the following text.

The research framework papers covered the following areas:

- Incorporation of professionalism and innovations in local management
- Innovations in mobilizing and managing local and regional resources
- Innovations in local service provision and related intergovernmental cooperative arrangements
- Innovations in mobilizing private sector development
- Innovations in local participation and public policymaking

The papers described the various steps taken to introduce new or reformed measures in order to improve efficiency in government and overall prospects for better service delivery and private sector development. Although in practice most innovations complement each other—innovations in area 1 may have caused innovations in 2 and 5, or the latter may have stimulated the others; innovations in 3 and 4 may be dependent on each other, and may have been linked from the very beginning, and so on—we tended, for the sake of comparative research and clear definition of areas of inquiry, to keep the categories distinct. In the case of write-ups, such distinctions were no longer fully necessary.

The review of documents allowed for an assessment of the economic and political environment of the selected cases (municipalities and regions) and, consequently, served to identify more easily the specific set of economic and political incentives triggering the behavior of local policymakers, entrepreneurs, and other social actors. As outlined in the first two chapters, this review process was to take into account a careful blend of different theoretical and conceptual approaches, such as political economy, new institutional economics, and neocorporatism, depending on the context.

Interviews with "key informants"—local decisionmakers (past and present), local experts, and other relevant actors—complemented the empirical reconstruction of cases and allowed for crosschecking and verification of the information gathered. Given the lack of previous documentation in some cases, qualitative interviews were one of the most important tools available to collect the required information. Because interviews were held with a variety of actors and focused on a cumulative knowledge of cases, they were necessarily based on a rather restricted set of open-ended questions. To allow for some intercountry comparisons, an interview format defining basic informational requirements and expected outputs was developed.

Field Guide for Case Studies

Researchers took six analytical steps in each case study:

- Identifying the context and origins
- Documenting the evolution of the idea—that is, the major transitional phase involving experimentation and implementation
- Describing and assessing the outcomes to date in terms of impact and degree of solution reached
- Analyzing the obstacles or pitfalls encountered during transition
- Describing the extent to which horizontal and vertical diffusion has taken place and sustainability has been achieved
- Addressing how obstacles might be avoided and successful outcomes enhanced in the future.

Each of the authors of the cases was to follow an analytical approach that incorporated these key areas of concern and to organize the inquiry and report writing in accordance with this broad structure. The field guides included specific instructions in several areas, as detailed in the following paragraphs.

SYSTEMIC CONTEXT AND ORIGINS. Researchers had to recognize that a broad, circumspect approach should be taken to understand not only the mechanics of how new managerial styles work, but also to clarify and document the conditions—political, institutional, civic—under which these styles were brought into being. The cases followed the broad outlines—and much of the detail in the areas of context and evolution—of a method reported in, for example, *The Life Cycle of Urban Innovations*, a review of selected urban innovations compiled by the "Mega-Cities project"(see Hopkins 1995, pp. 6–7, 15–19, 29–31).[3]

As suggested earlier, innovations in management, and particularly the separation of technical from political functions in the management of cities, flow as a consequence of the decentralization process in the country. Our hypothesis is that these impulses arise in response to a felt need for more effective government, including, in part, greater accountability and clearer transparency. In addition, the circumstances of change arise from more intense and richer horizontal interactions in political, economic, and business affairs among actors at a regional level than were true before decentralization. The case studies explored political, economic, social, and civic dimensions of these horizontal linkages. They are equivalent to Hopkins's "networks of groups and intersectoral linkages" (Hopkins 1995, p. 29), or with alliances of political, public, and private sectors (Putnam 1993). In other words, the dimensions of analysis are strongly sociopolitical in content, and these should be treated with sensitivity to historical factors (for example, to contemporary history with occasional reference to tradition and identity where such concepts are immediately relevant to understanding the innovation under review).

EVOLUTION, OBSTACLES, AND TRANSITION. Researchers were to define in comparative detail the innovation under consideration. Examples could include such innovations as city manager (compared to the city manager paper by Katz 1994); financial reform (compared to Dillinger 1992), or political reform (for example, Bland 1994). Field researchers were to seek out what was distinct about a particular municipal or regional reform in comparison to the literature and to other cities or regions in the country. What have been the achievements in terms of efficiency, equity, or accountability of the reform? What is left to achieve?

Case analysts were cautioned to understand that the innovations they reviewed most probably had evolved through many stages. This evolution contains many of the secrets to successful innovation and reform because

---

3. Consultants had to take note of the drawbacks of adhering too rigidly to the lifecycle format, as described in Hopkins (1995). Had we tried to force fit the experiences we wished to document into our preconceived format, we could have distorted the true course of evolution in a particular case. Therefore consultants should feel free to change the order of treatment or combine sections. It is important to ensure that the conditions and context are described so that one experience can be compared and understood in the context of similar or contrasting experiences in other countries.

each change in the original idea is introduced to overcome some obstacle. The case investigations were to be seen, fundamentally, as historical analyses to understand the sequence of changes and to fill in detail about how the innovation was kept alive.

Conception is one of the most important of the phases. Our research sought to examine whether the origin of the idea had a long gestation period, was brought in from outside (as in the case of city managers to Honduras), or was hatched from necessity (the betterment levies following disastrous floods in Tijuana). The analysis was to trace these origins into phases of formulation and champion, that is, to identify who synthesized and refined the idea and what actor or actors kept it moving and promoted it. The research takes note of what local and regional allies helped in the promotion of the innovation, and how the innovation might have evolved or been redesigned to accommodate outside interests or to improve acceptability.

An important part of the story is to gauge the barriers and natural resistance to risk and the opposition that might arise when vested interests are threatened. Such obstacles could take the form of political party interests, council opposition, questions of cost, or resistance of entrenched interests. Research sought to identify both the forces of opposition—misunderstanding, lethargy or social drag, vested interests—and the collective, horizontal support mobilized to overcome these barriers. How important were outside forces from the region, the nation, or other nations, in overcoming them?

The research reports were to begin with a timeline, eventually to appear as an annex, that would trace the evolution in notational form. Typical cases were to start with a statement of the problem organically conceived as the objective of the innovation and to indicate the major dates and events that shaped the course of evolution. The cases do have key dates, but not always detailed timelines.

OUTCOMES: IMPLEMENTATION AND IMPACT OF INNOVATIONS. Analysts were to evaluate the tangible impact of the innovation, that is, whether it had achieved the desired success or had mutated into a fundamentally different, but still useful, innovation. They were to examine whether local circumstances or more powerful underlying needs pushed reform and innovation into something more useful. Accordingly a more objective, outside measure might conclude that different levels of success, or qualitatively unexpected results (or failure) were achieved and were perhaps worthwhile. In this measurement the "reach" of the innovation—the savings in money, the qualitative change in management, the sense of ownership in participation—is important to document and, if possible, to evaluate.

Once the first several steps in the field guide had been achieved, two other sets of questions were to be addressed. In essence, the case studies were to document whatever full or partial success a particular case might have had, then to identify what was left to accomplish, and, finally, summarize what conditions needed to be met for replicability.

DIFFUSION AND DISSEMINATION. The purpose of this phase of work was to understand whether the innovation had spread "horizontally"—that is, to other equivalent levels of government, such as municipalities—as well as whether it had spread "vertically," or diffused up or down to other levels of government or out to other countries. The agent of transmission was important here. International agents can parachute ideas into the setting—as in the case of city mangers—and can lift good ideas. But it may be more important if some internal transmission mechanism is at work. Both extent of diffusion and transmission mechanism were cited as important areas to document.

REPLICABILITY AND RECOMMENDATIONS. A final, but linked, set of questions was to determine whether the circumstances that had led to innovations could be sustained. Equally important was to gauge the extent to which the innovations could be replicated. Part of the answer to these questions depends on whether the terms and circumstances of innovation (in city management, for instance) are amenable to policy levers immediately available to local leaders, and whether leaders can manipulate them. For instance, the Colombia study of local capacity (World Bank 1995) has shown that changes in electoral rules, and nomination by civic alliances in particular, led to new crops of leaders not tied to traditional party elites. This innovation was triggered by electoral reform at the national level. Employing city management professionals has become an option to mayors newly freed from traditional bonds of patronage. The case analysts were to explore the extent to which this freedom was essential to replicability. Do some cases show that the professionalization of management need not depend on political independence? A similar, and possibly less rigorous, set of questions holds for the introduction of objective, transparent, and modern financial management systems.

Conclusion

Some 17 cases were explored and documented, with extensive field visits and original materials from each case. Following successive rounds of research, field seminars—one in Cartagena in 1995 and a second in Caracas in 1996—were held to discuss clusters of cases. The chapters in the following sections benefited from these discussions and from participant feedback at the seminars.

As indicated, the study was not intended to lead to a monolithic review of decentralization policies, but rather to a set of smaller, mutually linked, standalone studies designed to document best practices experiences of innovation in selected countries. The study also identified gaps that remain in current decentralization practice. Since the extent and scope of such policies, and the overall political and social context for them, differ from country to country, no quick fix, cross-country, or cross-sector solution was expected from this research. Rather, the study identified the set of institutional factors that have made some cases of decentralization and decentralized decisionmaking more successful than others. The case studies document innovations and achievements, accumulating knowledge about the requirements for successful and sustainable institutional change. In a constructive manner, and with a sharper view toward sectoral issues, the study contributed to ongoing discussion of the opportunities, costs, benefits, and perils of decentralization in Latin America and the Caribbean.

References

Bardach, Eugene. 1994. "Comment: The Problem of 'Best Practice' Research." *Journal of Policy Analysis and Management* 13(2): 260–68.

Bland, Gary. 1994. "Local and Intermediate Level Electoral Policy in Latin America and the Caribbean." Processed for the Latin America and the Caribbean Technical Department, World Bank, Washington, D.C.

Campbell, Tim, Harald Fuhr, and Florence Eid. 1995. "Decentralization in LAC: Best Practice and Policy Lessons." Initiating Memorandum for LATAD Regional Study. Washington, D.C.: World Bank.

Dillinger, William. 1992. *Urban Property Tax Reform, Guidelines and Recommendations.* Washington, D.C.: U.N. Development Programme, World Bank, and U.N. Centre for Human Settlements.

Guillen, Tonatiuh. 1995. *Innovaciones y Conflicto—Sociedad Civil y Gobierno Local.* Tijuana, Mexico: *Colegio de la Frontera Norte.*

Hopkins, Elwood. 1995. "The Life Cycle of Urban Innovations." Vol. 1. Urban Management Program Working Paper Series, World Bank, Washington, D.C.

Katz, Travis. 1994. *The City Manager Experience in the U.S.* Washington, D.C.: World Bank, LATAD.

Putnam, Robert D. 1993. *Making Democracy Work. Civic Traditions in Modern Italy.* Princeton, N.J.: Princeton University Press.

World Bank. 1995. *Colombia Local Government Capacity: Beyond Technical Assistance.* Washington, D.C.: World Bank.

Part 2

Cases

Some of the illustrative cases discussed in this volume were prepared several years prior to publication. In a number of instances the discussion has been left in the present tense to preserve the immediacy of the description. Thus readers should be aware that the case studies do not necessarily reflect the present conditions in those areas under review.

Part 2

5

*Fiscal Management and Local
Resource Mobilization*

5-1

The Politics of Participation in Tijuana, Mexico: Inventing a New Style of Governance

Tim Campbell, World Bank
Travis Katz, McKinsey & Company

The case of Tijuana is an amalgam of a half-dozen innovations, rather than just one (see box 5-1.1). The direct and indirect connections among the innovations in Tijuana built upon, and then helped advance, a qualitative change in the style of governance of the municipality. In fact, innovations in the city—first in property tax increases, then in management of income and expenditures—occurred during several political administrations. The administration of Héctor Osuna Jaime (1992–95) built upon groundwork of the previous administration of Carlos Montejo Favela (1989–92). By increasing revenue and gradually heightening discipline in spending, and then modernizing cadastre and management information systems, the two successive administrations brought city government back into the black despite having borrowed several million dollars for cadastre improvements.

Although the Urban Action Program (Plan de Activación Urbana, or PAU) was perhaps the most audacious of all the innovations in Tijuana's city government, it must be seen in the context, and sequencing, of other innovations (see figure 5-1.1). The PAU was designed to be financed by a betterment levy, accompanied, for purposes of decisionmaking, by a citywide public referendum. But the PAU could not have been formulated without the cadastre improvement program, which generated detailed land use and financial data. Then, after the peso crisis and other major national-level

---

Box 5-1.1. *Innovations in the Municipality of Tijuana*

Cadastre Modernization: In October 1993, the city of Tijuana signed an agreement with BANOBRAS (Mexico's national credit agency for state and local governments) for a loan to fund modernization of the city's cadastre. The result is a high-tech, fully digitized map and database system, which places information—from the size and value of a property to its electricity, water, and sewage connections—at the fingertips of city agencies and property owners.

The aim of the cadastre modernization was to improve municipal revenue collection. Its impact, however, has extended to many areas of public and private management. The modernized mapping system made possible the identification of works and the estimation of beneficiary contribution that formed the basis for the city's urban rehabilitation program. In addition, the new system allowed municipal officials to rationalize solid waste collection and disposal systems, improve police protection, monitor growth, and plan proactively, as well as quickly provide citizens with up-to-date information about properties.

Financial Management Improvements: During the administrations of Carlos Montejo Favela and Héctor Osuna Jaime, the municipal government implemented a series of measures to improve the management of the city's finances. Increased property tax collections, buttressed by the new cadastre, caused the municipality's own-source revenue to climb more than 65 percent over six years. Corresponding improvements in spending restraint, plus increased efficiency of service provision, generated savings that were channeled into a number of community and social programs, including ¡Manos a la Obra!.

Urban Action Program (Plan de Activación Urbana, or PAU): This comprehensive, large-scale public works program was designed in the wake of torrential flooding in 1993, which, combined with a severe lack of basic infra-

---

political events derailed the PAU, the city focused on developmental efforts it could afford. The city increased the emphasis on a popular small-scale civil works program (¡Manos a la Obra!, or Hands to Work) for low-income communities. At a very different level of action, the city also mobilized prominent private citizens in a deliberative process about Tijuana's future through a strategic plan (Plan Estratégico de Tijuana, or

structure, cost more than 60 people their lives. The program was backed by a public referendum and included 40 major works, to be financed largely by beneficiaries through a betterment levy. Beneficiaries would be charged differential rates based on the size of a property and its proximity to the works. Due to the severe devaluation of the peso in December 1994, however, the program was put on hold indefinitely.

¡Manos a la Obra!: This was a small works program involving beneficiaries in the selection of works, contracting of services, oversight, and cost recovery. Manos was similar in function to a program by the PRI, or Revolutionary Institutional Party, called the National Solidarity Program (Programa Nacional de Solidaridad, or PRONASOL) and, not coincidentally, initiated in an election year. Communities were asked to elect local works committees and submit proposals for projects to be cofinanced by the municipality. More than 2,400 proposals were submitted, mostly for paving, drainage, stairs, and other basic infrastructure. For approved projects, the municipality provided partial funding (ranging from 80 percent of the project cost in poor neighborhoods to 20 percent in upper-income areas) and limited technical assistance to the community. The works committee itself was then responsible for the contracting of labor, collection of beneficiary contributions, oversight, and payment of bills.

Strategic Plan (Plan Estratégico de Tijuana, or PET): The PET is a process through which business and community leaders can come together with the city to develop a long-term vision for Tijuana. Andersen Consulting developed the PET using Bilbao, Spain, as a model. Andersen conducted an analysis of the challenges facing Tijuana that was published in March 1995. With this analysis in hand, the leaders involved in strategic planning were expected to seek medium- and long-term solutions to these challenges.

PET). Throughout the two administrations covered in this study, the city managed to keep spending within the limits set by its income.

The PAU was the innovation of greatest scope, widest visibility, and most intense public debate, and it was central in the sense that it built upon the reforms of the previous government and laid the groundwork for deepening the political process in the city. The PAU also featured the most novelty

Figure 5-1.1. *Schematic Sequence of Tijuana's Innovations*

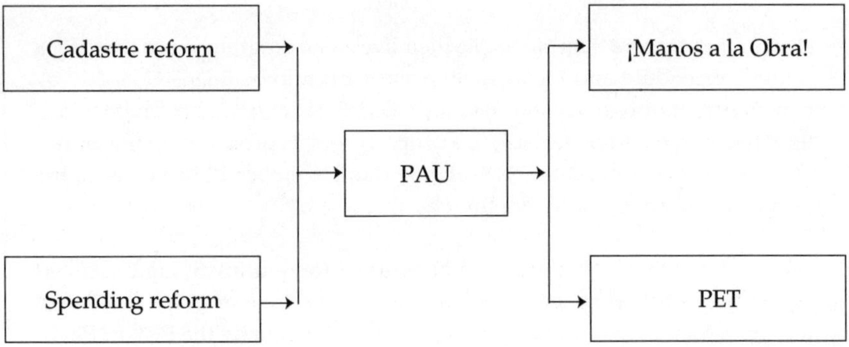

Source: Authors.

in terms of finance and fiscal choice. Although it was conspicuous in many ways, the peso crisis and a change of Tijuana's political administration (in December 1995) demolished prospects for moving ahead with the PAU. But the innovations before it, and those afterward, are also an indispensable part of the story of change in the city (see box 5-1.1).

Systemic Context and Origins

In an abstract way, it might be said that the innovations in Tijuana developed from a fundamental desire to take control of a city that had grown far faster and wealthier than nearly all others in the country in the past 20 years. Population growth from the mid 1970s to the mid 1990s averaged 5 percent in many years. This growth overwhelmed the transport corridors of the city and left nearly a third of its residents without water and connections, and 40 percent without sewerage. Many residents lived in substandard and precarious shelters awkwardly situated in a cityscape marked by steep, barren hillsides that were difficult to access and highly vulnerable to subsidence and floods. Industrial parks and *maquila* (foreign manufacturing) facilities leapfrogged over residential areas crowded in and around the city center and commercial zones. The industrial areas in turn became surrounded by overnight settlements of newly arrived populations seeking employment and wages much higher than the national average (see box 5-1.2 for an overview of Tijuana.)

Box 5-1.2. *Managing the Urban Stresses of a Frontier Metropolis*

In a state separated from the rest of Mexico by the Gulf of California, Tijuana is a frontier town in several respects. The U.S.-Mexican border slices across its northern flank in a straight east-west line that divides such features as a watershed, a tourist beachfront, and miles of industrial corridor. Tijuana is a city of immigrants from virtually every Mexican state—60 percent of its residents were born elsewhere and drawn to Tijuana by the promise of high wages or passage to the United States. Although Tijuana employs 51 percent of its working-age population (as opposed to 43 percent nationally), 70 percent of the work force is immigrant labor. Seasonal laborers are funneled through Tijuana to work in the fields and orchards of California. *Maquila* investments starting in the 1960s also accelerated immigration to the city. By 1970 the population had passed 600,000, and it reached more than double that number by the 1990s.

Tijuana's 1990 population of 1.2 million made it the largest city in the state. It is one of the most urbanized municipalities in the country, with nearly 99 percent of its population living in an urban setting, as compared with 90 percent in the state and 72 percent in the country as a whole. Tijuana has also been one of the fastest growing and most dynamic cities in Mexico over the past two decades. The rapid growth and prospects for rising incomes have made Tijuana a kind of labor reservoir, replete with skilled and semi-skilled laborers ebbing and flowing with seasonal agricultural activity as well as with very high turnover in the *maquilas*.

Tijuana's proximity to the U.S. border has profoundly influenced its character. Approximately 40,000 people cross the border to work legally in the United States each day. Tourism on both sides of the border provides for a constant exchange of culture and ideas. Residents have grown up watching American television and hearing American radio. This close association, combined with increased trade flows due to the North American Free Trade Agreement, has caused many in the Tijuana-San Diego area to view their destinies jointly. Indeed, exercises in joint planning and environmental and border management have become common practice for the two cities. The high degree of cross-cultural exchange and the lack of a deep-seated traditionalism makes Tijuana, in many senses, an ideal breeding ground for innovations.

On the flip side of Tijuana's unique demographics, however, is a troubling deficit in basic services. As the population of Tijuana more than doubled between 1970 and 1990, Tijuana built up a massive backlog of desperately needed infrastructure. The municipal census of 1990 showed that only 68 percent of residents had access to running water in their homes and, of these, many had running water only on certain days or during certain hours of the day. Some 64 percent of respondents had no access to municipal sewage services and, perhaps most telling, 76 percent of the population had no access to paved roads or roads in good condition. Despite a higher than average level of income and employment, Tijuana's explosive growth left it vulnerable.

Decentralization

In 1983, the first modern era of decentralization began to affect local governments in Mexico. In that year, responsibilities for property taxation were shifted to local governments. In 1985, modifications to Article 115 of the national constitution transferred more responsibilities to Mexican municipalities, making them fully or jointly responsible for a variety of local services (World Bank 1991).

Soon after, the opposition National Action Party (Partido de Acción Nacional, or PAN) won the governorship in the state of Baja California (see box 5-1.3). Then, in 1989, PAN's Montejo was elected mayor in Tijuana. PAN's strategy in Tijuana and other cities was to promise a record of good government following the principle of *subsidiarity*, under which assistance of the state in civic affairs is allowed only insofar as it is really needed. Although this demarcation of government is difficult, perhaps impossible, to define in theory, in practice it becomes defined by degrees of importance

---

Box 5-1.3. *The State of Baja California*

The 32 Mexican states form the second tier of government under the Mexican federal constitution of 1917. States are equivalent to federated units found in other countries in the region (such as Brazil, República Bolivariana de Venezuela, and Argentina). They have their own executive and legislative branches (to which representatives are elected) that pass laws, raise revenue, and implement state programs. In fact, the Mexican federal system has been strongly central since 1917, buttressed by an unusually strong political party and institutionalized in the political and governmental life of the country. In the 1990s, this dominance was challenged by competing parties in state and local elections. Two successive opposition governments have been elected in Baja California and in the city of Tijuana.

Baja California lies at the extreme northwestern corner of the country in a semiarid region. The state covers about 70,000 square kilometers, making it about the size of Nicaragua. Baja California and its principal city, Tijuana, have been affected heavily by Mexico's promotion efforts and particularly by the *maquiladora* program, in which foreign companies are allowed duty free import of manufacturing facilities and export of products in exchange for Mexican labor inputs. Manufacturing growth adds to the attraction of Tijuana for migrant streams already drawn by agricultural jobs and cross-border trade with California.

given to the individual, as opposed to the state, in the context of political opposition. In general, the PAN seeks to curb the role of the public sector in private life more sharply than the Revolutionary Institutional Party, better known as PRI.

Ironically, in the eyes of PAN leaders, fiscal reform and more, not less, activism in the state were required to gain fiscal and policy control of the city. Soon after taking office in 1989, Mayor Montejo proposed to improve the city's fiscal situation by increasing property taxes and improving collections efforts and management of municipal records and finance. Financing the infrastructure backlog in the city and improving city services were widely recognized as important objectives. In addition to the opposition, Montejo faced a challenge throughout his administration caused by an internecine struggle in the PAN. He did manage to secure revaluation of property and to achieve increases in collections and expenditure controls. Table 5-1.1 and figure 5-1.2 present these steps and their results.

Catalytic Role of the Flooding of 1993

The impulse to control the city's rapid growth, coupled with federal decentralization and the city's own management reforms, might not have produced

Table 5-1.1. *Municipal Income and Expenditures, Tijuana, 1989–94*
(millions of 1995 new pesos)

Year	Montejo administration			Osuna administration		
	1989	1990	1991	1992	1993	1994
Total revenues	264.1	313.5	343.0	366.5	425.6	437.9
(percentage change from prior year)	—	(18.7)	(9.4)	(6.8)	(16.1)	(2.9)
Own source revenues	154.5	180.8	201.4	206.4	249.3	243.7
(percentage change from prior year)	—	(17.1)	(11.4)	(2.5)	(20.8)	(–2.3)
(percentage of total revenues)	(58.5)	(57.7)	(58.7)	(56.3)	(58.6)	(55.7)
Expenditures	292.8	313.3	339.0	367.0	430.5	416.6
(percentage change from prior year)	—	(7.0)	(8.2)	(8.3)	(17.3)	(–3.2)

— Not available.
Source: Project files, Municipal Treasurer's Office, City of Tijuana.

Figure 5-1.2. *Municipal Income and Expenditures, Tijuana, 1989–94*

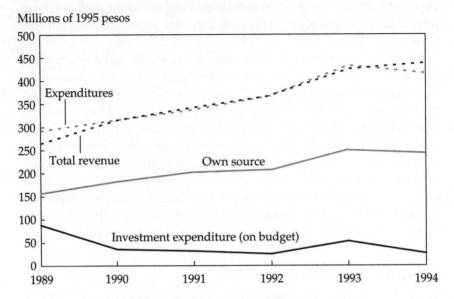

Source: Project files, 1995, Municipal Office of Public Works, City of Tijuana.

such an ambitious innovation as the PAU, even under ideal circumstances—
a reform-minded mayor in a city open to new ideas. As in other cases (such
as the Programma Social de Infrastructure de Mendoza, or Mendoza Social
Infrastructure Program, in Argentina), it took a crisis to spark innovation.
Less than two months after taking office, Montejo's successor, Héctor Osuna
Jaime, was confronted with storm damage and flooding of crisis propor-
tions. Heavy storms dropped more rain in three days of January 1993 than
Tijuana normally had in an entire season. Flash floods washed shanties down
steep gullies and killed more than 60 people, mostly low-income residents.
Some places in the city were buried under six feet of mud. A large backlog of
infrastructure, after two decades of rapid growth, left the city vulnerable to
this natural disaster. Damages were estimated at around US$170 million.

The havoc wreaked by floods left the city in a state of disaster, forcing
the new mayor to seek new ways of addressing the urban infrastructure
problem. From this crisis sprung two innovations. One, the PAU, was aimed
at addressing large-scale infrastructure needs with broad impact, including the paving of major thoroughfares and boulevards. The second, ¡Manos
a la Obra!, was conceived as a tool to provide desperately needed social
infrastructure in the districts of Tijuana.

The Urban Action Program (PAU)

The torrential rains triggered an emergency reaction in the city in the form of a plan to restore urban infrastructure. The PAU, in principle, was conceived rapidly. But it emerged only gradually from a stop-and-go process of deliberation and planning. Furthermore, the PAU evolved in surprising directions as its dimensions and the methods for sharing its financing were presented to the public. As mentioned earlier, the PAU became critically dependent upon a cadastre modernization program, which was undertaken concurrently with Osuna's ascension to office in December 1992 (see box 5-1.4).

Box 5-1.4. *Cadastre Modernization*

Tax and spending reforms carried out by Mayor Carlos Montejo Favela were taking place while his eventual successor, Héctor Osuna Jaime, was serving in the statehouse as representative of a central district in Tijuana. In this capacity, Osuna grew increasingly aware of the ample scope for improvements in spending and management and of the potential for increased revenues through property tax modernization.

During his campaign for mayor, Osuna began laying the groundwork for this modernization by asking the head of the cadastre office to prepare a modernization program. From November 1992 (before the election) to April 1993 (several months after Osuna took office), officials prepared a US$1.1 million program, to be financed by borrowing from BANOBRAS (Mexico's national credit agency for state and local governments). The program would completely overhaul the 215,000 legal and physical records of the city. It would gather and input entirely new databases on modern, integrated computer systems. This in turn would allow greater property tax revenues and nearly instantaneous turnaround of zoning and property transactions at public terminals in the cadastre office. The modernization program also offered great promise for agencies working in water, power, planning, transportation, and housing.

Osuna signed the four-year BANOBRAS loan in October 1993. Technical work began the following month, while the details of the PAU were being worked out. The data acquisition and mapping produced results at the very moment they were needed to begin detailing the locations and impacts of the works proposed for the PAU. Maps and data arising from the cadastre modernization were instrumental in planning and costing out the PAU and in educating the public about the geographical location and costs of the proposed works.

Launching the PAU

A quasi-public agency of the city, the Urban Mobilization Unit (known as the Unidad de Movilización Urbana, or UMU) developed an engineering proposal for the mayor. The unit, which was set up by Montejo as a way to execute projects quickly, operated as a private sector enterprise, because it would contract with labor without the encumbrances of public bidding, clearances, and other bureaucratic requirements. The UMU's chief engineer worked closely with the mayor to develop a plan of action for recovery from the floods, taking advantage first of previously developed state projects, and later of physical data and maps gradually emerging from the cadastre modernization.

Initially, the UMU conceived of limited works focused on the most heavily damaged areas, including some form of limited financial and organizational participation by residents. But as they worked, the mayor and his technical staff became drawn to the idea of scaling up their plans to achieve broader objectives. Because drainage in the city was a key to flood control, and drainage was integrated with the city's fragmented road system, building roads would make it possible to address the multiple objectives of city transit and flood control on a larger scale. The investments planned under the PAU involved a step-by-step extension of key stretches of road. Later, on an even larger scale, these extensions could be connected and integrated into the grid of urban infrastructure.

Major components of the city's road system were absent in the same places drainage was critical, causing major traffic snarls. These areas experienced the worst flood damage during the rains of January 1993.

Services to industrial and manufacturing installations that had leapfrogged one another during the 1980s were poorly linked to residential areas, commercial markets within the city, and international markets across the border. The prospects for opening these bottlenecks generated pressure and then support from businesses to scale up the proposed works in the PAU. The program began as a remedial effort to address flood damage, and it grew by stages with the help of maps and detailed data on infrastructure. First the program expanded to include selective strengthening of weak points in the city's transport grid and then transformed into a strategic effort to dramatically improve the city's infrastructure. The objective of the resulting strategic effort was not only to improve traffic circulation but also to foster trade.

The PAU consisted of more than 40 distinct public works strategically linked to open major bottlenecks, correct danger spots, and integrate the city's infrastructure. Nearly 90 kilometers of streets and boulevards accounted for about two-thirds of the value of the PAU works (see table 5-1.2). In addition, another 10 percent was devoted to purely flood control, not counting drainage works embedded in roads. Improvements of existing roads plus equipment and facilities made up the balance. The total projected cost of the PAU reached US$170 million. The production of maps and land-use data emerging from the cadastre modernization program removed one of the most serious obstacles to planning and costing out works. In the end, the PAU comprised streets, paving, drainage, culverts, bridges, sidewalks, and other works.

Taking the PAU to the City

Shaping the PAU became a technical process distinctly different from the customary consensual deliberations in Mexican municipalities. Normally, local governments develop and adopt proposals through intensive deliberations of local planning councils, known as *comites de planificacio de municipio,* or COPLADEMs. The COPLADEMs and their counterparts at the state level (*comites de planificacion del estado,* or COPLADES) are broadly representative of a city's technical, social, economic, and political forces. The committees operate like a planning department, providing technical inputs and policy advice and reflecting the will of the community. (Municipal planning councils, in turn, represent the city in parallel state organizations and play a key role in handling matching grants through PRONASOL.) Osuna commissioned Tijuana's COPLADEM to review the needs of the city following the January storms, even though the UMU had already done this. The COPLADEM produced a predictably long, detailed list of needed city infrastructure, in contrast to the integrated package developed by the UMU.

Table 5-1.2. PAU Investment Profile

Investment categories	Percentage
Boulevards	48
Streets	22
Drainage works	8
Street improvements	14
Protection works	2
Urban facilities	6

Source: Project files, 1995, Municipal Office of Public Works, City of Tijuana.

Partly to avoid the dangers of pork-barrel trading in the COPLADEM, the mayor opened up the deliberation process by mounting a publicity and educational campaign aimed at the private sector. This transparency in design and choice posed dangers. It hampered the mayor by removing options to buy off opposition with bargaining and concessions. But going public offered advantages of direct, broad-based political support, which the mayor would need to make his own case and to win statehouse approval for indebtedness. Although Osuna was well aware of the pitfalls of partisan political influence in the COPLADEM, he could not avoid them entirely. In fact, the COPLADEM met on 25 occasions during 1994 alone to consider the city's infrastructure needs and the PAU. The smaller and more technically oriented UMU continued to provide more purely technical criteria to guide strategic integration of different works. Subjecting these decisions to the COPLADEM would give sway to political interests in the choice or routes, sequence of works, and even choice of contractors. The risks of eschewing the traditional modes of consensus seeking were offset by an unusual publicity campaign.

CONSULTING STAKEHOLDERS. Even before the PAU was completely defined, Osuna launched the publicity and education campaign, a departure from usual procedures in municipal governance. The purpose of the campaign was not only to garner broad-based support from the community or even to secure the agreement of the interest groups—private sector, business associations, neighborhood and other organizations—although these objectives were critical to the program's success. Rather, the overriding objective was to mobilize public commitment to pay for the works proposed in the PAU. Although Tijuana received emergency aid from the federal government immediately after the floods, assistance in reconstruction and improvements was slow in arriving. The mayor felt that the burden of reconstruction and renewal would fall mainly on the state and the city.

Consulting with stakeholders was difficult, because details of finance and execution were not only technically complicated, but also politically unusual: the PAU sought to spread the cost directly and indirectly among beneficiaries in proportion to the impact on property values. The city struggled with ways to express a very broad principle in terms that could be understood by an average property owner in average circumstances. Officials used eye-catching graphics and well-chosen examples. But clever illustrations could not encompass the variety of individual lot layouts and idiosyncrasy of urban circumstances.

Significant opposition arose in citizens' organizations and was voiced by an association of property owners, service users, and later by a Citizen's Defense Front. Proponents of the PAU presented their arguments in small, local meetings, where residents could view maps and drawings and pose key questions relating to the number of works, location, costs and benefits, property owners' financial obligations, and the like.

WINNING OVER THE MEDIA. Explaining the PAU's theory and practical applications required intensive use of visual aids and oral briefings in many forums. The publicity campaign was measured in hundreds of community meetings, scores of press conferences and feature articles, a plethora of informational pamphlets, production of several videos, and weekly appearances on radio talk shows. According to Guillen (1995), much of the press coverage was unfavorable in a partisan way. Three of the four television stations, an equal ratio of the radio stations, and all of the daily newspapers were opposed to the PAU, or at least gave more weight to opposition opinion. This generally negative coverage prompted the city to publish its own newspaper and to produce posters, bumper stickers, and other publicity aids. The mayor countered the generally negative press by participating in radio talk shows, using the opportunity to field questions and explain his program. City staff also held small-scale neighborhood meetings—Guillen (1995) reports that more than 100 meetings were held and 6,000 people were contacted during the campaign.

LINKING COST RECOVERY TO FINANCE. After studying a variety of similar experiences of U.S. cities, the mayor's office adopted the concept of a betterment levy, complemented by contributions from commercial, business, and industrial interests and from the statehouse. The betterment levy appealed to the *subsidiarity* concept central to the political philosophy of the PAN. Betterment levies, or improvement taxes, also offered the advantage of scaling individual contributions in proportion to the proximity and size of beneficiaries' property. Although simple in concept, such schemes were practically unknown in Mexico.

Perhaps the toughest challenge was to convince residents—rich and poor, old and young, recent arrivals and long-time dwellers—that property owners adjacent to the works should accept new levies to offset part of the costs for improvements. It is difficult to overstate the departure this arrangement represents from customary fiscal arrangements in Mexico. Most large works—water, roads, buildings, and bridges—are the domain of state and federal government, and residents rarely know that such works are planned until heavy machinery appears in the area. Small local works, such as those under PRONASOL or ¡Manos a la Obra!, do hold groups of residents responsible for making joint financial contributions, but these contributions are small and go toward neighborhood improvements proposed by residents themselves. In the PAU, works were developed and proposed by the city. They were citywide in scope, did not involve the central government, and depended critically on the approval, even vote, of the entire citizenry. Table 5-1.3 shows the sources of PAU finance.

To educate the public, the city prepared attractive graphics that showed the cost-sharing proposal in accordance with benefits received. A typical example (see box 5-1.5) was portrayed in posters and newspaper and television advertisements: the city calculated that a boulevard or street adjacent to an average parcel of property of about 200 square meters would increase property value by about US$500 over a period of five years. Indirect benefits would accrue citywide to all properties. For a typical street or boulevard (with attendant drainage and other works), indirect benefits were calculated to be in the range of US$20–$33. The cost-sharing proposal asked property owners to pay an amount equal to the increase in property value that would result from the investments. Several options for repayment (terms from 12 to 60 months) were illustrated in tables published in local newspapers, handbills, and pamphlets.

None of the published information we could find disputed the UMU's assumptions or calculations to illustrate cost and incidence. Most opposition arguments were rooted in principles of fairness. Residents' associations felt that a betterment levy for works of citywide benefit should not be imposed on the poor. According to some sources (Guillen 1995), private sector groups—real estate interests, associations of downtown businesses,

Table 5-1.3. Sources of PAU Finance

Source of finance	Percentage
State	15
Municipal	10
Community	
Private business	15
Betterment levy	20
Indirect	40

Source: Project files, 1995, Municipal Treasurer's Office, City of Tijuana.

Box 5-1.5. *Sample Graphics, PAU Publicity Campaign*

The graphics on this page are based on those published in 1994 during the PAU publicity campaign.

Decision Process for the PAU

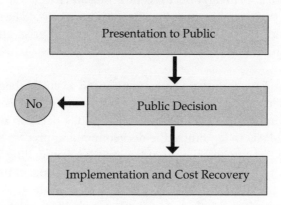

Cost-Recovery Terms

Indirect Beneficiaries			**Direct Beneficiaries**		
Improvement	*Boulevard*	*Street*	*Improvement*	*Boulevard*	*Street*
Rate/m²	US$1.8	n.a.	Rate/m²	US$29	US$23
Typical lot size	200m²	120m²	Typical lot size	200m²	160m²
Monthly payments	*Total payment amounts (US$)*		*Monthly payments*	*Total payment amounts (US$)*	
12	33.35	20.00	12	537.28	340.89
24	18.32	10.99	24	295.20	187.30
36	13.38	8.03	36	215.55	136.76
48	10.95	6.57	48	176.50	111.98
60	9.54	5.70	60	153.66	97.50

n.a. Not applicable (streets were not believed to have indirect benefits).
Note: 3.54 pesos = US$1 in March 1994.
Source: Project files, 1995, Municipal Treasurer's Office, City of Tijuana.

and industrialists—supported the proposal, but not vociferously. Only the chamber of industry and construction declared open support. The national chamber of commerce, led by a then-candidate for federal deputy (and member of the PRI), opposed the PAU.

An interesting proposal for implementing the PAU arose from the deliberations and was adopted by Osuna. Business groups proposed the creation of a trust (*fideicomiso*) to carry out the contracting and execution. Placing PAU resources in a trust would ensure that these resources would be spent for the PAU alone, not other political purposes that might arise after Osuna's administration.

HOLDING A REFERENDUM. Osuna announced from the beginning that the PAU would depend on broad-based public support. His administration decided in spring 1993 that an explicit public decision would be required on the PAU to legitimize the decisionmaking process and to build confidence in the city and the program. Another compelling reason for a strong show of public support was the need to win support from the state legislature so that it would authorize the city to incur debt.

But city authorities felt that special efforts would be needed to get reliable results in a referendum. For one thing, public distrust in the electoral process began to rise sharply after the presidential elections in 1988. Also, the federal elections in August 1994 were disputed in many states of Mexico. And although Mexico had a long tradition of popular elections, electoral machinery had been used only extremely rarely for public choicemaking; in fact, Mexican law did not allow public referenda. But the mayor, feeling that a direct and individualized consultation would provide the strongest support for the PAU, organized a citywide vote as a *consulta popular* (referendum). *Consultas* are a familiar practice widely used in Mexican civil and political life but usually implemented in the form of community meetings and advisory groups. Osuna's concept of a citywide referendum was drawn from an earlier experience in Mexicali, the state capital, as well as from other Latin American countries and neighboring California.

The referendum was organized under the auspices of a bipartisan supervisory committee (*comité de vigilancia*) of 30 members, which received technical support from the state electoral commission. The committee used the state's modern, electronic voting machinery and computerized registration and identification systems. Identification cards linked to photographs and bar codes matched those stored in computerized voter registration files, making fraudulent voting extremely difficult. Polls were open to all registered voters, whether they owned property or not. The computerized systems made it possible for voters to be identified in any 1 of the 16 polling places, while for most local elections, voters marked ballots at predesignated voting stations. The vote was scheduled to be held March 24–28, 1994.

Unfortunately, the referendum had to be postponed following the tragic assassination of presidential candidate Luis Donaldo Colossio on March 23, 1994, in a working class neighborhood of Tijuana. Although it was rescheduled and held a month later (April 21–24), much of the momentum of the PAU campaign and the focus of public attention on it were lost after the assassination. Local elections usually draw 60 to 80 percent of registered voters. The referendum drew less than 8 percent of registered voters, although two-thirds (64 percent) of those voting cast ballots in favor of the PAU.

Securing Credit

To buttress his case before the legislature, Osuna commissioned the *Colegio de la Frontera Norte* (Northern Border College), a respected regional institution of research and education, to conduct a public opinion poll from a representative sample of city voters. The poll mirrored the outcome of the referendum. By the end of November, the state legislature, following a bipartisan recommendation but on a straight party-line vote (the PRI deputies abstained), authorized half the indebtedness Osuna sought.

Osuna extended an invitation to local credit institutions and within a month had discussions with representatives of 20 lenders to explain his deliberative process and to request proposals. Domestic and international banks with local affiliates expressed strong interest. They showed signs of competing, privately promising to meet or better other offers and making their interest known to the media. By this time, the public was aware of the city's strong financial position, and Osuna's popularity was well established.

On December 19, a few days after Osuna had completed his discussions, the Ministry of Finance devalued the peso. Within a month, the exchange rate fell from around 3.5 to over 8.5 pesos to the dollar (and eventually to more than 11). Market interest rates doubled between December 1994 and January 1995, reaching more than 50 percent. In January, Osuna announced the indefinite suspension of the PAU.

Transforming the Mode of Governance: Results of the PAU

Although the PAU was developed in crisis conditions, and then demolished by national tragedies, it forms part of a mosaic of related innovations (see box 5-1.6 for a timeline of innovations). It might be said that these innovations emanated from a common impulse to reform the character of

---

Box 5-1.6. *Timeline of Innovations in Tijuana*

December 1992	Héctor Osuna Jaime takes office.
January 1993	Torrential rains flood Tijuana, causing scores of deaths.
	Study by Municipal Planning Committee (COPLADEM) states the need for more community works.
February–April 1993	Conception of the Urban Action Program (Plan de Activación Urbana, or PAU).
January 1994	Comité de Vigilancia established, composed of 30 people—business, academic and community leaders—to oversee referendum.
April 1994	PAU referendum: 8 percent of the population vote; 64 percent vote in favor.
September 1994	Osuna presents idea for the Strategic Plan (Plan Estratégico de Tijuana, or PET) before group of business leaders.
September–October 1994	State and municipal governments co-organize Foros de Consulta Popular para la Planeación Democrática (Peoples' Consulting for Democratic Planning) in Tijuana's 16 administrative districts. More than 6,000 citizens participate.
November 1994	Federal elections held.
	¡Manos a la Obra! initiated.
	State congress votes to authorize municipal borrowing to finance the PAU at less than half the requested level.
December 1994	First election of neighborhood committees for ¡Manos a la Obra!
	15,000 people sign agreement in support of the PAU, to be presented to congress.
	Osuna meets with representatives from 20 private banks about financing the PAU.
	Devaluation of the peso begins.
March 1995	Phase I of the PET is published.

local government in Tijuana, or that they merely reflected the style of a particular leader. The changes were mutually reinforcing and exhibited a pattern of three essential features:

- The style of governance was transformed.
- Open communications engaged the public in decisionmaking.
- Fiscal linkages featured a two-way accountability through prices, voices, and votes.

A NEW STYLE OF GOVERNANCE. Normally local governments, like their counterparts at other levels in the Mexican federal system, work through institutionalized channels, such as the local COPLADEM and its counterpart at the state level, to incorporate public opinion and consult with local stakeholders before reaching consensus. The customary role of government is to sustain the dialogue, working as hard to reach mutual accord as to press its own point of view. In part, this traditional governmental posture is imposed by the dictates of party interests. Although the process is laborious, it is at once a communication and education process, and the result represents the community's will.

In the case of the PAU, the municipality played a more executive, proactive role, defining the program on technical grounds and then presenting the results not for consensus and negotiation, but for a straight yes-or-no vote on its cost implications. The change in emphasis and sequence of public dialogue stood in marked departure from customary government roles in Mexico.

COMMUNICATION WITH THE PUBLIC. Public debate over the PAU was carried out through an intense, and sometimes bitterly fought, media campaign, as well as through extensive neighborhood and community meetings. The complicated concepts and details of the PAU were not easy to grasp, even for the well-educated citizens of Tijuana (50 percent have an eighth grade education, a ratio well above the national average). For example, interpreting the property value impact of a given group of works at any given location was as much a matter of guesswork as calculation. The very idea of asking voter-taxpayers to say yes or no to the PAU lay at the heart of the city government's character change. Placing this question to the public reversed customary practice in Mexico. It put responsibility for consumer choice squarely in the hands of the people. In effect, it was the kind of choice—transparent, democratic, decisive—that gave real meaning to sometimes faddish terms such as "empowerment" and "autonomy."

FISCAL LINKAGES AND ACCOUNTABILITY. Although the referendum was not entirely unprecedented, it is the first we know of in Mexico to involve questions of payment and price, factors that in the customary style of governance are divorced from the principles that guide consensus seeking and negotiation. Rarely are the terms of a political bargain placed so squarely before the voters for decision. The significance of this bargain is the implicit fiscal and financial tie binding elected officials to taxpayers. In this linkage lies the most essential elements of government—synthesizing the wishes of the collective and equating these not only to an agreed price, but also to an implicit agreement to meet a debt burden, individually and collectively.

Few, if any, of the architects or observers of the PAU delved into the political theory of this bargain or stopped to consider its impact on local government beyond the city. Nor were the PAU's architects in a position to see the common traits in governance style that Tijuana shares with a score of innovative cities in the region. Many of Tijuana's innovations—the PAU, the cuts in spending, the steps to increase income, and the consultation on spending—shared a common denominator: they linked responsibility and accountability of government with the governed. The accumulated impacts of these experiences laid the groundwork for a sharp turn toward more participatory forms of accountability in governance in Tijuana.

¡Manos a la Obra!

In the wake of the floods, the mayor commissioned the COPLADEM to analyze the most pressing needs of the city. The survey found that small community works, including constructing ramps, stairs, and community centers and paving streets, were clearly a priority. Many of Tijuana's poor lived in clustered settlements along barren hillsides and valleys. Most settlements were accessible only by crude dirt roads, which turned quickly to mud and became impassable with even a normal amount of rain. The lack of social infrastructure could turn a two-mile walk to work or school into a difficult, often impossible task.

The COPLADEM survey provided dramatic evidence of citizens' demand for social infrastructure. Between January and July 1994, the COPLADEM distributed 1,261 questionnaires to neighborhood committees and officials in each of Tijuana's administrative districts. Approximately three-fourths of respondents rated the level of community works in the municipality "deficient" (see table 5-1.4). In comparison, most respondents (63 percent) felt that the municipality provided an "acceptable" level of basic public services (water, drainage, garbage collection, and lighting).

Table 5-1.4. Results of COPLADEM Municipal Opinion Survey, January–July 1994

(percent by category)

Category	Deficient	Medium	Acceptable
Public services[a]	26	11	63
Community works[b]	74	12	14
Community development[c]	77	8	15
Public security	75	14	11

a. Water, drainage, garbage collection, lighting, etc.
b. Ramps, stairs, paving, community centers, etc.
c. Scholarships, clinics, community journals, adult education, etc.
Source: Project files, 1995, Mayor's Office, City of Tijuana.

Municipal officials began to seek innovative solutions to maximize the impact of limited resources. To fund larger projects, the municipality developed a package of improvements valued at US$170 million to be funded by the state, city, and stakeholders through a betterment levy. This solution became the PAU.

To fund smaller-scale community infrastructure, Osuna turned to his Department of Social Development. Over the next several months, the department developed the concept for a participatory program similar to the federal government's PRONASOL (see box 5-1.7). Such a program offered several benefits. First, requiring beneficiary contributions would allow the municipality to build more community works and would give the program a broader impact. In addition, the program would provide a high-visibility channel for incorporating citizen participation—a stated priority of the administration—into municipal governance. Finally, by placing responsibility for the contracting of works into the hands of citizens, Osuna could put into practice the PAN principle of subsidiarity, differentiating the program from PRONASOL by removing some of the upper layers of bureaucracy.

Launch

Municipal and state officials initiated the Manos program in September 1994 by holding a series of public forums—one in each of Tijuana's 16 administrative districts—in which citizens were asked to submit proposals for small infrastructure projects via previously existing neighborhood committees.

Box 5-1.7. *PRONASOL: Mexico's National Solidarity Program*

In 1989 the administration of President Carlos Salinas de Gortari initiated PRONASOL, whose goal is to alleviate poverty by providing social infrastructure and supporting income-generating activities. The program focuses on three major groups: the rural poor, indigenous peoples, and urban poor. It is designed to replace top-down federal assistance with a participatory approach, and its projects emphasize community initiative, shared responsibility for implementation, transparency, and efficiency. Between 1989 and 1993, over US$8 billion in federal funding went into the program, matched with varying levels of state and local funds. The program has reached nearly every municipality in Mexico.

PRONASOL is actually an amalgam of roughly 30 subprograms funded by federal budget line item (*ramo*) 26, which allows federal funds to be matched by state and local funds, or by credits from BANOBRAS, Mexico's national credit agency for state and local governments. Regional branches of the national Secretariat for Social Development manage the program. There are subprograms for municipal funds, urban development, education, water supply and sanitation, rural roads, and a number of other areas.

It is PRONASOL's municipal funds that operate most like the ¡Manos a la Obra! program in Tijuana. Approximately 11 percent of Solidarity financing is earmarked as municipal funds, providing municipalities with annual grants amounting to approximately US$5 per inhabitant. A Municipal Solidarity Council selects projects after holding community assemblies to gauge community demand. For selected projects, a Solidarity committee is formed at the community level and given budgeted resources for the project. Committees are then responsible for procurement and implementation of the work, with communities contributing at least 20 percent of the cost in unskilled labor, materials, or cash.

As with Manos, there has been some criticism of the technical quality of projects constructed under PRONASOL, as well as allegations that funding decisions are subject to political maneuvering. Nevertheless, PRONASOL is generally regarded as having had a positive impact on poverty in Mexico (Campbell and Freedheim 1994; Silverman 1995).

The enthusiastic response surprised even the project's initiators: more than 6,000 citizens participated in the forums, submitting more than 2,400 requests for works.

Two months later, the municipal and state governments hosted a citizens' participation congress. The municipality reported that 15,000 people attended.

The event was essentially a political rally in support of the new government's participatory programs. Osuna used this opportunity to announce, with the state governor, his commitment of US$4.2 million for community works.

Selection of Works

The municipality analyzed the requests submitted through the forums for technical feasibility, reducing the number of possible projects to around 1,300. Then, in early 1995, it established councils in each of the 16 districts to determine which works would be funded. To insulate the program from political influence or entrenchment, officials agreed that councils would be dissolved at the end of each project cycle. Each council was made up of 32 members, divided evenly between community representatives elected in an open community assembly and officials appointed by the municipality.

Once these councils were established, the municipality provided them with a list of project proposals and a budget. Municipal officials then worked with their elected counterparts to decide which projects would receive Manos funding.

Essential Features: Community Organization and Works Committees

The cornerstone of ¡Manos a la Obra! is the participation of citizens in the implementation, oversight, and repayment of community works. In Tijuana, as in much of Mexico, traditional community leaders are rarely elected. Community organizations are often more clientelistic than democratic. Recognizing the potential limitations of relying on these arrangements, the municipality chose not to use existing community organizations (as is common in similar programs in the region; see the Conchalí case study in chapter 6). Instead, new "works committees" were elected in participating communities for the single purpose of managing the projects. To ensure a project rather than political orientation, each committee would dissolve once the construction and repayment of the work was completed.

To initiate community involvement, municipal staff drove through the neighborhoods for which proposals had been approved, using a megaphone to announce that a meeting with the community would be held on a specified date. The meetings were held outdoors in neutral territory, typically a public plaza or schoolyard, to promote openness and inclusion in the program.

At the first meeting, municipal representatives provided a briefing for the community on the works selected in their area and what was needed to build them. Communities were expected to elect a council to contract the works, oversee their construction, ensure that contractors were paid, and contribute financially to the cost of the works. Neighborhoods were classified into four groups, based on ability to pay. The lowest-income neighborhoods would be responsible for 20 percent of project costs, while those in the higher-income brackets would be expected to pay up to 80 percent.

Communities were then asked to decide whether to participate. For interested communities, two more open-air meetings were held, this time supervised by representatives from local, state, and national levels of government. In the first meeting, citizens nominated candidates for office. In the second, citizens elected works committees by popular vote.

Results

Once a community had elected a works committee, the municipality issued a check directly to the committee for its share of the approved works. Committees contracted workers and oversaw construction. Upon satisfactory completion of the project, the committee went door-to-door to collect beneficiary contributions and pay the contractors.

In the year in which it was in operation, ¡Manos a la Obra! completed 659 projects (see table 5-1.5). More than half (accounting for more than 75 percent of costs) involved paving streets and boulevards. Others involved constructing stairs, terracing, sports facilities, and schools. The projects proceeded efficiently, with work being completed an average of three months after checks were issued to neighborhood committees.

The residents we interviewed expressed enthusiasm about the improvements to their neighborhoods resulting from Manos. In the Cañon de los Laureles, where flooding was severe, the federal government built a spillway to channel water out of the canyon, and Manos followed with a paved access road running along the spillway. A woman whose family participated in the program explained that the road provided the first reliable access and drainage to their house in the 25 years she had lived there. Their family contributed US$250 to the project, which she considered a worthwhile investment.

Some questions have been raised (particularly by the local society of engineers, which was not involved in the project) about the technical quality of the works constructed by the Manos program. It also has been argued that the works constructed under Manos provided local, rather than systemic, solutions to Tijuana's lack of social infrastructure. Although a formal investigation had not been carried out to investigate the validity of

Table 5-1.5. Number and Type of Works Built by ¡Manos a la Obra!

Type of work	Number	Percentage of total
Paving	382	58.0
Stairs	38	5.8
Terracing	42	6.4
Athletic courts	32	4.9
Community centers	5	0.8
Schools	46	7.0
Flood protection	21	3.2
Electrification	22	3.3
Bridges	7	1.1
Drainage	11	1.7
Other	53	8.0
Total	659	100.0

Source: Project files, 1995, Municipal Office of Public Works, City of Tijuana.

these claims, the works we visited appeared to be of high quality, particularly given the difficult terrain over which they were built. We saw several cases in which roads built by Manos joined existing municipal boulevards, with no apparent disparity in quality in terms of thickness, width, materials, or general appearance.

In total, more than US$14.9 million was invested in community works through ¡Manos a la Obra!, 42 percent of which was paid by beneficiaries. The program successfully targeted the poorer sectors of the society, with 75 percent of funding going to neighborhoods in the low-income and medium-low-income categories.

The Role of Political Competition

Whether Manos was conceived to compete with PRONASOL, imitate it, or complement it is unclear. While conceding similarities, Osuna answered comparisons by saying that Manos aimed to be more "representative" and less political than PRONASOL. He supported this claim by citing a number of cases in which members of PRI and PRD (Partido Revolucionario Democratico, or Revolutionary Democratic Party), rather than members of PAN exclusively, headed elected works committees—a fact that, he argued, was uncommon in PRONASOL.

Although we found no data to support or refute this claim, a healthy competition clearly existed between the two programs. The fact that Osuna initiated ¡Manos a la Obra! at the same time that federal elections were held is a likely indicator of the political significance of the program to the municipality's PAN government.

In addition, the municipality invested significant resources in public promotion of the program. Each work in Manos was inaugurated with a municipally sponsored party, complete with brightly colored banners, photos, live music, and tamales. A representative from the municipality, often either Osuna or his director of social development, Luis Bustamente, was present at each event.

A walk through the city highlighted the competition between the programs. On corners and signposts, the blue, red, and yellow logo clearly marked Manos works, whereas works built by PRONASOL were often painted in the PRI colors of red, white, and green with government-supplied paint. We encountered one road, in fact, which was built in sections, part by Manos and part by PRONASOL. Although the road itself had no visible seams that would indicate a division, all of the houses along the PRONASOL section were painted in PRI colors, while houses along the Manos section retained their original coat of paint.

This example, however, brings to light an interesting point. Although there was a high degree of political competition between the programs, at least from the policymaker's perspective, there was actually a high degree of coordination between the two—so much so, in fact, that one municipal official admitted, "they should be the same program." The programs were so well coordinated because both took responsibility for the implementation and oversight of the projects out of the political arena and placed it in the hands of the beneficiaries themselves. For residents of Tijuana's neighborhoods, the need for social infrastructure transcended political affiliations. Stakeholders chose to broker partisan rivalries to ensure that their needs were served, regardless of the source of funding. Indeed, in the eyes of the residents, there was often little distinction made between the two programs except as a source of funding. We visited one neighborhood in which residents elected the same committee to oversee two projects: a Manos project to build a bridge and a PRONASOL project to build an athletic court. Although no figures were available, we were told that such overlap was common.

Taken together, the two programs built 1,010 works (nearly double that of Manos alone), investing approximately US$22.6 million in the municipality.

Outcome and Fate

Héctor Osuna Jaime's term ended in December 1995, and it appeared unlikely that the Manos program would continue without the support of his successor, Guadalupe Osuna Millán. Unlike the Mendoza Social Infrastructure Program in Argentina or the Neighborhood Development Fund in Chile, the high degree of politics surrounding Manos probably undermined the program's chances of survival. As with most successful innovators, Osuna took personal risks to implement the program and was rewarded through public recognition of his accomplishments. Although it is argued (Hopkins 1995) that such recognition provides important incentives for the innovator to take risks, personalizing a program may also weaken the incentives for the successor to pick up the torch. For Guadalupe Osuna, the risk of continuing Manos was that it could undermine his ability to establish a political identity distinct from his predecessor. Indeed, were Manos to continue, the success would likely be attributed to Héctor, not Guadalupe, Osuna. The risk of not being recognized for continuing an innovation, combined with the political baggage attached to Manos, made it unlikely that the program would continue in the municipality, at least in name.

Even if ¡Manos a la Obra! were to end with Héctor Osuna's term in office, the program broke important new ground in Tijuana, planting the seed for future innovation in the municipality. First, Manos followed the PAU's lead by actively engaging citizens in a dialogue and, eventually, a partnership with their municipal government. By requiring participants to articulate their needs, elect representatives to choose projects, and organize themselves around these needs to ensure their implementation, Osuna's administration put into action a new way of governing at the municipal level—one in which citizens could and must play an active role. Through participation in all aspects of the program, citizens learned how to engage their local governments and how to organize around common needs, and they saw the fruits of their labor in an improved quality of life. This is a particularly important lesson in Mexico, where a long tradition of centralized governance and single-party rule weakened the ties between local government and citizens.

At the same time, Manos confronted citizens with the costs of their demands—first by conditioning participation in the program on a willingness to pay and, second, by requiring beneficiaries to provide counterpart funding. As with the PAU, these steps established a new, direct linkage between citizen-taxpayers and local government. This is particularly important in the Latin American context, where popular resistance to paying taxes often stems from citizens' perception of a disconnect between the taxes they pay and the services they receive. Manos worked to counteract this sentiment, offering citizens a concrete program that they themselves oversaw. Citizens were able to see where their money went and the resulting benefits in their city. According to Campbell (1996, p. 18), "in this linkage lies the most essential elements of government—of synthesizing the wishes of the collective, and equating these not only to an agreed price, but an implicit agreement to meet a debt burden, individually and collectively." As with civic engagement, establishing this fiscal linkage involves a learning process that must evolve over time. Manos provides a successful model. Whether future administrations or citizens will carry this process further remained to be seen.

The demand for social infrastructure in Tijuana will certainly continue. Manos provided citizens and officials of the municipality with a proven model to use as a tool in satisfying this demand or as a building block for further innovation in this area.

Conclusion

The Tijuana case supports the argument that specific circumstances involving pressing needs (such as the flooding in Tijuana or the cholera scare in Mendoza) may play a pivotal role in sparking innovation. Past cases have also suggested that some features of innovation are more influenced by policy variables than others. For instance, the complexity and social dimensions of an innovation and the circumstances of its incubation can be influenced by public policy. Tijuana also unveils factors generally considered outside the realm of policy manipulation, including political rivalry and northward-looking attitudes, which played important roles in the success of Manos.

The multiple innovations in Tijuana, one laying the groundwork for the next, allow us to take a step further in analyzing the innovations process and begin formulating hypotheses about the dynamics of sustained change. Each change in the city builds and extends the climate of expectations and eventually produces a qualitative change. In the case of Tijuana, we refer to this qualitative change as a transformation in the character of government.

The Tijuana experience allows new insights into the policy options and conditions of civil society that donors must understand to foster reform in decentralized systems of government. Above all, the new style of governance is marked by the terms of a new political contract forged in Tijuana.

In it, the links between public works and the voter-taxpayer are made more explicit and subjected to public debate. This relationship goes to the heart of governance and offers a rare glimpse into the making of a new political process at the local level.

Tijuana's change in style of governance parallels in many ways local reforms in other Latin American countries. But rather than the stroke-of-the-pen reforms of civil service or tax reform, city reforms are stepwise and labor intensive. Jacobs (1968) reminded us decades ago that economic growth in cities depends on innovations achieved not by giant leaps, but rather by small extensions of something already established—a marginal change in a product, a process, or an organization. Slight modifications enable something familiar to serve new, sometimes entirely different, purposes. The case of Tijuana reflects some of this stepwise flavor. Its cumulative effects provide insight into the policy options and conditions of civil society that must be understood if financial and technical assistance organizations are to foster reform in decentralized systems of government.

References

The word *processed* describes informally reproduced works that may not be commonly available through libraries.

Campbell, Tim. 1996. "The Politics of Participation in Tijuana Mexico: Inventing a New Style of Governance."World Bank, Latin America and the Caribbean Technical Department, Washington, D.C. Processed.

Campbell, Tim, and Sara Freedheim. 1994. *Basic Features and Significance of PRONASOL, Mexico's National Solidarity Program.* Washington, D.C.: World Bank.

Guillen, T. 1995. *Innovaciones y Conflicto—Sociedad Civil y Gobierno Local.* Tijuana: Colegio de la Frontera Norte.

Hopkins, Elwood. 1995. *The Life Cycle of Urban Innovations,* vol I. Urban Management Program Working Paper Series. Washington, D.C.: World Bank.

Jacobs, Jane. 1968. *Life and Death of Great American Cities.* New York: Doubleday.

Silverman, Andrea. 1995. "National Solidarity Program." Mexico Strategy Papers. Washington, D.C.: World Bank.

World Bank. 1991. *Mexico—Decentralization and Urban Management Urban Sector Study.* Report 8924. Washington, D.C.: World Bank, Latin America and the Caribbean Technical Department Infrastructure and Energy Operations Division.

5-2

Tax Management in the Municipalities of Valledupar and Manizales, Colombia

Alberto Maldonado,
Departmento Nacional de Planeacion, Colombia

A major goal of territorial decentralization in Colombia is to strengthen the financial situation of the municipal governments.[1] The ultimate objective is for the municipalities to be able to adequately carry out the functions transferred to them and to broaden their capabilities to solve the problems of their citizens. The tax decentralization regime combines measures such as a substantial increase in national transfer payments and the introduction of mechanisms that seek to increase collections arising from local sources. Critics of the adopted system (Maldonado and Ospina 1997) thought that the rapid growth in national resources transferred to the municipalities would lead to a reduction in local governments' tax collection efforts. They believed that local governments would prefer to rely on national resources to avoid facing the political costs of a greater mobilization of municipal resources.

However, the municipalities of Manizales and Valledupar were innovative in demonstrating an enormous capacity to increase their own resources,

1. This publication was prepared under the research project Transferencias y Esfuerzo Fiscal Municipal (Transfer Payments and Municipal Tax Effort), carried out by the research department of Central University in Bogotá, with the support of the Columbian Scientific Research Institute and the regional and urban planning unit of Colombia's National Planning Department. Enrique Rodríguez participated in data collection and organization.

both in terms of traditional tax revenue sources as well as newer instruments (see boxes 5-2.1 and 5-2.2 for an overview of the municipalities). Since the popular election of mayors began in 1988, and coinciding with significant growth in national level transfer payments, the municipalities have substantially strengthened their own resources, thus achieving growth in expenditures and investment to provide the services under their charge. Total income for the central administrations grew at a real rate of 22.5 percent in Valledupar and 16 percent in Manizales between 1988 and 1994. This growth resulted from using a combination of current revenue and credit. A similar, very high growth rate was visible in tax and transfer incomes within current revenues. This means that in spite of a significant increase in national resources, the municipalities were able to maintain a higher growth rate in own tax revenue resources. This behavior has entailed a significant increase in per capita taxation and a slight reduction in the rate of dependence on national resources.

Fiscal management has been characterized by complementary actions taken on different fronts, which together have produced very significant

---

Box 5-2.1. *The Municipality of Valledupar*

The municipality of Valledupar is the capital of the department of Cesar, and it is located in the northeastern part of the country, 105 kilometers from Bogotá, in the Atlantic coastal region. According to the 1993 census, the municipality had a population of 235,993. Of these, 209,231 lived in the city center. The municipality was founded in 1550, and in recent years it has undergone notable urban growth. It has a total area of 25 square kilometers and is 126 meters above sea level.

The land around Valledupar is predominantly dedicated to agriculture and cattle raising, and the urban area is the center for trade and services for a large region of the department. Very limited industrial activity exists. The most important agricultural product has traditionally been cotton, but the cotton sector is undergoing a severe crisis.

Among medium cities, Valledupar stands out for its good public management and adequate urban organization, which has enabled it to achieve levels of public service coverage and physical infrastructure far superior to those of the other municipalities in the Atlantic region. The central administration consists of 20 departments with a staff of 520, and there are four decentralized entities in charge of residential public services, housing, public works (funded by assessments), and the transportation terminal.

Box 5-2.2. *The Municipality of Manizales*

Manizales, with a population of approximately 380,000 (1993 census), is the country's sixth largest city and the capital of the department of Caldas. Some 92 percent of the population reside within the city limits. Manizales is a relatively new city, founded in 1848. It developed as a result of coffee-growing activities, and it is one of the major centers for this activity. Manizales has a total area of 50,788 hectares; of these, 4,488 constitute the urban zone. The political divisions comprise 11 urban communes and 7 rural boroughs.

In addition to coffee, agricultural crops that are significant to the local economy include plantains, sugar cane, corn, and beans. The city also has a significant amount of industrial activity, with around 400 firms employing approximately 13,000 people.

The administrative structure of the municipality consists of the 19-member municipal council, which elects the comptroller and the solicitor, and the municipal executive branch, which includes the mayor and 11 secretariats. The municipality also has six decentralized primary agencies, which include the public service companies, and five decentralized secondary agencies.

---

results. With the emergence of new, directly elected leaders and the larger commitment by public management to the community, local government has ably taken advantage of the instruments made available to it by the decentralizing reform. These experiences demonstrate the potential for strengthening local government tax bases even though the most dynamic taxes are concentrated at the national level.

Origin and Context

The tax base strengthening reported here occurred between 1988 and 1994, which coincides with the terms of mayors elected by popular vote. National regulatory factors as well as local provisions influenced the innovations.

National-Level Factors

The decentralization process provided new instruments and incentives for improvement of local management overall and strengthening of the tax base in particular. Since the beginning of the 1980s, a series of measures have been developed to strengthen local governments in various ways.

POPULAR ELECTION OF MAYORS. Legislative Act 1 of 1986 decreed the popular election of mayors in all Colombian municipalities, and the first such election was held in 1988. This measure produced a substantial change in the role of mayors, who had previously been appointed by governors and did not have fixed terms. Aside from the political implications, the election of mayors generated new possibilities for improving management, arising from the greater commitment to the voters and the option of carrying out planning activities over a specific period of time. To strengthen the local leader's commitment to the community, all candidates were required to present a plan of governance that would be the basis for evaluating their performance if elected, and whose results could even serve as grounds for removing them from office. Additionally, the regulations established mechanisms for fostering greater citizen participation in the municipality's affairs.

LOCAL REVENUE INSTRUMENTS. The decentralization process granted new revenue instruments to the local governments. Municipal resources were strengthened by the introduction of taxes such as those on real property, commerce, and industry. Of special note is the demand placed on the Augustín Codazzi Geographical Institute (IGAC), the national institution responsible for cadastral appraisals. The IGAC had to carry out these appraisals within certain time limits and update the cadastral values based on the consumer price index. Similarly, the 1986 law authorized a municipal surtax on gasoline, which was a potentially important source of additional funding for transportation systems.

INCREASE IN TRANSFER PAYMENTS. In addition to the strengthening of their own resources, municipal governments received a substantial increase in transfer payments. These were initially calculated as a percentage of the value added tax collected at the national level, and later as a proportion of total current revenue. Municipal participation in these revenues was slated to increase from 14 to 22 percent between 1994 and 2002, representing a significant increase in municipal resources. Additionally, the municipalities may have access to national resources through cofinancing in certain sectors—health, education, roads, waterworks, and agriculture. Municipalities also have credit resources available from the Territorial Development Finance Institute (*Financiera de Desarrollo Territorial,* or FINDETER), which was established to grant credits to territorial bodies.

DECENTRALIZATION OF SERVICE PROVISION. In the administrative area, functions were transferred to local governments in areas such as potable water, basic sanitation, health, education, agriculture, and transportation. A majority of the resources transferred along with these functions had to be oriented to investment or preparation of investment development plans, which specified the local priorities and the programs and projects to be implemented.

The set of decentralizing measures granted opportunities to municipal governments for substantial improvement in their management. However, adequate use of these measures depended on local circumstances.

Local Factors

Since the decentralization process began, municipal income policy has been characterized by the utilization of available instruments. The efforts to increase revenue, especially from taxes, relied on a combination of techniques, ranging from exclusively administrative measures and campaigns to promote responsible citizenship to new taxes, such as the gasoline surtax. These techniques have made it possible to substantially increase revenues and thus increase and improve the services provided to the community.

Valledupar and Manizales have made good use of the opportunities offered by decentralization. In Valledupar the first elected mayor, who won a second term, imprinted a special dynamic on his administration, combining elements of citizen participation, planning, and budgetary efforts. But even before the decentralizing reform, the municipality's commitment to local development was expressed in the quality and coverage of public services and in the plans for urban organization. The elected mayors merely reinforced a tradition of good management in the municipality. This tradition makes Valledupar and Manizales unusual in Colombia's Atlantic region, where public management has been characterized by notorious deficiencies and corruption.

Beside strengthening the tax base, the municipalities have demonstrated significant management capacity in other efforts. For example, Valledupar has:

- Carried out interesting experiments in the area of rural road management by creating a cooperative and dismissing the public officials previously responsible for that function
- Designed and put into effect a self-administered neighborhood paving program, which has achieved notable results
- Promoted the popular election of rural inspectors to increase their commitment to their communities and to enable greater participation

- Undertaken strategic planning while improving the professionalism of its personnel.

Among other achievements, Manizales has:

- Pioneered efforts to decentralize health services by implementing an arrangement for cooperation with the private sector
- Set up a municipal training institute, which operates primarily with its own resources and is in charge of improving the qualifications of personnel at all levels
- Created, with the participation of the private sector, the Verdant Manizales Corporation (*Corporación Manizales Reverdece*), an organization responsible for the parks and green areas throughout the city
- Privatized street-cleaning services, converting a service that usually ran at a deficit into a source of income for the public service company.

Essential Features and Evolution

Certain factors aided Valledupar and Manizales in improving their fiscal management. The significant growth of current revenues and investment was associated with low turnover in the staff responsible for local finance and planning, the effective use of available resources, and a considerable effort to increase efficiency.

During the period corresponding to the elected mayors in both cities (1988–94), tax revenue grew at a high rate, especially compared to the preceding period (1980–87). The municipalities' fiscal management made use of the financing system proposed by the Colombian decentralization process. This system included efforts related to real property taxes and to commercial and industrial taxes, the introduction of a gasoline surtax, improvement of systems and procedures, use of an assessment mechanism, improvement of expenditure planning, and efficient use of human resources.

The Valledupar Experience

Real Property Tax Increases. The management of real property taxes included activities such as cadastral training, rate increases, systematization, and improved enforcement. In 1988, cadastral training was carried out in collaboration with the IGAC, and this translated into an immediate improvement in collections. In 1994 the IGAC updated the cadastre, which once again led to a substantial increase in income. During the same period,

Valledupar also increased real property tax rates (see table 5-2.1), systematized the collection process, and enforced compliance with tax obligations.

With the slogan "Watch your taxes at work," the local administration undertook massive campaigns to promote compliance with tax obligations, appealing to the citizens' commitment to development of their city. During the third popularly elected administration (1992–94), Valledupar gave special emphasis to these campaigns because of the large number of delinquent taxpayers (see box 5-2.3).

COMMERCIAL AND INDUSTRIAL TAXES. These taxes grew in real terms during the period under study. The mayors elected by popular vote had a direct influence on this growth, similar to but much less than their influence on the real property tax. The administrations carried out activities that improved taxpayer registration and exercised greater pressure, both persuasively and coercively, for citizens to pay this tax on a timely basis.

The annual rate of growth of commercial and industrial tax revenue averaged 12.8 percent since 1988, partly due to a slight increase in rates (see table 5-2.2). The relatively modest growth of these taxes meant that they accounted for a declining share of total revenue, from 60 percent in 1988 to 38 percent in 1994.

In spite of the improvement in taxpayer compliance, the low collections meant that Valledupar still lacked the resources to pay all its bills. The municipality exerted pressure on taxpayers through a strategy that combined inspections of businesses with radio advertising campaigns. The administration also facilitated collections by reaching an agreement with a rural savings association *(Caja Agraria)* to accept tax payments in the outlying boroughs and by authorizing police inspectors to act as tax collection agents.

Table 5-2.1. Property Tax Rates, Valledupar City Council Resolutions, 1990–95

Type of property	Resolution 02/90	Resolution 059/91	Resolution 039/92	Resolution 01/95
Built-up urban	5	5	7	6.8
Rural	10	5	7	7.0
Borough	5	—	—	—
Urbanized not built-up	15	17	25	25
Urbanized not urban	15	17	25	18

— Not available.
Source: Project files, 1996, Finance Department, Municipality of Valledupar.

Box 5-2.3. *Potential and Effective Property Tax Collections*

According to information provided by the Municipal Tax Division, only 7,430 (12.2 percent) of Valledupar's 60,923 properties had fully paid their taxes as of May 15, 1995. Of the rest, 17,661 owed money only for 1995, while 35,832 were delinquent for preceding years. The delinquent portfolio amounted to Col$3.6 billion, which, combined with interest, totaled almost Col$6.8 billion—an amount that was slightly larger than the entire debt of the city's administration. As figure 5-2.1 shows, the delinquent collections had been accumulating for years.

Although collections were growing significantly in real terms, the true potential had still to be realized. For 1994, the effective potential tax collection amounted to Col$1.8 billion, whereas only Col$887.5 million (47.5 percent) was collected. In the opinion of the secretary of public finance, the high amounts of unpaid property taxes were the result of both the economic recession in the municipality and inadequate attention to communication with the citizens, which required promotional activities emphasizing the relationship between taxes and benefits.

As of July 1997, the municipality had 60,778 lots with a total appraised value of Col$478.8 billion. The total annual property tax should have amounted to Col$4.04 billion, but the 1995 budget had estimated collections of only one-third that amount, or Col$1.34 billion. According to Valledupar's development plan document, only about 14,500 (24 percent) of property owners pay their property taxes.

Figure 5-2.1. *Delinquent Collections of Real Property Tax*

Millions of Colombian pesos

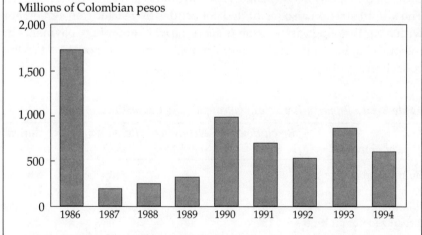

Source: Project files, 1996, Finance Department, Municipality of Valledupar.

Table 5-2.2. Industrial and Commercial Tax Rates, Valledupar City Council Resolutions, 1988–93

Activity	Resolution 10/88	Resolution 03/90	Resolution 029/90	Decree 153 of 1993
Industrial	4–5.5	4–5.5	4–5.5	4–7
Commercial	4.5–10	4.5–10	4.5–10	5–10
Services	5–10	5.5–10	5.5–10	5.5–10
Financial	n.a.	3–5	5	3–5

n.a. Not applicable.
Source: Project files, 1996, Finance Department, Municipality of Valledupar.

GASOLINE SURTAX. Using new powers granted by Resolution 43 of September 10, 1993, the Valledupar Municipal Council adopted a gasoline surtax for a 10-year period beginning January 1, 1994. The surtax was set at 6 percent of the public sale price of automotive gasoline, and the resulting revenue was allocated exclusively to the construction and maintenance of road infrastructure for mass passenger transit. During 1994, the revenue from the gasoline surtax represented 12 percent of tax revenues and 4 percent of the central administration's total current revenue.

SYSTEMS AND PROCEDURES. With technical assistance from the Directorate of Tax Support in Colombia's Ministry of Public Finance, Valledupar drafted and issued the municipal tax code and budgetary statutes that became procedural tools of vital importance. In addition, the city systemized daily reports for cash on hand. Local banks trained executive personnel at the Secretariat of Public Finance and implemented program-based budgeting. The secretariat's structure was modified in 1993 to define the functions of the tax division more clearly and make it more effective.

ASSESSMENT LEVIES. The municipality also employed a decentralized entity, the Municipal Assessment Fund, which is responsible for carrying out public works financed by assessment levies. During the period of the directly elected mayors, the plan for roads and highways relied heavily on these levies, and the city organized a broad advertising campaign. Although the levies generated some complementary resources, collections failed to achieve expected levels because citizens resisted paying. This nonpayment caused severe financial problems for the fund, which utilized credit resources to execute the projects.

PLANNING. Along with improving collections, Valledupar made efforts to improve expenditure planning and implementation, especially with regard to investments. In 1983, Valledupar prepared a development plan with the help of an outside consulting firm, according to an outline proposed by the municipal council's Decree 1306 of 1980. The first popular administration modified the plan to bring it up to date, with the support of the same consulting firm, and the municipal council adopted it in 1990. Known as Valledupar Century XXI, the plan focused on the different aspects of city development, and it fine-tuned sectorial strategies and actions based on these aspects.

In addition, the municipal administration, with support from consultant Carlos Matus, the Ministry of the Government, and the U.N. Development Programme, carried out a massive training project on strategic and situational planning for all supervisory personnel. Based on this project, many of Matus' recommendations were put into practice during the third popular administration. These included creating a central planning unit and technical-political processing unit within the city's planning office.

The first of these units oversaw the drafting of the general plans and closely monitored the officials responsible for implementation. The second unit supported the mayor in dealing with everyday problems, prioritizing them to separate problems that merited the mayor's direct intervention from those that could be delegated to other staff members.

In addition to these two units, the planning office is composed of two divisions: economic and social planning, and municipal organization. During Mayor Rodolfo Campo's second term, the units reported directly to the mayor.

In spite of the improvements, notable planning problems persisted. The planning office remained quite weak. It did not have a unit in charge of project formulation and follow-up, it lacked sufficient information on municipal development, and it rarely evaluated the impact of the administration's planning activities.

HUMAN RESOURCES. Valledupar accomplished its planning and management improvements with nearly the same number of staff as it had before undertaking the innovations. While overall staff size remained unchanged, more professional staff were added, replacing less-qualified persons. From 1985 to 1994, the number of professionals in the Secretariat of Public Finance's staff increased from 5 to 7, and the number of professionals in the Planning Office increased from 8 to 10. Valledupar's revenue was much higher in real terms than in 1988, but it was being managed by nearly the same number of staff.

The Manizales Experience

REAL PROPERTY TAX INCREASES. The efforts to improve the management of real property taxes, including developing and updating the cadastre, increased the tax base. The cadastral appraisals reached about 70 percent of commercial appraisals as of 1995 and, as a result, tax collections had a very high real growth. In 1989, Manizales contracted with the IGAC to set up the cadastre, which was updated in 1993, and these actions provided immediate results, according to available figures. Manizales subsequently held discussions with the IGAC to begin a new process of cadastre development. In addition, by using the individuals in charge of delivering the tax forms, cadastral information was updated for those lots whose land usage pattern had changed. Furthermore, the IGAC and the municipality implemented a periodic electronic input system to eliminate errors arising from manual data entry.

As table 5-2.3 shows, real property tax rates increased in 1991, when different rates were established according to the value of the lots by category. For example, dwellings went from a single rate of 7 per thousand (combining the taxes for real property, parks, and shade trees, which were unified in the unified real property tax), to rates of 7, 8, and 9 per thousand according to the value categories. A similar modification was made for lots dedicated to economic or institutional activities. Since 1991, in addition to issuing different norms, these rates had not been modified as of 1995, with the exception of urbanizable lots that had not been urbanized and unbuilt urbanizable lots. These lots initially underwent a rate increase to 16 to 20 per thousand and then were reduced to 12 per thousand. Similarly, the tax on rural properties initially had a single rate of 4 per thousand but decreased slightly when three rate levels were established in 1991.

The increase in the appraised value, and the stability and slight increase in rates, were partially counteracted by decisions on taxpayer exemptions. A review of council activities shows a large number of resolutions on particular exemptions, basically granted to religious and public service institutions. However, during 1989, exemptions were decreed in favor of low-cost housing and housing that did not exceed a value determined by mass assessment. This led to a high percentage of the lower-value lots escaping payment of taxes for several years.

COMMERCIAL AND INDUSTRIAL TAXES. With regard to these taxes, Manizales has concentrated on raising the rates, improving tax audits, and working with taxpayers both to facilitate the process and to provide incentives for fulfilling obligations.

Table 5-2.3. *Real Property Tax Rates, Manizales Municipal Council Actions, 1989–93*

Category	Resolution 11/89	Resolution 20/91	Decree 760/91	Resolution 073/93
Dwellings	4/1,000 and up 3/1,000[a]	<20': 7/1,000 20–25': 8/1,000 >25': 9/1,000	<20': 7/1,000 20–25': 8/1,000 >25': 9/1,000	<20': 7/1,000 20–25': 8/1,000 >25': 9/1,000
Economic activity[b]	4.01/1,000 and up 4.0/1,000	<20': 8.01/1,000 >20': 10.01/1,000	<20': 8.01/1,000 >20': 10.01/1,000	<20': 8.01/1,000 >20': 10.01/1,000
Institutional activity	n.a.	<20': 7.01/1,000 >20': 9.01/1,000	<20': 7.01/1,000 >20': 9.01/1,000	<20': 7.01/1,000 >20': 9.01/1,000
Lots	16/1,000	20/1000	20/1,000	12/1,000
Rural areas	4/1,000	4/1000	<100 mlms[c] Area <5 hectares: 3.8/1,000 100–150 mlms Area 5–10 hectares: 3.9/1,000 >150 mlms Area >10 hectares: 4/1,000	<100 mlms Area <5 hectares: 3.8/1,000 100–150 mlms Area 5–10 hectares: 3.9/1,000 >150 mlms Area >10 hectares: 4/1,000

n.a. Not applicable.

a. In 1989, a fee was levied for property tax and another for parks and shade trees. No differentiation according to cadastral appraisal was made until 1991.

b. In 1989, the economic activity category included economic and institutional activities. After 1991, this was separated into two categories.

c. The term "mlms" refers to minimum legal monthly salary. For rural areas, Decree 760 of 1991 differentiated lots according to their value in minimum legal monthly salaries and the areas of the lots.

Source: Project files, 1996, Finance Department, Municipality of Manizales.

Between 1991 and 1993, Manizales made several adjustments to the rate structure for industrial and commercial taxes, introducing a much more detailed classification of economic activities and increasing rates for certain groups of activities. These adjustments generally led to an increase in the ranges within which the rates could vary for each activity.

Tax audits for industry and commerce constitute one of the central opportunities for improving collections. The city's revenue unit improved its capabilities in this area by cross-checking information with different sources to put pressure on businesses to pay all taxes owed. The municipality has taken steps to manage information from different sources that will allow it to detect inaccuracies on the part of the taxpayers. These sources are annual values declared to the National Tax Administration, information on credit card payments made to establishments, information from large distributorships, information derived from the liquidation of other taxes or royalties, and monthly new registrations with the Manizales Chamber of Commerce. These cross checks serve as a basis for tax investigations.

Furthermore, the administration has carried out campaigns directed at making compliance with tax obligations easier. The goal of these campaigns has been to advise and support taxpayers in the payment process and thus generate a more positive attitude on the part of the taxpayers.

GASOLINE SURTAX. In order to finance mass transit systems, Manizales also took advantage of the previously described law authorizing municipalities to introduce a surtax on automotive gasoline consumption. Under Resolution 37 (passed on August 31, 1992), the council created a 6 percent surtax on automotive gasoline consumption to finance the execution of a transit plan designed to relieve congestion in the city center. The surtax was to be collected for a period of 12 years, starting in 1993.

Resolution 2 (February 16, 1993) regulated the collection of the surtax, directing wholesale distributors to collect the surtax on automotive gasoline sold by suppliers to filling stations. Similarly, the resolution stipulated that the wholesaler would forward the collections to the treasury on a biweekly basis. The local administration rapidly utilized the increased capacity for indebtedness allowed by the surtax.

SYSTEMS AND PROCEDURES. The municipality's income tax code regulates and systemizes tax collections. Likewise, all financial operations were systematized since the beginning of the elected administrations, and the capacity exists to draft financial plans. Manizales also has a highly developed accounting system, which handles not only budgetary accounting but also accounting of the municipality's assets and finances, as is set out in the municipality's own fiscal code.

ASSESSMENT LEVIES. The Municipal Assessment Institute, a technical unit devoted to analysis and forecasting of tax revenues, was of great help to the city. During the first elected administration, part of the road plan was financed by means of an assessment. In 1994, officials designed another assessment plan to help fund a citywide mass transit plan. Assessments had been an important source of revenue for some years; for example, in 1989, the assessment collections exceeded property tax collections.

PRIVATE SECTOR PARTICIPATION. To improve service provision and tap private sector resources, the municipality promoted the creation of a private entity responsible for maintaining and cleaning the city's parks and green areas: the Verdant Manizales Corporation (Corporación Manizales Reverdece). The city also created an "adopt a park" program whereby private firms assumed the costs for maintaining particular parks. Furthermore, the public service companies in Manizales, with private sector participation, took advantage of the options proposed by the new law on provision of residential public services by establishing a firm to administer the street cleaning service in the early 1990s. Traditionally, the public agency that oversaw this service had provided good coverage of the city but produced operational losses. After privatization, it was projected that the new firm would produce earnings while improving the level and quality of service.

PLANNING. Concurrent with the efforts to increase the municipality's own resources, the administration complemented fiscal innovations with steps to strengthen resource planning and programming. Even before mayors were popularly elected, the municipality had begun to prepare development plans, but planning practices became more formal after popular elections. This formalization involved not only general planning, but also sectorial planning and technical instruments such as project banks.

During the 1970s and 1980s, planning in Manizales had been piecemeal and disjointed, and it often failed to win consensus. In 1989, National Law 9 finally compelled the city to approve a plan by the new city administration. The mayor took advantage of this momentum to propose tax increases to solve nightmarish traffic congestion in the narrow, winding streets of central Manizales

In 1991, the council approved the Manizales Development Plan, Quality for the 21st Century. The process of developing the plan constituted one of

the main experiences in municipal planning because of the active participation of the planning department. One year later, officials incorporated a
mass transit plan into the Manizales Development Plan. This plan included
a package of works to be carried out during the administration of Mayor
Germán Cardona. Financing for the plan would be handled according to
the stipulations of a 1992 resolution. Furthermore, the mayor was empowered to pledge the resources from the gasoline surtax for up to Col$200
million for financing studies and designs of the proposed works. A municipal investment bank was set up in 1992 to facilitate financing of feasibility
and engineering studies.

HUMAN RESOURCES. Concurrent steps were taken to strengthen personnel in finance and planning. The municipal administration of Manizales
had a total of 839 workers in 1994, compared to 787 in 1988. The increase
(6.6 percent) is not very large, considering that during the same period
both investment and total resources grew substantially. Between 1988 and
1994, the percent of professionals also rose from 11 to 18 percent. In the
years following 1988, the Secretariat of Public Finance kept practically the
same personnel. In the mid 1990s it employed 67 staff members, compared
to 66 in 1989.

The planning department's staff grew slightly and became more professional. Similar to the Secretariat of Public Finance and the income unit, the
planning department maintained staffing practically at the same level, going from 33 staff members in 1988 to 38 in 1989 and 43 by the end of 1994.
Of those 43, 23 were professionals (54 percent). In 1988, just 12 of the 33
staff members were professionals (36 percent) and, in 1989, 13 of 38 employees were professionals (34 percent). This indicates that the personnel
increases were concentrated at the professional-level staff.

Personnel turnover was quite low. As of the end of 1994, the head of the
application unit had been at that post for three years and has worked in the
mayor's office for six. The head of the environmental unit had been there
for 15 years, and the head of project design had worked for 8 years in the
planning department and 11 years in the mayor's office. The group coordinators and other lower level staff had similar lengths of service.

Results

Although Valledupar and Manizales both made significant improvements
in tax management during 1988–94, these achievements were buttressed,
perhaps even made possible, by interlocking innovations in other areas.

Valledupar

National Law 12 of 1986 and, later, Law 60 of 1993 increased national transfer payments to the municipality of Valledupar by 198 percent in real terms during 1988–94. This figure is the equivalent of an annual average increase of 33 percent. In absolute terms, the municipality went from receiving Col$1.47 billion in 1988 to Col$4.39 billion in 1994. It could be expected that the municipal administration would respond to this automatic and growing influx of resources by reducing the collection of its own resources. However, this was not the case in Valledupar. The available figures for the 1988–94 period, which coincided with the administrations of the first three elected mayors in the municipality, show that a significant effort was made to manage tax revenues.

In spite of the growth of the transfer payments, tax revenues grew during the same period by 246 percent in real terms, while nontax revenues grew by 493 percent. Between 1980 and 1987, the tax revenues had shown a growth of a mere 42 percent in the face of a growth in transfer payments of 408 percent. An analysis of the behavior of the major taxes also shows that efforts to collect them increased; in fact, property taxes grew by 338 percent in real terms after 1988, whereas during 1980–87 they had declined by 26 percent. In the case of commercial and industrial taxes, the increase was 106 percent after 1988 compared to 62 percent in the 1980–87 period. Thus, it is evident that the municipal administration achieved a significant complement to the transfer payment resources by improving the collection of its own resources.

The most significant tax revenue change was the increase in the share of property taxes, which climbed from 26 percent in 1988 to 33 percent in 1994, while industrial and commercial taxes declined from 60 percent to 38 percent. Over the same period, property taxes represented 38 percent, and industrial and commercial taxes represented 47 percent, of total tax resources. The most significant change was the appearance of the surtax on gasoline, which in 1994 represented 13 percent of total tax resources.

This behavior allowed a significant increase in per capita taxation and a slight reduction in the rate of dependence on national resources. Per capita tax payments in constant 1994 values represented a 33 percent increase over 1991 (see table 5-2.4). Furthermore, the dependence rate dropped from 54 percent in 1988 to 44 percent in 1994, which attests to the greater growth of local resources (see table 5-2.5). Real growth was continuous throughout the whole period, which demonstrates an effort on the part of all the elected mayors to maintain tax revenues. However,

Table 5-2.4. *Total Tax Revenue and Tax Payments per Inhabitant, Valledupar, 1991–94*

Year	Tax revenue (millions of 1994 US$)	Population	Tax payments per capita (1994 US$)
1991	2,911	232,842	12.52
1992	2,869	234,412	12.24
1993	3,162	235,993	13.40
1994	3,958	237,585	16.66

Source: Project files, 1996, Finance Department, Municipality of Valledupar.

not all cities achieved the same overall impact in terms of improvements in infrastructure and services.

Paralleling this increase in tax revenue, the period of elected mayors saw a large increase in investment, thus fulfilling one of the main objectives of the decentralization process. As a result of elevated real growth, the share of investment expenditures out of total expenditures grew from 34 percent in 1990 to 46 percent in 1994, and per capita investment more than doubled from US$11 to US$26 (see table 5-2.6). Similarly, for the period as a whole, operating expenses were less than local municipal resources, which means that in the aggregate the total sum of national transfer payments was devoted to investment. The increase in investment also resulted from an increasing use of credit.

Table 5-2.5. *Degree of Dependence on National Resources, Valledupar, 1988–94*

Year	Current revenues (millions of 1994 Col$)	Total transfers (millions of 1994 Col$)	Total national transfers (millions of 1994 Col$)	Total dependence (percent)	National dependence (percent)
1988	2,731.6	1,472.5	1,472.5	53.9	53.9
1989	3,480.7	1,665.4	1,665.4	47.8	47.8
1990	4,226.4	1,760.8	1,760.8	41.7	41.7
1991	5,234.7	2,314.3	2,314.3	44.2	44.2
1992	5,921.9	2,897.7	2,897.7	48.9	48.9
1993	7,284.8	3,561.0	3,341.7	48.9	45.9
1994	9,982.3	5,059.6	4,388.2	50.7	44.0
Total	38,862.6	18,731.3	17,840.6	48.2	45.9

Source: Project files, 1996, Finance Department, Municipality of Valledupar.

Table 5-2.6. Investment Behavior, Valledupar, 1991–94

Year	Investment (millions of 1994 US$)	Population	Per capita investment (millions of 1994 US$)
1991	2,535	232,842	10.89
1992	2,014	234,412	8.59
1993	4,944	235,993	20.95
1994	6,178	237,585	26.01

Source: Project files, 1996, Finance Department, Municipality of Valledupar.

The most important effect of decentralization was the increase in local investment. Between 1988 and 1994 the municipal administration carried out investments in the amount of Col$14.33 billion. Most of this was concentrated in the last two years. Four sectors—roads, education, health, and recreation and sports—comprised 77 percent of the total, while the other 15 sectors or spending objectives shared the remaining 23 percent. The available figures show a significant concentration in favor of the roads and highways sector, which received 49 percent of the total investment between 1990 and 1994, with a minimum of 39 percent in 1991 and a maximum of 62 percent in 1990. These figures indicate the administrations' priorities in the area of infrastructure.

Manizales

Between 1988 and 1994, total municipal revenue grew from Col$10.63 billion to Col$26.2 billion (in constant 1994 pesos), a real growth of 146 percent for the period and 16 percent per year. This significant growth demonstrates the municipality's efforts to improve its income. The largest growth for the period occurred in 1993, when total revenue grew by 82 percent in real terms, increasing from Col$12.2 billion to Col$22.2 billion. The current income shows a total growth of 141 percent, concentrated principally in 1993 and 1994. Credit grew by 112 percent in real terms, but with very irregular behavior (see figure 5-2.2).

The trend for current revenue has been growth in real terms in each of the years under study, with the exception of 1992, when it declined by 1.4 percent. The largest growth was concentrated in 1993 and 1994, during the term of the third popularly elected mayor, with real growth rates of 55 percent and 21 percent, respectively. In absolute terms, current revenue climbed from Col$7.8 billion in 1988 to Col$9.2 billion in 1990, Col$10 billion in

Figure 5-2.2. *Total Revenue, Manizales, 1988–94*

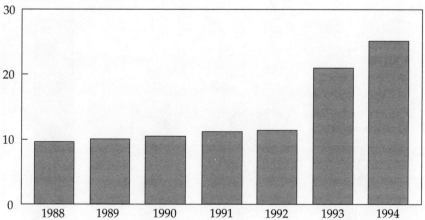

Source: Project files, 1996, Finance Department, Municipality of Manizales.

1992, and Col$18.8 billion in 1994. Within current income, the greatest growth occurred in tax revenues, which increased by 160 percent in real terms, while total transfers grew by 135 percent and nontax revenues by 94 percent. These figures clearly show that during the period of the elected mayors, Manizales was able to maintain a very high real growth of its own resources (see figure 5-2.3).

Although transfer payments grew at a high rate, tax revenues for the municipality grew at an even higher rate in the period under study. Thus, under popular administrations the fiscal performance of the municipality increased significantly. Between 1980 and 1988, growth in real terms was a mere 28 percent in the face of a 143 percent growth in national transfer payments. This change is clearly evident in the main local taxes; for example, the property tax went from 12 percent growth between 1980 and 1988 to 160 percent growth between 1988 and 1994. The growth in industrial and commercial taxes was less significant, because these taxes went from 85 percent to 111 percent real growth during the two periods under consideration. Finally, the "other taxes" line item went from 28 percent to 160 percent growth, mainly as a result of the introduction of the gasoline surtax.

Taken together, tax revenues grew by 160 percent between 1988 and 1994 in real terms, while during 1980–88 they grew only 28 percent. Average

Figure 5-2.3. *Current Revenue, Manizales, 1988–94*

Billions of 1994 pesos

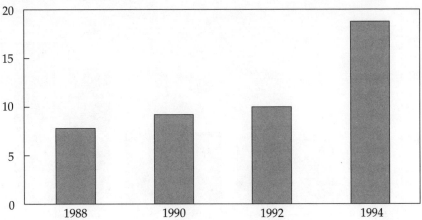

Source: Project files, 1996, Finance Department, Municipality of Manizales.

annual real growth was 17.3 percent, but with significant variation from
year to year (see table 5-2.7). The important real increases were concentrated in the first and third popular administrations. In 1989, which showed
the highest growth, the cadastre was developed, and between 1993 and
1994 the growth stemmed from a combination of actions related to property taxes, industrial and commercial taxes, and the gasoline surtax.

The growth in local resources allowed a notable increase in per capita
taxation and the maintenance of the rate of dependence on national transfer payments between 1988 and 1994. In effect, during this period, the tax

Table 5-2.7. *Growth Rates of Tax Revenues, Manizales, 1989–94*

Year	Growth rate
1989	49.3
1990	−7.0
1991	3.3
1992	1.7
1993	48.0
1994	20.0

Source: Project files, 1996, Finance Department, Municipality of Manizales.

revenue per inhabitant grew from Col$10,700 to Col$24,400 in real terms, while the rate of dependence on automatic transfers decreased slightly from 28.8 percent to 27.8 percent. This dependence ratio is based only on revenue from the central administration, which means that taking into account the resources coming from the public firms and other decentralized entities, the dependence of Manizales on transfers was much lower than 27.8 percent.

Along with the increase in current revenues, the municipality utilized significant amounts of credit, especially during 1993–94, to increase investment substantially. Although between 1989 and 1991, total transfers surpassed investment, in 1994, transfers represented only 58 percent of investment. Similarly, after 1989, the municipality's own resources (tax and nontax) surpassed operating expenses, leaving an additional margin for financing investment.

The strengthening of the municipality's fiscal base and the use of credit resources allowed a substantial increase in local government investment. In 1980 the municipality invested Col$1.5 billion (in 1994 pesos); in 1988 the figure was Col$3.8 billion, and by 1994 it had climbed to Col$13.7 billion. As a result of a higher rate of growth, investment went from representing 34 percent of total expenditures in 1988 to 56 percent in 1994, with an average of 41 percent for 1988–94. On the other hand, operating expenses dropped from 51 percent in 1988 to 28 percent in 1994, with an average of 42.1 percent during the period. The expenditures related to debt service represented 15 percent throughout the whole period.

There is not as much evidence of efficient use of resources. However, in general, the popular administrations made significant efforts to improve the planning, programming, project formulation, and investment control processes, which were required for the rationalization of expenditures. The mayors' efforts helped produce a positive image of the city's activities among its citizens, according to the surveys carried out by the municipality (World Bank 1995). According to the available information, the substantial increase in national transfer payments had not been translated into a reduction in fiscal effort. Rather, during the period under study, Manizales significantly increased its revenues by better use of local revenue sources.

Sustainability and Replicability

The tax management experiences in Manizales and Valledupar include all the conditions for sustained fiscal health, as long as efforts are kept up and weak points are improved. The potential tax revenue was still not fully exploited; however, the municipalities' ability to reach the full revenue potential may be constrained by tax inelasticity over the medium term, the degree of indebtedness, and especially the nation's economic crisis of the mid 1990s. The following are the key factors in the performance of public management in the municipalities of Valledupar and Manizales, which can act as an example for other municipalities:

- **Use of the instruments offered by decentralization.** The presence of instruments and options in the area of fiscal strengthening is a basic requirement for good administrative management.
- **Activities on different fronts.** The experiences are not characterized by a fundamental change or a radical reform of the municipalities' fiscal management. On the contrary, the results obtained were the product of various changes and adjustments, some of them minor, in the different sources of financing available.
- **Continuity in personnel.** Low turnover among tax management personnel was a key element in the observed results.
- **Leadership and commitment of the mayors.** The results achieved in fiscal management in Valledupar and Manizales depended to a great extent on the capability and leadership of the popularly elected mayors, as well as on their ongoing commitment to strengthen the fiscal bases of the municipality.

Conclusion

A special set of contextual factors were important in the genesis and promulgation of innovations in Manizales. Most notable among these factors were (a) new incentives for mayors to implement innovative policies created by the resumption of elections and reinforced by new measures of accountability; (b) various national policies that were intended to enlarge the fiscal base of municipalities, both by increasing the sources of own-source revenue and by augmenting central government transfers; and (c) the transfer of additional responsibility for service delivery to municipal governments in areas such as water and sanitation, health, education, agriculture, and transportation. Another factor in the success of these cities' financial innovations is that both cities approved these measures in their respective municipal councils, acts that accorded additional degrees of visibility and formality. Also in Manizales, the municipality extended the mentality of own-source revenue raising in the realm of modernized financial management within the municipality.

But many of these same factors were present in cities all across Colombia. Why then were they so prominently exploited in these two cities? One answer is that the innovations were launched by mayors who were elected into an environment of good management, and therefore into an atmosphere of expectation for good government on the part of the electorate. Another part of the answer is that the innovations were launched by newly elected leaders who were able to see the promise and potential of efficient city management. The mayor of Manizales, for example, spoke (in personal communication) of "delivering the goods" and confronting taxpayers with the costs of city services. This new vision of government came with the headiness of new municipal autonomy accorded during Colombia's decentralization. Similar changes were apparent in Valledupar where popular election was extended even to county police officers. The concepts and techniques of financial management were widely disseminated, but not adopted everywhere in Colombia. Many municipalities took advantage of the prerogatives given to local governments by national law. And while own-source revenues grew across the spectrum of local governments in Colombia, not all local governments innovated in fiscal management to the extent shown in Manizales and Valledupar.

References

Maldonado, Alberto, and Carlos Moreno Ospina. 1997. *"Transferencias y esfuerzo fiscal municipal." Nomados* 3 (October).

World Bank. 1995. *Colombia—Estudio sobre la Capacidad de los Gobiernos Locales: Más Allá de la Asistencia Técnica.* Washington, D.C.

6

Administrative Performance and Management

6-1

Modernizing a Provincial Public Sector: An Experiment in Mendoza, Argentina

Harald Fuhr, University of Potsdam

This case study describes two innovative experiments in public administration at the provincial level that, interestingly, took place during a time of political uncertainties and persistent macroeconomic instability at the national level. One was an approach to modernize budgeting and make the provincial budget more results-driven. Results-oriented budgeting—in Argentina as in many other countries—was expected to lead to a profound and dual change: to better inform decisionmakers within the provincial government and, at the same time, improve the quality and efficiency of service delivery for the provincial population. And while government officials and experts in the capital were still discussing new options for fiscal federalism in the country, Mendoza pushed forward another reform: a new performance-driven, revenue-sharing system between the provincial government and its municipalities.

As in Brazil and other Latin American countries, provincial politics in Argentina became more important during the 1980s. The failure of previous national governments to achieve economic and political stability gave some strong civil society movements in the provinces room to maneuver. Both of Mendoza's reforms started in the late 1980s within a broader context of public sector reforms in the province, which was one of the most advanced in Argentina. And many of those public sector reforms were associated with an interesting political movement and strong leadership by a charismatic governor, Octavio Bordón, who later ran for president against Raúl Menem.

The province of Mendoza (population about 1.4 million), located in midwestern Argentina, has some notable features compared to other provinces in the country. First, the province's finances and economy seem to be in better shape and, second, the size and growth of its public sector, as table 6-1.1 shows, seem comparatively small:

- After a decade of stagnation in the 1970s (0.1 percent annual loss in Gross Provincial Product, or GPP), GPP increased during 1980–92 by 3 percent a year. Annual GPP growth rates per capita during the same periods were –2.1 and 1.3 percent, respectively. Since the 1980s, all figures have been significantly above the national average.
- Mendoza is among the country's top four producers of petroleum; in 1993 the province settled a dispute with the national government, which had owed Mendoza royalties totaling nearly US$630 million. A compensation arrangement provided for US$450 million to be paid in several annual tranches.
- With federal transfers representing only 7.8 percent of Mendoza's GPP, the province has a large degree of financial independence.
- Unemployment figures in Mendoza during the late 1980s and early 1990s (3.3–6 percent) were among the lowest in the country.
- Public employment grew by just 25 percent from 1983 to 1994, compared to the national average of approximately 50 percent.
- In 1995–96, the province of Mendoza had 29 public employees per 1,000 people (compared to a national average of 57); public employees received average monthly salaries of 1,230 pesos in 1995, significantly above the country's average (1,057 pesos).[1]

Context

Historically, development in Mendoza advanced more rapidly than in other Argentinian provinces. Two factors accounted for Mendoza's early success: irrigation and immigration. Overall provincial development and, eventually, innovation in Mendoza's government were based on strong middle-class development, patterns of local participation, and public-private partnerships. Throughout Mendoza's history, these conditions provided a credible framework for both public and private actors to engage in local resource mobilization and growth, invest in education, and occasionally generate innovations in local government.

---

1. The exchange rate at the time was approximately one peso to US$1.

Table 6-1.1. *Argentina: Comparative Provincial Indicators, 1995–96*

Indicator	Mendoza	Argentina's other 24 provinces (average)
Public employees per 1,000 population	29	57
Average salary of public employees (pesos)	1,230	1,057
Deficit pension system (million pesos)	30.4	39.9
Ratio of provincial revenue to total expenditures (percent)	29.5	19.5
Ratio of personnel expenditures to total expenditures (percent)	51.5	53.2
Ratio of capital expenditures to total expenditures (percent)	16.5	15.9
Total provincial expenditures per capita (pesos)	875	1,360
Current provincial expenditures per capita (pesos)	730	1,126
Provincial revenues per capita (pesos)	295	313
National revenues per capita (pesos)	380	710
Provincial personnel expenditures per capita (pesos)	450	700
Federal transfers to Mendoza per capita (pesos)	297	525

Note: One Argentine peso equals US$1.
Source: Ministry of the Interior, 1995 project files.

Mendoza's history began in the mid-nineteenth century when European settlers migrated to the eastern slope of the Andes and created irrigation systems to turn thousands of square kilometers of desert into one of the most productive agricultural areas in the country. Today, all green spaces and trees along the streets of Mendoza still need irrigation; the forests that surround the city have all been planted by people.

Immigration and the Winemaking Industry

Mendoza's formidable economic growth was made possible by a great influx of European immigrants around 1890. The highest level, about 12,000 immigrants a year, was reached during 1906–13. By 1914, 32 percent of the 278,000 inhabitants of Mendoza were foreigners, almost all of whom were Europeans.

Wine became Mendoza's favorite product and source of income, and a corresponding pattern of middle-class development emerged along with it. With the explosive growth of wine production between 1883 and 1914, grape growing and wine production became the basis of Mendoza's economy and society, tying the province firmly to the swelling coastal market (Mörner 1993).

Italians, Spaniards, and other immigrants were particularly important to the grape and wine sector. In 1895, foreigners controlled only 29 percent of 1,770 vineyards; in 1914, they controlled 52 percent of some 6,160 vineyards. Wine production underwent as much as a tenfold increase between 1895 and 1914. By the latter year, immigrants comprised the majority of the population in the northeastern and southern areas of the province. In Mendoza, foreigners dominated the industrial sector as well, accounting for 74 percent of all industrial owners. Similarly, they dominated the commercial sector (Mörner 1993).

Traditional politics in Mendoza were family-based. Prior to 1912, a small number of upper-class families controlled political life. This elite had long been surprisingly open toward foreigners, who they regarded as well behaved. The upper-class families had even tried to attract immigrants, but had little success prior to the railroad (which was built in the 1890s) and to viticultural opportunities (Fleming 1987).

During the 1902–11 period—coinciding with the peak of immigration—more than 23 million hectares of land were sold in Mendoza, more than in any other province of the country. The number of landholders increased from 6,700 in 1901 to 18,000 in 1915. When the immigrants did arrive en masse, they were well received, especially those who had viticultural or technical skills (Fleming 1987). Agriculturalists, engineers, and enologists were drawn to Mendoza by the lure of cheap land and economic opportunity. Once established in Mendoza, they demanded a voice in the provincial government, and Mendoza's Argentine-born leaders could not survive the transformation of the province that they themselves had encouraged (Supplee 1988).

David Rock (1987) points to some of the sociopolitical patterns that evolved with wine production:

> Tariff protection and the coming of the railroad, which reached Mendoza from Mercedes in 1885, greatly benefited the new wine economy, as did an interventionist provincial government, which created local banks, instituted tax exemptions for farmers, organized irrigation schemes, and laid down roads between the vineyards and the railheads. As in Tucuman, seasonal contract labor was used, for

grape picking, but Mendoza managed to attract and retain European immigrants and thus largely avoided the acute social disparities of Tucuman. The distinctive feature of society in Mendoza was the emergence of a rural and urban middle class. Middle class politics and participatory policies seem to be particularly obvious in Mendoza's democratically elected *comités de agua* [water committees] that helped ensure equal access to irrigated water and to establish early forms of civic culture and exchange (p. 152).

Public-Private Partnerships

Small and medium enterprises—as many studies around the world have shown—participate in various institutions that involve collaboration not only with each other, but also with local governments, educational institutions, research centers, and organized labor. The presence and strength of these institutions create an information-rich environment, fostering the exchange of information, continuous interaction among different social actors, and the development of trust-based relations (Schmitz 1990).

Santos Martínez (1994), in his historical account of Mendoza, refers to many examples of successful public-private partnerships that have endured since the 1930s. Effective literacy campaigns and investment in education (such as the founding of the University of Cuyo in 1939) took place during the 1930s. With the government playing an active role in promoting local economic development, production of wine almost doubled, and energy and oil production quadrupled, between 1954 and 1965. Uranium production began in the mid 1960s. Local oil fields helped finance public investments in transport. In 1964, the Mendoza government expropriated Bodegas y Viñederos Giol, a wine marketing and regulatory agency that had previously been a private enterprise. In 1972, the provincial government supported a provincial civic alliance (which included the business community) that protested a national increase in electricity prices. The protest eventually led to military intervention by the national government.

These examples illustrate the long tradition of effective public-private partnerships in Mendoza. The civil society of the province is characterized by strong government support of industry, free movement of decisionmakers between the public and the private sectors, well-developed participatory channels, and a strong middle-class orientation. As some studies have pointed out, persistent macroeconomic instability has put enormous pressures on such "traditional" civic alliances, often leading to their disruption (for good or bad).[2] Such pressures emerged in the second half of the 1980s, particularly during the period of hyperinflation (1987–89). These pressures, however, can also provide incentives to create new types of civic alliances, as demonstrated in Mendoza in recent years.

Origin and Conception

Governor Octavio Bordón became the champion of Mendoza's innovations. With his background as professor of sociology at Mendoza's University of Cuyo during the 1980s and representative of the *Justicialista* party in the National Congress of Argentina, Bordón received support for his gubernatorial campaign from both the academic and political communities. His platform also represented the aspirations of Mendoza's middle-class citizens—particularly entrepreneurs and professionals—who had been severely affected during the country's economic crises. Thanks in part to his charisma, Bordón was elected governor of the province of Mendoza in December 1988, and he promptly launched a variety of innovations in local policymaking (see box 6-1.1).

The ambitious reform program of the incoming government addressed key problem areas and sectors, striving for better transparency and accountability of public administration, better management and increased effectiveness of provincial finances, effective use of provincial resources (particularly the promotion of wine exports), investments in basic education and health, and new incentive structures for provincial-municipal cooperation and transfers. The government in these years was keen to stress that the province of Mendoza had started an adjustment process and modernized its public sector with its own resources (Government of Mendoza 1991a), while other provinces had largely resisted such efforts.

In sociological terms, Bordón was a visionary governor spearheading a group of dedicated middle-class reformers, many of whom were linked to his former employer (the University of Cuyo) and to the private sector. Most of Bordón's professional supporters later held ministerial positions in the provincial administration; two (Rodolfo Federico Gabrielli and Arturo Pedro Lafalla) became governors of Mendoza, and others served as technical advisors to assistance projects of international organizations, such as the Inter-American Development Bank and the World Bank.

---

2. See Casaburi (1994) for an interesting comparative study on two commercial-industrial districts in Chile and Argentina during phases of recession and liberalization.

Box 6-1.1. *Timeline of Events in Mendoza*

1985	National Stabilization Plan, or Plan Austral, developed.
1987–89	Period of hyperinflation in Argentina.
Early 1988	Budget process reform launched.
Late 1988	Introduction of Revenue Collection and Control System (Sistema de Recaudación y Control), a reform of provincial tax administration.
Late 1988	Introduction of the Revenue-Sharing System of Provincial Resources (Régimen de Coparticipación de los Recursos Provinciales), based on new incentives for provincial-municipal transfers, which replaced the transfer system of 1975 (Law 1268).
Late 1988	Restructuring and privatization of Giol, Mendoza's former public marketing company for grapes and wine.
December 1988	José Octavio Bordón elected governor of the province of Mendoza (Arturo Pedro Lafalla, vice governor; Juán Argentino Vega, minister of finance; Rodolfo Federico Gabrielli, minister of economy).
1990	First full cycle of the new budget process.
April 1991	National Convertibility Plan (Plan de Covertibilidad) developed.
January 1992	Rodolfo Federico Gabrielli elected governor of the province of Mendoza.
August 1992	National Provisional Fiscal Agreement (Convenio Fiscal Transitorio) restructures intergovernmental transfers in Argentina.
1992–95	Victor Manuel Fayad serves as mayor of Mendoza.
January 1996	Arturo Pedro Lafalla elected governor of the province of Mendoza.

Launch

Among the first and most important of the many reforms the provincial government initiated was the privatization of Giol, the public enterprise for marketing grapes and wine. Giol had annual operating deficits throughout the 1980s of some US$20 million. The financing of these deficits was not transparent, yet it was made easy through the involvement of provincial banks. At the end of 1987, Giol's deficit amounted to US$35 million, an amount equivalent to 90 percent of expenditures for public security, 77 percent of health expenditures, or 27 percent of total expenditures for public works in Mendoza in 1988. In late 1988, Giol was sold to a cooperative of provincial winemakers. The privatization of Giol, which was carried out quickly and without major conflicts, marked the first visible success of the new government (Juri and Mercau 1990).

The efforts to modernize the provincial public sector ranked among Mendoza's more innovative approaches. The provincial government started with five major administrative reforms:

- **Results-Oriented Budgeting (ROB).** Results-driven annual exercise in budgeting, with a clear set of priorities, goals, implementing agencies, costs, costs per unit, and more.
- **Municipal Revenue-Sharing System (Régimen de Coparticipación Municipal, or RECOMU).** Computerized, transparent, and incentive-driven revenue-sharing system for municipalities within the province.
- **Revenue Collection and Control System.** Computerized system that allowed for better collection, monitoring, and control of provincial revenues.
- **Territorial Information System.** Computerized system with continuously updated information on provincial land use and land ownership.
- **Database of Investment Projects.** Database on provincial investment projects for long-term expenditure planning and better identification and monitoring of public investment.

This case study discusses the first two of these reforms in detail. The first related to internal financial procedures, and the second to the administration's external financial relationships. Mendoza undertook these key innovations—ROB and a new municipal revenue-sharing system—to improve control of provincial expenditures and make the budget and revenue sharing more transparent.

Results-Oriented Budgeting

In early 1988 the provincial Ministry of Finance presented a plan to introduce ROB with very sophisticated financial management techniques. The overall goal of the reform was to better link assessed needs of the citizenry to policies, policies to provincial resources, and these, in turn, to well-defined objectives with quantifiable results (see box 6-1.2).

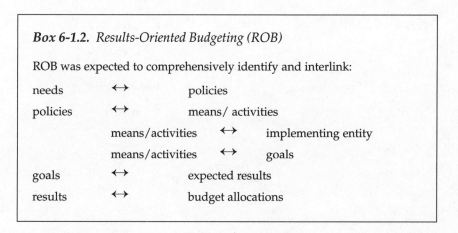

Box 6-1.2. *Results-Oriented Budgeting (ROB)*

ROB was expected to comprehensively identify and interlink:

needs	↔	policies
policies	↔	means/ activities
	means/activities ↔	implementing entity
	means/activities ↔	goals
goals	↔	expected results
results	↔	budget allocations

ROB was developed originally as a research project (called Proyecto de Presupuesto y Tarifas en el Sector Público de Mendoza, or Project on Budgeting and Fees in Mendoza's Public Sector) in the Economics Department of the University of Cuyo between 1983 and 1987. Economics professor Orlando Braceli was its principal developer (Braceli 1995). With some of his teaching assistants and students, Braceli formed an effective and motivated "change team" that became involved in ROB's implementation and operation in early 1988. Team members were later hired as full-time professionals in the provincial administration, and Braceli himself became minister of finance in early 1991.

ROB represented a new approach to defining and expressing government policies and preferences. The new administration expected it, in particular, to increase transparency and accountability of policymaking, underscore prioritized policies, measure policy outputs and performance, and serve as a vehicle for the subsequent overall modification of public administration.

As figures 6-1.1 to 6-1.4 show, the budgeting process comprises four distinct steps. The cycle starts with a preliminary gathering of information and programming, bringing in line responsible units, activities, and territorial information. Then implementing units are assigned tasks. In the third step, targets and indicators are defined. In the last step, resource needs are defined, different alternatives for achieving targets are discussed, and resources are programmed.

ROB puts strong emphasis on good data. Information gathering quantifies the social and economic living conditions of the provincial population and specifies the citizens' needs. Needs are addressed through different policy options with quantified goals and targets.

Figure 6-1.1. *Step 1: Collect Information and Prepare Preliminary Program*

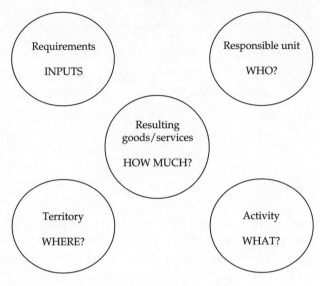

Source: Author.

Figure 6-1.2. *Step 2: Identify Implementing Units and Assign Tasks*

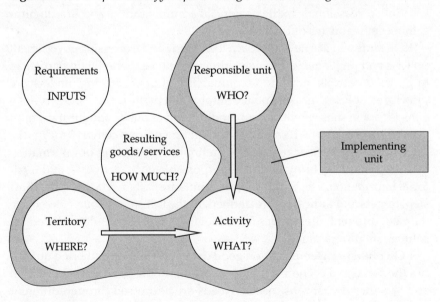

Source: Author.

Figure 6-1.3. *Step 3: Identify Goods and Services to Be Produced and Define Targets and Indicators*

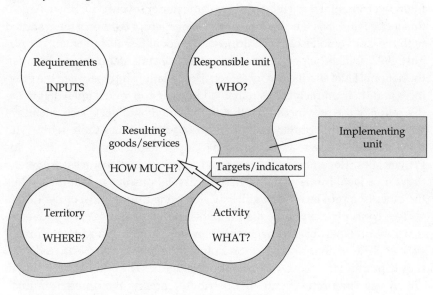

Source: Author.

Figure 6-1.4. *Step 4: Define Resource Needs and Assign Resources*

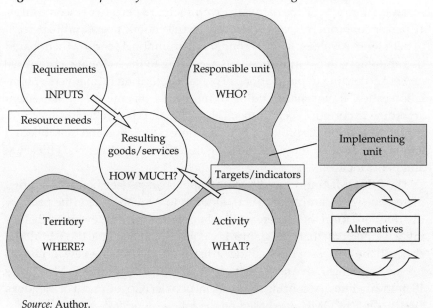

Source: Author.

Innovative Revenue Sharing with Municipalities

Intergovernmental fiscal relationships came under severe criticism in Argentina in the late 1980s. The first major national attempt to reform them started with the Convenio Fiscal Transitorio (Provisional Fiscal Agreement) of August 1992, which helped restructure intergovernmental transfers between the national level and its provinces. Yet, fiscal relationships between the provinces and their municipalities remained unclear and were largely left to the discretion of the provinces. Together with Chubut and del Chaco, Mendoza was one of the first provinces that addressed these issues thoroughly. With the 1988 law known as Régimen de Coparticipación de los Recursos Provinciales (Revenue-Sharing System for Provincial Resources), Mendoza drew up a legal framework for these fiscal relationships in late 1988, while the other two provinces were still experimenting during most of the 1990s.

Two concepts need to be distinguished: *primary* and *secondary* revenue distribution (sharing) arrangements between provinces and their municipalities. The primary distribution defines the amount to be shared with municipalities; the secondary distribution defines the criteria according to which this amount is eventually distributed among the different municipalities within a province.

Before the RECOMU was introduced in 1988, the primary distribution consisted of 10 percent of the revenues that the province received from revenue sharing with the national government, 10 percent of income taxes, 10 percent of property taxes, 70 percent of automobile taxes, and 10 percent of petroleum royalties. In the secondary distribution, Mendoza then shared this amount with the municipalities according to the following criteria: 30 percent according to population, 10 percent according to an inverse population ratio, 30 percent according to municipal revenues, and 30 percent according to current expenditures. The system thus favored developed municipalities within the province that had more population and that collected and spent more, without considering criteria of effectiveness, efficiency, and performance.

The RECOMU introduced two principal changes (see box 6-1.3). It first increased significantly the overall amount to be distributed (the primary distribution) from the 10 percent to a 14 percent share in revenues, including a 14 percent share in stamp tax collections. Second, the RECOMU changed the criteria of the secondary distribution, stressing new incentives for good administrative performance and capital expenditures in Mendoza's 18 municipalities. According to an official booklet (Government of Mendoza 1991b), the RECOMU was based on the following ideas:

Box 6-1.3. Mendoza's Revenue-Sharing Arrangements
Before and After RECOMU

Primary distribution (as percentage)

	Province of Mendoza		Municipalities	
Category	1975–88	RECOMU	1975–88	RECOMU
Federal revenue sharing	90	86	10	14
Income tax	90	86	10	14
Stamp tax	0	86	0	14
Property tax	90	86	10	14
Automobile tax	30	30	70	70
Petroleum, uranium, and gas royalties	90	88	10	12

Secondary distribution

Revenues from federal revenue sharing, income tax, and stamp tax, as well as 50 percent of royalties, are distributed as follows:

• Property tax and automobile tax revenues are distributed in proportion to de facto registration of property and vehicles in each of the municipalities (departments).
• Fifty percent of the royalties are distributed in proportion to the annual production of petroleum, uranium, and gas in each municipality (department).

Criteria for secondary distribution (as percentage)	1975–88	RECOMU
1. Population	30	35
2. Inverse population ratio	10	3
3. Municipal revenues	30	15
4. Current expenditures	30	15
5. Ratio of municipal tax revenues to current expenditures	n.a.	20
6. Ratio of capital expenditures to total expenditures	n.a.	5
7. Ratio of municipal personnel to population	n.a.	7

n.a. Not applicable.
Note: Three percent of the overall primary distribution amount is reserved for an assistance fund for municipalities (Fondo de Apoyo Municipal); 97 percent is distributed according to the secondary distribution criteria.
Sources: Bertranou (1993); Government of Mendoza (1991b); Vega, Ojeda, and Russo (1995).

- Increasing the amount of revenue to be shared with municipalities with the overall objective to provide "more resources to *do* more"
- Channeling *all* resources for municipalities according to clearly established criteria, thus avoiding discretion in the distribution of revenues
- Incorporating in the secondary distribution of revenues a variety of new, measurable criteria, such as quality in conducting municipal administration and managing local finances, fiscal effort, municipal investment, and poverty in municipalities
- Implementing a system of incentives that encouraged good performance in local administration and service delivery.

It is important to note that 3 percent of the overall amount after primary distribution is reserved for a special assistance fund for municipalities (Fondo de Apoyo Municipal); 97 percent of the amount is then shared with the municipalities according to the secondary distribution criteria in box 6-1.3. The municipal assistance fund is supposed to support municipalities in crisis with grants, credits, or both. Since 1994, five poorer municipalities have been entitled to receive contributions from this fund on a more permanent basis, according to criteria established by a joint provincial-municipal committee.

The RECOMU, although conceptually embedded in Mendoza's broader reform strategy, was not just introduced from above, but discussed and agreed upon in several joint sessions between the provincial government and elected mayors. Such discussions reflected the consensual leadership style of Bordón's government.

Results

Mendoza's efforts to improve its public sector had many positive results, which are detailed in this section.

Results of Results-Oriented Budgeting

ROB was introduced in 1988 with a major public relations effort and with strong involvement and top-down support of both the minister of finance and Bordón. Massive advertising campaigns in the departments, face-to-face interactions among decisionmakers, and a well-designed information strategy assisted dissemination efforts.[3]

---

3. Most information in this section is based on Government of Mendoza (1992) and on interviews in 1995 and 1996 with staff and managers of Mendoza's provincial administration.

Managers in departments had to phase out traditional program budgeting and specify results of their annual operations. Working with staff, they defined expected results, activities, units of production, and, eventually, resource allocation. ROB was a radically different approach to budgeting that required extensive staff effort—during sessions lasting from July to November—and massive training or retraining. ROB training programs were designed and implemented to shift course in the first year, and then offered continuously. Mendoza planned to provide assistance in ROB techniques to its municipalities later on.

ROB introduced a variety of new tools to assist Mendoza's decisionmakers (see box 6-1.4). Decisionmakers in the Ministry of Finance stressed that, for the first time, ROB processes allowed them to clearly translate assessed needs in the province into targeted policies, and individual policies into a set of specified activities and subactivities. They could then define measurable targets associated with these activities, define responsibilities of implementing units and managers, and assign financial and human resources. Under ROB, output and performance indicators helped

---

Box 6-1.4. *New Tools Introduced under Results-Oriented Budgeting*

ROB helped introduce several new, successful forms of doing business in the provincial administration:

- The input classification system
- The system for purchasing inputs
- The activity classification system
- The systematization of responsibilities and functional entities
- The systematization (and interconnection) of territorial information
- The decentralization of financial management, particularly accounting procedures, at department and unit levels
- The development of a new personnel administration system
- Better options for managing and training staff
- New options for monitoring, evaluating, and adjusting the budget
- Sophisticated, administrationwide computer networks and new options for exchange of information among units
- Enhanced management information systems for improved decisionmaking
- New performance indicators
- New options for output measurement
- Better follow-up of provincial investment projects
- New legal procedures.

them monitor progress, guide and evaluate implementation, and eventually quantify policy impact. The increasingly detailed information on impacts helped decisionmakers adjust policies at the end of each ROB cycle and translate those into new sets of activities for the next cycle.

The sheer mass of information that was generated in the first decade since ROB began is impressive. Some 14,000 activities—including related indicators—had been specified and responsibly managed by nearly 6,000 operational units within the provincial administration.

Change is particularly evident in Mendoza's education and health sectors. Starting in 1989, hospitals and schools were expected to provide detailed information on their services. Health problems detected in the province, such as infant and maternal mortality rates in the rural areas, were assessed carefully. Provincial health policies then defined targets and respective activities to reduce such problems over a specified period of time. The activities—such as preventive measures, injections, and operations—were classified (see table 6-1.2). Required inputs for these activities, such as tools and drugs, were eventually given eight-digit input codes. Similarly, schools took stock of their annual outputs and defined required inputs to meet certain educational targets, such as attendance rates in primary education, girls' education, and scoring and achievement rates of pupils.

In addition to establishing new standards in input and output classification, provincial health and education administrations were able to monitor overall costs and individual expenditures by location. Classified information and indicators helped quantify unit costs—for example, the cost of educating one pupil in a certain municipality or district, or of one patient-day in a provincial hospital, or of preventive care procedures, such as anti-cholera injections. Such data, consequently, also helped to reduce costs on the input side, sometimes simply by providing better knowledge of expenditure composition and single expenditure items, sometimes by providing price comparisons that led to lower-cost or higher-quality options. Expenditures for hospital care per patient, for example, decreased between 1991 and 1993 by approximately 23 percent, saving the provincial administration nearly 24 million pesos.

Under ROB, the decentralization of the financial management system and the encouragement of decisionmaking within the units (constrained by budgetary ceilings), led to a significant decrease in processing time for administrative procedures, thus saving time and resources. Simple accounting procedures, for example, that formerly involved 8 separate administrative steps and lasted at least 10 days, were now reduced to 4 steps and a minimum of 4 days; more complex procedures that involved 12 steps and a

Table 6-1.2. *Mendoza Ministry of Finance 1995 Budget Activities and Expenditures (Excerpts)*

	Activities	Current expenditures					Capital expenditures				Total expenditures
		Staff	Goods	Services	Transfers	Sub-total	Goods	Public works	Others	Sub-total	
1	Promote overall general welfare	118,800	38,830	42,637	6,768	207,035	830	2,400	26	3,256	210,291
2	Provide final public goods	118,753	38,799	42,637	6,768	206,957	830	2,400	26	3,256	210,213
3	Guarantee health of citizens	106,110	29,403	40,884	734	177,131	828	2,400	6	3,234	180,365
4	Guarantee preventive health of citizens	5,973	365	691	139	7,168	n.a.	n.a.	n.a.	n.a.	7,168
5	Promote and protect health of target groups	5,354	331	672	139	6,496	n.a.	n.a.	n.a.	n.a.	6,496
6	Promote and protect health through preventive programs	4,065	214	501	2	4,782	n.a.	n.a.	n.a.	n.a.	4,782
7	Promote and protect health of infants and young children	28	0	192	1	221	n.a.	n.a.	n.a.	n.a.	221
8	Promote and protect health during pregnancy	28	0	n.a.	1	29	n.a.	n.a.	n.a.	n.a.	29
9	Train staff	28	0	n.a.	1	29	n.a.	n.a.	n.a.	n.a.	29
8	Promote and protect health of mothers and infants	n.a.	n.a.	192	n.a.	192	n.a.	n.a.	n.a.	n.a.	192
7	Assist preventive programs against cholera	840	37	17	n.a.	894	n.a.	n.a.	n.a.	n.a.	894
7	Assist preventive programs against AIDS	29	0	1	0	30	n.a.	n.a.	n.a.	n.a.	30
7	Provide education and orientation for health at work	444	n.a.	112	n.a.	556	n.a.	n.a.	n.a.	n.a.	556
8	Check psychological and physical conditions	444	n.a.	112	n.a.	556	n.a.	n.a.	n.a.	n.a.	556
9	Check and monitor absenteeism at work	444	n.a.	112	n.a.	556	n.a.	n.a.	n.a.	n.a.	556
7	Promote and protect oral/dental health of staff	56	2	n.a.	n.a.	58	n.a.	n.a.	n.a.	n.a.	58
7	Promote and protect health through clinical exams and other preventive measures	1,235	126	13	n.a.	1,374	n.a.	n.a.	n.a.	n.a.	1,374
8	Provide laboratory services and X-ray services	725	106	n.a.	n.a.	831	n.a.	n.a.	n.a.	n.a.	831
9	Provide laboratory services	425	58	n.a.	n.a.	483	n.a.	n.a.	n.a.	n.a.	483
9	Provide X-ray services	297	48	n.a.	n.a.	345	n.a.	n.a.	n.a.	n.a.	345
8	Reduce effects of TBC infections	37	n.a.	0	n.a.	37	n.a.	n.a.	n.a.	n.a.	37

n.a. Not applicable.
Source: Project files, 1996. Data provided by the Finance Department of the government of Mendoza.

minimum of about 30 days for processing (and usually much more) now had only 6 steps and required 6 to 10 days to complete. Most important, accounting could be monitored in real time: technology allowed for improved management of the tax department. The number of identified and registered taxpayers increased from 30,000 in 1990 to 100,000 in 1993, which helped diminish tax evasion.

ROB required high-end data processing equipment and an overall computerization of government departments. Before ROB started, the provincial administration in 1987 owned just two personal computers. In the first year of operation (1988), the department had approximately 40 computers, in late 1990 it had 220, and by the mid 1990s it had nearly 1,000 personal computers and workstations—plus 300 computers exclusively for ROB purposes. The quality and the speed of data processing were stunning. Fiber optic technology was introduced at the system's inception, and officials planned to implement satellite technology to facilitate budgeting processes in Mendoza's municipalities.

It is interesting to note that the broad introduction of computer technology in the late 1980s helped jump start a variety of additional tools to modernize public administration in Mendoza, such as e-mail and other Internet resources. These tools gave departments new options for informing the public. The ministries of finance, education, and health, for example, developed their own home pages and provided information on their work at a Web site.

Results of the RECOMU

Some studies, such as Bertranou (1993) and Vega, Ojeda, and Russo (1995), discuss the effects of the RECOMU for participating municipalities. One can raise six interesting questions about the RECOMU. Has it resulted in:

1. **More transfers for municipalities?** Probably yes. As table 6-1.3 indicates, transfers to municipalities rose significantly throughout the early 1990s. Although mainly due to a rise in national transfers to the province (from US$240 million in 1989 to US$440 million in 1994), municipal transfers rose much faster than national transfers to Mendoza, almost tripling from US$60 million in 1989 to US$175 million in 1994.
2. **A larger share of revenues for smaller municipalities?** Mixed scenario. Vega, Ojeda, and Russo (1995) indicate that after secondary distribution, the share in revenues for the larger municipalities (Capital, Godoy Cruz, Guaymallen, and San Rafael) first decreased significantly from slightly above 50 percent of total transfers before the reform to 41–45

Table 6-1.3. *Mendoza: Provincial Finances, 1984–94*
(million pesos convertibles)

Category	1984	1985	1986	1987	1988	1989	1990	1991	1992	1993	1994
Total revenues	513	561	732	740	688	638	438	602	882	1,076	1,123
Current revenues	358	507	614	533	523	502	410	575	841	964	999
Provincial	129	157	217	174	182	171	136	205	324	385	436
National	229	349	397	359	342	331	274	370	517	580	562
Revenue sharing	100	218	235	224	206	240	202	282	415	428	440
Others	129	131	162	135	136	91	73	88	101	152	123
Capital	3	3	1	1	2	2	0	0	2	63	71
Contributions	152	51	117	206	163	134	28	27	39	49	53
Total expenditures	601	569	835	776	763	502	452	574	865	1,110	1,294
Current expenditures	520	454	688	576	550	427	402	513	785	953	1,081
Personnel	303	255	388	308	258	201	215	305	468	549	666
Goods and services	48	51	63	59	91	65	39	53	87	122	138
Interest and debt	0	1	15	5	11	16	0	1	8	2	14
Transfers	169	148	222	204	190	145	148	154	222	281	263
Municipalities	65	55	87	61	69	60	60	88	115	168	175
Social security	67			122	86	73	65	43	42	64	30
Others	36	94	135	21	35	13	23	23	64	49	58
Capital	81	115	147	200	213	75	50	61	80	157	213
Deficit (total revenues – total expenditures)	–88	–8	–103	–36	–75	136	–14	28	17	–34	–171

Source: Government of Mendoza (1995, table 1.1.1.1).

143

percent shortly after. The same holds true for the municipalities that form the Mendoza capital region, which faced a decrease from 70 percent to approximately 65 percent under the RECOMU. The larger municipalities, however, caught up quickly after 1992, and the overall situation changed drastically with the beginning of stabilization policies and the introduction of a new transfer system.

3. **More rational use of municipal expenditures?** No. Bertranou (1993) and Vega, Ojeda, and Russo (1995) indicate that de facto constraints on spending due to stabilization policies after 1991 influenced municipal spending behavior more than incentives provided by the RECOMU. Investment ratios in municipalities—although they had increased during the five years since the RECOMU began, particularly in the larger municipalities—went up and down without clear trends.

4. **Incentives for better fiscal autonomy?** Mixed. Analysis in Vega, Ojeda, and Russo (1995) and Bertranou (1993) shows no clear trend. During the first years of the RECOMU, the indicator "own-source revenues/current expenditures" shows that larger municipalities first seemed to lose importance, but then recuperated toward 1993. Small and medium municipalities increased their revenues in 1992 and 1993, but also increased current expenditures, which gave them a more favorable participation ratio. Again, the incentives provided by the RECOMU did not seem to make a large difference.

5. **More rational management of human resources?** Probably yes. As table 6-1.4 indicates, employment figures increased by 57 percent (8 percent per year) in the years preceding the reform. Employment levels markedly slowed down after 1989 with an annual increase of 1 percent, significantly below population growth. Employment growth was significantly below average in larger municipalities and above average in the small and medium municipalities of Mendoza. Although these indicators are very promising, it is questionable if the slowdown in employment was due to RECOMU's incentives. The slowdown more likely occurred because of the overall macroeconomic situation of the country during these years. In any case, because the indicator reflects public sector growth to a certain extent, it became very important in the debate on reforming fiscal transfers in other provinces.

6. **Municipalities providing information on time?** Yes. Past experience indicates that quarterly information on the status of municipal finances, investment, and human resources is provided to Mendoza's Ministry of Finance in a reliable and timely manner. New data requirements as well as procedures have also helped improve management of data, which can be used for administrative purposes as well.

Table 6-1.4. Employment in Mendoza's Municipalities, 1982–93

Year	Number of employees	Index
1982	8,531	100
1983	9,159	107
1984	10,374	122
1985	10,548	124
1986	11,195	131
1987	12,215	143
1988	13,357	157
1989	13,401	157
1990	13,499	158
1991	13,580	160
1992	13,880	163
1993	14,170	165

Note: Annual population growth 1982–92: 1.7 percent.
Growth of employment 1982–88: 57 percent (8 percent annual); 1988–92: 5 percent (1 percent annual).
Source: Government of Mendoza (1991a); Vega, Ojeda, and Russo (1995).

Lessons Learned and Next Steps

This section describes the experience gained from ROB and the RECOMU.

Results-Oriented Budgeting

Mendoza's experiences with ROB are somewhat mixed (see box 6-1.5). On the one hand, implementation has been successful from a purely technical point of view. Annual budget formulation and execution follow the new guidelines, criteria for monitoring performance have been established, policymakers have more control of provincial expenditures, budgetary and financial management are more transparent, and computer technology has spurred many positive changes. ROB has also induced change in some of the surrounding municipalities, although these efforts could not be sustained.

On the other hand, discussions with staff pointed to some serious short-comings that need to be addressed more thoroughly. One major shortcoming is poor staff management. Although staff and managers work for months to define annual targets and performance indicators in their departments, these figures do not imply any rewards if the targets are achieved or sanctions if they are not. Because salaries are largely fixed in negotiations with

---

Box 6-1.5. *Results-Oriented Budgeting Successes and Shortcomings*

Successes:

- Eight budgets have been implemented.
- Extensive high-end information technology (such as fiber optic interconnections) has been introduced.
- Departments have options to calculate unit costs of services (such as hospital services).
- Expenditure control and options for reducing costs for both inputs and services are technically feasible.
- Criteria to assess performance and detect efficiency gaps in the provision of public services have been established.

Shortcomings:

- No supporting framework of incentives exists to employ new techniques effectively—for example, there are no rewards for goal achievement or sanctions for failure to achieve set targets. Personnel policies are rigid and professionalization remains weak.
- Budget modernization remains isolated. It is not part of an overall effort to thoroughly redefine the functions and missions of the provincial government or of government intervention in general.
- Collection of data to effectively assess results and monitor performance is often very burdensome and leads to high overhead costs.
- In the absence of sound incentive structures, ROB can degenerate into symbolic annual exercises. Simple administrative rituals seem to erode both credibility in ROB and the commitment and dedication of staff. In addition, rapid inflow of revenues from the federal level discourages performance, leads to high spending (particularly on personnel), and deters the few incentives set up by ROB.

---

unions and salary scales are inflexible, the hiring and firing of staff and managers reflect these rigidities. Hence, there are few incentives to meet achievement targets. Mendoza's ROB is only weakly linked to ideas of "new public management," under which managers manage within strict budget constraints and face incentives that reward good performance and sanction bad performance.

Other shortcomings include ill-defined job descriptions and career paths. These problems increased with the introduction of information technology.

Limited career paths tend to lead to misplacing staff in higher job positions for which they do not have appropriate skills in order to permit increases in remuneration not allowed by the present salary scales. This process is aggravated by limited labor mobility within the provincial administration, which prevents staff from seeking new qualifications and thus upgrading positions and salaries. Within inelastic employment structures, staff motivation is likely to decrease in the medium to long term.

The introduction of information technology in an organizational environment that is largely traditional has not been accompanied by appropriate measures to ensure its institutionalization. Its very success has led to pervasive technology that has been more quickly implemented than normal, exceeding the capacity of the organization to adapt. For example, technology has required staff to learn new work procedures, which are not reflected in job descriptions and hence in staff performance reviews. A demand for new job functions has been created, which is insufficiently addressed. In some cases, new job functions are fulfilled temporarily by using consultants. An overlap of functions is one result, as the new function (and consultant) coexist with the old function (and staff). Adequate career paths and respective compensation levels demanded by the new procedures are mostly absent. In some cases, these deficiencies and rigidities in existing job descriptions have led to a demand for new units, in particular to manage the ROB information generated at headquarters as well as in the decentralized agencies. Hence, contrary to management intentions to streamline the organization and reduce the number of units, there is a strong tendency to create new units.

The systems and procedures themselves have been affected by the modifications and have been integrated into the government structure in a largely ad hoc manner. Units, functions, and job descriptions have not yet been redefined systematically and comprehensively. This affects the development of training plans and the establishment and measurement of performance indicators. Isolated attempts to solve these problems have created incompatibilities and unfavorable comparisons between the traditional provincial administration and the more modern organizational, financial, and human resource management introduced in some of the ROB areas. Hence there is considerable risk that low-performing units will adversely affect high-performing units, thus scaling down success achieved and probably having an adverse impact on morale.

As table 6-1.3 indicates, the province of Mendoza in the early 1990s had huge inflows of resources from revenue sharing with the federal level and from past petroleum royalties that had been irregularly withheld by the federal government. Total current income doubled in the first half of the 1990s from 410 million pesos to 999 million pesos. Annual federal transfers also increased from 202 million pesos to 436 million pesos in the same period. In addition, Mendoza obtained revenues from privatization and delayed royalties that—in 1993 and 1994 alone—amounted to some 838 million pesos. With these extra amounts on top of already rising revenues, Mendoza may have had limited motivation during these years to save, use resources more effectively and efficiently, and encourage staff performance.

The effects of easy money made it difficult for Mendoza to establish hard budget constraints and ceilings essential for new public management and make it difficult to assess ROB's success in economic terms. Without effective ceilings, spending increased sharply during the 1990s. For example, the provincial wage bill climbed steadily since 1990, increasing by more than 300 percent from US$215 million to US$666 million by 1994 (see table 6-1.3), accounting for more than 50 percent of total expenditures.

One of the key lessons of ROB, however, is that efforts to use resources more effectively need to be accompanied not only by early top-down support but also by overall organizational change that provides a new set of incentives. This holds true in particular for employment of staff, remuneration, rewards, benefits, and sanctions. Otherwise, ROB targets and performance indicators are likely to create additional units and costs and gradually degenerate into ineffective symbolism. Lacking a supporting framework of incentives, ROB seems rather alien to the rest of the provincial administration.

The RECOMU

Given the macroeconomic conditions and the changes that occurred in the national-provincial transfer system after 1992, it is difficult to assess cause-effect relationships of the RECOMU properly. Although the reform itself has not caused clear-cut, empirically-measured change, most observers in Argentina agree that the incentive system that the RECOMU provided pointed in the right direction. The RECOMU simplified and streamlined revenue sharing with municipalities. It eliminated the distortionary criteria of giving higher transfers to municipalities with higher wage bills and made the total flow of resources to the local level more transparent.

Options for Replication and Conclusions

In terms of diffusion, the RECOMU had an interesting impact. Juan A. Vega was the first minister of finance in the Bordón provincial government; he also introduced the RECOMU. In the mid 1990s he became program coordinator of a World Bank–supported reform project for Argentina's provinces. The incentive-driven formula developed under Mendoza served as a preliminary model in the debate over Argentina's reform of intraprovincial transfers.[4] In a sense, the RECOMU highlighted some minimum requirements that revenue-sharing systems may need to include. More important than the RECOMU's own results in practice was its effect on the conceptual discussions and the reform process in Argentina during the 1990s. The RECOMU innovation jump started a necessary debate.

In the long run, as debated within Argentina, it may be desirable to simplify transfers even more and use them only for sharing federal funds with municipalities. Any other formula-driven transfer system could then include some measure of poverty in order to address inequalities across municipalities.

Although successful, Mendoza's innovations need further refinement. In general, the innovations showed that reforming fiscal relationships can have— at least in the short term—a discouraging effect on performance, especially in the case of rapidly rising revenues at subnational levels. A steady realignment of revenue and expenditure authorities, an effective incentive- and formula-driven system of transfers, and sound institutional reforms need to accompany such changes in intergovernmental relationships.

References

Bertranou, Fabio. 1993. *Descentralización fiscal en Argentina desde una perspectiva local: el caso de la provincia de Mendoza.* Santiago, Chile: Economic Commission for Latin America/German Technical Cooperation.

Braceli, Orlando. 1995. "*El Presupuesto Nacional de 1995, un analisis no convencional: lo que es y lo que debe ser.*" *Perspectiva* 7(8): 85–89.

Casaburi, Gabriel. 1994. *Dynamic Production Systems in Newly-Liberalized Developing Countries: Agro-Industrial Sectors in Argentina and Chile.* Ph.D. dissertation, Yale University, New Haven, Conn.

Fleming, William J. 1987. *Regional Development and Transportation in Argentina: Mendoza and the Gran Oeste Argentina Railroad.* New York: Garland Publishing.

Government of Mendoza. 1991a. *Mendoza 1987–91. Cuatro años de esfuerzos compartidos.* Mendoza.

---

4. See Vega, Ojeda, and Russo (1995), which compared Mendoza favorably to the provinces of Chubut and del Chaco. See also Braceli (1995) and Bertranou (1993).

————. 1991b. *Participación municipal en los recursos de la provincia de Mendoza.* Mendoza: Ministry of Housing.

————. 1992. *El presupuesto. Una estratégia para la transformación del sector público de la provincia de Mendoza.* Mendoza: Ministry of Finance.

Juri, Maria E., and Raúl Mercau. 1990. *"Privatización en Argentina: El Caso de Bodegas y Viñederos Giol." Estudios* 13(53): 3–20.

Mörner, Magnus. 1993. *Region and State in Latin America's Past.* Baltimore, Md.: The Johns Hopkins University Press.

Rock, David. 1987. *Argentina 1516–1987. From Spanish Colonization to Alfonsín.* Berkeley, Calif.: University of California Press.

Santos Martínez, Pedro. 1994. *Historia de Mendoza.* Buenos Aires: Editorial Plus Ultra.

Schmitz, Hubert. 1990. "Small Firms and Flexible Specialization in Developing Countries." *Labour and Society* 15(3): 257–85.

Supplee, Joan Ellen. 1988. *Provincial Elites and the Economic Transformation of Mendoza, Argentina, 1880–1914.* Ph.D. dissertation, University of Texas at Austin.

Vega, Juan Argentino, J. Carlos García Ojeda, and Eduardo Adolfo Russo. 1995. *Relación fiscal provincia-municipios. Analysis de tres régimenes de participación de recursos.* Buenos Aires: Ministry of the Interior, Secretariat for Assistance to the Provincial Economic Reform.

6-2

Changing the Managerial Mindset: The FONDEVE in Conchalí, Chile

Florence Eid, American University of Beirut

This case study focuses on a participatory local government investment program that came about in Chile in 1991 and has spread to an estimated one-third of the country's 335 municipalities.[1] The Neighborhood Development Fund (Fondo de Desarrollo Vecinal, or FONDEVE) finances small infrastructure and neighborhood works projects, such as small parks with lighting and irrigation, football and basketball fields, playgrounds, meeting houses, and small libraries for community groups. In some municipalities, the FONDEVE also finances environmental, cultural, and social projects, in addition to preparing feasibility studies and proposals for larger sectoral projects and presenting them to line ministries for funding. In each of the municipalities studied—Conchalí, Rancagua, and Viña del Mar—the average number of projects financed is 80 per year with an average annual budget of US$200,000.

The principal focus of this case study is the FONDEVE of the municipality of Conchalí, because it is the most-replicated model, and because it has evolved significantly since it was established. This case study discusses the origins of the FONDEVE, its initial design and evolution, and its impact on

1. Much of the information is drawn from interviews conducted in 1995 with four sources: former Conchalí Mayor Maria Antonieta Saa; Katia Reimer, director of the Neighborhood Development Fund, or FONDEVE; Miriam Orrego, FONDEVE program assistant; and Victor Hugo, director of the Communal Planning Secretariat (SECPLAC).

relations between the municipality and its citizens and on the organization of local public administration. The other two municipalities, Rancagua and Viña del Mar Certain, each have a FONDEVE that offers interesting contrasts to the FONDEVE of Conchalí. These serve as examples of forms the FONDEVE can take after it is diffused and suggest ways in which governments might further the policy implications of such programs.

Two conceptual concerns are central to analyzing the Conchalí case. First, the potential benefits of participation in improving the quality of public service delivery have been well documented (Ahumada Pacheco 1994; Basu and Pritchett 1995; Isham, Narayan, and Pritchett 1995). What follows instead is a study of some challenges, setbacks, and opportunities involved in engendering participation. Second, this case study presents counterevidence to what has become the standard dismal view of bureaucracies in developing countries. From Chile we have a public sector example where, instead of finding the symptoms of bureaucratic inefficiency and rent seeking that we have come to expect, we encounter a local public administration endowed with highly motivated staff, moving toward more efficient public service delivery, and interested in undertaking innovative and sophisticated policy initiatives.

The FONDEVE as an Innovation

From the standpoint of both the recent history of local government in Chile and local government development in Latin America, the FONDEVE is innovative for the following reasons:

- The FONDEVE is funded from municipal own-source revenues.[2]
- In a centralized unitary state, the FONDEVE is a purely local initiative that does not belong to, nor depend on, any national program.
- The FONDEVE pays for services that are otherwise not funded, except through sporadic municipal appropriations.
- The FONDEVE fundamentally affects the organization of local government.

---

2. Up to 7 percent of municipalities' own-source revenue can be transferred to community organizations (or other private sector actors) according to Chilean municipal law. This stipulation is especially important in cases in which the municipality neither implements nor contracts out project implementation itself, but transfers funds to community organizations, which take charge of all subsequent steps of project realization. From 1992 to 1996, the size of the FONDEVE budget in Conchalí varied from 2.5 to 5 percent of own-source revenue.

The following analysis focuses on the way in which the last two points relate to the conceptual concerns mentioned previously—participation under decentralization and public sector performance.

The approach taken in this case study falls under the category of best practice research. The study seeks to describe how the FONDEVE was conceived and initiated and how it evolved, and to analyze what impacts its evolution had on relations between the local government and its citizens. To answer these questions, the study focuses on the following aspects of the FONDEVE: (a) project initiation and allocation of funds, (b) project evaluation and selection, (c) project implementation, and (d) program administration and management. The latter aspect seeks to underscore the impacts that the FONDEVE has had on the local public sector.

Origins of the FONDEVE

In Conchalí (see box 6-2.1), leadership by Mayor Maria Antonietta Saa, combined with the transition to democracy, was crucial to the innovative period during which the program was first conceived and implemented. As a step in Chile's transition to democracy, Saa was among the last group of 15 mayors appointed to office by the president of the republic following Augusto Pinochet's defeat by Conciliation Party candidate Patricio Aylwin.[3] Preparations were underway for municipal elections amid high expectations about democracy.

As a political activist opposed to the military regime, Saa had not left the country during the Pinochet period but had adapted to working alongside the regime and grew to understand its limitations. This experience worked

---

Box 6-2.1. *The Municipality of Conchalí*

Located in the Santiago metropolitan area, Conchalí was a municipality of 415,000 inhabitants and contained 78 *Unidades Vecinales* (neighborhood units) until the end of 1991. In 1992 its territory and population were reduced when it was divided into three municipalities. By 1995 the population of Conchalí was 140,000, and it contained 40 neighborhood units. Conchalí is home to lower middle- and low-income residents.

---

3. According to the 1980 constitution, the president had the right upon taking office to appoint new mayors to the 15 largest municipalities in the country.

to her advantage in several ways when she took public office during the transition to democracy.

First, Saa was especially sensitive to the fact that she would need to establish the legitimacy of her administration in the eyes of the public, especially given that neither she nor members of the local Community Development Council (Consejo de Desarrollo Comunal, or CODECO) were elected. For example, she repeatedly reminded the CODECO of the care with which the municipality had to handle public trust (CODECO 1991). The mayor translated her concerns about legitimacy and trust into a series of policy actions, including establishing the FONDEVE, that aimed to open city hall to the citizens.[4]

Second, as a center-left mayor imposed on a predominantly far-right CODECO by a rightist central government, Saa was aware that it was important not to alienate those with whom she had to work with internally. This strategic political concern is what caused her to seek the participation of all members of the administration in her initiatives. She also included both old and new members in her board of policy advisors to minimize confrontation while promoting her vision of more open and inclusive municipal governance. The Conchalí experience during this period illustrates the importance of drawing on latent capacity in the public sector. Through their active involvement in discussions of important policy initiatives, older members of the administration facilitated, for instance, the CODECO's approval of the FONDEVE, which was problematic because it entailed the unprecedented transfer of public funds to private hands.

A third important aspect of Saa's policy choices relates to her professional background before taking office and is true of a number of mayors elected to office since the resumption of democracy in Chile. Saa had worked in the nongovernmental organization (NGO) sector for over 15 years at a time when this was the only alternative for those who were interested in public affairs but were outside the ideological camp of the military government. She brought this experience to public office and incorporated NGOs into the management of Conchalí in several ways:

- As a source of funds (especially international) for programs that the municipality could not afford to finance and that the CODECO was not accustomed to approving

---

4. This was important practically as well as symbolically. During the interviews conducted for this case study, members of community organizations referred to the fact that they no longer needed to request a pass to enter city hall. To them, this obviously had been a significant change.

- As a fresh, external base of expertise on public sector issues that provided such services as consulting, training, and information dissemination
- As a vehicle for articulating demand and bringing grassroots concerns to the public sector
- As a mechanism of dialogue between the local government and citizens.

The use of NGO resources proved central to the initiation and evolution of the FONDEVE. Although many new mayors, especially those of the center-left, were able to establish such ties with NGOs, the intensity and volume of such exchanges in Conchalí were impressive. At one point Conchalí had signed agreements with 60 NGOs, and at one meeting during the early period of Saa's tenure, representatives from 30 NGOs were present (Sepulveda and Alvarez 1995).

How did the decision to form a participatory investment program come about? The idea emerged in 1990, Saa's first year in office, when she was making presentations about the municipal budget to the citizens. The objectives of these *jornadas informativas* (informational conferences) were to (a) respond to citizens' desires to have a say in local policy, (b) create an appreciation of financial transparency, and (c) create an awareness of the possibilities and limitations of municipal investments.

The process of preparing municipal staff for the *jornadas* had an important effect within the municipal administration. As in most local governments in developing countries, Conchalí's municipal staff had never before discussed municipal finances with the citizens. Also, for the 17 years of the military regime, the Department of Finance and the mayor's office had largely handled the budget process, with very little input from other departments. With the assistance of an NGO called Education and Communication (Educación y Comunicación, or ECO), the administration held internal discussions involving staff from all municipal departments to prepare for these *jornadas.*

Conchalí's municipal administration held a total of nine *jornadas,* which became forums for heated debates about the administration's role in virtually every aspect of development, reflecting the high expectations that accompanied the return to democracy. It was during these debates that the idea arose to create an instrument that would respond to the expectations about local democratic government by giving citizens a say in the municipal budget process.

In only a matter of months, the FONDEVE evolved from an idea into a policy action. In preparing the budget proposal for her second year in office, Saa decided to transfer 40 percent of the municipality's investment budget to the FONDEVE (a much higher initial percentage than in other municipalities). Over the following six months, her board of policy advisors designed the program and proposed it to the municipal council, which, having been impressed by the impact of the *jornadas*, voted to accept it as an item in the 1991 budget. As a result of its assistance in preparing the *jornadas*, the ECO was the natural partner to assist in various aspects of the program's development. In fact, the ECO-Conchalí partnership became central to the evolution of the FONDEVE. The Communal Planning Secretariat (Secretaría de Planificación Comunal, or SECPLAC) formulated the guidelines and regulations for participation in the FONDEVE, and the Community Development Division (División de Desarrollo Comunitario, or DIDECO) disseminated information on the FONDEVE among community organizations and their leaders through another series of *jornadas*.

Agents of Participation

In designing the FONDEVE as a participatory program, the municipality selected the *juntas de vecinos*, or neighborhood councils, as its counterparts because these were the most visible and established community organizations. This choice later had important implications for the evolution of the FONDEVE in Conchalí.

The origin of the neighborhood councils dates back to the presidency of Christian Democrat Eduardo Frei Montalva (1964–70), who was elected on a political platform promising economic growth for all societal elements. In its efforts to strengthen its electoral base, the Christian Democratic Party under Frei sought to attract marginalized urban groups living in squatter settlements around Santiago. These citizens constituted a potentially significant base of electoral support but had not been successfully mobilized by the traditional left. Once in office, Frei launched a program to help marginalized groups organize themselves to demand resources and change from the state. The idea was to encourage grassroots activity that would also be capable of placing pressure on government to satisfy demands. As part of this program, neighborhoods were encouraged to elect councils that would represent their communities in local governmental matters (Oppenheim 1993).

In keeping with the legal tradition of Chile, a law on neighborhood councils was passed in 1968 "to grant these organizations legal status and to encourage their creation" (Government of Chile 1993). This law defined neighborhood councils as territorial community organizations that represented the citizens of their jurisdiction—the *unidad vecinal*, or neighborhood unit. As part of this legal structure, all municipalities were divided into neighborhood units.

Under the government of Salvador Allende (1970–73), neighborhood councils increasingly supported state agencies in the delivery and improvement of local health care and housing services, literacy programs, and vocational training (Graham 1994). The disadvantage was that the neighborhood councils had begun to work in close cooperation with political parties and were losing some of their credibility because they were beginning to be seen as politicized. The Pinochet regime further reduced the councils' representative power through a decree that replaced elected council representatives with "directors," who tended to be Pinochet loyalists appointed by the mayor. For the 17 years of the Pinochet regime (1973–90), the neighborhood councils no longer represented the community in the government; instead, they represented the government in the community. As the neighborhood councils continued to lose legitimacy and become less representative of the public, those interested in contributing to community development began to work through either NGOs or popular economic organizations.

The return to democracy in Chile focused heavily on the role of participation in promoting social equity. As part of the effort to reinvigorate community life, two new laws governing neighborhood councils were passed in 1989 and in 1995, and the heads of neighborhood councils were once again selected by popular vote of the neighborhood unit. Although it may be early to draw conclusions, the general consensus among those interviewed for this case study was that the loss of legitimacy suffered by legally registered organizations such as neighborhood councils under the military regime and their gradual politicization have precluded them from fully reassuming the representational functions for which they were designed. The FONDEVE experience has exposed the inability of neighborhood councils to represent community interests.

Initial Design: The First Year (1991–92)

The following sections outline the initial design of the FONDEVE in Conchalí, the setbacks it encountered, and the manner in which it evolved. The analysis seeks to show what adjustments the administration made in the design and management of the FONDEVE to respond to previous years' problems.

Project Initiation and Allocation of Funds

The FONDEVE cycle in Conchalí begins in the winter (June) and ends during the fall of the following year. For the first cycle, the neighborhood councils represented all residents of their neighborhood unit in proposing projects to be financed by the FONDEVE. The administration allocated a set amount of one million Chilean pesos (US$2,864) to each neighborhood unit, regardless of surface area or population, since there was not yet any method for determining needs more precisely.

A municipal FONDEVE commission, with representatives from the SECPLAC, the DIDECO, and the Public Works Division, was in charge of evaluating the technical feasibility of proposed projects and of selecting those that would be financed. The number of projects financed during the first year was 115, the most ever undertaken by the FONDEVE of Conchalí. When two or more organizations represented a neighborhood unit and could not agree on a single project to present to the FONDEVE, the commission accepted all proposed projects that were technically feasible and divided the funds allocated to the neighborhood unit among the projects. This policy resulted in many small projects of minor impact. In terms of the technical viability and efficiency of the investments, this created an immediate concern, and the policy was adjusted in the program's third year.

Project Implementation

During the first FONDEVE cycle, the municipality contracted out the selected projects directly to private contractors. There were many delays in implementation during the first year because it was difficult to find contractors interested in such small projects. In addition, the lengthy bureaucratic process of the municipality discouraged small contractors. By April 1992, only 63.5 percent of projects financed had been implemented, according to the Public Works Division, compared to the impressive 95 percent that the FONDEVE later achieved.

Most notable during this period was the burden that the program placed on the municipal administration. Four aspects illustrate the FONDEVE's impact on the administration's usual ways of carrying out its work:

* The FONDEVE commission created a forum that forced municipal staff to negotiate and discuss the administration's priorities in ways that had not existed previously. In the old administration, divisions typically worked with little coordination. The FONDEVE, however, cut across divisions and depended upon coordination between them for success. For example, officials in the SECPLAC and the DIDECO, the two divisions from which the FONDEVE originated, thought that projects proposed by community organizations were an excellent idea.

They believed that such projects served the dual purpose of providing needed neighborhood works and promoting participation and community development by presenting municipal staff with the opportunity to work with the people. By contrast, the Public Works Division had much less enthusiasm for the FONDEVE. The most notable source of resistance was the engineers, who, for good reason in the early stages, hesitated to take technical responsibility for projects proposed by community groups.

- The large number of projects required a different and faster way of conducting municipal business that would still comply with central regulations and procedures defined by the Comptroller General's Office, such as those for competitive bidding. In 1992, competitive bidding had to be carried out for 115 projects as opposed to the traditional 10 to 15 per year. The impact of the increased number of transactions was most visible in the public works and finance divisions.
- The evaluation of most proposals involved a field visit by municipal technical staff to ascertain the feasibility of the proposal. This involved much more interaction between municipal staff and citizens than had previously been the norm.
- The FONDEVE required a cultural change. The municipal staff were not accustomed to the types of contracts being signed under the FONDEVE—transferring public funds to community organizations—and had difficulty accepting them. The most evident cultural change developed among the staff of the Public Works Division, who had to grant technical clearances before funds were transferred (Parraguez 1993).

The FONDEVE clearly exacted a way of doing business that was alien to the administration. The five division directors interviewed for this case study estimated that the bureaucracy's adjustment problems lasted about one year. It is interesting to note that the remainder of the municipal bureaucracy often regarded those promoting the FONDEVE as entrepreneurial idealists.

It is difficult to measure the degree of organizational pressure that the FONDEVE created; however, the following information might be one indication. When the FONDEVE was being launched, 10 new staff members formed the core group in FONDEVE. The incumbent staff in the social services and planning departments, approximately 100 people, were from the old regime. Most of these staff members received the FONDEVE with some skepticism, if not outright resistance.

Results of the First Year

Because of insufficient technical preparation of projects, inadequate evaluation of proposals, and long delays in project execution, an estimated 80 percent of FONDEVE projects failed to reach project design or the intended objectives during the program's first year. This first year can be considered a learning period, as became apparent in the second iteration of the program.

Interviewees attribute the survival of the FONDEVE beyond the first year to Saa's leadership and management style. She was particularly successful in winning over the Public Works Division, whose director, a member of the old guard of the administration, became convinced that the FONDEVE would benefit Conchalí. He helped lobby for the FONDEVE's acceptance by the nonelected municipal council and then worked to ensure that his own skeptical staff adjusted and contributed to furthering the program.

One question often posed during the program's first year related to whether the small sum (US$2,864) allocated to each neighborhood unit was significant, especially compared with the energy expended to process the many transactions that were managed by the FONDEVE. The FONDEVE's supporters defended the small sum, contending that the budget allocated per neighborhood unit was less important than the process involved in proposing a project. That process entailed negotiations among neighborhood groups in order to select a project the neighborhood unit would propose. This forced citizens to debate local infrastructure decisions among themselves in unfamiliar ways. In fact, because the culture of discussion and negotiation over public affairs was weak, at the beginning citizens would get tired and upset during negotiations, and the process created tensions among neighborhood groups and their leaders.

In addition, the first year served to demonstrate that (a) the program was of interest to community organizations and had the potential to be accepted by old guard municipal staff; (b) the small projects financed by the FONDEVE were needed but had few other sources of funding; (c) it was possible to implement projects based on the needs and requirements of the population, instead of basing infrastructure decisions exclusively on the plans of municipal and central government technical staff; and (d) an improvement in municipal organizational efficiency would be required to administer and improve the FONDEVE.

Evolution of the FONDEVE, 1992–95

The FONDEVE evolved significantly after the first year of its implementation (see box 6-2.2). By the second year (1992–93), Conchalí had been split into three municipalities. Conchalí then had a population of 140,000 people instead of 415,000 and 40 neighborhood units instead of 78. This made the FONDEVE less difficult to administer and encouraged certain improvements. Several notable adjustments took place over the next three iterations of the program:

Box 6-2.2. FONDEVE Timeline, Conchalí

1990	Augusto Pinochet's military regime ends. Mayor Antonietta Saa takes office in Conchalí, nominated by President Patricio Aylwin Azócar.
1991–92	Conchalí develops the idea for the Neighborhood Development Fund (FONDEVE) and implements it, jointly managed by the Communal Planning Secretariat (SECPLAC) and the Community Development Division (DIDECO).
1992	Conchalí is divided into three municipalities.
1992–93	Conchalí transfers responsibility for FONDEVE project implementation to the community organizations. The SECPLAC manages the FONDEVE.
1993–94	The FONDEVE requires recipients of funding to sign a contract. The FONDEVE committee is created to select projects, and the FONDEVE operational unit is created with staff to manage the program. Allocation of funds is based on criteria of technical feasibility, participation, and need.
1994–95	Municipal staff take over provision of technical assistance from the Education and Communication NGO (ECO). Supervision of project implementation is delegated to the Waste Collection Division.
1996–97	The FONDEVE may be divided into two annual cycles, with additional criteria that proposed projects address certain priority themes.

- **Smaller community groups.** By changing the FONDEVE's requirements for project initiation and allocation of funds, the municipality
  slowly began to encourage smaller and less-established community
  groups to participate in the program. The evolution of the manner in
  which projects were initiated and funded chronicles the difficulties of
  extending participation to groups that have not traditionally had relations with the public sector.
- **Rigorous criteria.** Although during the first year virtually all projects
  that community groups proposed were accepted, over the next three
  years the process of project evaluation and selection became defined
  by rigorous criteria regarding technical feasibility, participation, and
  need. In addition, community organizations were invited to play a
  formal role in the project selection process as part of the FONDEVE
  commission. Considering that these changes were carried out in close
  consultation with a third player, an NGO, they allowed Conchalí to
  define a new set of relations with its citizens. This behavior was a
  departure from the municipality's traditional insularity as an administrative extension of the central government, and it represented a
  move toward a willingness to invite the opinions and criticisms of
  two other types of players and shape its policies based on their input.
- **Responsibility for implementation.** Participation in the FONDEVE
  after the first year placed an increasingly heavy burden on community organizations as responsibility for project implementation was
  transferred from the municipality to FONDEVE participants. This step
  signaled that participation came with responsibilities as well as privileges and required the building of new capacities, both within the
  local public sector and among community groups, to accomplish the
  tasks involved.
- **Program administration and management.** As the municipal administration made these changes in the FONDEVE, it made concomitant organizational adjustments for program administration and
  management.

Project Initiation

It became evident that extending contractual relations with the municipality to all interested community organizations would require more than
the stroke of a pen and a few training sessions, and more time and bargaining than anticipated. After the FONDEVE's first year, the declining
legitimacy and efficacy of neighborhood councils had become clear, and

FONDEVE staff sought to reduce the councils' control over project initiation and proposal.

Transforming the FONDEVE into a more participatory program required the councils to cede some of their local hegemony over relations with the municipality. A more participatory FONDEVE also required that other groups trust the municipality enough to participate in its programs. After 17 years of insularity, the municipality had the burden of proving its commitment to better relations with its citizens.

The municipality first signaled this commitment through a series of adjustments in the operation of the FONDEVE, carried out over three years, which aimed to address the obstacles to participation. The initial step created one FONDEVE commission per neighborhood unit, formally representing all community groups within the unit. During the second year these commissions were headed by the presidents of neighborhood councils only, but after that, they were required to be headed jointly by the other established groups as well—the mothers' centers and the sports clubs. The purpose was to gradually dilute the influence of the neighborhood councils and allow other actors to participate. Nonregistered organizations like environmental, AIDS awareness, and youth ecological and musical groups presented a dilemma to the municipality. The municipality encouraged their participation but had difficulty lobbying the local commissions for their formal inclusion. To ensure a minimum of equity in representation, the FONDEVE commissions were required to consider proposals made by all nonregistered community organizations.

The purpose of the FONDEVE commissions was to encourage open and fair project selection at the neighborhood level. The new system limited proposed projects to a maximum of four per neighborhood unit—an arrangement that forced the neighborhood councils to work with other community groups during the project proposal stage. But the new rules came at a cost: negotiation among larger numbers of community groups with different objectives and interests created tensions, requiring a further period of adjustment and assistance from the third player: the ECO.

Allocation of Funds

To create stronger incentives for joint efforts among community groups, the FONDEVE made changes in the allocation of funds. After the second year, it became clear that allocating a set amount of funds per neighborhood unit not only made the FONDEVE a very blunt instrument of local development, but it also had a series of undesirable effects. First, it created an expectation that the residents of each neighborhood unit would be entitled to a set amount of funds every year. This created an incentive to propose projects with little regard for need or feasibility. Second, in the first and second iteration of the FONDEVE, the allotted funds were split among the various projects that a neighborhood unit proposed. This led to fragmentation of funds and smaller projects of lesser impact, created an incentive to found new neighborhood councils, and decreased the incentive for groups to collaborate in proposing projects. By the program's third year, the policy of dividing funds in case of failure to reach agreement was abandoned. In addition, project selection was based on a point system created to favor projects of larger impact and projects proposed by larger numbers of community organizations.

Another way in which the municipality conveyed its commitment to new rules of the game was the aggressive and creative communication strategy it employed to disseminate information about the FONDEVE. In addition to the *jornadas informativas* put out every year to launch the FONDEVE, the municipality developed other communication tools after the second year. The most interesting of these was an easy-to-read illustrated brochure in color that was produced and disseminated widely every year. This brochure listed prerequisites, amounts, procedures for filling out FONDEVE applications, implementation schedules, and responsibilities. It also included a simple, detachable one-page application. So successful was this brochure that the heads of two community groups interviewed for this case study referred to it first when asked about the steps involved in undertaking a FONDEVE project.

Although the communication strategy was aimed primarily at ensuring that all community groups were aware of their rights, opportunities, and responsibilities, it also served to alleviate pressure on the municipality as it made changes in the program. Because people were informed ahead of time, and were represented at discussions of policy changes, they were not surprised when the municipality made changes in the program, although they resisted at times. Communication and representation were important for the municipal government to regain its legitimacy and credibility. Making sudden changes to procedures that people had come to expect was simply no longer feasible, regardless of how necessary and economically efficient the changes would be.

After 1993, the start of the FONDEVE cycle consisted of much more than an announcement and information sessions. The launch of the FONDEVE also entailed the signing of a year-long contract (*convenio*) between the municipality and community groups. This contract not only

signaled the willingness of both parties to be held accountable and responsible, but also a noteworthy change in the municipality's role from
paternalistic provider to equal partner. This contractual arrangement did
not begin smoothly, however. In both 1993 and 1995 the neighborhood
councils refused to sign the FONDEVE contract when it became clear that
the FONDEVE's next iteration aimed to reduce their influence. The deadlock was broken after a series of negotiations between the neighborhood
councils and the FONDEVE office, eventually necessitating the intervention of the mayor, with small compromises on both sides. The most interesting achievement of the latest round of negotiations was that nonregistered community organizations could now present projects directly to the
FONDEVE office if they felt the FONDEVE commission was not handling
their inputs fairly. Whether this marked the beginning of a formal system
of grievance remained to be seen.

Project Evaluation and Selection

The municipal administration also altered the process of project evaluation
and selection in keeping with its new interface with citizens. During the
first year, this stage of the FONDEVE cycle was virtually nonexistent—all
projects proposed were accepted. As of the second year, however, this stage
involved debates on the merits of FONDEVE projects within the administration and, eventually, jointly with community groups.

Again, the administration made these changes in close collaboration with
the third actor, the ECO. By this time the ECO had developed a close relationship with the municipality. ECO staff members took part in internal
discussions and gave advice on problems, more as insiders than as external
observers or consultants. The depth of their involvement in Conchalí's
FONDEVE was crucial to its survival and evolution. It is not clear that the
human resource and technical capacity within the administration of
Conchalí would have been sufficient to improve the program and implement the changes with the same speed and continuity.

The project evaluation and selection process evolved through trial and
error. First, the administration created a municipal FONDEVE committee,
comprising the FONDEVE directors and representatives from DIDECO and
the Public Works Division. After the second year, in an effort to underscore
its commitment to the participatory aspect of the FONDEVE, the municipality invited representatives of community organizations to sit on the committee and turned it into a board that would govern the operation of the
program in partnership with its users. The new members were from the

Unión Comunal de Unidades Vecinales (representing all neighborhood councils in the municipality), the Unión Comunal de Centros de Madres (representing mothers' centers), and the Consejo Local de Deportes (representing sports clubs). The committee selected projects by consensus, or by a majority vote in case of deadlock.

As the FONDEVE became a sharper, more selective instrument, more projects were rejected for failure to meet the announced criteria. During 1993–95, for example, in the spirit of opening participation to less-established actors, the administration made an effort to reduce the level of funding for meeting houses of neighborhood councils. A survey carried out by the municipality concluded that an excessive number of these meeting houses had been constructed in Conchalí through the FONDEVE in its first two years of the program, and that many of them were underutilized. In the 1995–96 cycle, the FONDEVE planned to further reduce the number of projects accepted (to 15 to 20 for the entire municipality) and increase their size and cost for more impact and better correspondence with the projections of the municipal development plan.

Project Implementation

The process of implementing projects also evolved. During the first year the municipality's goal was to encourage participation in a very general sense, and it invited citizens to present their ideas. In the second year, the municipality made efforts to define participation in narrower and more concrete ways. In practical terms, the municipality achieved this by transferring the responsibility for project implementation to community organizations. This step meant that program participants both enjoyed the privileges and bore the liabilities of participation.

The ECO, in conjunction with municipal technical staff, organized a series of training programs in project formulation for heads of community groups. These training programs, which were part of an effort to avoid the failures of the first year, aimed to make sure the community groups were aware that turning an idea into a viable project was substantially more difficult than proposing ideas. By the fourth year, municipal staff in the line divisions had assumed the ECO's responsibility for technical assistance on a demand basis. Although the transfer of responsibility signified maturation and self-sufficiency in managing community relations, it placed an added burden on the local administration. This added burden had an impact on Conchalí's public sector, as described in the following section.

Program Administration and Management

Three main aspects of the management of the FONDEVE had an impact on the public administration of Conchalí. First, the strategy of internal diffusion of the program among municipal divisions required municipal staff to negotiate and discuss priorities within the administration in new ways. Most notably, the preparation and launching of the FONDEVE project cycle required continual interaction, coordination, and rapid information exchange between staff across divisions.

Second, because the FONDEVE became a contract between the municipality and its citizens with fixed start and end dates to which both parties had to adhere, the local administration was under pressure to get the job done. When delays occurred, citizens knocked on the door of the FONDEVE office and demanded the projects that they had worked to prepare and felt entitled to receive. The impact of this new accountability was evident in the informal and unconventional methods used to process FONDEVE transactions faster than those of other programs. For example, a standard investment project entailed sending a document through the legal department, the accountant's office, the finance division, and the mayor's office to get the necessary approvals, which took over a month. FONDEVE contracts, however, were often processed in less than 10 days, because the program's staff members hand carried documents from one municipal office to another and then called to follow up on the status of their paperwork until it was completed. Likewise, in preparation for the launching of the FONDEVE, the administration would initiate an internal information campaign along with the external one. FONDEVE staff members would call the divisions that served them with a reminder that the FONDEVE was about to begin and that the program staff would need their cooperation soon.

Third, the organizational pressure to perform and, indeed, the very survival of the FONDEVE necessitated changes to fit within the rigid structural constraints imposed on Chilean municipalities. During the first year, the SECPLAC and the DIDECO jointly managed the FONDEVE. By the second iteration, the SECPLAC had exclusive responsibility for the program but continued to draw on the assistance of the DIDECO. To consolidate the program and grant it credibility with the administration, there was a need to centralize it and give it an identity. In response, the FONDEVE Operational Unit was created, with special staff exclusively focused on the FONDEVE. The unit is not part of the municipal organization chart, but it is an interesting example of adapting the rigid organizational structure defined by the law to respond to local exigencies. The decision to create the unit appears to have been crucial to maintaining FONDEVE's momentum.

Improvements in the Design

By 1993, Conchalí policymakers became concerned that the FONDEVE might have become too centralized and "personalized," or exclusively associated with the FONDEVE's three staff members. Accordingly, the municipality took steps to depersonalize and institutionalize the FONDEVE by delegating various aspects of the project cycle, such as field supervision, to the line divisions of the municipality. This entailed a learning process for municipal staff, who were not accustomed to demanding field visits or constant interaction and negotiation with citizens. The 1994–95 experience of delegating supervision of project implementation to the Waste Collection Division was regarded as a success, and the city moved to replicate it in 1995–96.

A second step in improving the design of the FONDEVE relates to project maintenance. Because the program was relatively recent, no clear assignment of responsibility for project maintenance existed. The municipality and community organizations shared the maintenance of FONDEVE projects in an ad hoc manner. Although some other municipalities had experimented with contractual arrangements for project maintenance, policies in this area are not consistent.

The FONDEVE was the only municipal program open to redesign every year. For 1996–97, Conchalí considered dividing the FONDEVE cycle in two and launching two separate annual competitions for projects with specific themes, such as health education and youth environmental initiatives. The project funds would amount to around US$100,000 for each cycle. The municipality would also attempt to fund cultural and social projects, which were more difficult to evaluate and account for, to promote local civic life. These types of projects would constitute a dramatic departure from the small works that the FONDEVE financed during its initial stages. Such an evolution in the objectives of the program could carry its impact beyond that of small neighborhood works.

Through such changes, the FONDEVE had become a mechanism for flexibility in an otherwise rigid and centralized municipal structure.

Conclusion

Some 95 percent of the projects financed by the FONDEVE of Conchalí had been implemented as of the mid 1990s. Table 6-2.1 summarizes the program's budget in its early years.

In a centralized unitary state, the FONDEVE is a purely local initiative that does not belong to any national program. On the contrary, it was formed because, during the period of transition from authoritarian to democratic rule, municipalities took advantage of new opportunities to exercise autonomy in an otherwise very legalistic constitutional structure. The innovation was first diffused horizontally between municipalities, then diffused vertically and subsequently incorporated into national legislation in 1995. The lack of a national program governing the FONDEVE has allowed various permutations in design and impact to result from its diffusion. Boxes 6-2.3 and 6-2.4 compare key points of the FONDEVE of Conchalí with those of Rancagua and Viña del Mar and underscore the areas that require careful attention in operational work and policy design.

The FONDEVE has changed the types of interactions and the nature of the relationship between the municipal government and its citizens, altering the local rules of the game. Such changes range from more frequent and open dialogue between municipal staff and citizens over matters of local policy to negotiation with municipal managers over the speed and efficiency of public service delivery and expenditure allocation decisions. The history of the FONDEVE's development offers an opportunity to chronicle and analyze the difficulties involved in implementing the broad and somewhat idealized notion of "participation."

Table 6-2.1. *Historical Data on the FONDEVE of Conchalí, 1991–94*

Year	Number of projects financed	Total budget (Chilean pesos)	Total budget (US$)	Maximum budget per neighborhood unit (US$)
1991	115	78,000,000	223,355	2,864
1992	96	58,188,332	160,484	4,137
1993	84	67,994,388	168,232	4,206
1994	75	64,498,985	176,701	5,479

Source: Project files, 1996, Department of Finance, Municipaliy of Conchalí.

Box 6-2.3. *The FONDEVE of Rancagua*

Rancagua is a municipality of 250,000 inhabitants, predominantly middle and lower-middle class. Its main industry is mining. By the mid 1990s, under the mayor elected to office in 1991, the FONDEVE of Rancagua had become a principal component of the municipal development strategy, with an impressive implementation rate of 95 percent. In 1994, the budget allocation for the FONDEVE was US$139,000, which amounted to 18 percent of the total municipal investment budget. It financed 81 projects. Highlights of the program include:

- *Flexible Organization.* The FONDEVE of Rancagua disregards the legally defined neighborhood units and focuses instead on the urgency and severity of needs, regardless of their location. Project initiation, selection, and funding do not take the neighborhood unit into consideration. This is a clear departure from the legalistic structure governing local territories, and is instead a more flexible form of organization that has better potential to respond to local needs. There is no maximum budget allocated per neighborhood unit, nor per project.
- *Project Selection Process.* In Rancagua, all community organizations present projects directly to the FONDEVE office, eliminating the need for neighborhood-level preselection through an institution such as Conchalí's FONDEVE commission. This arrangement may result in fewer tensions among community organizations, with the net effect of encouraging participation by newer, less-established groups. However, this arrangement may also place a heavier burden on the local administration than the arrangement in Conchalí. Once the FONDEVE office receives proposals, technical staff evaluate and prioritize them based on an elaborate point system that favors projects affecting larger numbers of beneficiaries and poorer neighborhoods. The municipality contributes up to 60 percent of the cost of projects to be implemented in middle-class neighborhoods and up to 70 percent for those implemented in poorer neighborhoods. The selection process favors

---

Under certain conditions, the FONDEVE can also have an impact on the operation of the local public sector, because the administration of the program demands new ways of processing transactions between and within municipal divisions.

By the end of 1994, the FONDEVE had become established as the principal mechanism of interface between the municipality and community

projects with higher proposed contributions of cash or labor and weights projects according to priority problem areas identified in the municipal development plan.

- *Community Relations.* Does the requirement that community organizations contribute to the cost of projects they propose result in more ownership and better implementation? Does the project evaluation and selection process achieve its aim of making the FONDEVE into an integral component of the municipal development strategy? The mayor of Rancagua planned to commission an evaluation of the FONDEVE to address such questions.

Another notable feature of the FONDEVE of Rancagua, owing partly to the municipality's large size, is the group of *sectorialistas* (sector specialists) who constitute the public face of the program. These are 10 staff members who are, or once were, heads of community organizations. Their primary responsibility is to present and "market" the program to community groups, register community organizations, and encourage them to promote projects that make sense in terms of the municipality's development strategy. Of the three FONDEVEs studied, Rancagua's system of *sectorialistas* is the most proactive method of managing community relations.

Unlike the FONDEVE of Conchalí, the program in Rancagua has no specified time period, nor does it involve the signing of a contract. This could imply that the pressure created by the yearly launch date and contract signing in Conchalí is nonexistent in Rancagua and thus that the program may not have had the same effect on the internal management of the administration. It is important to note that the entire administration of Rancagua is often cited as one of the most proactive and efficiently run administrations in the country largely because of its young, entrepreneurial mayor. Hence, if the FONDEVE has had a positive effect on local public management in Rancagua, it may be difficult to isolate.

organizations. The FONDEVE was a small program in budgetary terms but had high visibility—the citizens knew about it, felt entitled to it, and looked forward to it beginning every year. In 1995, the FONDEVE was the only participatory program that involved community organizations in all phases of the project cycle, and it was forcing a change in the social compact between the local government and community organizations.

Box 6-2.4. *The FONDEVE of Viña del Mar*

Viña del Mar is a city of about 318,000 inhabitants. It is endowed with a thriving tourism industry run by an entrepreneurial sector that operates the center and more scenic areas of the city. In 1995, Viña del Mar allotted US$600,000 to the FONDEVE, which amounted to 18 percent of its total investment budget. The number of projects financed that year was 149.

In contrast to the cases of Conchalí and Rancagua, preliminary research indicates that the FONDEVE of Viña, which was also formed in 1991, has not been of primary interest to the municipal government. This conclusion is based on the following findings:

- Although municipal staff members recognize the inability of neighborhood councils to represent a plurality of local interests, and although they estimate that councils represent no more than 2 percent of the population, the councils still have exclusive control over FONDEVE project initiation and proposal. Other community organizations interested in participating in the FONDEVE are obliged to seek to be represented by a neighborhood council, but there is no formal mechanism for this purpose. The councils are encouraged, but not required, to take into consideration the demands of other community organizations. The implication for the participation of less-established and nontraditional community organizations such as youth musical groups or AIDS awareness groups is obvious. Although such groups are active in Viña, they rarely benefit from FONDEVE initiatives.
- The allocation and use of funds is less rational than in the other two cases. In Viña, each neighborhood unit receives a set amount of CP 1.5 million each year (US$4,110 in 1995), regardless of the type or number of projects funded. In cases in which there is more than one neighborhood council per neighborhood unit and no agreement is reached on a single project, funds are divided among the projects proposed. This often results in many small projects of little impact. Prevention of the

---

References

Ahumada Pacheco, Jaime. 1994. *Planificación descentralizada y participación social en el nuevo contexto del desarrollo.* Division of Policies and Social Projects, Latin American Institute for Economic and Social Policy. Santiago: Economic Commission for Latin America.

Basu, Ritu, and Lant Pritchett. 1995. "The Determinants of the Magnitude and Effectiveness of Participation: Evidence from Rural Water Projects." Background note for the *World Development Report,* World Bank, Washington, D.C.

fragmentation of funds is subject to municipal staff members being willing to engage in informal negotiations with heads of neighborhood councils. Although the municipality has provided some technical assistance to community groups in project selection and negotiation, the two staff members responsible for the FONDEVE feel that their office is understaffed and cannot provide the assistance required to improve participation in the program. Because each neighborhood unit receives a guaranteed budget every year, there is a tendency to create virtually fictitious neighborhood councils in order to benefit from the program. These councils often make conflicting demands on the FONDEVE, which municipal staff then have to resolve.

- Municipal staff, especially in the Community Development Division, are dissatisfied with the way the FONDEVE functions in Viña. The opinion of those interviewed is that the program suffers from not having its own office. Instead it is administered jointly and in a part-time capacity by staff from the community development and planning divisions. The municipal council received at least one written proposal to make improvements during the program's first four years, but rejected it. It is not clear that the FONDEVE of Viña has had any effect on the internal management of the local administration or changed any part of its organizational structure.

In drawing conclusions on the FONDEVE experience in Viña del Mar, it is important to point out that the local government of Viña del Mar has lacked political continuity in the program's first four years because the last appointed mayor was of a different political party than the mayor elected in 1991. The result, in terms of municipal management, has been a lack of uniformity in the prioritization and level of commitment to policy initiatives, one of which is the FONDEVE.

CODECO. 1991. *Actas del CODECO de Conchalí*. Conchalí, Chile.

Government of Chile. 1993. *Manual de Gestión Municipal*. Santiago: Ministry of the Interior, Undersecretary for Regional Development and Administration.

Graham, Carol. 1994. *Safety Nets, Politics, and the Poor: Transitions to Market Economies*. Washington, D.C.: The Brookings Institution.

Isham, Jonathan, Deepa Narayan, and Lant Pritchett. 1995. "Does Participation Improve Performance? Establishing Causality with Subjective Data." *The World Bank Economic Review* 9(2): 175–200.

Oppenheim, Lois Hecht. 1993. *Politics in Chile: Democracy, Authoritarianism and the Search for Development*. Boulder, Colo.: Westview Press.

Parraguez, Darvich Jorge. 1993. "Fondo de Desarrollo Vecinal-Programa de Inversion y Participacion: Una alternativa de accion." Unpublished article, Santiago.

Sepulveda, Leandro, and Jpilar Alvarez. 1995. *La gestion de los vecinos: El program Fondeve en la comuna de Conchali*. Santiago: ECO.

7

Participation in Local and Regional Decisionmaking

7-1

Participatory Budgeting in Porto Alegre, Brazil

Zander Navarro, Federal University of Rio Grande do Sul, Porto Alegre, Brazil

Processes of political transition in Latin America have been based on conflicting trends in recent years.[1] On the one hand, the political system throughout the region now resembles a typical democratic regime, featuring open, quasi-free elections, unprecedented freedom of press and political party organizing, and relatively weak influence of the armed forces. But on the other hand, democratization in these societies has not been accompanied by substantial economic transformations intended to integrate larger social sectors into economic life. As a result, the region is marked by poverty, poor living conditions, and a striking inequality of income and land ownership.

Brazil is perhaps the country that best illustrates these trends. Its political vitality has spread democratic values and ideas, leading to actions that clearly demonstrate the changing political environment toward democratization

1. The following citizens of Porto Alegre were instrumental in the preparation of this paper, and I am most grateful to them: Nilton Bueno Fischer, who was the municipal secretary for education in 1994; Gildo de Lima, head of the Coordenação de Relações com a Comunidade (Community Relations Coordinator) in the 1990s; Itamar Spanhol and Marlene Steffen, CRC officials; Clovis Ingelfritz da Silva, municipal secretary of planning in 1989–90 and elected city councilor for the 1993–96 term; Ubiratan de Souza, coordinator of Gabinete de Planejamento, the planning agency in charge of participatory budgeting; Luciano Fedozzi, who headed the planning office in charge of participatory budgeting during its initial implementation; and Tarso Genro, who was mayor of Porto Alegre. In addition, Márcia Hoppe Navarro provided insightful comments on an earlier draft of this paper.

(McCoy 1995; Schmitter and Karl 1991). Social scientists have observed that even long-term results of the political transition in Brazil, namely behavioral changes and a new political culture, have surfaced in recent years (Avritzer 1995; Gay 1995; Moisés 1995).

However, economic growth in Brazil has been uncertain and slow, reflecting inappropriate macroeconomic policies of the government as well as international changes over the same period. Thus, Brazil has been unable to produce a steady pattern of development. Citizens have been dissatisfied with public policies and public management because of the government's failure to reduce widespread poverty and social inequalities. A report published by the World Bank, for example, notes that the level of poverty in Brazil is well above the norm for a middle-income country and identifies deficient public policies as the cause (World Bank 1995).[2]

Offering reasons for Brazil's poor macroeconomic performance is beyond the scope of this case study. Yet it is relevant to note the virtual disappearance of a strong and centralized state in recent years. The fading of this model and a persistent fiscal crisis have reduced the level of state intervention and diminished public investments and services, including many social safeguards supported by the national budget. As a consequence, political responsibility for basic social policies became increasingly less clearly defined during the 1990s.

Brazilian states and municipalities were given power and new responsibilities under the new federal constitution signed in 1988. Some corresponding resources were transferred, but these have been insufficient, resulting in growing difficulties for the cities.[3] Under these resource constraints, Brazilian cities have developed many promising innovations. *Orçamento participativo* (participatory budgeting, or PB) is one of these innovations that has grown to play a role in allocating tens of millions of dollars per year in community investments.

Enabling Environment

The contextual origins of PB as a generic idea can be traced back to the political history of the city of Porto Alegre over the last three decades. Distinctive features of the city itself may have contributed (see box 7-1.1). Broader conditions may also have been factors in the innovation (Genro 1994, 1996).

---

2. For further discussion of the abysmal social situation prevailing in the country, see World Bank (1995).

3. In 1988, Brazilian municipalities received 11.4 percent of national revenues, and the federal government received 61.3 percent. In 1992, after decentralization, these figures were 17.2 percent and 53.8 percent, respectively (PMPA 1995a, 1995b, 1995c).

Box 7-1.1. *The City of Porto Alegre: Main Features and Recent Developments*

With a population of 1.3 million and an area of 489 square kilometers, Porto Alegre has a major economic impact on the state of Rio Grande do Sul. Porto Alegre's 1994 gross domestic product was estimated at US$6.7 billion. Porto Alegre is the biggest urban and industrial municipality in Rio Grande do Sul, producing 12.4 percent of the state's gross industrial product and nearly a third of the income from the service sector, according to 1992 figures. The city accounted for 18 percent of Rio Grande do Sul's total population in 1992 (Oliveira 1995).

Like other Brazilian capitals, in the last few decades Porto Alegre has experienced an accelerated process of urbanization. Its population doubled between 1960 and 1980, but in the 1985–95 period the total population grew only 12 percent, because new industrial centers in the state diverted migrants who would otherwise have gone to the capital. Porto Alegre's economic activity is concentrated in the service and government sectors. In 1980, 78 percent of the city's income came from the service sector (compared to 57 percent nationally). The industrial sector is still important in Porto Alegre, although less so due to the recent slowdown in immigration (Oliveira 1995). The city was named as the Brazilian state capital with the highest standard of living.

Porto Alegre's and Rio Grande do Sul's social indicators are also impressive compared to similar national indicators. For example, among the 50 Brazilian cities with the highest literacy rate, 32 are in the state. Life expectancy in the state is 70 years for men and 75 years for women, the highest of all Brazilian states. Infant mortality rates also fell in the state in the 1980s and 1990s, dropping from 52.6 to 16.5 deaths per thousand children. In the city of Porto Alegre, the infant mortality rate declined from 37.2 deaths per thousand in 1980 to 13.8 in 1994, the best performance among Brazilian state capitals.

In contrast, there are also negative indicators, in particular related to housing. A third of Porto Alegre's population lives in slums, and the total population in slums appeared to more than double between 1981 and 1990. Nonused urban land represented 41.8 percent of the total urban area of the city in 1989, and the 100 biggest landowners owned some 47.8 percent of this area (Fedozzi 1994).[a] In the 1990s the housing problem was aggravated by the growing lack of productive employment.

Despite some positive indicators, Porto Alegre is as marked by social contrasts as deep as the rest of Brazil, with acute inequality of income, property rights, and—except in the municipal domain—political power.

a. Some statistics were provided by Clovis Ingelfritz da Silva, city councilor and former municipal planning secretary.

New Constitution

Among national political factors, the signing of the new Brazilian constitution in 1988 had the greatest influence on Porto Alegre's decision to implement PB locally. The constitution transferred substantial power to the states and the cities, thereby (a) signaling new political and administrative decentralization with the goal of meeting citizens' needs more effectively, and (b) giving citizens more influence in the management of the state. The constitution also legislated new channels for citizen participation in government decisionmaking, such as the referendum, the plebiscite, and citizen-initiated legislation (or the popular initiative of law). These mechanisms were not widely used at first because they needed further refinement. The importance of the new constitution on PB was the document's influence on the strong local traditions of social participation in many areas of Rio Grande do Sul, including Porto Alegre.

Political Opportunity

The previous administration's failure to integrate citizen participation into its decisionmaking also influenced the introduction of PB in Porto Alegre. The administration of Mayor Alceu Collares (1985–88) took office on a strongly participatory platform, amid the democratic fervor and excitement generated by the end of the military regime in 1985. Collares's party, the *Partido Democrático Trabalhista* (Workers' Democratic Party), which easily won the 1985 election with 42 percent of the vote, is heir to an old pro-worker tradition, which remained strong in the state of Rio Grande do Sul. This political orientation usually supports popular interests and participation. During his administration Collares did go so far as to issue a decree establishing popular councils around the city to allow community organizations a voice. Broadly speaking, however, the majority of Collares's campaign promises were never implemented. His administration frequently practiced clientelism (the exchange of political rights for material rewards) and failed to allow the participation of community associations.

The citizens showed their disappointment in 1988 by electing a coalition of various left-wing parties commanded by the Workers' Party (Partido dos Trabalhadores), which won 34 percent of the vote. The Workers' Party victory led directly to the implementation of PB in Porto Alegre because of the party's ideological emphasis on participation, democratization, and the political necessity of a stronger civil society.[4] Capitalizing on the growing

---

4. Keck (1990) provides an in-depth discussion of the history and internal development of the Workers' Party.

success of PB, the Workers' Party coalition won a second term, with its candidate amassing 41 percent of the votes in the 1992 elections. This marked the first time in Porto Alegre that a party won two elections in a row, suggesting that one result of the PB innovation may be to produce enormous political benefits for its champions.

Political Ideology

Prevailing political ideology also played a role in the PB innovation. The political transition in Brazil has focused on democratization through decentralization. But positive results from political decentralization require other political changes, such as devolution of resources. In theory, decentralization is associated with improved responsiveness and accountability by the public sector, thus creating better mechanisms of resource allocation and provision of public services. However, concentrated market power, rent seeking, and other kinds of market failure may impede efficiency. Experience has shown that a democratic history is the fundamental requirement for success in decentralizing processes (Fox and Aranda 1995).

The administration that gained power in 1988 had general ideas about democratization, strengthening civil society, and sharing management of the municipality, but it possessed neither previous administrative experience nor a model to follow. This created an opportunity to break away from left-wing orthodoxy and develop innovative theories as well as practices. The administration realized that democracy necessarily recognizes social conflicts not only as a legitimate aspect of modern societies, but as the form of a complex polity and the foundation of politics. These are crucial political concepts, especially in unequal societies like Brazil's, because such a view of modern democracies makes it possible to understand that the political participation of poorer social groups can result in concrete changes. In the long run, new rights may gradually materialize—which is, after all, the major objective of any democratic polity.[5]

These theoretical notions about PB were not necessarily shared by all those implementing the innovation, however. The parties that comprised

---

5. Consider, for example, Lima (1995): "A radical democratization of the State and politics demands direct and organized participation of the population in government decisions . . . it demands that the abyss between the state and society no longer exist and incites permanent control of citizens over the state's affairs. This is the ultimate meaning of the Participatory Budgeting experiment . . . one of the most fruitful experiences of constituting a nongovernmental public sphere of decisionmaking, control and action over the state" (pp. 1–2).

the winning coalition in 1988 achieved no political consensus. Even those within the Workers' Party could not reach a consensus on how to put some general ideas into practice. This characteristic may have been beneficial, for it prevented a given "model" from being imposed on the process unleashed by PB. Each step was taken after lengthy negotiations among the political factions in power and, most important, after a dialogue with community associations. Once community members gained a share of power, the PB process quickly became based on real experience and not only on a theoretical orientation, enlarging its chances of success.

Community Associations

The strength of community associations in Porto Alegre contributed to the municipality's readiness to implement PB. Community associations have long been active and influential in Porto Alegre and Rio Grande do Sul (Navarro 1994). As early as 1956, a municipal decree opened the door to various councils. The state federation of community associations (Federação Rio-Grandense das Associações Comunitárias e de Bairros) was founded in 1959 and has been quite active since the 1980s. In 1979, the federation had 65 member associations in Porto Alegre. In 1983, the Community Associations' Union of Porto Alegre (União das Associações de Moradores de Porto Alegre, or UAMPA), a very politicized organization, was established as a direct result of political liberalization in the country. The UAMPA became intensely involved in housing, education, health services, human rights, and lobbying the municipal administration for broader popular participation (Menegat 1995). Eventually, approximately 500 community organizations developed in Porto Alegre.

The associational strength of the city, as well as the desire of some leftist groups to establish popular councils, resulted in an openness to new participatory experiences and proposals in Porto Alegre. In fact, the ideas about PB that the new administration introduced in 1989 were not entirely novel for a population with such a solid history of community associations. As soon as citizens realized that the municipal authorities' offer to share decisionmaking on the budget was sincere, PB's success ignited a sort of participatory fever that was unprecedented in the city's history. A great number of councils were formed—for example, the Municipal Council on Social Assistance. As with all the councils, the municipality has fewer representatives on this council than do nongovernmental organizations.

Initial Efforts

The new administration of Porto Alegre faced the following problems when it took office in January 1989:

- Nearly 98 percent of revenues were needed to pay the municipal staff. The number of personnel had substantially increased in the previous administration, and the former mayor had also approved a major pay increase just before leaving office, which jeopardized the municipality's plans for the coming year.
- Executive control and financial management were weakened by several procedural loopholes.
- The tax system was not indexed to inflation, preventing the city from coping with the high inflation rates at that time.
- Under decentralization, the municipality had received many new responsibilities but lacked sufficient financing for them.

These problems jeopardized the administration's ability to fulfill its campaign promise of implementing policies to help poor citizens and left it uncertain of a proper course at the beginning of its tenure. In this context of administrative confusion and lack of resources, the administration initiated *SOS Porto Alegre,* whose objective was to demonstrate to the city that the new administration truly wanted to serve its citizens. Staff members went "to the streets" in an effort that involved approximately 200 to 500 civil servants working each week in a specific area of the city. The purpose was not only to become visible but to conduct inexpensive public works and to cement personal contacts with citizens and leaders of community organizations. The municipality relied on the network of relationships fostered by *SOS Porto Alegre* to solicit public participation in the first meetings on PB in April 1989.

At the same time, the new administration tried to mitigate the problems it faced and regain its capacity to invest by implementing rigorous financial controls, going after debtors, devising new ways to prevent tax evasion, and attempting to increase revenues. The administration submitted various proposals to the city council for new laws related to revenue, the majority of which were approved. One of these laws modified the property tax, a major source of municipal revenues, to make it comparable to the property tax in other Brazilian cities and also to make it progressive. Other modifications that the new laws introduced included the indexation of taxes such as those for waste collection and water. Obtaining the City Council's agreement to index taxes was a major factor in improving Porto Alegre's financial health, given the high inflation at that time—more than 1,000 percent a year between 1989 and 1993. As a result of indexation, municipal tax revenues rose 132 percent in real terms between 1991 and 1992.

In its first year, then, the administration's priorities were to increase revenues and try to establish ties with the citizens. In this environment, the administration presented the proposal for PB in April 1989.

After deciding to introduce PB, the administration's first challenge was to propose a set of actions based upon community identity. Accordingly, it divided the city into communities to allow existing community associations to represent their constituents and take advantage of local social and economic homogeneities.

The only previous division, which officially took effect in 1979, split the city into four regions. Each region elected one councilor, and the four councilors constituted a community council. With the increased number of community associations formed in the 1980s, the format of this council proved entirely inappropriate, and it had little influence on the municipal government. Therefore, one of the first actions proposed for PB was to reorganize this council with one important difference: community associations themselves would decide how the city should be divided. Also, the new administration promised that the newly formed council would not be ignored in local decisionmaking processes.

Community associations then participated in a debate coordinated by their union (UAMPA) and determined that the city would be divided into 16 regions according to community identities (see table 7-1.1). The proposal for division into regions was not formally submitted to the city council but rather was agreed upon by community associations and approved by the mayor's office. Later on, when the PB process proved successful and attracted growing participation, the initial division required gradual modification. Nine regions have subdivided themselves into "microregions" for a total of 28 small regional communities.

Two characteristics of the preparations for PB should be mentioned. First, the decision to integrate community associations into the municipal decisionmaking structure may have produced some debate but no significant conflicts between local authorities and the community movement. This dialogue was made smoother, because many of the new municipal leaders had been community leaders themselves. The people involved in the dialogue already knew each other and were familiar with local conditions.

Second, the community associations, with their traditional suspicion of government promises, decided that the PB process should have complete

Table 7-1.1. Population of Participatory Budgeting Regions in Porto Alegre, 1991

Region	Population	Percentage of total
Humaitá-Navegantes/Ilhas	52,260	4.2
Noroeste	110,618	8.8
Leste	102,293	8.2
Lomba do Pinheiro	36,488	2.9
Norte	93,001	7.4
Nordeste	19,572	1.6
Partenon	127,096	10.2
Restinga	38,961	3.1
Glória	41,633	3.3
Cruzeiro	59,231	4.7
Cristal	25,166	2.0
Centro-Sul	102,560	8.2
Extremo-Sul	19,387	1.6
Eixo Baltazar	95,387	7.6
Sul	53,202	4.2
Centro	275,300	22.0
Total	1,251,902	100.0

Source: Brazilian Institute of Geography and Statistics; municipal government of Porto Alegre.

autonomy. The city council had no say, and PB received no official approval other than the autonomous approval of the associations themselves. This was a landmark decision, and one that was in agreement with the new administration's political views.

The preparations for PB demonstrated the numerous difficulties of starting up such a process. First, a political culture historically based on clientelist relations may weaken popular participation in politics (Fox 1994). The majority of citizens in the country had little faith in government proposals and political institutions, and this distrust had been reinforced by a series of incompetent and corrupt government administrations (at all levels). Other barriers to starting PB included the initial inexperience of the new municipal authorities (Genro 1994), the lack of resources in the first years, conflicting demands from the regions, uneven strength of associations in the PB regions, and a persistent dependence of many community organizations on the municipality's officials.

Format and Methodology

Since it first started, PB in Porto Alegre has consisted of a series of initial meetings occurring annually from March to June. Two main meetings co-ordinated by the municipality, called *rodadas*, are preceded by several smaller meetings organized by the communities themselves. Many meetings also take place in between the two main *rodadas*. The extent of these unofficial meetings depends on the organizational strength of each region, and community leaders are entitled to summon technical help from the municipality. Starting in 1994, *plenárias temáticas* (theme-oriented meetings) have also been held to attract other associations, such as trade unions and professional organizations, as well as middle-class sectors not interested in ordinary PB *rodadas*. The annual cycle of PB is summarized in box 7-1.2 and described in the following section.

Rodadas

The agendas of the two *rodadas* are determined by government officials in charge of a specific region and by the community leadership, and they are not restricted to votes on public works. Since 1994, the *rodadas* have become more sophisticated and animated: a skit is used to introduce all discussions, and photos of public works are presented to demonstrate the status of the previous year's investments.

The *rodadas* are a special opportunity for the municipal government to present its ideas. Municipal officials, technical staff, and even the mayor attend all *rodadas*. Any proposal they submit will be discussed by the attendees and can be accepted by a simple majority vote. All participants, the citizens and the government alike, feel that the presence of government authorities at the *rodadas* is beneficial. Direct, constant relations between high-level government personnel and the community are vital, because they indicate that the government is open and democratic and respects its citizens. Contact with citizens also has a profound impact on educating officials about citizens' wishes and on educating citizens about government programs (Lima 1995).

During the first *rodada*, the municipality:

- Presents the previous year's activities and accounts, explaining in particular how the approved capital investment plan (CIP) did or did not work and the reasons for any mid-year changes.
- Explains the status of the CIP for the current year, with a detailed progress report about public works projects approved in the previous year.

Box 7-1.2. *The Annual Participatory Budgeting Cycle*

Government	Civil Society
	March Citizens prepare for the first *rodada* (a meeting organized by the municipality).
	March/April The first *rodada* and *plenárias temáticas* (theme-oriented meetings) are held.
May–June Government agencies prepare sectoral demands.	*March–June* Delegates meet with citizens in their regions to discuss priorities. Additional problem-solving meetings are held.
	June–July The second *rodada* and another round of *plenárias temáticas* are held. Participants establish budget priorities, make a list of demands, and elect PB Council (COP) representatives.
August The Planning Cabinet (GAPLAN) coordinates internal demands with regional and theme-oriented demands and develops the budget proposal with the COP. The budget undergoes internal review.	*July–August* The COP is seated and meets to discuss criteria and allocation of resources.
	August–September The COP discusses and approves the budget.
September The mayor reviews the budget.	*September* The COP submits the budget to the city council by September 30.
	September–November The COP discusses sectoral investments and continues meeting until the new COP is installed.
November The city council votes on the budget.	

Source: Adapted from Cidade (1995).

- Announces the potential level of financial resources available for the next year and discusses new criteria and methods of implementing PB in each region.

In short, the municipality every year must coordinate information about three years of PB, an undertaking that requires significant staff resources and technical expertise.

The community's task in the first *rodada* is to elect the delegates who will represent the region, choosing one delegate for every 10 citizens (over 16 years old) attending the meeting. PB regulations forbid any municipal employee or any person holding a position in another municipal council or any public office to be elected as a PB delegate. In 1995, a total of 1,311 delegates were elected to represent all regions. To make the ensuing meetings less unwieldy, one delegate was elected for every 20 attendees beginning in 1996.

Between the two *rodadas*, the delegates contact citizens and discuss their demands in light of the municipality's projected investment capacity. Most important, they decide on general priorities (such as education, health services, and street paving) and also on specific priorities within each category—which street should be paved first, whether a new health facility must be built instead of an existing one being renovated, and so on. Because demands must fit within the projected investment, this is a time of negotiations on priorities and demands. If a consensus cannot be reached, any issue still under dispute will be voted on during the second *rodada*.

Citizens attending the second *rodada* elect the members of the *conselho do orçamento participativo* (PB council, or COP). In this second meeting, the citizens also choose the investment priorities for their regions.

Budget Preparation

After the second *rodada* is completed in all regions (usually in July), the COP meets once a week to coordinate preparation of the budget, which includes the CIP. The meetings are open to any interested citizen.

The COP and the Planning Cabinet (Gabinete de Planejamento, or GAPLAN) consider regions' priorities, the availability of financial resources and, when necessary, technical opinions. Municipal agencies and their directors then provide appropriate data and technical studies. If initial decisions do not prove viable, the COP must choose from viable options prepared by departments in the region. The main goal is to prepare a detailed budget that balances demands and financial viability.

The COP prepares the CIP based on a set of general criteria. The criteria, which aim to balance funding priorities among the regions, are:

- Lack of public services, infrastructure, or both in the region
- Total population in the region
- Priorities of the region in relation to the city's priorities.

Initially, there were additional, politicized criteria that took account of the level of citizen participation in the region and the importance of the region for the organization of the city, but these were later replaced by criterion 3. Another criterion measured the proportion of the region's population who lived in areas with extremely deficient services, infrastructure, or both, but this was abandoned in 1996 because it was largely fulfilled by criterion 1.

The procedures for developing the CIP are as follows:

- Each region chooses and ranks four of the seven standard priorities (basic sanitation; land and settlement regulation; transport and circulation; education; health services; street paving, including water and sewerage systems; and city organization). The priorities each region selects are graded from highest (4) to lowest (1). The remaining three priorities are also ranked but are not given grades.
- After the second *rodada,* all 16 regions' grades are added to determine the overall highest priorities for the following year. For 1994, for example, the regions decided that land and settlement regulation (including housing construction, land regulation, and resettlement of marginalized populations) would be the top priority. For 1995 and 1996, the top priority was determined to be street paving (which often includes basic sanitation, because any paved street must have water and sewage systems).
- Each region's priorities are compared with regional parameters to establish a distribution of financial resources. These regional parameters (or criteria) have become more and more sophisticated in order to make the final resource allocation as fair as possible. In 1996 the criteria were subdivided, and different weights were attributed to each (see table 7-1.2).
- After the weight of each criterion is measured and grades are obtained for each region, the COP determines a final grade that indicates the region's funding in proportion to the total city. This proportion indicates the allocation of resources for that region for each priority. Table

Table 7-1.2. *Regional Criteria and Relative Weights*

Lack of public services and/or infrastructure (Weight 3)	
Up to 25%:	grade 1
26 to 50%:	grade 2
51 to 75%:	grade 3
76 to 100%:	grade 4

Total population of the region in thousands (Weight 2)	
Up to 49.9:	grade 1
50 to 99.9:	grade 2
100 to 199.9:	grade 3
Above 200:	grade 4

Priority of the region in relation to the city's priorities[a] (Weight 3)	
Fourth and up:	grade 1
Third priority:	grade 2
Second priority:	grade 3
First priority:	grade 4

a. This is a comparison between the region's priorities and those for the city as a whole.
Source: Municipality of Porto Alegre, 1995.

7-1.3 illustrates this complex mechanism, using 1995's highest priority: street paving. According to the weight of this priority measured against the others, it was concluded that a total of 23 kilometers could be paved. Weights and grades were applied to distribute this total among the regions.

By law, the COP must submit the final budget document, with the accompanying CIP, to the city council no later than September 30. If the city councilors approve the budget, it becomes law and put into practice the following year.

To achieve such sophistication, the PB process underwent many changes in its first seven years. For example, the COP initially decided to concentrate a major part of the total investment in the five poorest areas of the city, allocating 70 percent of total investment to these areas in 1991. This allocation, based mainly on income, proved highly controversial and was not repeated. COP councilors concluded that municipal resources alone could not eradicate any social needs among the poorer sectors, and if they continued concentrating resources it would be unfair to the other regions. From 1991 on, the COP followed the steps listed previously.

Table 7-1.3. *Planned Street Pavement by Region, 1995*

Region[a]	Grades 1[b]	2[c]	3[d]	Priority[e] (3)	Total grade[f]	Distances[g]
1	3	4	2	3	12 (4.4)	1,004
3	3	6	3	6	18 (6.5)	1,505
4	9	2	1	12	24 (8.7)	2,007
5	3	4	2	12	21 (7.6)	1,756
6	6	4	1	9	20 (7.2)	1,673
7	3	4	3	12	22 (8.0)	1,840
8	3	2	1	6	12 (4.4)	1,004
9	6	2	1	12	21 (7.6)	1,756
10	3	4	2	6	15 (5.5)	1,255
11	3	2	1	9	15 (5.5)	1,255
12	6	2	3	12	23 (8.4)	1,924
13	12	2	1	12	27 (9.8)	2,257
14	3	2	3	6	14 (5.1)	1,171
15	3	2	2	12	19 (6.9)	1,589
16	3	2	4	3	12 (4.4)	1,004
Total	n.a.	n.a.	n.a.	n.a.	275 (100.0)	23,000

n.a. Not applicable

a. Region 2 did not plan any street paving projects in 1995.

b. Criterion: "Lack of public services and/or infrastructure" (Weight 3).

c. Criterion: "Proportion of population in areas of extremely deficient services and/or infrastructure" (Weight 2). Not used in 1996.

d. Criterion: "Total population in the region" (Weight 1).

e. Criterion: "Priorities of the region in relation to the city's priorities" (Weight 3).

f. Total grade obtained and its share of the total.

g. Total distance to be paved in the region, in meters (calculated by multiplying the share of the total grade by the total 23 kilometers).

Source: Adapted from Andreatta (1995).

Plenárias Temáticas

Meetings to discuss themes of general interest (as opposed to purely local interests) were promoted by the administration elected in 1992. In the following year, with growing participation and interest in PB, the municipality proposed to apply lessons learned from PB in other areas, such as overall city planning. To do this the municipality implemented a project called Porto Alegre Mais—Cidade Constituinte (Porto Alegre Plus—Constituent City). Broadly speaking, this project attempted to resolve issues concerning the city as a whole, thereby providing a definite orientation for the future of Porto Alegre.

As part of the project, discussion groups produced dozens of proposals, which were presented at the First Congress of the City of Porto Alegre, held in December 1993. This experience demonstrated that it was feasible to increase interest and attract sectors (especially the middle class and the business sector) from outside the PB structure. Typically, middle-class participants in the initial phases of the process were also involved in politics, and their participation increased only marginally. Among business people, only entrepreneurs have shown increased participation in the process. According to a survey conducted in 1993, 67 percent of those attending the *rodadas* were low-income wage earners (Fedozzi 1994).

Using the experience gained from the project, the municipality introduced *plenárias temáticas* into the PB process to attract participation of other sectors. *Plenárias* originated with the 1994 PB cycle. They were organized along the same lines as PB meetings, and each obtained the right to appoint councilors to the COP. To some extent, *plenárias* have succeeded in attracting new sectors to the process, and their qualitative approach has deepened the process, thus acting as a complement to the localism typical of *rodadas*. Meetings are held on the following five themes: (a) city organization and urban development; (b) health and social assistance; (c) economic development and tax systems; (d) transport and circulation; and (e) education, culture, and leisure.

Organizational Structure

An extensive network of people and institutions (illustrated in figure 7-1.1 and described in this section) implements the PB process in Porto Alegre.

Government Institutions

MAYOR. The mayor oversees PB-related activities of all local government bodies. The mayor also attends the *rodadas* and reviews the budget before the COP submits it to the city council. An initial veto by the mayor may be reversed by the COP, forcing negotiations, but the mayor's second decision is final.

Control of PB is concentrated in the mayor's office. It would have been logical to expect the municipal planning secretariat to coordinate the implementation of PB, but the secretariat did not demonstrate sufficient flexibility during the initial phases of PB in 1989. The ensuing decision to centralize all PB operations in the mayor's office proved crucial to PB's success.

Figure 7-1.1. *Organizational Structure of PB, 1996*

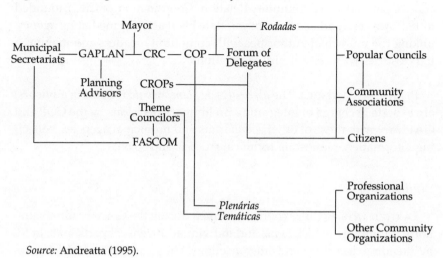

Source: Andreatta (1995).

MUNICIPAL SECRETARIATS AND COMMUNITY ADVISORS. The secretariats provide technical information on proposed works as requested. They also prepare sectoral demands and participate in a forum of community advisors. The forum brings together all municipal staff in charge of any kind of relations with the community. This forum's goal is to harmonize actions and implement a global policy supported by the municipality.

PLANNING CABINET. The GAPLAN, which is directly linked to the mayor, was established in 1990 to coordinate the PB process. It provides technical support to the COP in preparing the budget by translating community demands into technical formats, producing studies of technical and economic viability, and evaluating projects to ensure that they comply with the municipality's technical criteria. For example, the GAPLAN ensures that all street paving projects include necessary water and sewerage systems and take account of drainage conditions in the area, which may involve enlarging the scope of proposed works, particularly in peripheral and poorer regions of the city.

The GAPLAN also produces the budget booklet, which gives details on the budget and all approved public works, including the names and addresses of local councilors and regional coordinators of the PB process. This document is distributed in all meetings so that citizens may verify that their decisions have been incorporated.

COMMUNITY RELATIONS COORDINATION. The Coordenação de Relações com a Comunidade (Community Relations Coordination, or CRC), founded in 1981, was reorganized to accommodate PB. It acts as a mediating agency, linking the municipal authorities with community leaders and maintaining close ties with community associations.

PLANNING ADVISORS. The *assessores de planejamento* (planning advisors) are experts in charge of integrating preliminary decisions by the COP and GAPLAN with those of other secretariats and municipal agencies, collecting information, requesting technical studies, and so on.

Civil Society

PARTICIPANTS. Popular councils (formed during the Collares administration), community associations, and individual citizens all participate in PB by attending the *rodadas* and other meetings. The participants elect delegates and COP members and vote on investment priorities. Members of professional and other community organizations may attend *plenárias temáticas* geared toward special interests. At these meetings the participants elect theme councilors, who help coordinate PB efforts throughout the regions.

DELEGATES. These are elected at the first *rodada* to represent the regions. They discuss priorities with citizens, channel new demands to the COP, monitor all public works in progress, and maintain close contact with the region's elected PB councilors. The delegates comprise a body called the Forum of Delegates, which meets once a month to discuss how public works are being developed in the region. The delegates may also inspect investments and works, and they should divulge the inspection results to their constituents.

COP. The COP, whose members are elected at the second *rodada*, is responsible for preparing the budget and the CIP. The COP was initially composed of two councilors (and two substitutes) elected by each region, one representative of the civil servants' trade union, one representative selected by the UAMPA, and two nonvoting government representatives. Starting in 1994, the COP also included two elected councilors from each *plenária temática*. As a result, it has 44 members. The members serve for one-year terms, with a maximum of two consecutive terms. The COP has the final say on budget-related issues (except for the mayoral prerogative of final approval once the budget is submitted to the council), and over time it has become involved in other issues, such as sectoral policies, pay policies, and a career system for government employees.

REGIONAL COORDINATORS AND THEME COUNCILORS. The PB regional coordinators (*coordenadores regionais do orçamento participativo*) coordinate the regions' PB efforts. Each PB region has one coordinator, who maintains relations with the community associations and leaders, collects demands and local initiatives, helps organize meetings sponsored by local associations, and supports association leaders' preparations for the *rodadas*. Coordinators must be prepared to offer any information required by the community associations as well. Their counterparts in the *plenárias temáticas* are called theme councilors.

Results and Impacts

The application of PB methodology and the implementation of PB proposals have had impacts on citizen participation, politics, administration, and infrastructure in Porto Alegre, as described in this section.

Citizen Participation

A key result of PB is its effect on local participation and interest. In the first two years of PB, the new administration faced a number of difficulties and was unable to implement it consistently. As a consequence, citizen participation was low in the first year and even lower in the second. After 1991, however, revenues recovered and the level of investments increased; hence, citizen participation also increased (see table 7-1.4 and figure 7-1.2).

Table 7-1.4. *Number of Participants in Participatory Budgeting, Rodadas, and Plenárias Temáticas, 1990–95*

	Rodadas		Plenárias		
Year	I	II	I	II	Total
1990	348	628	n.a.	n.a.	976
1991	608	3,086	n.a.	n.a.	3,694
1992	1,442	6,168	n.a.	n.a.	7,610
1993	3,760	6,975	n.a.	n.a.	10,735
1994	2,638	7,000	598	1,011	11,247
1995	6,855	4,957	1,640	806	14,258

n.a. Not applicable.
Source: Community Relations Coordination.

Figure 7-1.2. *Number of Participants in PB (First Rodada), 1989–96*

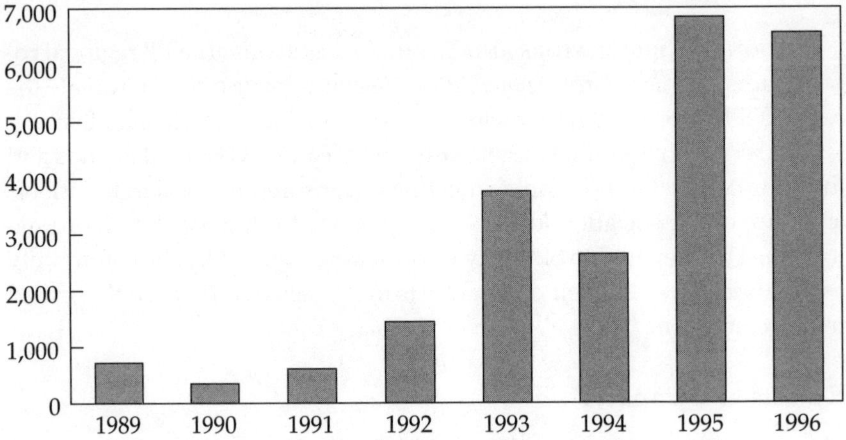

Source: Community Relations Coordination.

The administration initially measured participation by the number of attendees at PB activities and meetings. In some regions, however, many residents were urged to attend PB meetings in order to "get the numbers up" and therefore to elect more delegates and exert more pressure to define local priorities. The administration subsequently made efforts to refine the notion of representation, paying close attention to the emergence of new associations and to regional disputes and conflicts, and such maneuvers have gradually diminished.

Politics

Political results of an innovation are rarely evident in the short run. But one generally perceived result of PB is a higher level of political practices in terms of the content and sophistication of party proposals, issues, and so on. Specific political results are:

- **Increased approval ratings.** The party commanding the administration in the mid 1990s, the Worker's Party, achieved increased approval ratings resulting from the success of PB. Porto Alegre's administration at the time ranked third in approval among Brazilian state capitals, having received an approval rating of 65 to 75 percent for nearly two years (Folha de São Paulo 1996a,b). As a consequence, other political parties that wanted to challenge the Workers' Party were forced to permanently refine their practices and proposals for the city.

- **Decrease in clientelism.** One significant consequence of PB has been a reduction in clientelist practices, because the PB processes that contribute to budget decisionmaking result from impersonal mechanisms. Under PB, decisions are the outcome of open debate, which weakens mechanisms that are not socially legitimate. Clientelist practices persist only in areas of the city where the PB structure has not yet mobilized the local population.
- **Increase in democratic practices.** A democratic citizenry is being formed as a direct result of PB. Low-income groups, in particular, are becoming increasingly accustomed to participating in intense negotiations, dealing personally with city authorities, and facing complex issues related to the budget and its mechanisms.
- **Reverse trend in emancipation.** Because of loosened constitutional control, the number of new municipalities since 1988 has increased remarkably in Rio Grande do Sul and in many other Brazilian states. Before 1988, Rio Grande do Sul had 224 municipalities; that number increased to 427 by the end of 1993. On the local level in Porto Alegre, however, the trend was reversed. In Belém Novo, for example, a community 30 kilometers from the center of Porto Alegre, an emancipationist movement faded away after the advent of PB. Approximately 30 community-organized PB meetings were held in Belém Novo in preparation for the 1993 *rodadas* (Andreatta 1995). Near the borders of Porto Alegre, many regions organized to emancipate themselves from their municipalities and join Porto Alegre. As of the mid 1990s, only one of these areas had succeeded.

Administration

The new administrative practices implemented under PB have visibly improved the functioning of the entire municipal government. Among the results:

- **Improved staff morale.** Employees have benefited not only because they have a pay policy that is unique among Brazilian state capitals (wages are adjusted for inflation every two months), but also because their services are now more highly valued by citizens as a result of closer interaction.

- **Improved monitoring.** With the proliferation of councils and other collective bodies, more external eyes are inspecting the government's performance. For example, elected PB delegates and local Comissões de Obras (Works Commissions) constantly monitor progress on public works approved by the COP. Many times these commissions have prevented waste and delays in the development of planned works, exerting constant pressure on the private builders or public officials in charge.
- **Reduced costs.** Observers agree that PB activities have reduced the costs of public works. In the past, the total costs of most works were inflated due to frequent payments to corrupt municipal staff—to facilitate permits and allow fraud of all sorts—as well as to chronic inflation. With PB and a price stabilization that began in June 1994, these practices diminished substantially.
- **Improved effectiveness through decentralization.** Administrative decentralization, a medium-term objective of the municipal government to increase its rationality and effectiveness, is gradually becoming feasible. Now that Porto Alegre's citizens are accustomed to government routines and requirements, they are willing to take part in new decentralized regional administrations.
- **Increased transparency.** Governance in Porto Alegre is now transparent as a result of the PB process. Availability and allocation of resources are public knowledge, and no internal secrets prevail in the day-to-day workings of the administration. Many citizens now understand the relationship between taxes paid and services rendered. For the first time in many years, the municipal administration in the mid 1990s was not being accused of corruption, nepotism, or other unethical practices.

Infrastructure

The increased investment funds that Porto Alegre made available for infrastructure through the PB process resulted in improved basic services. PB's initial successes in infrastructure also facilitated the development of public-private cooperative efforts.

SERVICE IMPROVEMENTS. With a priority on basic services in the peripheral regions of the city, Porto Alegre's infrastructure has noticeably improved during the seven years since PB began. For example, expansion of the sewerage system has been extraordinary. In 1989, only 46 percent of the population was served, but by the end of 1996 the system was expected to serve 85 percent of the population. Before the launch of PB, all previous administrations combined had built approximately 1,100 kilometers of sewerage systems, while the two administrations alone in the early years of PB built 900 kilometers (*O Estado de São Paulo* 1996).

In addition to these changes, street pavement is expanding rapidly, with 25 to 30 kilometers paved each year. Slums have been upgraded, and housing has been built for the homeless. Also, the number of students enrolled in school doubled between 1989 and 1995 (PMPA 1996).

INCREASED INVESTMENT FUNDS. Between 1991 and the middle part of the decade, the municipality was able to offer a rising level of investments (in proportion to total revenues), exceeding the level in other Brazilian capitals (see figure 7-1.3). This level was not expected to rise any further unless taxes were raised or funds were borrowed. As a result, PB seemed to have reached an investment ceiling. With an enlarged agenda of demands, it appeared possible that resource disputes would intensify with the passing of time.

PB's transparency and efficient allocation have attracted the attention of international multilateral banks. For example, Porto Alegre requested a loan from the Inter-American Development Bank (IDB) to build a turnpike

Figure 7-1.3. Investment Resources, 1992–96

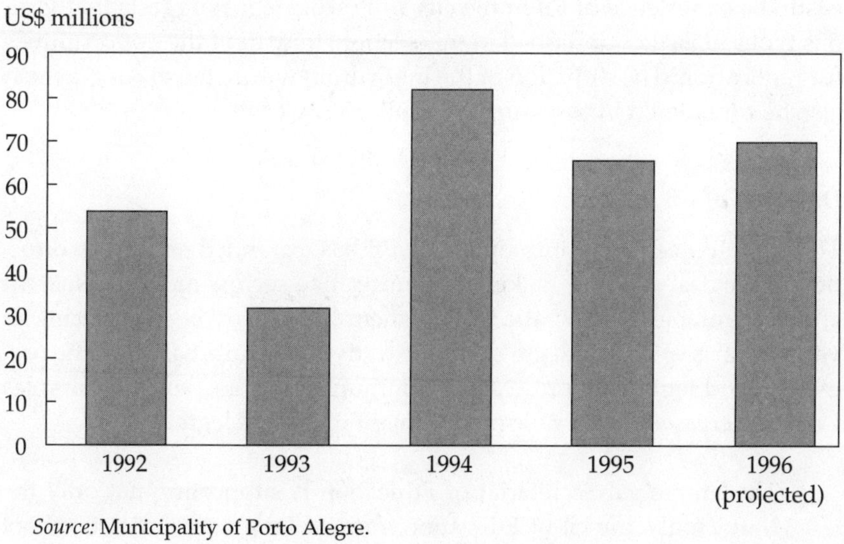

US$ millions

Source: Municipality of Porto Alegre.

around the city (the III Perimetral). The IDB granted preliminary approval for an additional loan for unspecified street pavement around the main road. The streets and distances (up to 100 kilometers) to be paved would be decided later through the PB process.

PUBLIC-PRIVATE COOPERATION. The municipality has pursued a range of initiatives with the private sector in a sign of growing cooperation between city agencies and civil society. Among the initiatives is "Trade Point," a project that aims to channel new opportunities for foreign trade. This effort has brought together the municipality, industrial and commercial organizations, and state agencies. Another project is the creation of a municipal bank (Banco Municipal do Porto Alegre), formed in 1993 as a partnership between associations representing private interests and government agencies. Finally, the Tecnópole Project is a multi-institutional project involving the city, local universities, and private sector organizations to stimulate technological innovations. The project is modeled on the research parks in Europe and the United States and is the first initiative of this type in Brazil.

Replicability

PB has had important repercussions in Brazil and abroad, inspiring approximately 70 attempts at replication in other urban contexts, mainly in small, rural towns and medium cities in the Brazilian South and Northeast. The experience of PB in the city of Porto Alegre suggests that various types of issues, described in this section, may limit the opportunities for replication. The diffusion of the innovation within Porto Alegre must also be considered in assessing the replicability of PB.

Diffusion of PB

The participatory fever introduced by PB has expanded and given direction to sectoral reforms, making administrative sectors more transparent and accountable. Democratic management has slowly been surfacing in various parts of Porto Alegre's administrative structure, based on the permanent and legitimate presence of community sectors. Several examples exist of increased democratic management in Porto Alegre:

- The Municipal Secretariat of Education is supporting not only the Municipal Council of Education, formed long ago, but also school councils in each school, comprising teachers, employees, parents, and students. The councils directly elect the school board and make decisions on a wide range of issues.

- Communities are managing nursery schools (see box 7-1.3).
- The newly formed Municipal Council on Land Access and Housing is devising Porto Alegre's housing policy.
- Municipal authorities have attempted to incorporate citizen participation into the city's master planning processes. The First Congress of the City of Porto Alegre passed a resolution to create the Municipal Council for Urban Development that would use the PB model. The Second Congress of the City laid down formal guidelines to shape the new *plano diretor* (master plan) of Porto Alegre.

Box 7-1.3. *Community Nursery Schools: Lower-Cost Services, Community Control*

The application of PB to improvements in the city's system of community nursery schools (*creches comunitárias*) illustrates the appeal and effectiveness of PB. Porto Alegre's first elected administration (1989–92) devised an ambitious plan to offer full-time municipal nursery schools as part of its education policy. PB participants gladly approved the construction of nursery schools and hiring of employees (amazingly enough, to the point of one employee for every three children). Thirty-one of these nursery schools were built, but they soon proved too expensive to operate, and the federal resources to maintain them were erratic.

In 1993, the region of Vila Cruzeiro, one of the poorest in the city, was facing increasing difficulties in operating the community nursery school. A group of citizens asked the municipal government for money. After intense discussions, it was decided that money would be transferred to private nursery schools in the community, and the community associations would be required to manage the schools under the educational and financial supervision of the Municipal Secretariat of Education. Thus, the community nursery school system was born, and the municipality immediately renounced the previous, expensive policy of building new schools. The new system involves the community, which is obviously interested in the higher potential quality of the new community nursery schools, and has increased the number of places available. Whereas the 31 nursery schools built through the PB process had room in 1996 for an estimated 6,243 children at a very high cost, 62 smaller community nursery schools (usually in adapted private houses) were offering, as of May 1996, a total of 4,513 places at a much lower per capita cost.

Despite increased opportunities for citizen participation, some sectors (especially the middle class and residents of poorer areas) still have not shown an interest in citywide affairs. This difficulty of overcoming such apathy may pose a problem for the overall strategy that municipal authorities envision for the city, as well as for further diffusion of PB and perhaps even for the future of PB itself.

Political Issues

Political issues are critical because they determine the initial impulse for the innovation.

POLITICAL WILL. The founding presupposition of PB is that the municipal government has the political will to share decisionmaking. The application of PB in a specific urban context depends on the political will and determination of the municipal government's leadership and the support of the prevailing political forces. In some unusual cases, like Porto Alegre, a government will agree to share its mandate with no preconditions other than a legitimate participation of organized and autonomous urban groups. In other cases, however, the municipal government will keep a fraction of power under its own control.

ADMINISTRATIVE DECENTRALIZATION. After decentralized decisionmaking structures are established, in particular for the budget process, an administrative decentralization should gradually follow, thus allowing organized sectors of the population to take more control of public resources. The decentralization will enable communities to determine sectoral policies as well as to monitor the internal workings of the municipal administration.

POLITICAL CENTRALIZATION. The administrative decentralization must be preceded by a political centralization within the municipality itself, concentrating control of the PB process in the hands of the mayor. Other municipal administrators may not strictly adhere to the whole program established by the mayor, and their alterations may prove fatal for such an ambitious proposal as PB.

Social participation in PB appears proportional to the government's seriousness in adhering to the established process, especially in observing the calendar of public works. As such, a government structure beset by lack of coordination will fail to implement an innovative approach to budgeting. The risk of the initial centralization is that it may hinder the gradual loosening of control that is supposed to develop after the process becomes routine.

NEW POLITICAL BEHAVIOR. If successful, PB stimulates a new political behavior. A firm adherence to democratic practices in negotiating diverse social demands and a repeal of traditional clientelist practices are only some of the changes that PB and related innovations may provoke. Although idealistic, the long-term political objective of PB is to radically transform the municipal government into a strictly public and impersonal institution in which particularistic interests will hold no sway. The new political behavior also affects community leaders, among whom authoritarian and clientelist practices have been pervasive, as proven by the early history of PB.

SOCIAL INEQUALITY. In societies marked by blatant social inequality, immediate demands prevail when an opportunity like PB is offered to social groups living in dismal conditions. This may antagonize the interests of other groups. Fitting local demands into citywide priorities is difficult, and communities need many incentives to improve their sense of fairness when negotiating their demands with other communities. The complete autonomy of community organizations, a precondition of PB, will often generate parochial demands, but these will be balanced by other organizations' demands and technical arguments furnished by the local government's staff.

CONFLICT WITH OFFICIAL POLITICAL STRUCTURE. Another political issue is the inevitable conflict between the traditional political structure of representative democracy and the structure of direct democracy used by PB, at least in its initial phases. In Porto Alegre, the officially elected city councilors not linked politically to the current administration saw their political influence erode after the success of PB. As a result, the PB process introduced new themes to the old discussion of representative versus direct democracy.

Perhaps PB is showing that a third alternative may be possible, blending elements of representative and direct democracy systems. In fact, the PB experience in Porto Alegre has demonstrated that when the level of participation increases too much, a version of representative democracy *inside* the PB structure must be offered, or else the process will become unmanageable.

NEED FOR AGREEMENT. Other conflicts may emerge in the city if there is no broad social harmony. In *plenárias temáticas,* for example, conflicts may arise between social groups proposing works that benefit the city as a whole and local community groups proposing works that benefit a specific area. This is not an implausible scenario in a city with a large population. Pent-up demand may lag behind investments and influence the whole PB process, even if the mayor has the final say in all disputes.

Another potential scenario is a dispute between richer areas where no significant improvements in infrastructure or services are needed and poorer areas that could benefit from a transfer of revenues collected from the richer areas. Residents of the richer areas perceive the benefits of PB more as a token pattern of changes based on an expensive property tax system than as an improvement in their quality of life.

Operational and Administrative Issues

Although the favorable conditions in Porto Alegre have enhanced PB's results in the city, the PB experience has confronted some operational and administrative issues.

EXISTING SOCIAL ORGANIZATION. The PB experience presupposes a minimum background of social organizational traditions in the city, especially in the poorer regions. If no such traditions existed, PB's development in Porto Alegre would have been slow and difficult, opening the way for possible conflicts involving the distribution of resources and making the process somewhat unstable. As a consequence, it seems clear that in a context of weak organizational history, the PB process should be under the command of the municipality, which would gradually introduce the newly formed citizen organizations into the PB structure. In contexts of widespread illiteracy and social pauperization, the process may become even more complex to manage, for these are contexts in which large social groups become easy prey for political opportunists.

EFFECTIVE GOVERNMENT INTERACTION. Another prerequisite of PB is the municipal government's effective participation. It should offer precise information when required as well as technical and economic evaluations of public works decided on by community organizations. In addition, the government must develop an efficient methodology for interacting with local citizens, especially when a significant proportion of them are illiterate. The city of Porto Alegre developed a series of educational techniques and methods (such as videotapes and skits), learning how to present diverse themes clearly to the citizens and to help them face difficult issues in the PB meetings.

SKILLED MUNICIPAL STAFF. A staff with expertise in new fields is required to make the PB process proceed smoothly. Above all, the staff must have a thorough command of budget techniques. In attempts to replicate PB in Brazil, a lack of professional staff to organize the list of social demands to be transformed into a budget may have slowed the implementation of the process more widely in the country.

REGIONAL ORGANIZATION. The division of the city into regions should not follow traditional borders but should be based entirely on social, community, and organizational homogeneity. This will greatly increase the citizens' potential support for PB.

APPROPRIATE SCOPE. Another operational issue is the scope of PB. The maximum or minimum size of a population for which PB is effective remains unknown. But there is an objective ceiling that must be considered when implementing PB, and that is the potential level of investments offered by the municipality. There seems to be a limit of investments, which varies from region to region, below which the population will not engage in a participatory movement organized by the municipal authorities. The irresistible attraction of PB, in particular in depressed areas, is a growing perception that resources are available, that they will be used according to decisions made by the community residents, and that citizens who fail to participate will therefore risk forgoing quality-of-life improvements.

Porto Alegre experienced the effects of the lower limit of investments in 1990, when promises made during the PB process in the previous year did not materialize due to lack of resources. The citizens' interest in the process diminished as a consequence.

IMMIGRATION. Another social pressure on PB is the rate of immigration, which increases with news of improved living conditions. Porto Alegre has received an impressive contingent of immigrants, not only from rural areas but also from other cities of Rio Grande do Sul. A vicious cycle can result, in which the positive impacts of PB attract people to move toward the capital, which, in turn, brings local demands to unsustainable levels.

Economic Issues

The introduction of PB must be founded on an existing economic structure whose growth creates employment (to reduce pressures on social assistance and to produce income tax revenue) and on revenues from taxes imposed on local firms. Many economic issues are beyond the control of the city.

REVENUE GENERATION. The city must have the capacity to generate revenue to fund PB. If not, the budget will depend on an erratic transfer of resources from the state, the federal government, or both. These transfers are subject to delays and to negotiations that are not always in favor of local governments, especially the smaller ones with little political influence.

As a capital, Porto Alegre has an advantage in implementing PB, because the city houses all government services, the headquarters of many important firms, and the largest commercial and service sectors in Rio Grande do Sul. In consequence, the city's capacity to produce revenues is larger than many others', thus allowing reasonable room to maneuver in implementing an innovation such as PB. For the majority of other Brazilian municipalities, however, the level of investments may be too low to entice their citizens to participate in the process.

NATIONAL ECONOMIC FACTORS. Some issues stem from outside decisions and economic movements. These outside factors derive from federal government policies and national or even global processes of economic adjustment. For example, a national policy during sky-high interest rates in Brazil in the mid 1990s claimed to be a precondition to price stabilization. But it also led to a semirecessionist situation, forcing many small businesses to close down—with inevitable impacts on Porto Alegre's economy.

Another trend prevailing in Brazil since the 1988 constitution is that the states and the federal government have increasingly transferred responsibilities to the municipalities' domain—but without corresponding financing. A PB cycle that results in a "grand pact" to be implemented in the following year may prove worthless if the city finds itself with sudden new and expensive duties (such as health care services) that it inherited from the federal government.

GLOBAL FACTORS. Global changes also cause unexpected problems in local experiences, but the effects of global changes may not be immediately visible. Unemployment due to new technology is the most obvious example of such a change. In the case of Rio Grande do Sul, however, the Common Market of the South (*Mercado Comum do Sul*, or Mercosul) posed a more relevant economic problem. The formation of Mercosul and its regional free-trade processes was not accompanied by appropriate mechanisms of economic adjustment. As a result, especially in the state of Rio Grande do Sul, Mercosul had negative impacts on some agricultural sectors, forcing many small producers out of the market and thus contributing to migration to the urban centers, especially Porto Alegre.

Legal Issues

Legal issues sometimes prevent planned works, even if financially supported, from materializing due to juridical barriers that can delay a project or require its modification. An illustrative example in Porto Alegre was a decision made during the PB process to pave the main street in Region 1. Paving the main street had the potential to benefit a great number of residents, because water and sewage disposal systems would be installed as well. However, the paving project was vetoed by the state agency in charge of environmental affairs, which alleged that the area was legally under "environmental protection" and that the agency could not approve the planned work because of its possible impacts.

Another example is that immigrants often illegally occupy plots of land in depopulated areas of the city and later demand urban infrastructure through the PB process. It is improbable for such demands to be legally permissible.

Geographical Issues

A city's inability to control geographical issues outside its own borders restricts the PB decisionmaking process. Events in neighboring municipalities have various repercussions for Porto Alegre, but such events are not addressed jointly. The frequent floods, for example, have not been mitigated, because there is no joint flood control effort, and the inability to control flooding makes local works senseless in some parts of the city.

The most serious problem is pollution of the Guaiba river (which is, in fact, an estuary), which borders Porto Alegre, thus preventing the use of the river for leisure or other purposes. This pollution comes particularly from agricultural areas in remote municipalities that use large amounts of pesticides and from the neighboring industrial municipalities. Discussions in PB meetings about cleaning up the river only illustrate the futility of most cleanup efforts. Perhaps if the PB structure was formalized at the state or national level, a solution could be found for crucial issues like water pollution.

Controversial Issues

Beyond the specific types of issues mentioned above, the Porto Alegre experience has isolated several generally controversial issues:

OPTIMISM ABOUT PARTICIPATION. The proponents of PB persist in manifesting an unfounded optimism regarding social participation. This optimism reflects the leftist political orientation of those in power in the early years of PB, which usually magnifies the role of popular involvement in social change. It appears that PB is based on a belief in limitless interest in participation. Empirical evidence from other social experiments founded on participatory elements, however, has shown that there is a limit to citizens' interest in participating even when revenues are sufficient to fund needed works. This limit is reached when material demands have been met, and remaining cultural or symbolic demands can be expressed through the PB process but encounter a diminished motivation and interest of participants. Even when the issues raised involve the city as a whole (through *plenárias temáticas*, for example) the level of popular interest sometimes plummets.

FORMALIZATION OF PB. Formalizing the innovation would guarantee its continuity, yet the two administrations that created the process resisted any attempt to codify PB in the law. They were inspired by a strong notion of associational autonomy and by the concept of "nongovernmental public spheres" (Lima 1995). This meant reducing the presence of state institutions and maintaining social and public controls in areas chosen by the population. As such, the administrations argued, creating an institutional umbrella for PB would in fact endanger it under any future administration not committed to the ideals of autonomous participation and democratic principles.

LACK OF CITIZEN INITIATIVE. The fragile state of social commitment to the process is evidenced by the continuous dependence on municipal officials to organize meetings, manage local discussions, and define local priorities. There is a consensus that the citizens depend too much on their regional representatives—a clear indication of how loose the citizens' ties are to PB.

THE STATE VERSUS CIVIL SOCIETY. Experts disagree over the proper role of the state as opposed to the role of civil society. On the one hand, some social groups have an excessively generous opinion of the municipal state, to the point of idolizing it (Oliveira 1995), putting any notion of social control of state decisions at risk. On the other hand, many see civil society as a necessarily "good" social entity, whose actions will irreproachably reflect collective interests.

Conclusion

With a growing level of participation and an increasingly sophisticated process, the PB innovation has shown itself to be an enormous success. Porto Alegre emerged as one of the few Brazilian capitals with healthy financial management and a smooth administrative routine commanded by an autonomous, non-institutionalized council chosen outside the formal electoral system.

In the years since its inception, PB trained hundreds of citizens to act as decisionmakers, weighing the interests of their constituencies against the interests of the whole city. The city residents were able to decide on virtually any use of municipal resources—from streets to be paved to reform of the city's main public market, from cultural initiatives in peripheral areas to the publication of a book on community history, from sanitation systems to pay policies for municipal civil servants.

In terms of its innovative aspects, PB raised the general level of governance to a state of excellence that was only limited by local technical and financial constraints. Transparency, greater rationality in administrative procedures, strict control of finance, constant public monitoring of governmental performance, and an established routine of efficient allocation of public resources were some of PB's impacts. These changes allowed the level of investments in the city to increase significantly. With this record, the municipal government received not only greater popularity, as expressed in approval ratings, but also the recognition and cooperation of the private sector.

PB created new economic opportunities for many, and small businesses in particular benefited from the innovation. PB principles also embodied a notion of social justice, transferring taxes collected in the richer areas to improve services and general quality of life in the poorer parts of Porto

Alegre. Long-term results may demonstrate an enormous indirect benefit of this transfer in terms of social indicators, for the general level of infrastructure, education, and health services markedly improved since PB began. Another result of PB is the increasing control of government by an autonomous citizenry, a classic condition of a political democracy.

Lessons learned from PB indicate issues for its replicability. Some initial requirements for PB are a political will to cede significant power to community associations and a disciplined political posture that avoids customary clientelist practices. PB must be based on a rigorous financial control of the municipal budget and offer a relevant minimum of resources to be invested. In Brazil, with striking variations, approximately 70 other municipalities were implementing PB in the mid 1990s, and empirical evidence suggested that PB could become a widespread format for municipal administration in Brazil.

The issues for replicability summarized here indicate that more investigation must be carried out, possibly comparing PB cases implemented in Brazilian cities of varying socioeconomic status and comparing PB cases to other Latin American cases of successful fiscal management. These comparisons of innovative experiences may bring to light the universal requirements that must be present in a useful innovation applicable to a variety of urban contexts.

References

Author's Note:
Although in-depth analytical sources about PB are virtually nonexistent, various institutional materials produced by the municipal authorities in Porto Alegre proved useful. See, for example, Orçamento Participativo *(Boletim), published in 1995 (two issues) and 1996 (one issue to date). There are many scattered materials produced for such purposes as meetings or as generic documents or pamphlets explaining PB, and they also provided background for this chapter. They are not listed here but could be easily obtained at the* Prefeitura Municipal de Porto Alegre *(Municipal Government of Poroto Alegre). An NGO called Cidade* (Centro de Assessoria e Estudos Urbanos, *or Center for Urban Policy and Studies), based in Porto Alegre, has also produced useful materials, in addition to collecting documents related to PB processes. It publishes two periodicals (De olho no orçamento and De olho na Cidade) with many interesting articles that are instrumental to understanding the PB innovation.*

Andreatta, Humberto. 1995. *Orçamento participativo. Porto Alegre*. Porto Alegre: Municipal Government of Porto Allegre (Department of Culture).

Avritzer, Leonardo. 1995. "Models of Civil Society: An Analysis of the Emergence of Civil Society in Brazil and the Problems for Its Institutionalization." Paper presented at the XIX International Congress of the Latin American Studies Association, Sept. 28–30, Washington, D.C.

Cidade (Centro de Assessoria e Estudos Urbanos). 1995. *De olho no orçamento* 1(1). Porto Alegre: Cidade.

Fedozzi, Luciano. 1994. "*Poder local e governabilidade: o caso de Porto Alegre.*" *Proposta* 22(62): 23–29.

Folha de São Paulo. 1996a. São Paulo. January 1.

———. 1996b. São Paulo. April 29.

Fox, Jonathan. 1994. "The Difficult Transition from Clientelism to Citizenship: Lessons from Mexico." *World Politics* 46(2): 151–84.

Fox, Jonathan, and Josefina Aranda. 1995. "Decentralization and Rural Poverty in Mexico: 'Municipal Solidarity Funds' and Community Participation in Oaxaca." Paper presented at the XIX International Congress of the Latin American Studies Association, Sept. 28–30, Washington, D.C.

Gay, Robert. 1995. "Between Clientelism and Universalism: Reflections on Popular Politics in Urban Brazil." Paper presented at the XIX International Congress of the Latin American Studies Association, Sept. 28–30, Washington, D.C.

Genro, Tarso. 1994. *A utopia possível*. Porto Alegre: Arts and Guild.

———. 1996. "*Entre a solidão e a solidariedade.*" Folha de São Paulo, April 14: p. 5–8.

Keck, Margaret E. 1990. *The Workers' Party and Democratization in Brazil*. New Haven, Conn.: Yale University Press.

Lima, Gildo. 1995. "*A política de relações com a comunidade e o orçamento participativo.*" Unpublished paper, Porto Alegre.

McCoy, Jennifer L. 1995. "Political Learning and Redemocratization in Latin America." Paper presented at the XIX International Congress of the Latin American Studies Association, Sept. 28–30, Washington, D.C.

Menegat, Elizete M. 1995. "*Fios condutores da participação popular em Porto Alegre: elementos para um debate.*" *Proposta* 23(67): 34–40.

Moisés, José Álvaro. 1995. *Os brasileiros e a democracia*. São Paulo: Editora Ática.

Navarro, Zander. 1994. "Democracy, Citizenship and Representation: Rural Social Movements in Southern Brazil, 1978–1990." *Bulletin of Latin American Research* 13(2): 129–54.

O Estado de São Paulo. 1996. São Paulo. March 17.

Oliveira, Carlos Afonso da Silva, coordinator. 1995. *Democracia nas grandes cidades: a gestão democrática da prefeitura de Porto Alegre.* Rio de Janeiro: IBASE (*Instituto Brasileiro de Análises Sociais e Econômicas*).

PMPA (*Prefeitura Municipal de Porto Alegre*). 1995a. *Orçamento Participativo. Como aumentar os investimentos?* Porto Alegre.

————. 1995b. *Orçamento participativo. Regimento Interno.* Porto Alegre: Coordination of Social Communication.

————. 1995c. *Orçamento público.* Porto Alegre: Planning Cabinet.

————. 1996. *Plano de investimentos 1996.* Porto Alegre: Planning Cabinet and Coordination of Community Relationships.

Schmitter, Philippe, and Terry Karl. 1991. "What Democracy Is . . . and Is Not." *Journal of Democracy* 2(3): 75–88.

World Bank. 1995. *Brazil. A Poverty Assessment.* Report 4323-BR (two volumes). Human Resources Operations Division, Country Department I, Washington, D.C.

7-2

Improving Basic Infrastructure in Mendoza, Argentina: MENPROSIF

Tim Campbell, World Bank

Although many national and local programs in Latin America aim to build social infrastructure, such as water distribution and wastewater disposal systems, gas lines, storm drains, and other small-scale works, few utilize the elements that have been successfully incorporated into the Mendoza Provincial Program for Basic Infrastructure (*Programa de Infrastructura Social de Mendoza*, or MENPROSIF). MENPROSIF's chief innovation is its reliance on social censure to secure credit for low-income residents, rather than on pledges of capital that the residents rarely have. This system enables the poor to afford 70–80 percent of total project costs and minimizes state subsidies for improvement works of broad social interest. Other innovative features of MENPROSIF include collaborative arrangements among public agencies, private contractors, NGOs, and neighborhood organizations. High levels of community organization among beneficiary groups have also been a key ingredient in achieving extensive participation in the selection and implementation of works.

In the first four years after its inception in 1991, MENPROSIF implemented 274 small-scale works projects in over half the municipalities in the province of Mendoza (see box 7-2.1). In each case, beneficiaries took part in identifying needs, finding solutions, taking individual responsibility for short-term (two-year) credits, selecting contractors, and overseeing implementation of works.

The significance of MENPROSIF is its creative reformulation of public-private partnerships in a manner that takes advantage of each partner's

---

Box 7-2.1. *The Province of Mendoza*

Mendoza, with a population of 1.4 million in 1990, is one of 22 provinces that form the second tier of government under the Argentine Federal Constitution of 1853. Provinces are equivalent to states in other federated republics in the region (such as Brazil, República Bolivariana de Venezuela, and Mexico). They have their own executive and legislative branches (to which representatives are elected), which pass laws, raise revenue, and implement provincial programs. The 16 municipal governments in Mendoza are called *departamentos*. The population of the province's capital, also called Mendoza, and three surrounding *departamentos* totaled nearly 840,000 in 1990.

The province of Mendoza covers about 149,000 square kilometers, nearly the size of Uruguay. It is located on the western edge of Argentina, where the fertile agricultural plains begin their rise to the Andean foothills. Although most of the province lies under the Andean rain shadow, careful management of hydraulic resources has yielded productive viticulture and other agricultural output. Argentina's per capita gross domestic product was in the range of US$5,500 in 1993. At that time, the latest poverty data available (1980) indicated that a fifth of Mendoza's population had unsatisfied basic needs (as compared to nearly half the population in poorer provinces such as Formosa and Jujuy). Most of the beneficiaries of the Mendoza Provincial Program for Basic Infrastructure (MENPROSIF) earned US$250–300 a month.

---

comparative specialization. In the MENPROSIF formulation, individual beneficiaries run credit risks, contractors bid competitively for the works, the state assembles relief measures and offers them to residents and builders alike, and the provincial bank takes a commercial risk of nonpayment. Although the province is still indispensable to MENPROSIF's success—the provincial Ministry of Environment, Urbanism, and Housing (Ministerio de Ambiente Urbanismo y Habitación, or MINEUH) plays a strong fostering and brokerage role—MENPROSIF is geared to elicit preferences of individual residents and verify their willingness to pay, thereby moving these and other key responsibilities away from the state. By incorporating socially based market signals—which residents express in open, participatory meetings—and securing consensus, MENPROSIF obviates such key public sector tasks as cost-benefit evaluations of projects. In the process, MENPROSIF has reduced the costs of projects and enjoyed a high success rate. The next stages of evolution would include reducing the role of the state in organization and launching projects; more explicitly, targeting sub-sidies to the poorest residents; and securing longer-term, more market-based, credit.

Systemic Context and Origins

The MENPROSIF innovation dates to the cholera epidemic in Latin America, which first broke out in the Peruvian seaport of Callao in January 1991. The epidemic ravaged Peruvian shantytowns, killing hundreds of residents and infecting additional thousands. In a matter of months, the epidemic spread north and south along the Pacific Rim. Argentine and Chilean authorities began to take precautionary measures to arrest the spread of the disease, but a major highway link and shared border with Chile put Mendoza squarely in the path of infection. This public health crisis was among the first challenges to test the mettle of the provincial administration that took office in January 1992.[1] Several factors influenced the government's reaction to the crisis.

First, Argentina was in the process of redefining the very nature of the public sector following years of military rule in the late 1970s and 1980s. The restoration of democracy began in earnest with the election of President Raul Alfonsin in 1983. A new generation of leadership in Mendoza had already made substantial strides in state reform, and political leadership and innovative programs in the province were part of this political renaissance. Officials made two major reform efforts in Mendoza, aiming to (a) promote social welfare in a new, decentralized manner; and (b) "de-institutionalize" the state (that is, dismantle large state institutions, some of which dealt in social welfare). Moreover, the province was already known for its strong regional identity and had proven innovative under previous administrations. Cooperation between public and private entities dated to before World War II in such areas as water basin management and irri-gated agriculture (see box 7-2.2).

Another factor conditioning the province's response to the cholera scare was the strong public demand, expressed during the gubernatorial election campaign in 1987, for improvements in coverage of water, wastewater disposal, stormwater drainage, and other services, particularly in low-income communities. Ironically, the earlier privatization of the provincial water authority had weakened the province's ability to respond to this need.

---

1. In the end, the cholera outbreak did not become epidemic in Argentina.

Box 7-2.2. *Regional Identity and Innovation in Mendoza*

Mendoza, like many subnational regions in the Latin American and Caribbean region and elsewhere, exhibits a distinct identity dating from the early nineteenth century. In part, Mendoza's identity is rooted in its struggle for self-reliance and survival in adverse environmental circumstances of aridity, geographic distance from centers of power, and proximity to the Andes Mountains and to Chile. Mendoza was the staging ground for San Martín's campaign across the Andes to help drive the Spanish from Chile in the early nineteenth century. In the twentieth century, agriculture and mining grew to account for over half of the province's gross domestic product.

These factors appear to be underlying conditions for the many successful experiments launched in Mendoza since 1983. These include the privatization of public enterprises with the active collaboration of unions and, in the public sector, the introduction during Governor J. Octavio Bordon's administration (1988–91) of "budgeting by results." Using budgeting by results, the province of Mendoza became a nationally recognized leader in the budgeting process.

Mendoza has launched several other experiments with varying degrees of innovation and effectiveness. The public and private sectors reached an especially strong consensus on the management of water resources, particularly for irrigation in the semiarid environment. Nongovernmental organizations and the private sector have also collaborated on public education and the financing of schools, as well as the organization of social programs through community-based facilities run by nongovernmental organizations with local governmental authorities.

Since about 1990, the water authority had been undergoing a transformation from its former role as provider of multiple public services, including small-scale water and sanitation works, toward a more purely regulatory function. This transition left the public sector in a weaker position to respond quickly to the public demand for better services and unable to respond to the threat of a health crisis posed by the cholera outbreak.

Administrative and contractual delays were common in the government-run water system before 1991, due to excessive divisions of labor and poor coordination among ministries. These delays, combined with political interference, changing priorities, and occasional lapses in budgetary allocations, led to serious cost overruns, particularly during the inflationary period of 1987–91. In short, partisan interference and bureaucracy produced not water services, but public frustration and a large unmet demand for services, particularly in low-income areas. Census data for 1990 showed that fewer than 70 percent of structures had water connections.

The provincial government had also experimented with *ahorros previos* (prior savings), a successful program similar to those in other Argentine provinces. Under this program, community organizations grouped by city blocks collected and deposited beneficiary contributions—30 to 40 percent of the total cost of works—in advance of, and as a condition for, construction of civil works. This mechanism effectively rationed provincial expenditures on water and other infrastructure to neighborhoods that proved their interest. Many, if not most, of the *ahorros previos* programs withered under the effects of hyperinflation (about 4,000 percent a year) in the late 1980s.

Program Conception and Launch

The genesis, launch, and first project of MENPROSIF provided the foundation for the innovation's success.

Genesis

The combination of the cholera scare, inflationary environment, public clamor during the political campaign for water and wastewater services, and poor past performance of the public agency responsible for sanitation led Governor-elect Rodolfo Federico Gabrielli to propose a program for social infrastructure in 1991. But both his conception of the program and his method for launching it were unusual. First, Gabrielli's social infrastructure program was not conceived as a massive frontal assault, as in Peru, where President Alberto Fujimori asserted central government control in a gigantic social fund. Rather, Gabrielli envisioned a program heavily dependent on social organization and local control. Although housed in the MINEUH, MENPROSIF's central premise was to invert the conventional public sector formulation—state planning and execution with minimal beneficiary inputs—that was typical of most local governments in Latin America and the Caribbean.

The new approach was aimed at fixing the problems of traditional public works systems—slowness, tendency to overrun the budget, and inability to respond flexibly to the special needs of low-income areas. Strong, single-purpose neighborhood organizations were to be the bedrock of MENPROSIF. These organizations had a mandate to reach agreement on needs and to channel popular expression of demand. As conceived in MENPROSIF, the neighborhood organizations were also to take part in other aspects of the project cycle. With coaching and advice from MENPROSIF program officers, neighborhood organizations eventually became effective in increasing beneficiary involvement in securing credit, selecting contractors, supervising and signing off on works, and laying the groundwork for future projects.

Launch

Gabrielli formed the embryo of the program using his own staff, and later housed the program in the MINEUH. The governor started with a staff of one—a government official with training in title survey and strong experience in local public works. This official was a former director of works in the Municipality of Las Heras (see box 7-2.3), where poverty and population pressures fostered innovation. Many of the programs in Las Heras required frequent and close contact with neighborhood organizations in a variety of municipal works, and the former director of works had experimented with assorted participatory approaches in project identification, self-help labor, and *ahorros previos*.

Officials did not launch MENPROSIF with the ribbon cutting and fanfare common in many programs with populist appeal. The evisceration of public agencies had already done away with flashy, specially targeted, public sector interventions, customary in some countries. In such interventions, some with financing from the World Bank, beefed-up special units of highly

---

Box 7-2.3. *The Municipality of Las Heras*

Las Heras (population 174,000 in 1990) is a bedroom community for the low-income working class of the city of Mendoza. It serves as a regional reception center for the economically displaced, and the recession of 1987–91 made it one of the fastest growing communities in the province. The city's mayor, in his second term, took advantage of MENPROSIF and of many other opportunities he found or created to combat the problems of Las Heras. Community participation had long been a hallmark of many of the programs in Las Heras. Some of the experiences in Las Heras served as seeds for MENPROSIF, and the city became a training ground for its officers.

qualified professionals successfully carry out special-purpose programs, fueled by resources diverted from other programs. Many of these special-purpose programs far exceed the standard terms of reference and performance records of core ministries. Few of them are replicable over the long term, however. The transitional circumstances of the public sector in Argentina reinforced the drive to adopt a new approach.

First Project

The first project to be financed under the collective credit arrangements of MENPROSIF was a wastewater disposal system for 71 families in 1991. The project was located in a small neighborhood known as Bancarios, a residential district of former bank employees, mainly low-skilled and unskilled workers, such as custodians, clerks, and night watchmen. Officials chose the neighborhood to capitalize on the reservoir of trust built up over previous years between the provincial bank and neighborhood residents. Trust produced rapport, thus enabling program officers, bank authorities, and residents to communicate effectively and reach a mutual understanding. The chief obstacle was the bank's and the residents' unfamiliarity with the idea of credit for the poor. Rapport with the residents of Bancarios made it easier for both sides to overcome their uncertainties about the risks. Officials also thought that residents would feel a stronger than customary commitment to make good on their credit obligations and thereby reinforce the neighborhood bond with the bank.

The strategy of beginning MENPROSIF in this friendly pilot community paid off. But the project ran into delays caused by many obstacles in addition to the uncertainties of borrowing. For example, the then Ministry of Works undercut the overtures of MENPROSIF by launching its own program of basic infrastructure. Nevertheless, the first few MENPROSIF projects produced results and were completed more quickly than comparable projects under ministerial control. The Bancarios project was completed in about three months, far longer than later projects but far shorter than the standard then maintained by the provincial ministry. Demand from other communities began to build immediately after completion of the Bancarios project.

Essential Features and Evolution of MENPROSIF

Although MENPROSIF has evolved over time, its essential features have been retained. These features are:

- Community organization
- Design simplicity and cost transparency
- Credit securitization
- Financing and cost recovery
- Contractor competition and selection
- Rapid works implementation.

Community Organization

Local organizations are a customary feature of urban life in Argentina. In MENPROSIF, neighborhoods are organized around natural residential groupings. (Mendocinos use the term *unidades vecinales*, literally meaning neighborhood units, but referring in practice to block organizations.) These groupings are typically composed of several hundred households on one or more city blocks. MENPROSIF has implemented projects for as few as 5 and as many as 4,000 households.

Under MENPROSIF, neighborhood units (some already organized, others encouraged to do so) are invited to identify priority needs and to pledge individual and collective responsibility for improvements. The neighborhood unit must be legally formalized before registering to participate in MENPROSIF. In the early stages of the program, a MINEUH officer participated actively in the assembling and education of neighborhood units. With time, these groups have become aware of the rules, and now they approach the mayor's office or the MINEUH unsolicited to sponsor their own projects. In practice, neighborhood units engage in an iterative process of discussion and clarification with program officers, and often with each other, to determine objectives, define the scope of work they wish to complete, define their own contributions to it, and confirm personal and collective liability for completing the works.

Design Simplicity and Cost Transparency

Once a project idea is formulated—for infrastructure such as water connections or wastewater disposal systems, as were first given preference under MENPROSIF—the MINEUH helps arrange for concept and working drawings. The designs are typically simple, block-by-block schematic diagrams that clarify technical constraints, refine alignments, and determine costs. These are calculated with the help of provincial engineers. Later, communities that are well organized or that are carrying out a follow-up project have often been able to arrange for the design drawings on their own. The neighborhood units have found experienced third parties, such as a contractor or a municipal or public works engineer, to perform this design service.

Credit Securitization

The critical feature of MENPROSIF is the collective security of credit. Credit is offered to neighborhood residents at 15 percent interest with 24 months to pay. During the years of hyperinflation (about 4,000 percent annually), bank loans were available for about 35 percent interest. MENPROSIF offered most low-income residents their first experience with institutionalized credit—that is, from a faceless, impersonal institution—as opposed to credit from family networks, work colleagues, or other personal sources. For many poor people, accepting credit is extremely risky, particularly from formal, impersonal institutions, For one thing, low-income residents may have irregular property titles. Even when that is not a problem, offering their property as collateral represents a very large risk for the residents. Also, irregular or insufficient income makes borrowing flatly infeasible for the poor. Many other social and cultural obstacles, well documented elsewhere (World Bank 1991), stand in the way of borrowing as a way to finance anything, much less large projects such as wastewater disposal systems and other basic infrastructure. The lack of collateral and low or intermittent income pose correlative risks to lenders, and these obstacles prevent state and financial institutions from offering credit to the poor.

One of the great breakthroughs of MENPROSIF has been its adaptation of a well-known mechanism—securing credit through a kind of mutual solidarity—to offset these risks for both borrowers and lenders. The network of neighborhood organizations, local government agencies, and private sector companies emulates the "comfort" and "securitization" concepts of high finance. The compact begins with a community organization. This entity partially collectivizes debt obligation by spreading credit risk, and it acts as a sovereign consumer. MENPROSIF extends the community organization by incorporating the principle of social censure to maintain a web of mutually reinforcing promises to make good on the debt. This provides comfort to financiers and leads, in turn, to secure deals for the building industry and borrowers. Private contractors trust credit guarantees, which open the way for a partnership of the public sector, the provincial bank, and the neighborhoods. Although the idea of cross-securitization is not new—it was popularized with the success of Grameen Bank in

Bangladesh, for instance—it had not been adopted as a means of security by public institutions in Argentina.[2]

To determine a household's share of credit, cost estimates based on preliminary designs are converted into unit costs and announced in open meetings. Projects often have to be scaled down to make them more affordable. With a cost figure in hand, each member household—usually in another open assembly—agrees to take a unit share in credit to cover the cost of proposed works. Each household must then identify two and sometimes three co-signers to secure the credit risk. In practice, this process can take weeks or months to sort out. The credit share of residents who are retired or otherwise impeded from earning income sufficient to cover unit costs is often underwritten by third parties.

Over time, project manuals and an extensive community education program in consciousness-raising (*concientización*) have been developed to familiarize neighborhood residents, bankers, local government officials, and private sector officials with the essential trust needed to offset risks. The program is continuously applied as new neighborhoods participate in MENPROSIF.

In a typical MENPROSIF project, the community pays more than 70 percent of the total project costs. The balance is mobilized from third parties. In some cases the municipality offers a lump sum to cover the poorest group of residents. In other cases, residents themselves, and on occasion a business or one of the builders interested in securing a contract, will contribute the needed amount.

The province plays a facilitating role. It convenes meetings, offers technical assistance, helps with design revisions and cost calculations, and arranges co-signing. Once the province has vouched that co-signing is complete, the MENPROSIF office issues a letter of credit. This signals a creditor (initially the provincial bank, later the World Bank, and in the future perhaps private financiers) to establish a line of credit. An account is opened in the name of the community, and the funds are made payable only to the contractor selected for the project.

---

2. Grameen Bank has reversed conventional banking practice by removing the need for collateral and creating a banking system based on mutual trust, accountability, participation, and creativity. The bank has provided credit to 2.4 million of the poorest borrowers in 41,000 villages in Bangladesh without any collateral (Yunus 1997).

Financing and Cost Recovery

Until the onset of a World Bank loan in the third year of MENPROSIF, the provincial bank, according to the governor's instructions, set aside financial resources for the program. On several occasions, when demand for funds exceeded supply, the governor injected additional funds from the provincial budget to support the line of credit. Other tasks of the provincial bank under MENPROSIF are to verify credit conditions, open and maintain accounts, print payment vouchers for beneficiaries, and disburse payments to contractors, among other things. For these services, and for running the commercial credit risk of nonpayment, the provincial bank charges a 5 percent spread over interest.

To recover costs and facilitate monthly payments, the neighborhood organization issues a payment booklet to each household. Payments may be made at any of the branch offices of the provincial bank and range from US$20 to $40 a month. This represents a substantial amount for poor households, whose monthly incomes average about US$250–300. Yet arrearages have never exceeded 30 percent over 60 days, and incomplete payments at project's end represent only a few percentage points of the total number of loans.

Contractor Competition and Selection

Neighborhood organizations play an active role in selecting contractors, often interviewing and sometimes negotiating with competing firms. MENPROSIF officers organize and facilitate this process by providing lists of contractors, calling meetings, and advising and coaching the community. The guaranteed payment arrangements, based on the *ahorros previos* system of earlier years, have been sufficient to attract building contractors from the many based in and around Mendoza. Some of these builders have operated for generations, and a few have expanded their businesses due to MENPROSIF. Many builders make it a point to be known in neighborhoods and have built up reputations with block organizations. About 10 to 15 building contractors bid routinely on MENPROSIF projects.

Over time, contractors have bid down the cost of works. Competition in bidding has resulted in costs substantially below those of early MENPROSIF projects and as much as 35 percent below comparable works previously carried out by the public works ministry. Contractor bidding has entered a new stage of competition, going beyond price alone. Increasingly, contractors are offering warranties of up to five years on their work. The small scale of works and the reputations of firms have made warranties more reliable.

Rapid Works Implementation

Execution of works proceeds quickly; most are completed within a month or two of the contract award. Much of this speed can be attributed to the transparent and, from the point of view of contractors, secure financing. Upon selection of a contractor, 40 percent of the total estimated cost of the project is disbursed in advance for acquisition of materials and site preparation. Because financial resources are protected from misuse (in an account in the community name), contractors are safeguarded from partisan interference and bureaucratic delays. Contractors face little risk of nonpayment except in cases of nonperformance.

At the same time, contractors cannot be paid until community representatives, often with the help of provincial or other authorities, have signed off on the completion of works. State regulatory authorities with competence in the relevant subsector (the municipal agency for solid waste, drainage, and sidewalks; a ministry for natural gas; the public sanitary works agency for water and sewerage) verify physical progress and ensure that the technical standards have been met. More recently, under the World Bank loan, the provincial bank has contracted engineers to inspect physical progress on a weekly basis.

Upon completion of the project, an inauguration ceremony is held in the community to transfer the assets. This act has both social and fiscal significance. First, the ceremony allows residents to celebrate their achievement, consolidate their system of mutual support, and mark the completion of their collective effort. Second, it is at the inauguration ceremony that the assets of any public works—water, sewerage, and gas lines, for instance—are turned over to the local government as required by law. Operating authorities of water and gas utilities routinely assume the costs of services for a period of six months to a year in recognition of the value added to capital assets by completion of the project.

Project Record and Diffusion

MENPROSIF's successful project implementation record has resulted in the program's diffusion throughout Mendoza.

Project Implementation Record

From its inception in 1991 through 1995, MENPROSIF completed or launched 274 projects in all 16 of the province's departments (see table 7-2.1).

Table 7-2.1. *Implementation of MENPROSIF, 1991–95*

Feature	Water	Sanitation	Gas	Other	Total
Number of families	1,393	17,038	25,590	4,763	49,054
Number of projects	31	85	114	44	274
Project cost (in US$000)	606	8,298	10,280	8,688	27,872

Note: Exchange rates have remained at parity with the dollar since 1991. They moved from 0.042 in 1989 and 0.487 in 1990. Inflation in 1993 was 7.4 percent.
Source: MENPROSIF, government of Mendoza.

It produced over 60 projects a year averaging US$100,000 each. Because of administrative or financial delays, program spending was below commitment, averaging around US$5 million per year. But provincial bank set-asides, or budgetary allocations for these amounts, have sometimes been insufficient or delayed, holding up effective implementation of works. World Bank financing of the Provincial Strengthening Project has offered a new, and in some ways more secure and predictable, financing source.

Two points should be noted about the implementation record of MENPROSIF. First, MENPROSIF's emphasis on sewerage and wastewater disposal reflects the strong popular concern for sanitation around the time of the cholera scare. Eligibility restrictions confined early projects to sanitation (collection only, not treatment). After the cholera danger passed, other works, such as gas distribution pipelines, drainage systems, sidewalks, and community centers, became eligible for the program. Second, the large number of works reflects a willingness to pay for services that governments and planners often assume are of low priority for low-income households. The large number of natural gas projects reflects the demand for heating during Mendoza's cold winters, during which temperatures frequently reach the freezing point.

Diffusion

The diffusion of MENPROSIF can be gauged in several ways. First, the news of, and enthusiasm about, the program has spread quickly to neighborhoods in virtually all municipalities in the province. Many neighborhood organizations soon undertook, or prepared for, a second round of projects (see box 7-2.4).

The confederation of the more than 130 neighborhood organizations in Mendoza is another measure of diffusion. Neighborhood organizations

---

Box 7-2.4. *The Neighborhood of Piccione*

Piccione, a neighborhood community of about 140 households on the out-skirts of Mendoza, is one of the most successful cases in the Mendoza Provincial Program for Basic Infrastructure (MENPROSIF). Under the program, Piccione constructed its own water system in 1991, added gas in 1994, and built a health and community center on a vacant lot in 1995. Community organizers operate their own water system under the regulatory guidance of provincial authorities. The community center and clinic were built adjacent to the water tower and pumps.

Piccione has raised enough recurrent financing from monthly membership dues to cover the costs of health care facilities and equipment for an examining room. The Piccione organization also pays for the services of a part-time physician who makes regular weekly calls at the community center. Emergency first aid and prenatal counseling are the main health concerns in Piccione, where most households are headed by women. The center is also used for meetings, parties, raffles, and office space.

---

formed an association capable of representing the interests of neighborhood groups before municipal and provincial authorities. The association of neighborhood organizations is chartered under a provincial law (Ley de Asociaciones Comunales sin Fines de Lucro, or the Law on Nonprofit Community Associations). The association has elected officials, bylaws, an income in dues of a few dollars per month from 86 of the neighborhood organizations, its own building, and a program for job creation and local economic development.

Municipalities within the province of Mendoza have been equally quick to take up the challenge of fostering community organization and to sponsor credit for the most vulnerable populations. Some municipalities have launched programs of their own, either modeled on MENPROSIF or extending its principles to smaller-scale works or to other sectors, including health care and education. These other programs do not involve the collective credit features of MENPROSIF, but they do build on collaborative arrangements among private, public, and "independent" sectors, such as the university. These arrangements provide, for example, financing of schools, clinics, or women's services (such as programs for battered women, early childhood education, and child care for working families).

Several provinces have inquired about MENPROSIF and how the program is organized but, to the authors' knowledge, these inquiries have not resulted in replication. This is partly because the Provincial Strengthening Project, financed by the World Bank and the Inter-American Development Bank, began in 1993 and filled a similar financing gap while meeting some of the need for financing of local infrastructure. At the same time, the incorporation of MENPROSIF into the World Bank project is in itself an interesting illustration of upward diffusion. The origins of this stage of MENPROSIF may be traced to a 1992 oral briefing about the program that Governor Gabrielli gave to President Menachem Menem's cabinet. The future head of the World Bank's project coordinating unit was present at the briefing and recognized immediately the good fit of MENPROSIF with the World Bank project. He acted quickly to gather more details and incorporate MENPROSIF as an eligible component of the project.

Outcomes and Impacts

No systematic, comparative data have been collected in this case study to demonstrate the reduction in costs under MENPROSIF. However, private contractors, provincial and municipal authorities, and neighborhood groups uniformly report cost savings in the range of 30–35 percent.

Private building contractors report a further benefit: the basis of competition for contracts has moved from price to quality of service. One contractor reported that competition is routinely expressed in terms of warranty on products and service; for instance, builders promise to repair breaks or correct faulty performance for a specified time period, usually three to five years. Potential health benefits are also possible—such as savings in lost work or school days, helping to prevent the spread of cholera, or even prevention of loss of life. But none of these benefits could be measured directly in this case study.

The MENPROSIF innovation has reinforced the spirit of reform in the province and produced ripple effects of its own. Participatory and collaborative arrangements have been structured in many other areas of public works. MENPROSIF can be seen as a vehicle for a new style of governance, one brought closer to neighborhood and community problems and responsive to local circumstances. A prominent feature of this innovation, like innovations launched in other cities for similar purposes, is the directness of the linkage forged between neighborhood works and service improvements on the one hand, and payments made by beneficiaries on the other hand. Customary fiscal models of government take the exchange of beneficiary payments for public goods and services as axiomatic, but four decades of centralized systems in Latin America and the Caribbean have broken the linkage between payment and services. MENPROSIF is but one of many innovations in the aftermath of decentralization in the region that has restored this critical fiscal connection.

The transfer of assets from beneficiary communities to local governments, a reverse of the customary model, underscores this change in community-government relations. The community participates more actively in the creation of assets than is normally the case in the modern concept of government. As central governments did in the case of self-help housing in the 1960s and 1970s, government agencies under MENPROSIF retain a regulatory and fostering role, even when they are unable to create public goods (Turner 1977). Neighborhoods in Mendoza are willing not only to undertake the risks of credit, but also to reverse the customary flow of social capital.

Subsequent Steps in MENPROSIF

The successful experience with MENPROSIF ripened conditions for extensions and refinements of the basic approach. Communities began to identify the need for longer-term credit to make payments easier for low-income households or to make it possible to undertake larger projects of broader impact. A second step could be a direct subsidy to reduce the costs of the most basic infrastructure for low-income families. The director of MENPROSIF felt that neighborhood organizations are best suited for, and capable of, identifying families eligible for a subsidy. The director proposed a mini-block grant (handled through account transfers) to cover the monthly payments of the poorest families.

A third step would be to make financing subject to stronger competitive terms and to further insulate the financing process from political interference. This is not to say that financing for these works should be entirely market-driven. Basic infrastructure, particularly sanitation works, is rarely competitive in purely financial terms with alternative uses of capital. But it should be possible to inculcate a deeper financial discipline and achieve greater efficiency in program execution by adopting a system of private banks to administer credit at the local level and by mobilizing municipal counterparts for neighborhood projects.

A fourth step would be to decrease the province's role in the program. The state has played an important fostering and custodial role to nurture the program into maturity. But it is evident from the widespread recognition enjoyed by MENPROSIF, and the strong demand for it, that neighborhood groups themselves, acting with individual municipalities, can do much more on their own to launch and implement projects.

Conclusion

Most of the unusual conditions in the social and political environment of Mendoza that helped precipitate MENPROSIF—the political renewal, the cholera scare, and other circumstances—lie beyond the scope of policy choices available under ordinary circumstances. Although the unusual conditions of Mendoza cannot be replicated, they should be noted as contributing factors to successful innovation, even if this only means recognizing that the existence of special circumstances creates a rare opportunity for innovation. At the same time, scores of new leaders are emerging at the local level with and without electoral reform, and this new generation of leaders has launched an impressive assortment of innovations, many of them involving community participation. These circumstances present a propitious environment of receptive clients for tested innovations.

What factors can play a role in replicating the MENPROSIF experience? Several are within the scope of policy manipulation.

- **Simplicity of social organization.** MENPROSIF began at the grassroots level with simple, single-purpose organizations formed around common needs. The community organizations have typically involved 100 to 300 families living in a contiguous neighborhood. The organizing principle is not an abstract political ideology or larger social concern, but rather the desire to create concrete improvements that can be seen, are subject to verification, and are linked to payments.
- **Social relations.** Correlatively, the architects of MENPROSIF were acutely aware of the importance of the organized community, and they possessed skills and experience in promoting organization and managing community relations. The organizational tools and techniques that were adopted and refined were critical inputs for the success of MENPROSIF.
- **Voluntary organizations and social communication.** World Bank experience with participation points to the same conclusion: voluntary organizations and social communication, along with particularly extensive involvement of beneficiaries in key aspects of programs,

are decisive in program success. MENPROSIF also teaches that unorganized communities, like leaderless communities, cannot be treated indifferently. Assistance has been offered only to neighborhoods that are ready—that is, organized. MENPROSIF has not required beneficiaries to participate equally in every aspect of the project cycle, as some project experience (low-cost sanitation, rural water supply, rural irrigation) appears to advocate. Beneficiaries have organized themselves; divulged information; and helped decide what to build, whether to assume debt, and whom to select as contractors. However, communities have not been involved in all policy and design questions, or even in manual labor.

- **Champion and visionary.** As reported elsewhere (for example, Hopkins 1995; Leeuw, Rist, and Sonnichsen 1995), a champion or visionary can visualize a new way of doing things and convert this vision into practical steps. In the case of MENPROSIF, the governor and his staff, particularly the director of MENPROSIF, have served as the champions. It is hard to imagine the successful outcome of MENPROSIF without the driving force of leadership, and hard to imagine this driving force without the larger imperative of political reform experienced in Argentina and Mendoza in the early 1990s.
- **Sustained commitment.** An extension of the importance of leadership, particularly in local governments, is that a leader must be able to convincingly articulate commitment and sustain public trust by periodic doses of direct contact with participating neighborhoods. The governor who took office in January 1996 had belonged to the Gabrielli administration and was therefore familiar with, and probably supportive of, MENPROSIF. It appeared unlikely, however, that MENPROSIF would continue to enjoy success unless the new governor demonstrated sustained commitment to the program.
- **Comprehensiveness of responsibility.** The architects of MENPROSIF were convinced by their experience with the Argentine public sector that division of labor, even within a single ministry, was a recipe for failure. Divisions of labor across different ministries and among governments posed an even greater threat to the smooth and timely operation of small-scale local works. Nor was consolidation of all the key phases of the project cycle sufficient to guarantee the success of MENPROSIF. Different actors performed their functions in different phases of the program, but all worked within a coherent and mutually interdependent system.

- **Appropriate scale.** Scale of operations is critical, especially for neighborhood works. The small, 200- to 300-family, block-by-block scale of MENPROSIF is important for several reasons. It encourages sustained personal contact between program officials and leaders, and hence makes legitimacy easier to achieve. Small scale also fosters a sense of partnership between neighborhood residents and program officers. Increasing the face-to-face contact among neighbors engaged in a project tends to heighten mutual responsibility, and this, in turn, is key to managing the risks for community members who undertake credit obligations. Finally, small works get built faster.
- **Start in a harbor.** The pilot community idea reflects a well-known practice in social action: innovations need an incubator. As an incubator, the MENPROSIF case selected a small community with a high confidence index between participants and sponsors.

References

Hopkins, Elwood. 1995. "The Life Cycle of Urban Innovations," vol. 1. Urban Management Program Working Paper Series. World Bank, Washington, D.C.

Leeuw, F., R. Rist, and R. Sonnichsen, eds. 1994. *Can Governments Learn? Comparative Perspectives on Evaluation and Organizational Learning.* New Brunswick, N.J.: Transaction Publishers.

Turner, John F. C. 1977. *Housing by People, Towards Autonomy in Building Environments.* New York: Pantheon.

Yunus, Mohammed. 1997. *Banker to the Poor. The Autobiography of Mohammad Yunus.* New York: Public Affairs.

World Bank. 1991. *Poverty Reduction Handbook.* Washington, D.C.

8

Public Service Provision

8-1

Innovative Urban Transport in Curitiba, Brazil

Roberto Santoro, Government of Parana
Josef Leitmann, World Bank

The Brazilian city of Curitiba has been successfully innovating in the transport sector for more than 25 years by challenging conventional wisdom: the city favors public transport over private automobiles, selects appropriate rather than capital-intensive technologies, and pursues strategic principles rather than rigid master plans. These innovations are rooted in a forward-looking, flexible master plan that matured during an incubation period of institutional development. The innovations have been bolstered by continued political support across municipal administrations and by the positive effects of Curitiba's relations with the central government and with other cities.

Curitiba's transport innovations evolved in several ways at the same time. The city developed its structural axis road system and carefully integrated it with land-use planning. The integrated public transport system that evolved relies on buses and public-private partnership. These transport innovations were implemented with the help of innovative enforcement measures and transport-oriented land-use policy.

Despite the challenges of rapid growth and inflation, Curitiba has met the typical developmental challenges in an environmentally sensitive manner (see box 8.1.1). Beginning in the 1960s, most Brazilian cities built highways and established the predominance of the automobile; Curitiba took a different path. This case study examines the development of Curitiba's transport system, which consists of more than a dozen innovations, including:

Box 8-1.1. *An Overview of Curitiba*

Curitiba is a southern Brazilian city of 1.6 million inhabitants (2.3 million in the metropolitan area). From the 1950s to the 1970s, it was Brazil's fastest growing city. The consequences of this rapid growth were typical: unemployment, squatter settlements, congestion, and environmental decay. Curitiba's poverty profile and rate of inflation were similar to those of other cities in the south and southeast of Brazil.

- Conscientious integration of land-use planning, road design, and public transport
- Joint public-private operation of public transit systems
- Capacity-expanding measures (special buses, boarding stations, and advance ticket sales)
- Emphasis on equity and affordability (measures to keep costs down and ensure high-quality service to the poor and to the less-populated areas of the city).

Although these innovations are part of a sophisticated and complex system, they had humble origins in the realms of city and land-use planning. Rooted in a forward-looking, flexible master plan, the innovations have been bolstered by continued political support across municipal administrations and by the positive effects of Curitiba's relations with the central government and with other cities.

The Planning Process

The first formal attempt to respond to urban growth in Curitiba was the Agache Plan, designed by French urban planner Alfred Agache in 1943. The plan proposed a well-defined central area surrounded by residential zones, with a traffic system composed of concentric (ring) roads linked to the central area by radial avenues—that is, the spoke-and-wheel design. This design reflected a classic planning concept but failed to predict the private automobile boom that began in Brazil during the 1950s. The plan was not implemented, except for the construction of radial avenues, mainly due to lack of public funds. The city subsequently grew beyond the physical limits envisioned by the Agache Plan.

The Agache Plan's main legacy was consciousness raising. It generated the perception that planning could help solve urban growth–related problems. Acting on this perception, the city government in 1964 commissioned the Preliminary Urban Plan, which later became the Curitiba Master Plan. Following a competition organized by city hall and local professionals, the Curitiba Master Plan was developed by a consortium of Brazilian consulting firms. The city then created the Curitiba Research and Urban Planning Institute (Instituto de Pesquisa e Planificacao Urbana, or IPPUC) in 1965 to implement the master plan.

The central tenet of the Curitiba Master Plan, which laid the groundwork for a range of transport innovations, held that commerce, services, and residences should expand in a linear manner from the city center along structural axes. The plan had the following guiding objectives:

- To change the radial urban growth trend to a linear one by integrating the road network, transport, and land use
- To decongest the central business district while preserving its historic center
- To manage, not prevent, population growth
- To provide economic support for urban development
- To support greater mobility by improving infrastructure.

Thus, the Curitiba Master Plan proposed not only a traffic management system but also its integration with land use to limit the physical expansion of the central city.

The planning process consisted of two important phases: an incubation period and an era of action. During incubation (1965–70), the IPPUC had time to further develop the ideas contained in the master plan. The IPPUC also served as a breeding ground for many actors who played key roles in the implementation phase. For example, Jaime Lerner served as president of the IPPUC in 1968–69 and later became the mayor of Curitiba. The era of action (1971 to the present) has been characterized by the political will and the commitment of the public administration to get things done. During this era the established practice has emphasized implementation led by city hall, with strategic coordination and guidance from the IPPUC.

The Political Setting

Wise planning and institutional development has assisted Curitiba's capacity to innovate. Political continuity and the peculiar nature of cross-jurisdictional relations has also played a role. During the era of action, the city benefited from a succession of mayors, beginning with Jaime Lerner in 1971, who consolidated, maintained, and added to key innovations (see box 8-1.2). At the outset of the action era, the mass media were under censorship, and public participation was minimal throughout the country. Public involvement gradually increased after 1979 to a point at which most programs in Curitiba depended on stakeholder participation.

The relationship between the city and other levels of government also changed over time and influenced Curitiba's approach to urban development. At the federal level, Brazil endured a military dictatorship from 1964 to 1979. This had two effects on innovation in Curitiba. First, cities became financially dependent on the state and federal governments, making them vulnerable to changing macroeconomic and political conditions. Curitiba responded by developing creative and self-financing programs, enabling it to gradually implement its own ideas without assistance from higher levels of government. Second, the military government gradually replaced import substitution policies with inflows of foreign capital and major infrastructure projects, including an increase in urban investment. Most Brazilian cities took advantage of that investment to build motorways and viaducts, thus establishing the predominance of the private car. Curitiba, however, developed an alternative course of action.

At the local level, Curitiba became part of a metropolitan region known as Area Metropolitana de Curitiba, created in the mid 1970s. In general, the metropolitan level of government in Brazil failed to bridge the horizontal gaps between local mayors and the vertical distance between mayors and state governments. Curitiba became an exception because of demographic and economic advantages: its population was more than twice that of the

---

Box 8-1.2. *Nontransport Innovations in Curitiba*

In addition to the structural axes; integration of road planning, land use, and public transport; key innovations during Mayor Jaime Lerner's terms included:

- Creation of the Curitiba Industrial City
- Novel waste recycling programs
- An integrated park creation–flood control program
- New sewage treatment
- Renovation of historical, cultural, and architectural sites
- Programs to educate and protect disadvantaged children.

combined population of all other municipalities surrounding it. Also, its status as the state capital lent it economic weight. Because of these advantages, Curitiba managed to achieve a higher degree of coordination with neighboring municipalities than the Brazilian norm.

Evolution of Innovative Urban Transport

Most modern cities have implicitly or explicitly geared urban growth strategies to meet the demands of the automobile. Private transport strongly influences the physical layout of cities, including the location of housing, commerce, and industry, and the patterns of human interaction. Urban planners design around highways, parking structures, and rush-hour traffic patterns. Urban engineers attempt to control these social and economic forces within the confines of the city limits, often at the expense of environmental quality. Urban officials typically rely on expensive technological solutions to developmental challenges.

In addition, most cities grow in a concentric fashion, annexing new districts at the periphery while progressively increasing the density of central commercial and business districts. Congestion intensifies with densification and increased commuter travel from the periphery to the center in private cars. Curitiba, however, with investment in mass transit, took a different approach.

The Road Network

HISTORICAL DEVELOPMENT. During the 1970s, city authorities began to implement an urban design structure that emphasized linear growth along structural axes to keep businesses, industries, and residences accessible to one another (see figure 8-1.1). Simultaneously, land-use legislation was enacted to guide this growth. The planned road network and public transport system that resulted have probably been the most influential elements in forming the present shape of the city.

Since then, Curitiba has encouraged urban growth along five main axes with "structural" roads. Each axis consists of a three-part road system (see figure 8-1.2). The central road has two restricted bus lanes in the middle for express buses, flanked by two lanes for local traffic. On each side of this central road, one block away, are high-capacity one-way roads, one for traffic flowing into the city, the other for traffic flowing out of the city. In the areas adjacent to each axis, land-use legislation has encouraged high-density housing, together with services and commerce.

Figure 8-1.1. *Evolution of Curitiba's Integrated Transport Network*

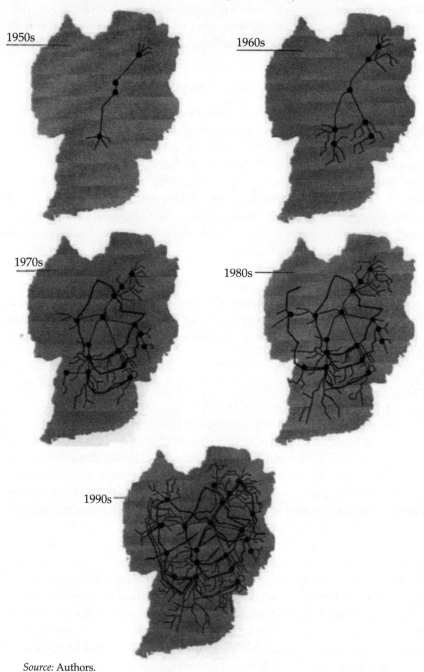

Source: Authors.

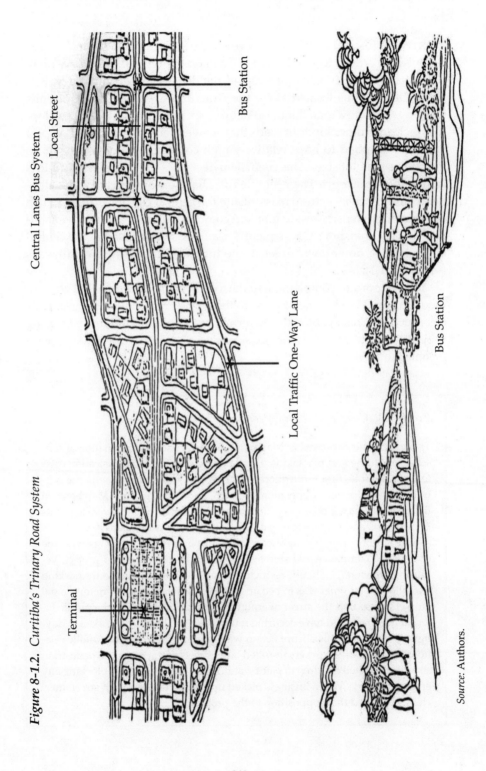

Figure 8-1.2. Curitiba's Trinary Road System

Central Lanes Bus System

Local Street

Bus Station

Local Traffic One-Way Lane

Terminal

Bus Station

Source: Authors.

INTEGRATION OF LAND USE WITH THE ROAD SYSTEM. Land use in Curitiba is zoned according to two basic parameters: the type of use (residential, commercial, industrial, or mixed) and the density of permitted development. On the sites located along the structural axes, legislation permits buildings to have a total floor area of up to six times the plot size. Developments close to other kinds of roads that are well served by public transport are also permitted to have relatively high coefficients (floor space up to four times the plot size). This coefficient decreases the farther a land site is from public transport. These simple rules have encouraged new development along each structural axis outside the central city, ensuring a match between high-density residential and commercial areas and the availability of public transport. Consequently, traffic has been eased in the central city, allowing downtown streets to be turned into pedestrian walkways (see box 8-1.3).

As an important complement to the road system, the municipal government acquired land along or close to the new transport axes prior to their construction. This enabled the government to build high-density housing projects close to the transport axes, providing housing for 17,000 lower-income families.

Box 8-1.3. *Creating the First Pedestrian Street*

To reach political consensus, Mayor Jaime Lerner used a combination of consensus building and risk taking. For example, when his administration tried to implement its first innovation—creation of a pedestrian zone in the central business district—opposition arose from powerful groups. Merchants in the affected area feared a loss of business if shoppers could not drive to points of purchase, and motorists threatened to ignore the traffic ban.

The administration sought consensus through many meetings with the chamber of commerce and storeowners to clarify the proposed project. Vehicle flows were gradually restricted to parallel streets, and only parking was allowed on what was to become the pedestrian street. Then, municipal workers closed off the street overnight to all traffic, avoiding the public interference that could have occurred if the move had been undertaken in daylight. The risks of this abrupt action were minimized through a public relations measure: city workers unrolled large sheets of paper on the pedestrian street and invited children to paint watercolors, thus effectively blocking any errant motorists. When business picked up along the pedestrian street, merchants dropped their opposition to the project.

Another important element of Curitiba's road system is the use of "road hierarchies." Each road is assigned a function in relation to its location and importance. There are the "structural" roads along the five axes described previously and "priority" roads that connect traffic to the structural roads. "Collector" streets have commercial activity along them with all forms of traffic, and "connector" streets link the structural roads to the industrial area. These four types of roads form the structure of Curitiba's road network.

System Development. Despite having some 500,000 cars (more per capita than any other major Brazilian city), Curitiba does not have a traffic problem. When the present transport system was initiated in 1974, city officials made a conscious decision to continue relying entirely on buses rather than accommodating automobiles, as did other Brazilian cities. A central lane was reserved for buses along the main axes of the city. New bus lines were created and expanded as the city grew (see box 8-1.4).

Box 8-1.4. *Timeline: Highlights in the Evolution of Curitiba's Public Transport System*

1974   Implementation of the first two express bus lanes along the northern and southern structural axes.

1978   Three new express busways added along structural axes.

Introduction of a computerized traffic control system.

1979   Introduction of a standard fare paid by all bus users. This "social fare" benefits those who live on the city periphery (predominantly low-income groups), as shorter journeys subsidize longer ones.

Introduction of circular interdistrict bus lines to complement the express busways.

1982   Opening of a new connection between the city center and the industrial area and improvement of the interdistrict routes.

1991   Introduction of the Rapid Bus System (direct lines) using boarding tubes.

1992   Introduction of bi-articulated buses.

1995   Operation of first "surface metro" line.

Curitiba's Integrated Transport Network (ITN) became the first—and only—example in Brazil of a mass transport system in which the bus routes and land use were more important than private vehicles.

Curitiba relies on buses rather than a more capital-intensive solution to public transport, because express buses on exclusive busways are far cheaper than subways or light rail. They also represent a more flexible solution for a medium-size city (see table 8-1.1). Another comparative advantage of the surface bus system is that it can be planned and built to operate on the existing street network (this is also generally true for light rail systems).

In the ITN, all lines interlink, allowing connections in up to four different directions at each transfer point for one flat fare. The ITN has grown to cover nearly 800 kilometers and provides service for 1.5 million trips daily. The structural axes cover 56 kilometers of roads exclusively devoted to express bus traffic. These roads are complemented by 300 kilometers of feeder lines, 185 kilometers of interdistrict lines, and 250 kilometers of direct lines. The fleet consists of 1,650 conventional 80-passenger buses and 160 articulated (double length) and bi-articulated (triple length) buses. Box 8-1.5 describes the economic benefits and environmental impacts of the ITN.

Approximately 90 percent of trips by public transport in Curitiba are made on the ITN, with the remainder on conventional lines (local and intermunicipal). The ITN consists of 20 transfer terminals and four types of lines:

- **Express:** 313 vehicles (both articulated and standard) that circulate in exclusive bus lanes and carry 600,000 passengers daily.
- **Feeder:** 310 standard buses that connect residential areas in the suburbs to transfer terminals and carry 300,000 passengers daily.

Table 8-1.1. *Relative Costs of Public Transport Options*

Option	Capital cost (US$ million/km)[a]
Underground subway system	90–100
Light rail system	16
"Surface metro"	0.9
Curitiba's direct bus system (using boarding tubes)	0.2

a. These do not include the economic costs related to construction of subway or light rail systems, or the capital costs of road building in the case of the bus system.
Source: Municipality of Curitiba.

Box 8-1.5. *Economic Benefits and Environmental Impacts of Curitiba's Integrated Transport Network*

The low standard fare of the Integrated Transport Network (ITN) contributes to reducing family expenditure on transport. Low-income residents of Curitiba spend only about 10 percent of their income on transport, which is relatively low for Brazil.

The ITN improves productivity by alleviating congestion of main arteries and speeding the movement of people, goods, and services throughout the city. The direct lines save the average passenger one hour per day in commuting time. The suburbs have become more important for commerce, education, services, and leisure because they are easily accessible via the ITN. At the same time, the downtown area has maintained its economic attractiveness, partly because of reduced congestion and easy access.

The ITN also generates private sector activity. For example, most of the investment for the "surface metro" was made by the company that held the concession for the line where it was first implemented. The city government invested US$2 million to install the 30 tubular boarding stations and restructure the transfer terminals. The private company spent US$9 million to acquire the new vehicles needed.

Integrating the road network, public transport, and land management has resulted in a more energy-efficient, greener city. From an airplane or the highest building in the city, it is possible to see the borders between different residential zones, distinguish commercial collecting roads from neighborhood ones, and view the separation between the built-up line of "structural sectors" defining urban growth and the protected green areas redirecting it.

Positive environmental changes are directly linked to urban management in the transport sector. Curitiba's public transport system is used by about 1.5 million passengers each day, or about 75 percent of commuters, which is much higher than other Brazilian cities; comparable ridership rates for public transport are 57 percent in Rio de Janeiro and 45 percent in São Paulo. Twenty-eight percent of direct route bus users previously traveled by car. The increased use of public transport has helped save up to 25 percent of fuel consumption citywide, with related reductions in automotive emissions. Curitiba's public transport system is directly responsible for the city having one of the lowest rates of ambient air pollution in Brazil.

Due to a good working relationship with the private sector, Curitiba has one of the newest bus fleets in Brazil, with an average of three years of use. The average for other Brazilian cities is around eight years. Curitiba's newer buses

(Box continues on the following page.)

Box 8-1.7 *(continued)*

and fare structure guarantee financial resources for proper maintenance of buses and help reduce the amount of air pollution from circulating buses. Recently, new engines that produce just half the emissions of the original engines have been installed in half the fleet.

Curitiba has created a positive feedback loop in its public transport system: increased ridership generates more resources, which are then reinvested in the system, improving the quality of service and causing even more people to use it. The International Institute for Energy Conservation (based in Washington, D.C.) gave Curitiba its 1990 global energy efficiency award in recognition of the environmental benefits of Curitiba's transport system.

- **Interdistrict:** 150 standard buses that connect the city's suburbs in a circular route without passing through the downtown area. They also connect the bus terminals with each other, and they serve 300,000 passengers daily.
- **Direct:** 156 specially designed vehicles that stop only at the tubular boarding stations. They operate along 14 lines and serve 300,000 passengers daily.

Buses in the conventional (feeder) system operate at 17 kilometers per hour, those in the express system operate at 20 kilometers per hour on exclusive lanes, and those in the direct system reach an average speed of 30 kilometers per hour. Buses are color-coded: the express buses are red, interdistrict buses are green, and the conventional buses are orange and yellow.

A key feature of the ITN is the ease with which passengers can transfer for a single fare. Large bus terminals situated at the end of the five express busways (see figure 8-1.2) allow passengers to transfer to interdistrict, feeder, or intermunicipal buses. Along each express route, medium-size bus terminals are located approximately every two kilometers and are equipped with newspaper stands, public telephones, post offices, and small commercial facilities.

The direct bus system, an innovation introduced in 1991, features fewer stops than express buses and runs along the one-way routes on the central roads that form the structural axes. In this system, passengers pay before boarding the buses in special raised tubular stations, which are platforms set at the same height as the bus floors. This greatly reduces boarding and unloading times. A bus system with these "boarding tubes" can carry three times as many passengers per hour as a conventional bus operating on a normal street (see figure 8-1.2). The boarding tubes also eliminate the need for a crew on the bus to collect fares, which frees up space for more passengers. In this way, one of Curitiba's direct buses does the work of several traditional ones, and at a faster speed (see table 8-1.2).

Officials constantly explore new initiatives to improve the system. Automatic fare collection, articulated buses, peak-load demand management, and priority traffic lights for buses (which the bus drivers operate themselves) have optimized the system's operation and resulted in lower operating costs. A fleet of 27 bi-articulated buses, each with a capacity for 270 passengers, began operation in 1992. These have five lateral doors for passenger entry or exit and significantly decrease boarding and unloading times, especially when linked to the new boarding tubes. The large vehicles were custom-built by Volvo's facility at the Curitiba Industrial City. To manage peak-load demand, Curitiba's administration has instituted different schedules for schools, commerce, and services, especially in the city's central area. This has helped spread demand for transport over a longer period each day, resulting in less congestion, faster travel times, and less crowded public transport.

Table 8-1.2. *Capacity of Bus Options in Curitiba*

Bus configuration	Capacity (passengers/hour)
Conventional bus on average street (80 passengers)	X
Conventional bus on busway (80 passengers)	2X
Double (articulated bus) on busway (150 passengers)	2.5X
Direct route with boarding tubes (110 passengers)	3.2X

Note: These figures are a simplification of operational data, taking into account the capacity of the vehicles and their respective commercial running time.

Sources: Muncipality of Curitiba; interview with Mayor Jaime Lerner.

In 1995, the first line of a "surface metro" was introduced. This system consists of a direct route serviced entirely by bi-articulated buses. The buses run along a 16-kilometer line featuring 30 tube stations for boarding and unloading passengers every 500 meters. The line has three transfer terminals where passengers can connect with other lines.

After years of successful experimentation and change, both the municipal government and the citizens have become proud of their spirit of environmentally responsible innovation. In addition, Curitiba tries to live up to its reputation as the "Ecological Capital of Brazil" by planting trees, creating parks, and striving for clean air (Rabinovitch and Leitmann 1996; Ravazzani and Fagani 1999). These factors—a history of success, civic pride, and external expectations—have made it easier to introduce multiple or successive innovations over time. In addition, many of the innovations have resulted in welcome improvements in the quality of urban life, such as less time spent stuck in traffic.

MANAGEMENT AND FINANCE. The ITN is managed by Urbanization of Curitiba (Urbanizaçao de Curitiba, or URBS), a parastatal company created by the city in 1963. Its responsibilities include calculating bus timetables, developing new bus routes, determining the necessary number of buses, monitoring the performance of the system, training drivers and conductors, and responding to suggestions and complaints from the bus users. The URBS also manages the Curitiba Taxi System, the municipal and intermunicipal bus terminals, the public parking system, and community paving programs.

The bus system in Curitiba is operated by private companies that receive licenses for specific routes. The licensed companies must abide by regulations developed by the URBS and IPPUC. The procedure for payment is simple: the daily revenue collected by each bus in Curitiba is immediately deposited in a bank account managed by the URBS. The companies receive their revenue 10 days afterward, according to the number of kilometers that they have operated. A 1990 law establishes that the city can use the revenue collected from the bus system only to pay for the system.

To ensure private sector accountability, the URBS monitors the system according to (a) the number of passengers, based on daily readings of sealed turnstiles; and (b) the number of kilometers operated, based on the length of routes, odometer readings, on-off surveys, and 24-hour surveillance of bus depots. This supervision also helps the URBS calculate the bus fare. The calculation of the fare takes into account operational, administrative, and capital costs, as presented in box 8-1.6.

Box 8-1.6. *Costs Used in Bus Fare Calculation*

1.   Operational Costs
      1.1   Dependent costs
             - Fuel
             - Lubricants
             - Vehicle depreciation
      1.2   Maintenance costs
             - Personnel
             - Parts and accessories
      1.3   Personnel costs
             - Drivers
             - Conductors
             - Supervisors
             - Porters
             - Uniforms
2.   Administrative Costs
      - Personnel
      - Equipment depreciation
      - Payments for equipment and installations
      - Payments for garages and repairs
      - Depreciation of buildings and infrastructure
3.   Capital Costs
      - Payments to private capital (1 percent of investments in new buses
        per month)
      - Amortization of private capital (depreciation of the bus fleet)

Source: Urbanization of Curitiba.

The flat fare of the Curitiba bus system varied between US$0.20 and US$0.25, as of the mid 1990s. It is one of the cheapest urban fares in Brazil, considering that the typical rider averages 2.4 transfers per day for one bus fare.

The monthly rate of return to the private bus companies is 1 percent of the capital invested in the bus fleet, which represents approximately 11 percent of the fare. The other component of the companies' profits is 3 percent of administrative costs for equipment and infrastructure, representing 0.39 percent of the fare.

Operating costs and fares are affected by Brazil's traditionally high rate of inflation. (For example, inflation averaged 25 percent a month in 1992.)

Even under these circumstances the bus system has operated successfully; however, fares must constantly increase to cope with inflating operating costs. Bus fares are a result not only of technical calculations but also of political negotiations. The bus companies exert pressure on the city to increase fares as often as possible, whereas riders demand constant or lower fares. City hall and the URBS have to contend with these two competing political forces and negotiate bus fare increases that are affordable to the public and profitable for the private sector.

The payment-by-kilometer system has many advantages. The quality of the service is regulated by the public sector, whereas investment originates with the private sector. The system minimizes financial risks for the private sector. Finally, the calculation of the revenue from fares is transparent, and collection is easily monitored.

Land Use and Enforcement

Curitiba's land-use policy is based on legislatively designated special areas that merit integration with the transport system or require special protection. These areas are geographically bounded by roads, zones within a district, or district boundaries. Box 8-1.7 outlines their main characteristics.

The basic philosophy for enforcement of innovations in the road system, public transport, and land use is that any change should be enacted in a self-enforcing way. Curitiba has used a variety of innovative instruments to direct urban growth by integrating land-use legislation and the public-transport network. These have included administrative, economic, physical, and informational tools for enforcement.

Regulatory and Planning Tools

- The land-use legislation requires that the structural sectors have a floor-to-area ratio of six, further enforcing urban growth and density alongside the structural axes.
- Anyone wishing to obtain or renew a permit to engage in commercial activity must provide the city's Urbanism Department with information needed to project traffic-generation figures, infrastructure needs, parking requirements, and other relevant impacts.

Economic Incentives

- Within the historic zone, owners of historical buildings can enter into a market of development rights, swapping or selling the rights to

Box 8-1.7. *Land-Use Designations in Curitiba*

The city of Curitiba is divided into several land-use designations:

- **Structural sectors.** Composed of the five structural axes in Curitiba. These accommodate segregated lanes for the express buses, high-density housing, commerce on the ground floors of new buildings, and services. They represent a linear extension of the central business district toward the north, south, east, west, and southeast (see figure 8-1.1), following the trinary road system (see figure 8-1.2).
- **Traditional center.** New commercial buildings are prohibited. Incentives are given to land-use conversion for housing. New parking areas are not allowed. An inner-ring road and pedestrian areas have been designated.
- **Priority areas for pedestrians.** Motor vehicles have partial or no access. No supermarkets, street parking, or parking garages are allowed. Banking, insurance, or financial institutions cannot occupy the ground floor of buildings in these areas. No new buildings with more than five floors can be constructed.
- **Historic zone.** All buildings in this area are classified into three categories: historical buildings, structures of general historical interest, and buildings without special historical value. Historical buildings may not be altered outside or inside without permission from public authorities. There are tax incentives for preservation of buildings with historical value. Buildings without special historical value may be demolished, provided the plot is used for a new building with no more than three floors. Construction projects, advertising, and other displays on buildings in the historic zone need to be approved by the Curitiba Research and Urban Planning Institute. Only the following uses are allowed: housing, cultural institutions, art galleries, restaurants, cinemas, theaters, small-scale commerce, and bars.
- **Connecting road zones.** Formed by the five axes that link structural sectors to the Curitiba Industrial City. These zones serve as small- and medium-scale service axes with medium residential density in the vicinity of the Industrial City. New development for this area must reserve 35 percent of public land for streets, public and community equipment (such as parks and benches), infrastructure, green space, and protected streambeds (if applicable).
- **Collecting road sectors.** Stretches of streets that "collect" and distribute the main traffic. They tend to be streets where the bus routes are located, offering more flexibility for commercial activities and mixed-land use.

(Box continues on the following page.)

Box 8-1.7 (continued)

- **River basins.** Linear stretches of land alongside rivers and streams that are preserved because of their particular importance for the hydraulic system of the region. Curitiba does not allow the building of roads, industrial plants, or warehouses in these areas. They are normally reserved for bicycle paths and greenbelts connecting parks.
- **Santa Felicidade area.** A traditionally Italian district of ethnic significance. The district also possesses substantial vegetation in the form of native woods. Legislation prohibits buildings of more than two floors and establishes compatible land uses.
- **Other special zones.** The Curitiba Industrial City, military facilities, universities and other educational areas, and green spaces or parks.

---

develop property to another area of the city. This means that, on the one hand, the law forbids owners of historical buildings to tear them down but, on the other hand, enforcement is achieved through a compensation mechanism.
- In specific areas of the city where existing infrastructure can cope with extra density, construction companies can "buy" permission to build up to two extra floors beyond the legal limit. Companies make payment for this permission to the municipal housing agency with money or land to be used for low-income housing, based on 75 percent of the market value of the extra floor area. This simple mechanism has generated land and resources for low-income housing in Curitiba.

PHYSICAL INSTRUMENTS

- Bicycle paths and bus lanes are physically segregated to maintain safe, dedicated routes.

INFORMATIONAL TOOLS

- Within minutes, city hall can provide information to any citizen about the building potential of any plot. A transparent information system helps avoid land speculation and has proven essential to the city budget, as the property tax is the city's main source of revenue.

Obstacles and Opportunities

Curitiba's innovations in urban transport have overcome a range of obstacles: the predominant thinking about how cities should respond to rapid
growth; the threats to long-term transport planning posed by short-term
political decisions; and the lack of finance. As discussed earlier in this
case study, conventional wisdom in the early 1970s favored the private
automobile over public transport, capital-intensive high technology over
more humble solutions, and master planning over strategic innovation.
Political continuity is difficult in Brazil, because mayors cannot serve two
successive terms in office. Thus, there is always the risk that a new administration will disregard the initiatives of the previous one and focus on short-
term actions rather than long-term solutions.

Municipal financing during most of the era of action has had to come
from the federal or state levels of government, making Curitiba dependent
on resources it does not control. The municipality has taken two steps to
finance the transport system itself. First, it created the Compensation Fund
in 1978, which allowed for a single bus fare and resulted in an expansion of
service, as more profitable lines subsidized less profitable ones. Second,
the municipality strategically invested in particular innovations in partnership with the private sector. For example, when the federal government
stopped making funds available for fleet renewal in 1986, the city purchased
89 articulated buses and distributed them among the operating companies
that did not have capital resources for renewing their fleets. City officials
have consulted private operators about new innovations and cosigned
loans for fleet renovation, with the private operators using their own assets (garages and buses) as collateral. Actions like these have kept interest
rates down and ensured continued cooperation from the private sector.

External finance has also played a critical role in getting key innovations underway. After 1979, a US$16 million World Bank loan was used
to build 13 important suburban transfer terminals and pave 150 kilometers of roads designed to be part of the feeder system and the interdistrict
circular system.

Horizontal and Vertical Diffusion of Innovations

Increasingly, other municipalities have studied Curitiba's system, offering
the possibility of a multiplier effect from technical interchange. Technical
planning teams from Brazilian and foreign cities have visited Curitiba at

the rate of two or three per week, and some of these teams have begun implementing similar projects in their cities. A few examples of ideas first developed in Curitiba and then spread to other Brazilian cities are segregated bus lanes, pedestrian streets, gradual development of land-use legislation, the Compensation Fund, and integrated surface transport networks. In addition, officials from cities as diverse as New York, Moscow, Buenos Aires, and Lagos have visited Curitiba and learned from its transport system. As an example, Cape Town has developed a vision for its metropolitan area that is explicitly based on Curitiba's system of structural axes.

The success of urban transport innovations has spurred Curitiba to implement many other successful experiments. For example, 70 percent of households participate in the recycling of municipal solid waste through two novel programs. From the mid 1970s to the mid 1990s, green space increased by a hundredfold per capita (from 0.5 to 50 square meters per citizen) despite rapid population growth; the city explicitly designed this expansion to benefit its flood control program and its diverse ethnic groups. Water and park development policies are integrated, and the city uses innovative sewage treatment to meet the needs of rapidly growing peri-urban areas. Curitiba has also facilitated industrial pollution control by creating the Curitiba Industrial City, an industrial park that attracts low-impact enterprises. Ecology is integrated into many facets of Curitiba's progressive education system for children and adults.

Lessons Learned and Next Steps

Curitiba's experiences with innovation in transport management demonstrate principles that may be applicable elsewhere. The municipality may benefit from the continuing momentum of its transport innovations to find solutions to its remaining problems.

Lessons Learned

ESTABLISH AN URBAN GROWTH PATTERN. Cities should establish an urban growth pattern in conjunction with a deliberate decision to integrate different elements of urban development. Local officials must be aware of their own growth trends and should make conscious technical, political, and economic decisions in response. Many urban problems linked to uncontrolled physical expansion (for instance, increasing infrastructure and service costs, loss of agricultural land, or inadequate open space) can be avoided by correct decisions at the right time. Cities should give top priority to public transport rather than to private cars, and to bicycles and pedestrians rather than to motorized vehicles. Curitiba's decision to give less attention to meeting the needs of private motorized traffic has reduced the use of cars. Curitiba has been at the forefront of integrated urban development: it was the first city in Brazil to implement not only pedestrian streets but also a whole pedestrian network. Curitiba was also the first with segregated bus lanes and a trinary road system.

CHOOSE APPROPRIATE TECHNOLOGY. Successful decisions are also related to conscious technological choices. In many instances, the most appropriate choice may be a low-technology solution that represents a challenge to certain technological dogmas. Curitiba has shown that a city with more than one million inhabitants does not necessarily need an underground transport system or a light rail system, and that surface solutions based on buses can be developed incrementally at a much lower cost.

INTEGRATE LAND USE. It is important to establish a close relationship between the public transport system, land-use legislation, and the urban road network. This can provide an integrated framework to guide development. Curitiba was able to guide development by:

- Demonstrating that innovations improve economic efficiency and profitability (such as the increase of business along the first pedestrian street)
- Using its high quality of life and economic efficiency to attract new investment
- Working with the business community (for example, in planning the Curitiba Industrial City)
- Providing direct support (such as purchasing articulated buses on behalf of private transport companies and contracting with the local Volvo plant to produce bi-articulated buses).

CONSERVE RESOURCES. A sustainable city seeks to conserve and recycle resources. In Curitiba, this is exemplified by the use of buses and installation of new engines to reduce air pollution and by the preservation of historic dwellings.

MAINTAIN AN INFORMATION SYSTEM. A good information system is essential: the better the inhabitants know their city, the better they treat it. Cities should establish an information center with a team of officials who know the city well and who are committed to developing it wisely. For example, Curitiba maintains a data processing center that develops and maintains information systems for use in municipal planning and administration, especially to give prompt service to taxpayers. Activities have included systems for integrated tax collection, personnel management and payroll, school registration and monitoring, simulation of the public transport network, and public housing administration. The IPPUC's Information Department collects, analyzes, and disseminates information through units for research, mapping, and communications and publications.

STRENGTHEN STAKEHOLDER INVOLVEMENT. Following the principle of subsidiarity, it is most appropriate for citizens to determine what is best for their own street or neighborhood. For example, Curitiba used consultations when creating pedestrian streets. Participation of stakeholders has steadily increased since the end of the military government; public involvement is now an integral part of each major innovation.

Curitiba has taken several steps to strengthen stakeholder involvement, and these could be applied in other cities:

- Curitiba has a policy of transparency with regard to the availability of information. City Hall's computerized system makes ownership, tax liability, infrastructure, zoning and other information about every plot of land in the city instantly available to the public.
- Motivated stakeholders are actively involved in many implementation efforts. For example, low-income residents collect solid waste in their difficult-to-service neighborhoods in exchange for bus tokens or surplus food, thus simultaneously improving hygiene in poor neighborhoods, reducing solid waste collection costs, boosting use of public transport, and avoiding waste of agricultural produce.
- Public education, starting at an early age, is actively used to improve awareness and the quality of public participation. For example, explanations of the benefits of the city's innovations have been added to the school curriculum.

SPEND MONEY WISELY. Creativity, public-private partnerships, and external support can overcome financial constraints. During the military dictatorship, Brazilian cities were dependent on the state and federal governments. Curitiba officials responded by developing creative and self-financing programs so they could gradually implement their own ideas without assistance from higher levels of government. The city has financed most of its innovations from its annual budget (US$250 million in the mid 1990s), much of which is raised from property taxes. Curitiba is no richer or poorer than other southern Brazilian cities; the difference is that Curitiba spends its funds on integrated, common-sense programs and environmentally sensitive projects.

ESTABLISH POLITICAL CONTINUITY. One feature of Curitiba's innovations that may not be transferable is the political commitment, leadership, and continuity that Curitiba has enjoyed over more than three decades. Much of this is attributable to one person—Mayor Jaime Lerner—who initiated and implemented many of these innovations during his three terms in office (1971–75, 1979–83, and 1988–92). Trained as an architect and planner, Lerner combined the skills of a professional with those of a charismatic politician to promote reforms and initiatives. This advocacy paid off: according to public opinion surveys, 99 percent of Curitiba's citizens would not want to live anywhere else (Lamb 1991), and Lerner maintained a 70 percent approval rating during most of his time in office (Maier 1991).

Unsolved Problems

Curitiba is not without its problems. Only half the population is connected to the sewer system, and much of the sewage is not treated prior to final disposal. This is the fault of the state government, which is responsible for urban sanitation throughout the state. In terms of problems within the city's domain, nearly half of the city's children do not complete grade school, and over 10 percent of its citizens live in slums. Thus, important problems still await innovative solutions.

Next Steps

The spirit of transport innovation continues in Curitiba. New programs that are planned or under implementation include:

- Expansion of the direct line network so that it will operate along 14 axes and serve 88 tubular boarding stations. These stations will also be increasingly used on the express lines along with buses specially designed for rapid exit and entry.
- Modernization of the north-south fleet with bi-articulated buses, new central bus terminals, upgraded suburban bus terminals, and tubular boarding stations.

- Introduction of a computerized central operations unit that will give passengers and drivers information on alternative routes in case of congestion and provide passengers waiting at bus stops with arrival time information.

Conclusion

Curitiba's innovations in urban transport have had to overcome a range of obstacles: the predominant thinking about how cities should respond to rapid growth; the threats to long-term transport planning posed by short-term political decisions; and the lack of finance. In overcoming these obstacles, several important lessons were learned.

First, even during a period of rapid growth, cities can guide physical expansion through integrated road planning, investment in public transport, and enforcement of complementary land-use planning. Second, the institutionalized capacity for planning and implementing works has been one of the least appreciated aspects of Curitiba's transit scheme. Third, the city was very creative in the use of public-private partnerships, resource conservation, and external support—and clever use of these factors helped to overcome financial constraints. Finally, the city proved that a broad range of stakeholders can be engaged in effective ways, but they must have transparent, up-to-date information.

References

Lamb, Christina. 1991. "Brazil City in Vanguard of Fight Against Pollution." *Financial Times*. Aug. 30.

Maier, John Jr. 1991. "From Brazil, the Cidade that Can." *Time*. Oct. 14.

Rabinovtich, Jonas, and J. Leitmann. 1996. "Urban Planning in Curitiba." *Scientific American* 274(3): 26–49.

Ravazzani, Carlos, and José Paulo Fagani. 1999. *Curitiba. A capital ecológica*. Curitiba: Natugraf Ltda.

8-2

Partnering for Services in Santa Cruz, Bolivia

Fernando Rojas, World Bank

Santa Cruz faced extreme challenges during the three decades from 1965 to 1995, including a restrictive political environment dominated by the central government.[1] The city has been forced to respond creatively to the challenges posed by accelerated urbanization, increased deconcentration and decentralization of the state, and widening globalization. Santa Cruz's strengths and weaknesses have shaped its efforts to meet these challenges.[2] Box 8-2.1 provides an overview of the city.

---

1. Information for this chapter came partly from interviews with José Blanes, director of the Bolivian Center of Multidisciplinary Studies; Fernando Calderón, advisor to the representative, U.N. Development Programme-La Paz; Roberto Laserna, director of the Center for Study of Economic and Social Reality, Cochabamba; Thomas Manz, director of the Latin American Institute of Social Research; Carlos Hugo Molina, national secretary of popular participation for Bolivia; Fernando Prado, director of the Center for Studies of Urban and Regional Development in Support of Decentralization; and Luis Verdesoto, consultant national secretary of popular participation for Bolivia.

2. Unless otherwise specified, the name of Santa Cruz as used in this chapter means the city of Santa Cruz. The term "municipality" refers to the territorial entity managed by the local level of government. There are more than 250 municipalities in Bolivia; the municipality of Santa Cruz, as that of any other major city, encompasses both the city and the surrounding rural areas. Because Santa Cruz is also the name of the department of which the city is the capital, this case study will prefix Santa Cruz with "the department of" Santa Cruz whenever there is a reference to the regional level of government.

Box 8-2.1. *The City of Santa Cruz*

The city of Santa Cruz de La Sierra is located in the vast plains of southeastern Bolivia, far from the mountain ranges that witnessed the turbulent development of the nation from colonial times to the revolution of 1951. With the exception of a few pre-established towns, the eastern plains of Bolivia constitute a new frontier where pioneers and colonizers settled during the second half of the twentieth century. The pioneers were attracted by jobs and investments in agriculture, cattle raising, gas and oil resources, and increasing trade along the new corridors that link Bolivia with the Southern Cone Common Market (MERCOSUR) countries (Brazil, Argentina, Paraguay, and Uruguay).

Bolivia's participation law is one of the most striking of any in Latin America. The Popular Participation Law, adopted in the Bolivian Congress in 1994, called for the creation of vigilance committees (*comites de vigilancia*) or watchdog groups at the municipal level. The Bolivian participation law was conceived as a means of opening government to disenfranchised indigenous groups in rural areas. For most of Bolivia's history, rural settlements with strong ethnic identities lived outside municipal jurisdictions in unincorporated areas governed by regional development agencies or by central government ministries. The National Participation Law was intended to incorporate these territorial "gaps." To buttress accountability of municipal administration, the *comites de vigilancia* became the bedrock of a system of accountability that included the rural poor and indigenous minorities. The *comites de vigilancia* were empowered to oversee all phases of municipal activities, from planning to implementation. Under the law, they were to report directly to the central government. They had the power to trigger suspension of revenue transfers when municipalities failed to carry out their functions.

Detractors of the Bolivian law point out that it sets up a mechanism for the central government to be present in, and to have a controlling influence over, local affairs. It is possible to imagine many other arrangements to achieve local accountability without the sharp imprint of presidential control embodied in the law. For instance, democratic election of local groups, parent-teachers associations, or local councils of broad representation, could, with bipartisan recognition based on objective criteria, serve the same watchdog functions envisioned in the law.

Urban Challenges Since the Mid 1960s

Between 1965 and 1995 the rate of population growth of Santa Cruz was either the highest or one of the highest among medium and large Latin American cities. The city had already been growing at more than 9 percent a year during 1950–76. Between 1976 and 1992 the population of Santa Cruz increased from 254,000 to 700,000, an average rate of 6.5 percent a year. During the early 1990s, the rate of growth decreased to nearly 4.8 percent—still a high rate. However, nearby towns like Montero, which are gradually forming a substantial metropolitan area with the city, are expanding at explosive rates (estimated at 8 percent per year or higher for 1993–95) as they begin to receive part of the flow of immigrants that had previously headed for Santa Cruz.

As the epicenter of a booming regional economy, based on agriculture and oil and gas resources, Santa Cruz also attracted miners from exhausted gold and silver mines and peasants forced to move due to land degradation and concentration processes in the more densely populated mountain areas of Bolivia. The construction of the first road that linked Santa Cruz to Cochabamba in the 1950s put the traditional and rather quiet Santa Cruz in contact with the complex and fragile mosaic of the Andean region of Bolivia, which comprised surviving indigenous communities, displaced peasants, powerful trade unions entrenched in exhausted mining exploitations, traditional agriculture, and conservative elites resistant to change. The road also opened markets for Santa Cruz's modern, industrial agriculture as well as a flourishing smuggling trade. As a result, Santa Cruz became a link between primarily peasant coca growers and worldwide drug traffickers. This initial link between Santa Cruz and the rest of the world was followed by the building of other roads, Bolivia's largest and most international airport, and good telephone communications (Calderón and Laserna 1983; Whitehead 1973).

Most immigrants were Bolivians of indigenous heritage from the mountain ranges, people who proudly maintained their cultural differences with the inhabitants of the lowlands when they moved into the Santa Cruz area. They also kept their ties with their kin in the mountains, continuing extended family arrangements that provided both sides with intrafamily social security. The indigenous peasants who were lured to the lowlands by the news of Santa Cruz's booming economy were not typical immigrants to a large Latin American metropolis. Bolivian immigrants did not come to Santa Cruz to beg; they came to work either to support themselves or through extended family arrangements in the city.

As a new center of development, relatively well connected with all the new trade corridors of South America, Santa Cruz attracted flocks of immigrants from neighboring countries, primarily Brazil, Argentina, and Paraguay. Most South American immigrants arrived in Santa Cruz since the mid 1960s and joined earlier immigrations of Japanese in the early 1940s, a few Germans after World War II, and Koreans and Chinese more recently. A few of the foreign immigrants were investors who brought capital to Santa Cruz, and most arrived in Santa Cruz with some entrepreneurial talent. The clusters of foreign immigrants have reinforced the ideas of community organization and community development as the nucleus for the formation of a new, mixed local culture and city identity. Fernando Calderón, one of the most prolific and respected Bolivian social scientists, captured this type of environment when he used the apparently contradictory term *cosmopolitas pueblerinos* ("cosmopolitan hicks") to describe a rapidly growing population that somehow combines local elites, who have traditions deeply rooted in oligarchic structures, with immigrants, who have more cosmopolitan views and are more open to adopting external innovations and interacting with other ethnic and cultural groups (Calderón and Laserna 1983).

Santa Cruz may be characterized as a frontier town that quickly developed into a city without suppressing the initiative of citizens and their desire for community participation, or the commitment of private organizations to local development. The city became a melting pot without significant disruption or turbulence. It mobilized residents to claim more local and regional autonomy from the national government, and it managed to accommodate some of the expectations that moved immigrants to settle in Santa Cruz. Long-term planning and commitment to the city as well as private initiative for public service delivery and infrastructure seem to be the main reasons behind Santa Cruz's relative success in incorporating new residents and creating an attractive environment for sustainable investments, jobs, and employment.

Continuous Expansion of the Urban Perimeter

Santa Cruz is one of the few Latin American cities that was planned as a concentric city, like Paris. The city rings are clearly divided by circular avenues; they are also linked by radial avenues that connect the center with the perimeter. The city spreads over a large area and has one of the lowest population densities among larger Latin American cities. Tall buildings are not popular, as the abundance of land with relatively easy access to other parts of Santa Cruz encourages businesses and residents to locate in the outskirts of the city.

The pattern of growth of Santa Cruz follows a continuous expansion of the urban perimeter to ever wider rings. This growth pattern poses a huge challenge for the city's investment in infrastructure and service delivery. As the city area expanded from the fourth to the eighth ring during the 1980s and early 1990s, low-income citizens sought preferential access to public utilities by occupying vacant—often public—land as close to the previously urbanized, more developed rings as possible. Santa Cruz's first urban plan (Plan Regulador), prepared in 1988 by the Regional Development Corporation of Santa Cruz (Corporación de Desarrollo Regional de Santa Cruz, or CORDECRUZ), covered only the areas between the second and fifth rings. No planner could have anticipated that, just eight years later, the city would already extend to the eighth ring. In 1994, under Mayor Percy Fernández, the planning of the city was extended to the tenth ring, essentially by drawing and gradually constructing new avenues, securing rights-of-way, authorizing privately owned transportation services, and building infrastructure (for electricity, street lighting, water, and sanitation) at a slower pace than land was actually being occupied. While private developers seek permission from city planners to urbanize land for high- and middle-income groups—thereby ensuring some orderly and rational development of public services—low-income groups have to pursue solutions on their own.

Because the city's expansion through illegal occupation of land has been checked neither by land tenancy regularization programs nor by drastic enforcement of property rights, city planning for services to irregularly occupied land lags well behind development. It is not until these irregularly born neighborhoods are well settled, housing has been significantly upgraded, and residents and private businesses have introduced some sort of public service arrangements of their own, that the city attempts to extend the public network of drains, pipelines, and cables and connect them with the diverse array of public and private arrangements. This was essentially the pattern of service expansion from the fifth to the eighth ring, and it was likely to continue for the newly developed ninth and tenth rings.

Extending the city from the fifth to the tenth ring in a period of only 10 years has meant a huge increase in local public investment in infrastructure as well as expanding the scale of garbage collection and wastewater disposal systems. Public investment requirements would have been much lower had the city adopted a different pattern of public service expansion and financing. The existing pattern of service development is chaotic from a technical point of view and inefficient from the point of view of the social allocation of resources for the medium and long terms.

Santa Cruz's Strengths

The exceptional capacity of Santa Cruz to innovatively respond to the daunting challenges of the last three decades is based on four factors that are rooted in the city's culture and history:

- **Cohesiveness.** The solid cultural identity of the city has not been eroded by the recent influxes of immigrants. On the contrary, the city is quickly incorporating immigrants into the local culture, social, and economic life.
- **Private initiative.** Deeply rooted social and economic elite members of society have made long-term private investments in urban infrastructure and have arranged for private or mixed (public-private) delivery of basic social services. Santa Cruz's new settlers, who often live in low-income communities, have developed their own strategies for self-provision of basic services and infrastructure based on Santa Cruz's early examples of private initiative.
- **Permeable local political system.** A relatively closed or exclusionary political system, generally controlled by a few families on the basis of patronage, has been permeated at times by local leaders' reform-minded programs aimed at reorganizing urban services—even when reorganization threatens long-entrenched private privileges.
- **Urban planning capabilities.** During the time of centralized regional planning, the privately formed Civic Committee of Santa Cruz (Comité Cívico de Santa Cruz, or CCSC) operated in close collaboration with the well-equipped CORDECRUZ. When regional corporations were dismantled and municipalities given more autonomy in the early 1990s, some of the planning capacity of Santa Cruz was transferred to the city planning units or to private research centers and consulting firms. These entities helped to anticipate and guide the accelerated growth of the city.

Paradoxically, each of Santa Cruz's strengths carries the risk of some perverse effects. If not adequately framed in an institutional environment that ensures effective checks and balances, private sector and community initiatives, city identity and cohesiveness, and elite urban planning can become sources of monopoly rents, administrative corruption, exclusionary politics, fragile finances, lack of transparency and accountability, and divisive policies. Overall, however, Santa Cruz fares much better in terms of local identity, service coverage, financing, and sophisticated urban planning than other rapidly growing cities in the new trade corridors of the Southern Cone countries, such as Ciudad del Este in Paraguay.

Santa Cruz's Weaknesses

In spite of Santa Cruz's relative success, it still suffers from deficiencies in service coverage, irregular land tenancy and inadequate land-use planning, weak staff professionalization, and underinvestment in infrastructure and public utilities. These weaknesses, in addition to those described in the following paragraphs, must be accounted for to draw more objective lessons from Santa Cruz's model of city management.

STRATIFIED AND EXCLUSIONARY PARTICIPATION. In Santa Cruz, traditional community organization is based upon exclusive fraternity-like clubs and committees that were initially restricted to the prominent families of the city and the region. Neighbors and classmates who grow up together develop the sense of loyalty and reciprocity that leads them to associate among themselves, even for purposes of public services and infrastructure. Often women of all socioeconomic groups are kept out of these exclusive organizations. When applied to Santa Cruz, the terms "civic committee" and "cooperative" lose their usual meanings. Although they still denote solidarity and public interest, they also imply elitism and patronage.

Aware of the natural and dynamic comparative advantages of the city and the region, the prominent families of Santa Cruz developed the restricted, powerful CCSC, which demanded resources and autonomy from the central government and became the most vocal regional and urban force lobbying for Bolivian decentralization. Not all members of Santa Cruz's prominent families joined the CCSC, however. Indeed, some of the top-level bureaucrats and technocrats coming out of Santa Cruz traditional families have pushed for more open, more transparent channels for citizens' participation in public affairs. A good example is Carlos Hugo Molina, a distinguished son of Santa Cruz and former national secretary of popular participation under the Sánchez de Losada administration, who was the single person most visibly responsible for the approval and early implementation of the laws on popular participation and decentralization.

UNREGULATED PRIVATE PARTICIPATION IN PUBLIC SERVICE DELIVERY. Santa Cruz underinvests in building and maintaining infrastructure and basic social services, as demonstrated by citizens' willingness to contribute to community cooperatives and private sector arrangements. In Santa Cruz, deficient provision of urban services under the centralized state has left an unmet demand that has been filled by private cooperatives, private corporations, and community arrangements. The relations between users and providers remain largely unregulated. They are often characterized by users' resistance to fees and charges, clandestine connections, and private sector abuses.

With few exceptions, the CCSC has been the primary city and regional decisionmaking body, often more important than local and regional authorities. It has also played a significant role in the planning, financing, and delivery of city services. Prominent members of the CCSC created so-called cooperatives of public services for potable water and water disposal. These privately controlled cooperatives actually planned city infrastructure, land use, and local services during the initial years of city expansion. Acting under an exceptional legal framework, these cooperatives enjoyed a monopoly position that has remained largely unregulated and uncontrolled. Not even the central government exercises real supervision over the cooperatives' budgets, investments, or rates of return.

UNEQUAL SERVICE QUALITY AND COVERAGE. More important, the overwhelming influence of the cooperatives debilitated the city's capacity to plan and finance the expansion of basic infrastructure and public services beyond the areas covered by the cooperatives. When immigration brought significant numbers of poor people into the city, the cooperatives were not prepared to expand their coverage. As a result, public services and infrastructure reached only as far as the first four rings of Santa Cruz's concentric urban space. The residents of the remaining six rings were left very much to their own initiatives. Residents—most often low- and middle-income families—promoted associations for public service delivery. Although the city was primarily responsible for building the basic infrastructure, communities and small businesses were in practice responsible for connecting to city pipes and sewers. This is how the city's pattern of community organization around civic committees and cooperatives was extended to new immigrants, who then became responsible for public services.

As a general rule, the division of responsibilities between the public and private sectors becomes more confusing as the radial distance from the city center increases. With the exception of high-income urban developments, service quality and coverage tend to decrease in proportion to the distance from the city center.

INEFFICIENCIES IN ALLOCATION AND PRODUCTION. Confusion in distribution of responsibilities leads to lack of accountability and coordination in investment and service delivery. The specifications of pipe sizes, water pressures, and the like vary from one initiative to another, making it practically impossible to integrate city services or implement environmentally sound policies for the protection of water resources.

Because no clear division of labor was established to define city, business, and community responsibilities, and because of the absence of a clear regulatory and institutional framework, prices do not necessarily reflect efficient cost structures or competitive rates of return. Nor do total contributions to city services reflect citizens' preferences and priorities for basic social services. Fees paid for public services primarily reflect monopoly rents or internal arrangements among members of public service cooperatives. Uncoordinated public-private investment fails to take advantage of economies of scale and leads to inefficiencies of various sorts and unused existing capacity. Although residents are willing to pay for basic services (as reflected by their initiatives to develop private arrangements), local authorities decline to raise the revenues needed to fund such services.

This situation has been aggravated by the charge of user fees for deficient services. When the private sector partially filled the gap left by the central government, monopolistic abuses and environmentally unsafe practices became common due to a lack of regulations and regulatory institutions. Abusive charges for deficient services led to users' resistance to payment, which in turn caused further underinvestment in water, wastewater, and other essential services as well as further deterioration of water sources and other damage to the environment.

Some small communities have attempted to follow Santa Cruz's pioneer example of creating cooperatives under the initiative of prominent families and have organized themselves, with or without city or central government support, for the construction or maintenance of water services. But their scale is usually insufficient and suboptimal for larger cities. And the accelerated rate of immigration to the cities makes it more difficult to develop a sense of belonging and mutual confidence among low-income communities, a feeling that is essential for community organizing.

Strategies to Expand Local Autonomy in a Restrictive Environment

The city's early initiatives to cope with the formidable challenges posed by exponential population growth clashed with the barriers of a highly centralized state in terms of the distribution of both financial resources and responsibilities. Santa Cruz might have been subdued by the pressures of external forces—accelerated urbanization, lack of autonomy, poor local social capital, and increasing vulnerability to international change—had it not been for the city's capacity to claim some degree of local autonomy from the national government.

Santa Cruz's response to the sudden and multiple challenges was a sustained, popular demand for autonomous management, more financial independence from the central government, and strengthened urban and regional unity. The city and the region identified the challenge of achieving local and regional autonomy as an intermediate goal on the way to more balanced development. Santa Cruz differed from other cities in that, when threatened by external, destabilizing factors, it opted to take on the challenge itself rather than resort to the protection of higher levels of government. Its proactive response to the risks and the opportunities of decentralization, urbanization, and globalization constitutes an innovation in itself.

During the 1970s and 1980s, mayors and civic leaders of Santa Cruz mobilized the citizens to lobby the central government for financial resources and autonomy in planning and service delivery. Above all, the traditional elite families of Santa Cruz became the driving force behind city and regional efforts to lobby for decentralization and state modernization.

Many of Santa Cruz's elite groups were members of the CCSC. The CCSC's capacity to effectively mobilize and act on behalf of the city, and even the entire region, was based on several of its achievements:

- Development of a regional identity and a common vision of the city through visionary planning
- Development of relatively strong planning capabilities at the regional and local levels
- Development of channels for public-private interaction that stimulated private investments in public utilities and city infrastructure
- Gradual expansion of local and regional public resources (even before decentralization, when public resources were almost exclusively provided by the central government and the rate of fiscal dependency was at its peak, the city was experimenting with innovative ways to capture local resources for public goods and services)
- Gradual strengthening of departmental and city management.

Santa Cruz championed the organization of civic committees and civic movements, and its precedent was quickly replicated in other parts of the country. By the early 1990s the civic committees were the most vocal organizations demanding resources and services from the central government. Civic movements in other parts of the country deviated from the Santa Cruz ideal of autonomy by channeling their efforts into making demands on the central government and the paternalistic, welfare state.

Santa Cruz's leadership role in state decentralization was so powerful that, in the 1980s, the city and the region were in practice granted more autonomy than other cities and regions in the country. The national government deconcentrated development planning through *corporaciones regionales de desarrollo* (regional development corporations). CORDECRUZ—the corporation for Santa Cruz—was technically better equipped than any other central government agency. Moreover, CORDECRUZ was largely managed and controlled by citizens of Santa Cruz. When Bolivia began its system of intergovernmental transfers, many believed that Santa Cruz received more than its share of the total amount of central transfers to departments and municipalities.

Santa Cruz's lobbying for state reform and decentralization was so significant that the nation's participation and decentralization reforms of the 1990s may be read as an attempt to eliminate civic movements like the one mobilized by the CCSC. On the national level, Bolivian policymakers specifically designed the laws on participation and decentralization that were finally passed under the administration of President Gonzalo Sánchez de Losada (1993–97) to eliminate elitist, corporatist city and regional organizations such as the CCSC. By expanding and guaranteeing participation at all levels while keeping final control in the hands of central institutions, the reforms of the 1990s aimed, and largely but not entirely succeeded, to subordinate powerful local and regional interests that were the primary force behind civic movements. Although muted and in weaker form, the influence of the CCSC is still an important factor in public policy in Santa Cruz.

In Bolivia, decentralization emphasized participation more than in any other country in the region. Decentralization also weakened the power of local and regional leaders in three ways:

- Mayors could be removed every year by the dominant political coalition in the city council—a coalition that was often dependent on national level politics.
- The *prefectos* (heads of departments) were agents of the president of the country.

- Popular organizations that objected to the local allocation of public resources could appeal to the National Congress. The Senate or higher chamber could then order suspension of central government transfers until local authorities amended the allocation of resources to take into account the interests of the complaining organization.

Response to the Challenges: Management Innovations

Santa Cruz's flexible responses to these challenges are a model of local and regional adaptation to the changing legal and institutional environment at the national level. The history of Santa Cruz's management consists of four phases:

- The early phase of the Comité de Obras (Public Works Committee) of Santa Cruz, a pioneer local response to central government negligence in infrastructure planning and investment.
- The CORDECRUZ phase of investment planning, contracting, and building. During this phase the city and the region were able to exercise enormous control over CORDECRUZ even though it was a central government agency for administrative deconcentration.
- The early years of decentralization and participation, characterized by tensions between citizens' demands for basic services and the city aristocratic structures and restricted urban services.
- The most recent phase, characterized by attempts to reconcile local traditional structures with the need to expand and regularize land tenancy and basic services.

Santa Cruz's management innovations may be seen as an uninterrupted process of adaptation to the changing institutional environment created by national policies. The common denominator of all management phases is the pursuit of local autonomy for planning and implementation of solutions adjusted to Santa Cruz's local and regional environment. Box 8-2.2 presents a timeline of important events in the city.

Innovations in Public-Private Interaction

The Bolivian institutional environment for local management changed dramatically during the 1975–95 period, from a highly centralized government to state deconcentration and—finally—to devolution. As a result of frequent policy changes at the national level, local management has been forced to adjust to a situation of constant institutional transition.

Box 8-2.2. *Timeline of Key Events*

1965   Santa Cruz's explosive growth begins.

Early   Santa Cruz receives foreign credit funds and transfers for oil
            and gas exploitations.
1970s   Civic Committee of Santa Cruz is formed.

1985   First municipal elections (department capitals only).
            Ley Orgánica de Municipalidades (Organic Municipal Law) is
            passed; devolves responsibilities but no corresponding
            finances to the municipalities.

1988   CORDECRUZ prepares the first urban plan, which covers the
            city's second to fifth rings.

1990   Percy Fernández is elected mayor, and he begins efforts to
            strengthen municipal management capacity.

1994   City planning extends to tenth ring.
            Law on System of Sectoral Regulation is passed to regulate local
            services.
            National Participation Law is passed.

1995   Real property cadaster is formed.
            Santa Cruz's property tax revenues peak at US$24 million.
            City prepares a 15-year, US$420 million infrastructure upgrading
            program.
            Law on National Administrative Decentralization is passed.

1996   Johny Fernández is elected mayor.
            Summit of the Americas takes place in Santa Cruz.
            Promulgation of National Decentralization Law.

1997   CORDECRUZ dissolved.

The history of public-private interaction in Santa Cruz depicts a linear transition, beginning with primarily private planning, then evolving to public regional planning highly influenced by local and regional leaders, and finally resulting in strengthened public sector management at the city level (see figure 8-2.1). Because this linear transition reflects adaptations to the changing emphasis of national government policies toward local institutional development, Santa Cruz's evolution in public-private interaction may be interpreted as a continuous and effective adjustment to the Bolivian institutional environment.

Figure 8-2.1. *Transition from Private to Public Service Delivery in Santa Cruz*

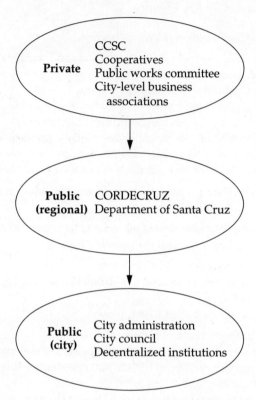

Source: Author.

Although the institutional context for managing the city has changed over time, the private sector has always been influential in local and regional policymaking in Santa Cruz. The role of the private sector in public service delivery has been so significant that some residents—including planners and former mayors—claim that the city has never had significant *public* institutions, capable of dictating and implementing local public policies. The truth is that Santa Cruz, more than any other city in Bolivia, managed to develop locally rooted institutions responsive to city demands during the times of centralization and deconcentration. Recent decentralization and participation policies have brought about changes in local management as the city is pursuing the transition from local, privately controlled institutions to a strengthened municipal government.

Evolution

Various institutional actors have reached prominence in Santa Cruz policymaking and service delivery since the mid 1960s: the Public Works Committee, CORDECRUZ, the early cooperatives, the later cooperatives, the municipality (both the city administration and the city council), the department of Santa Cruz, the CCSC, and other civil society organizations. Arrangements among these actors reflect the special inclination of Santa Cruz to form public-private partnerships for purposes of city management.

THE PUBLIC WORKS COMMITTEE. The committee was the highest expression of private sector management of public local and regional affairs. It preceded CORDECRUZ in investment planning and financing. Because it was primarily staffed by local leaders and technical experts who were responsive to local and regional priorities, it reversed the top-down (central to subnational) relationship that prevailed in Bolivia during decades of strong centralization and dictatorships. The committee developed investment plans and financial initiatives of its own; it was also instrumental in capturing significant transfers from the central government. Above all, the committee established a precedent of horizontal intergovernmental negotiations and planted the initial seeds of the ideological discourse that was to inspire regional and local identity in the 1980s and 1990s: developmental progress through local and regional unity.

CORDECRUZ. With CORDECRUZ, Santa Cruz established a division of labor that was unique in the country: the centrally created corporation became the technical arm of the regional elites, while the CCSC specialized in the political and negotiation functions. As CORDECRUZ gained significant technical capacity—many people would argue that it had at one point more planning capacity than the central planning office for the entire country—it quickly assumed the technical responsibilities for investment planning, financing, and contracting for the region and the city. The CCSC was responsible for strengthening local and regional identity as well as for bargaining for regional autonomy with the national government.

Because CORDECRUZ was technically competent, it became a symbol of public sector effectiveness in management. On the one hand, as a public institution, it also came to symbolize the relative autonomy of the technical side of public administration in relation to the primarily private interests of the CCSC. Some observers claim that CORDECRUZ's technically inspired judgments often prevailed over those of the CCSC. On the other hand,

CORDECRUZ promoted the formation of cooperatives for the private provision of basic urban services in Santa Cruz. When the role of cooperatives—and later the municipality of Santa Cruz—became more important for local management, CORDECRUZ withdrew from the urban scene. In fact, the role of CORDECRUZ was rendered obsolete by the tremendous development of the city.

EARLY COOPERATIVES. Three Santa Cruz cooperatives were, and still are, primarily responsible for water and wastewater disposal service to the four inner circles of the city. Other private sector arrangements take care of public transportation. Because an autonomous agency carries out urban planning, and service delivery of utilities is primarily private, the local administration is limited to providing street pavement and lighting, parks, and other public spaces.

With the decline of CORDECRUZ and the slow strengthening of local governments in the late 1980s and early 1990s, the existing Santa Cruz cooperatives filled the vacuum of responsibility for public urban services. These private cooperatives became the primary providers of city services and played a prominent role in city decisionmaking, planning, and service delivery.

The Santa Cruz cooperatives for the provision of basic urban services operate in a vacuum of central government regulations regarding quality, coverage, prices, control, and accountability. The national 1994 Law on the System of Sectoral Regulation was intended to fill this vacuum. However, this law has not effectively regulated the cooperatives. Part of the reason is it failed to take into account the precise role of municipalities in the provision of utilities and transportation, and the relationships of the municipalities with the central government or the agencies that provide local services.

The early Santa Cruz cooperatives came into being to fill the gap in urban infrastructure services for which no level of government was primarily accountable. No formal process existed for competition or for formal granting of concessionary rights. Many would argue that municipal laws (especially the national 1985 Ley Orgánica de Municipalidades [Organic Law of Municipalities]) were violated through these arrangements. However, the 1985 law preceded fiscal decentralization by more than eight years, making it difficult for municipalities to comply with it because they had practically no public resources to allocate.

Santa Cruz's early cooperatives are not cooperatives in the ordinary sense of the word. These cooperatives are closely controlled by a few entrepreneurial (often family-based) groups. Their internal structure and way of working make them more like family-held corporations than co-operatives. The Santa Cruz cooperatives are primarily capital ventures; hence, they have little or no concern for their current or potential low-income members. They do not follow legal procedures typical for private corporations nor fulfill the requirements for the creation of a public corporation. Rather, they behave more like private corporations "associated" with the municipality.

The cooperatives are natural monopolies that face little or no control by the city or its citizens, and they are not subject to rigorous scrutiny by any public agency. Some members of these cooperatives are profit-seeking private corporations. As no general law of the country seems to apply to these cooperatives, Santa Cruz has regulated them by special laws.

When not organized around cooperative lines for the provision of urban services, the private sector has resorted to the rather strong federations of private owners, as in the case of the intracity bus service in Santa Cruz. Both the cooperatives and the private federations, such as the public transportation federation, maintain unregulated relations with the city and effectively defend their private interests. Although Mayor Percy Fernández (1990–96) seriously challenged the power of the cooperatives, they maintained their monopoly over public service delivery.

NEW COOPERATIVES AND OTHER SPONTANEOUS ARRANGEMENTS. When the earlier cooperatives became incapable of extending their coverage to the newly developed areas of the city, new private initiatives materialized to provide such basic public services as water and wastewater disposal. Following the examples of the earlier cooperatives, some of these initiatives adopted the form and name of cooperatives. Other remained as de facto associations of neighbors or small business services. What makes these arrangements different from the earlier cooperatives is that they were not intended to serve the core rings of the city, nor were they organized by the powerful economic groups of Santa Cruz. In fact, many of these private initiatives for investment in city infrastructure and public service delivery originated in low- to middle-income neighborhoods.

Because the new cooperatives or similar private ventures have less capital than the traditional ones and are not technically well equipped, they could not meet technical standards and were unable to sustain an acceptable level of service. In view of this situation, the municipality has begun to recover control over basic urban services.

THE CITY ADMINISTRATION (THE MAYOR AND CITY STAFF).[3] The local government was essentially subservient to the interests of the private sector until the late 1980s. In Bolivia, the central and regional governments appointed local officers until 1985. The first elections for municipal authorities took place that year and were restricted to capitals of departments. Fernández, one of the first elected mayors of Santa Cruz and a prominent member of the civic movement, decided to organize a local administration capable of coordinating both public and private resources. He sought to reestablish the role and effectiveness of the city's public administration, as distinct from the role of business and the CCSC.

Santa Cruz had very scarce resources for a city growing at such an accelerated pace. The municipality had no real capacity to collect taxes or fees for public utilities. Nor did it have clout over reluctant taxpayers, because it could not suspend public services for nonpayment. The municipality's primary role was to grant concessions and privileges for the private sector to operate. Even these latter functions were carried out in an informal, disorganized manner.

Fernández imprinted a new character on the city administration. As mayor for three consecutive terms, he launched the citizen mobilization campaign that he named Santa Cruz Obra Gruesa, (Santa Cruz Major Works), which significantly advanced street paving and lighting and repaired the drainage system, while also beautifying the city.

The Fernández administrations overlapped with two developments at the national level that may have diminished the capacity and the relative autonomy of regional and local public authorities. One was the dismantling of CORDECRUZ, and the other was the implementation of new national policies for popular participation and deconcentration to the departmental level. As explained in the opening section of this chapter, the Bolivian process of decentralization has differed from similar processes in other Latin American countries in two main respects: (a) the emphasis on grassroots organizations, even at the cost of the coordinating capacity of local authorities, and (b) the so-called Decentralization Law. In reality, this law is a new deconcentration policy, away from the relatively more autonomous regional

---

3. Although, properly speaking, both the mayor's office and the local council constitute the local administration, this case study differentiates between those who administer the city on a day-to-day basis and the elected local council. The latter is primarily an elected political body that supervises the mayor and dictates the policy guidelines for city administration.

development corporations and in favor of the *prefecturas de departamento* (the regional government bodies).

Instead of succumbing to these policies, the mayor reorganized and strengthened the local administration to enable it to cope with the challenges of a rapidly growing city that could no longer be run by spontaneous private initiatives. Fernández's three successive administrations strengthened most areas of city management and elevated the capacity of the city to reorganize urban public services in several ways:

- The per capita tax burden per year increased to US$80, up from less than US$10 at the beginning of the first administration. Property tax revenues reached US$24 million in 1995.
- The city transformed its rather abstract urban plan into a truly operational one.
- Budget reform guaranteed fiscal equilibrium and serious fiscal management.
- Personnel reform created the basis for professionalization and technically oriented human resource management.
- The city publicized its investment plans and openly discussed investment priorities.
- New control mechanisms began to eliminate corruption.
- The city initiated the process of regularizing land ownership.

In the early 1990s the municipal administration began to deconcentrate into integrated neighborhood units that combined schools, health facilities, public libraries, police services, and maintenance of social and urban infrastructure. The initial goal of 200 neighborhood units for the entire city could not be completed by the time Fernández left office in 1996. In any case, Santa Cruz was divided into much smaller administrative units than other Latin American cities that had been partially deconcentrated or decentralized, such as Cali, Porto Alegre, or Quito.

With school attendance and performance data at the unit level, the municipality was then able to apply performance controls to such personnel as nationally appointed teachers. The local government went beyond the intergovernmental distribution of functions and took initiatives that corresponded to the city's priorities. It restored 270 school buildings, repaired school desks, and provided stationery supplies. Although the city was not primarily responsible for building and maintaining the educational infrastructure, the mayor went beyond his legal responsibilities in order to elevate the quality of education in the city.

Johny Fernández, who was elected mayor in 1995 after Percy Fernández, faced the challenge of managing a larger, more effective city structure, capable of leadership over the cooperatives, businesses, and the civic movement.[4]

THE MUNICIPAL COUNCIL. The distinguishing feature of the Santa Cruz council, an elected body that supervises the mayor, is that personal and political arrangements facilitate the linkages between the council and the mayor's office and ensure the stability of the administration. In Santa Cruz, in contrast to other large Bolivian cities, local policy concerns usually prevail over national political party divisions.[5]

THE DEPARTMENT OF SANTA CRUZ. The regional-level department was intended to be the primary source of public administration until Bolivia's 1994 Law on Popular Participation provided the basis for fiscal and administrative autonomy at the local level (through community organizations and municipalities). The departmental prefectures are the regional governing bodies in Bolivia. The prefects are not elected by the people, but are appointed by—and act as—agents of the president. A 1996 law on decentralization revived the prefectures as the official link between central and local governments and communities.

Both CORDECRUZ and the department were instrumental in expanding the horizons of the city—as perceived by the CCSC—to the nearby provinces from the perspective of a metropolitan area. This metropolitan perspective in city planning and interurban coordinated actions was introduced by former regional planners of CORDECRUZ, such as the architect Fernando Prado, who later became key urban planners during the expansion and professionalization of the city administration. Still, the department was notquite prepared to take initiatives for intermunicipal coordination, and the city had to negotiate on its own with neighboring municipalities for

---

4. The two men were not related. In fact, Johny was elected with the support of some of the traditional political leaders of Santa Cruz in a coalition that opposed Percy.

5. This is not the case, for instance, in the capital city of La Paz. There, Mayor Ronald McLean, who was well respected and widely regarded as an efficient manager, was suddenly replaced at the end of 1996 by a political coalition that responded primarily to the electoral interests of national political parties. Broadly speaking, the structure of the city council in Bolivia is similar to a parliamentary democracy, thereby jeopardizing continuity in management.

standardizing taxes (such as the vehicle tax), infrastructure (such as roads and bridges), and so on. This process gradually evolved into metropolitan area planning.

THE CCSC AND OTHER BUSINESS AND CIVIL SOCIETY ORGANIZATIONS. The CCSC became the enduring institution of local autonomy during the years of strong centralization and frequent dictatorships in Bolivia. For years it brought together many of the organizations of civil society in Santa Cruz. From the organization of local fairs and festivities to the mobilization of cultural identity for negotiations with the national government, the CCSC appears to be the undisputed leader of civic politics in the city and the region.

Nearly every sector of the economy has a *directorio* (board of directors), and the sum of these boards is a corporatist city structure. Some key business leaders or members of traditional families belong at the same time to the CCSC, the public service cooperatives, and the sectoral boards. This corporatist structure penetrates into public service delivery, policymaking, city planning, and contract allocation in ways that go beyond the formal organization chart of city administration. Unfortunately, this is a fertile field for monopoly rents and higher than necessary transaction costs. Mayors, planners, and other city leaders interested in developing their local administrations must try to challenge this corporatist structure of interest group representation that is parallel to the state and the political parties. This was the case with the first Mayor Fernández and the architect Prado. When the two of them decided to challenge the virtually unregulated monopoly of the cooperatives, a coalition of private interests and political parties strenuously resisted and finally brought them down in the 1996 election.

Although structured around corporatist lines, the unifying force behind the proliferation of civic associations in Santa Cruz is personal contacts. Friendships seem to prevail over political parties and sectoral divisions. The CCSC itself is based upon school and neighborhood ties. It is a heavily personalized organization that attempts to keep private influence and control over a given territory. Exclusively male and limited to schoolmates and neighbors, organizations such as the CCSC often behave in a reserved or secret manner. Secrecy and personal bonds are the basis for sharing privileged information and contacts that may lead to contracts with private or public parties. The three early Santa Cruz cooperatives combine the two driving forces behind Santa Cruz's civil society organizations: people growing together who are genuinely concerned for their neighborhoods, and the sectoral organization of the city along corporatist lines. (It is interesting to draw a parallel between the city cooperatives of Santa Cruz and those of Mondragon in the Basque region of Spain. Both grew out of a well-entrenched regional identity that supported a culture of self-development. However, while the Mondragon cooperatives gave themselves the mandate of comprehensive, integral regional development, the Santa Cruz cooperatives looked primarily after their members' interests.)

The tradition of exclusive organizations has extended to middle- and low-income groups, and the entire city has started organizing along neighborhood and friendship lines, thus restricting access to others or inhibiting the delivery of new services in areas of no interest to the organized groups. As some mayors and public officers have tried to reestablish the precedence of the entire city's public interest over neighborhood or sector associations, they have clashed with the CCSC and other traditional associations.

As the business associations and the CCSC prevailed on economic and political issues for a long time, the city may be characterized as a corporate city. Indeed, the civic movement went so far as to proclaim itself the "moral leader of Santa Cruz," and it dictated behavioral rules (particularly those involving regional and urban identity) for the citizens. It is often said that immigrants to the city quickly adopted the expected behavior as a means of incorporating themselves into the new environment and increasing their chances of reconciling their individual needs and interests with the public interest of the city and the region.

Although some traditional, landed families and larger business interests prevail, Santa Cruz's civic movement is a symbol for the entire city. It is only recently that friction and fragmentation have appeared within the movement. Workers' organizations, such as the regional branch of the Central Obrera Boliviana (the Workers' Confederation of Bolivia), do not easily fit within a regional movement based on neighborhood loyalties and led by the traditional families of the city. The emergence of fragments within this regional movement is evidence of the increasing diversification of centers of power in the city. As Santa Cruz's society becomes more complex, previously neglected institutions, such as the municipal government become alternative centers of power.

City-level business associations, primarily the Cámara de Industria y Comercio (Chamber of Industry and Commerce) and the Federación de Empresarios Privados (Federation of Private Firms), have played a major role in the delivery of basic city services through the three traditional cooperatives. The Confederación Agraria del Oriente (Eastern Agrarian Confederation), the major business association at the regional level, has been vocal concerning agrarian policies and agrarian reform issues. The CCSC has influence over a diversity of important city institutions, such as the regionally prominent hospital, which was founded with donations from the Japanese government. Indeed, the hospital is headed by Dr. Carlos Dabdoub, a former president of the CCSC and a former Bolivian minister of health. In this regard, the private sector influence in Santa Cruz is similar to that in Cali, where locally rooted private firms and foundations exert influence over every significant local and regional health and educational institution.

Rather than demanding more services from the central government, Santa Cruz took advantage of its civil society organizations to come up with solutions of its own. It may be argued that Santa Cruz did not initially stress the development of city management, because it was able to resort to the city's social capital. The private capital bridged the gap between an ineffective central government and a partially autonomous city administration; it ensured continuity in service in spite of the many discontinuities in public administration.

Scope and Significance

The creative—although disorganized, unregulated, and often inefficient—methods of public-private interaction in Santa Cruz have filled the vacuum left by a highly centralized government that is unresponsive to local needs. Were it not for this peculiar interaction between the public and the private sectors, it would be impossible to account for the gradual development of urban services in Santa Cruz. The private sector filled in for the state during the initial phase of cooperatives and regional development corporations, although at the cost of private control of public services. When the city outgrew local private capacity, it became necessary to professionalize the local administration, increase city revenues, differentiate the roles of the public and private sectors, and introduce competition and regulation. Santa Cruz has tried to cope with these challenges while gradually assuming its responsibilities with respect to basic urban services.

Unlike other cities, in which private investment may be deterred by uncertainties and the lack of an adequate legal framework, private businesses in Santa Cruz were motivated to invest in public services, because their capitals and returns faced no risk. The local elites' influence and control over every major public policy and institution—be it central, regional, or local—that might have jeopardized business investment prevented public sector interference or changes in policies.

The civic movement of Santa Cruz became a symbol of unity in relation to the central government. But it was also associated with investments in public services and urban and regional improvements. In this regard, the pioneer civic movement of Santa Cruz differed from other civic movements that appeared later and that were dominated by trade union and urban middle classes. The primary objective of these other movements, which were inspired by the Santa Cruz model, was to demand resources from the central government rather than to administer public-private resources for city development. Civic movements outside Santa Cruz had no capacity to contribute their own resources or to combine them with public resources to improve city services.

With the gradual strengthening of the city administration, the local government in Santa Cruz in the mid 1980s began approaching a new balance with the private sector. It also began to control and even regulate private investments in public services. Likewise, citizens' awareness of and vigilance over public service quality and prices increased.

Innovations in Planning

In 1988, CORDECRUZ prepared Santa Cruz's first urban plan, which was a landmark in urban planning for Bolivia and elsewhere. The plan covered the city's development from the second to the fifth ring. For the preparation of this plan, CORDECRUZ adopted city and regional priorities that Santa Cruz's local elites had identified over time. The staff of CORDECRUZ strictly followed regional criteria, as the creation and development of CORDECRUZ was a result of local and regional power and not—as in other regions of the country—a symbol of the central government's presence.

Santa Cruz's planning has been faithful to a few basic principles since the early days of the Public Works Committee. Continuity in planning was not essentially disrupted by the rapid turnover of the institutions primarily responsible for the city plans between 1986 and 1997. The passage from CORDECRUZ to the cooperatives, then to city hall, and finally to an independent agency appointed by city hall, was characterized by a striking continuity in the orientation and substance of the city plans. No matter who was primarily responsible for planning, each institution adhered to the following principles and applied them on the basis of its predecessor's achievements:

- The city structure is based on concentric rings.
- Effective planning is based on street construction. Initial investment in city infrastructure is also concentrated on the construction, lighting, and paving of streets and avenues.

- Street construction is soon followed by privately controlled public transportation.
- The city area keeps expanding on primarily public property as long as there is private demand for land and minimum capacity to pay for transportation services. The city is essentially tolerant toward irregular occupation of land, particularly public land. The continuous expansion of accessible land, combined with tolerance of irregular land settlements, maintains low densities.
- The expansion of urban land and public transportation is not immediately matched by public investment in other components of basic urban infrastructure, such as water and sanitation pipes, or social infrastructure, such as schools and health clinics. In the early years of new urban developments, residents are supposed to take care of these investments on their own, either according to urban regulations or under gradual and irregular arrangements. The city will try to connect, coordinate, and regularize these piecemeal investments at a later point.

Santa Cruz's planning is based on three major innovations. First, the city has demonstrated a remarkable ability for continuity and gradual strengthening of planning capabilities. Second, it has matched the demand for land with corresponding increases in the supply of urban land—even at the cost of tolerating irregular settlement. Finally, in a practical extension of private-public cooperation, Santa Cruz has been more able than most cities to explicitly mobilize residents' willingness and capacity to upgrade their own housing and neighborhood infrastructure.

Regarding the first innovation, several factors account for the stability of Santa Cruz's planning:

- Over the years, local and regional institutions such as the Public Works Committee and CORDECRUZ have received substantial technical assistance from international agencies.
- Key planners such as Prado have had a continuous influence. These planners are people whose technical expertise was respected by all sides, and even though Prado became involved in some political issues, for the most part the planners were seen as beyond petty political or economic rivalries.
- Percy Fernández served three consecutive terms soon after the introduction of elections for city mayors.
- An agency external to the mayor's office has always managed the urban plan.

- Surrounding provinces, such as Cordillera, have followed Santa Cruz's precedent of public-private interaction for planning and service delivery. Thus, neither the expanding scale of planning nor interjurisdictional planning disrupted the basic continuity in Santa Cruz planning. When some of the provinces achieved a planning capacity of their own, they found it easy to negotiate metropolitan and regional planning priorities with Santa Cruz.
- Above all, the local elites have controlled all agencies responsible for city planning, regardless of whether the planning agency has been primarily attached to the central, regional, or local government.

As for the second innovation, Santa Cruz's planning—like other Latin American cities—is not based so much on utilities (and their underground infrastructure) but on street design and public transportation. However, unlike most Latin American large cities, Santa Cruz has effectively anticipated population growth and prospective increases in the demand for urban land. In practice, it has been able to expand the supply of land—regular and irregular—according to increases in demand.

When land—even poorly developed urban land—is made accessible to new families and its occupation follows the rules of the most basic street planning and urban transportation services, the future costs of land readjustment, land rehabilitation for the prevention of natural disasters, or land property regularization are substantially reduced. This pattern of land supply also reduces the risk of later urban planners unsuccessfully imposing standard urban regulations on land that has been irregularly occupied and developed for years.

Expanding the supply of poorly developed land has prevented the dualistic growth that typifies most large Latin American cities (such as Rio de Janeiro): a relatively few regularized neighborhoods and a substantial number of irregular settlements that follow no preconceived urban design. In contrast, Santa Cruz has many intermediately developed areas that partially follow urban plans, thereby preventing the huge rents and administrative corruption experienced elsewhere in Latin America.

Regarding the third innovation, Santa Cruz has harnessed communities' potential contribution to the development of city infrastructure. Much earlier than most other cities, Santa Cruz perceived that Latin American cities are living entities, continuously being built by their residents, with or without public support. As has been demonstrated time and again, residents assign a high priority to housing and living conditions in the city and, for this reason, are prepared to invest their labor and savings in housing and city improvements as long as they reap tangible benefits. Some of the specific features of Santa Cruz's planning in this regard are:

- **A tradition of surveying its citizens' priorities.** For example, when one survey identified the citizens' concern for nutrition, the city prepared a nutrition plan. The plan was based on the availability and low prices of seasonal regional products, which are hard to market in full at the peak of the harvest. This plan included information on and incentives for consuming a balanced diet and was available from the Office of Citizen Information.
- **An insistence on the collective nature of the city's needs, challenges, and goals**. City planning is based upon comprehensive, intersector diagnoses of city problems that include environmental concerns, such as connecting the green areas of the city. As Percy Fernández put it in a personal communication in 1996, "the city is either good for all or is no good for anybody."
- **A structure for deconcentrated planning.** Neighborhood units for intersectoral planning identify priorities with the support and recognition of the mayor's office.
- **A center of community life.** Neighborhood schools effectively serve as the nucleus of community life. Local schools are a focus of neighborhood groups, and schoolrooms are convenient meeting places.
- **A justification of taxes.** Tax increases, particularly property tax increases, are carefully justified in terms of the specific benefits that will be brought to different areas of the city through the allocation of additional revenues. This system helps boost taxpayer compliance.

In sum, Santa Cruz has taken advantage of the three resources (land, people, and capital) available for city effectiveness in planning. As a concentric city situated in an enormous plain, Santa Cruz has practically limitless possibilities for land expansion just by paving and lighting the streets. As a city of immigrants and accelerated growth, it has been able to capture its residents' willingness and commitment to upgrading housing and infrastructure by themselves. As a city with deeply rooted, traditional families, Santa Cruz has been able to exploit social capital by effectively mobilizing private capitals to provide city infrastructure and public transportation.

However, Santa Cruz's urban planning does not effectively take into account the actual cost and the real possibilities of financing city infrastructure. This, combined with low densification and unregulated private utilities, makes it difficult to reorganize public service delivery at low financial or political costs.

The true meaning of Santa Cruz's innovations in planning cannot be measured against absolute standards or against the standards applicable to cities of more developed countries. Instead, it would be necessary to compare Santa Cruz with other Latin American cities that have gone through similar phases of accelerated growth to highlight its realistic and pragmatic approach to planning. However, this comparison is beyond the scope of this chapter.

Innovations in Professionalization

Santa Cruz exhibits a high degree of continuity in the gradual professionalization of the city administration. At the same time, its path toward professionalization is unique because of the city's willingness to share jobs and activities with the private sector.

The city has had neither a plan nor an explicit consensus that guarantees continuity in commitment and strategies toward professionalization of its staff. What exists in this area, as well as in other areas of city management, is the implicit commitment of all political and administrative leaders to strengthen the city's autonomy relative to the national government. Because strengthening city autonomy requires raising the standards of the public and the private staff who oversee the city, Santa Cruz has considerably elevated the professional level of its personnel.

CORDECRUZ provided on-the-job training, stability, and experience to young regional and city managers for over five years. The three early private cooperatives capitalized on some of the technical expertise and the enabling environment created by CORDECRUZ. The six years of Percy Fernández's administration also favored stability and professional development. These three institutional settings ensured nearly 12 continuous years of professional development for city managers and technocrats.

As mentioned previously, professionalization at CORDECRUZ reached levels well above those of other public agencies in Bolivia. However, Santa Cruz never planned a transition from the regional administration of the city by CORDECRUZ to local administration by cooperatives and the municipality. Therefore, the transfer of human resources from CORDECRUZ to the city did not take place in an orderly manner.

Instead, CORDECRUZ created an enabling environment for professionals trained in city and urban planning. Because CORDECRUZ and the central government emphasized physical planning and investment projects, the city has benefited over the years from a number of well-trained and experienced engineers. Similarly, the local universities—both public and private—have been oriented toward agricultural, engineering, and other technical training rather than the traditional Latin American concentration in law, medicine, and the social sciences.

There has also been a high degree of cross-fertilization between the modern business sector of Santa Cruz and the city administration. CORDECRUZ created the enabling environment for professionalization, and the private sector established the minimum standards that city staff should attain. The frequent flow of personnel between the public and the private administrations ensures continued cross-fertilization between the two sectors.

In the short span of 40 years, Santa Cruz evolved from a relatively neglected city and region into the most dynamic growth center of the country. During the last two decades of that period (1975–95), the entrepreneurial elites of Santa Cruz emerged as a significant economic power, as important as—or perhaps even more important than—their counterparts in the traditional Bolivian cities of the Andes. The Bank of Santa Cruz has developed into the largest bank in the country, and investments in urban infrastructure in Santa Cruz have consistently exceeded those of any other city. Private managers and professionals trained in negotiations and strategic planning have been in high demand. Many prominent members of the Santa Cruz civic movement and the local elites occupy key posts in the central government. In fact, the position of CCSC president is usually considered a step toward such posts. In its ongoing quest for control of private investment in public services, the city has had to emulate private sector standards of professionalism.

The same type of cross-fertilization is true for the professionalization of international negotiations. Because Santa Cruz is located at the crossroads of new trade corridors, both the private sector and the local and regional governments keep regular contacts with neighboring countries. City officials have even had direct conversations with governments from neighboring countries—and they have occasionally threatened to secede, mostly as a way of drawing attention to national policymakers.

Santa Cruz resorted to outsourcing many city activities long before the current wave of privatizing city services. The city contracts out most services except for physical and financial planning and administration. As a result, it has developed a relatively advanced contracting capacity.

Santa Cruz was the first large Bolivian city in which civic coalitions prevailed over political coalitions.[6] This de facto political reform has stimulated the necessary political basis for staff stability and conviviality, two

---

6. Cochabamba was also constructing this enabling city environment in the 1990s. La Paz, in contrast, continued to be heavily dominated by the maneuvers of national and local political parties.

preconditions for professionalization of the city administration. The prevailing civic spirit has also enabled routine exchanges between public sector and private sector staff.

Other significant innovations conducive to further professionalization include the simplification and technical evaluation of procedures, the deconcentration of the city to make city officers more responsive to citizens' demands, and an implicit policy of hiring women to fill key administrative posts as a strategy toward elimination of corruption. In fact, women outnumbered men in key city posts during the administrations of Percy Fernández.

Innovations in Financing

Santa Cruz's pressure for more independence from the central government has paid fiscal dividends since the times of highly centralized government finances. During the early 1970s, under the first presidency of Hugo Banzer—himself a prominent son of Santa Cruz—the government funneled foreign credit funds to Santa Cruz. Similarly, the city benefited more than other Bolivian cities from special central government transfers for oil and gas exploitation in the department of Santa Cruz. The CCSC utilized the significant bargaining power of Santa Cruz's regional movement to get central government concessions for revenue sharing from oil and gas exploitations.

Santa Cruz has demonstrated a higher capacity than any city in the country to plan and prepare large investment projects that comply with the technical and financial requirements imposed by external agencies. Because of this, the city has been privileged in the allocation of grant and credit resources by the financially powerful *Fondo Nacional de Desarrollo Regional* (National Regional Development Fund), the urban development fund of Bolivia. CORDECRUZ, during the 1980s, and the local government, during the 1990s, were able to capture more resources from the fund than larger cities such as La Paz or Cochabamba.

In addition to relying on central government transfers, the city has creatively raised local resources, both through local taxes and voluntary contributions or public-private partnerships. For example, property tax revenues increased as a result of the following improvements in tax administration during the first decade of popularly elected mayors:

- **Simplification of valuation methods.** The city adopted a new valuation method based on the number of square meters at different rates for different socioeconomic categories.

- **Estimation of the real property value of the entire city.** Santa Cruz in 1995 estimated for the first time the total number of real properties within the city (approximately 140,000 residential units with an average number of five persons per unit), the total value of real estate in the municipality, and the revenue potential of the tax (US$20–24 million; see table 8-2.1). These estimates gave the city the first rough measures of the combined effect of undervaluation, tax evasion, and tax expenditures (the cost of special tax exemptions and deductions).
- **Cadaster formation.** The city formed the initial property cadaster in one year (1995) by contracting out with a private firm. The initial cadaster covered 45,000 real estate units at a cost of US$3 per property. This initial cadaster could be refined later, if necessary, but what was important is that it gave the city, for the first time, a firm basis for collecting the property tax. Still, as in so many other Latin American cities, property tax administration is constrained by the fact that many land parcels lack legitimate title, and there is no connection between the property and the fiscal cadasters.
- **Maintenance of good relations with taxpayers.** The tax administration gave taxpayers opportunities to challenge the valuations of their properties and the option to pay their tax bills in several installments. More important, citizen education campaigns accompanied the processes of cadaster formation and property valuation. The city sought to persuade taxpayers to pay the property tax on the basis of the services it was already providing (street paving, park maintenance, and so on) and the connection between these services, the value of properties, and the quality of urban life. At the same time, those responsible for the processes of formation and valuation carried out the initial public relations campaign for the tax administration. The mayor also used a weekly two-hour television program to further publicize the new services approach to taxation.

Table 8-2.1. *Revenue Potential of the Property Tax, Santa Cruz*

Number of residential units	Average value (US$)	Percentage of total residential units
28,000	100,000	20
42,000	42,000	30
42,000	23,000	30
28,000	8,000	20

Note: Total value of the city's 140,000 residential units is US$5.8 billion.
Source: Municipality of Santa Cruz.

Santa Cruz has maintained the tradition of public-private partnerships for all sorts for financing collective goods and services.[7] Even Percy Fernández—who fought a long battle for city control of the public services delivered by the traditional private cooperatives—organized a public bid that included financing arranged through commercial banks. The purpose of the bid was to stimulate private companies to invest in equipment and infrastructure that would be repaid through taxes and fees over time. This financial scheme was not much different from municipal bonds underwritten by commercial banks, because commercial banks delivered the money to the private contractor as soon as the contract was signed.

The contracts were sufficiently large enough to attract both large contractors and big financial packages. The opponents to the mayor questioned the size of the contracts, as they seemed to favor large firms and reduce competition. However, the mayor insisted on large contracts as a means to ensure economies of scale and specialization.

Enemies of decentralization have long argued that cities are not as fiscally responsible as is the national government. The financial innovations, witnessed in Santa Cruz since the national government granted more autonomy to the region and the city, provide evidence against this argument. The financial management of Santa Cruz is not only innovative in terms of expanding public investment sources, but it is also becoming more responsible. For example:

- The city has prepared an intersectoral, long-term financial plan to cover the costs of full paving of all streets; cleaning, maintaining, and building drainage canals; street lighting; and building and maintaining plazas, parks, schools, sports arenas, neighborhood centers, and other public buildings. The estimated total cost for this major upgrading of city infrastructure is US$420 million (in 1995) and was to be distributed over a period of 15 years.

---

7. Unlike other Latin American cities that have distinguished themselves for their innovations in management, Santa Cruz has not resorted to the value added tax. This type of betterment levy has tremendous potential, but Percy Fernández did not want to introduce a value added tax for fear that it might drive public investments away from low-income neighborhoods. The city, however, has updated and maintained vehicle registration for purposes of the vehicle tax, simplified the tax structure to eliminate some obsolete taxes, and considered the possibility of making the property tax and the vehicle tax not just the dominant but, eventually, the sole sources of tax revenues.

- By the mid 1990s the city had reached a fiscal equilibrium by keeping current expenditures at around US$12 million a year and allowing only marginal increases in the city's payroll.
- The rate of public sector savings has gone up, and investments have continuously grown as a proportion of total budget.
- The credit policy has been carefully managed to ensure low interest rates and large, long-term financial packages. Credit is usually negotiated with private commercial banks, and private firms are tapped for building and maintaining city infrastructure.

The Need for New Innovations

As of the mid 1990s, the primary challenge of Santa Cruz seemed to be the transformation of civil society organizations into more open, transparent, and socially accountable institutions. The challenge was to properly exploit the associative tradition of Santa Cruz by abandoning the present structure of exclusionary associations and replacing them with organizations that invited membership, creativity, emulation, and replication. Because traditional, exclusionary organizations grew out of fraternity-like organizations at the school and neighborhood level, educational programs and incentives for interneighborhood exchanges and support appeared to be adequate tools to stimulate this transformation.

Santa Cruz officials face additional challenges:

- Public-private partnerships should be expanded at all levels, regulated, and made transparent. The city must make recent innovations in public works contracts subject to competition, publicity, and citizens' control by further developing the rules for accountability and contractualization. The central government must establish the legal framework for regulation and contractualization of public-private ventures at all government levels, including the city level.
- Because the Bolivian constitutional and legal framework weakens the stability of city administrations, Santa Cruz must ensure that city interests take precedence over the four major national political parties that are seeking control of city politics.
- Land regularization programs may help clarify land tenancy in the city. They will also expand the base for the property tax and other land-based levies.

- The city may further develop instruments that link investment planning and financing. The value added tax, if imposed in consultation with neighborhood priorities and with sensitivity to residents' willingness to pay, may be one of these instruments. Microregional planning, participatory budgeting, and regulated fees and prices may also be suitable instruments.
- The stability of mid-level public employees must be extended to all technical levels of city management; otherwise the benefits of professionalization and cross-fertilization with the private sector may dissipate. It must be kept in mind that high-level technocrats have exemplified personal commitment to public service since the time of CORDECRUZ.

Conclusion

Administering a rapidly growing city, in a context that is changing from state centralization to local autonomy, is a common challenge in Latin America. Retaining the cohesiveness of the city under these conditions, while expanding the urban area and gradually constructing urban infrastructure, as Santa Cruz has done, is less common and is a significant achievement. Avoiding the markedly dual structures of most Latin American large and intermediate cities is an even more exceptional result.

Driving forces have moved Santa Cruz to promote further decentralization, citizen mobilization, and the commitment of recently arrived immigrants to the development of the city—as well as the city's willingness to serve as a trade corridor and cultural melting pot. Accounting for these forces sheds some light on the prerequisites and the potential for decentralized urban development under conditions of globalization, modernization of the public sector, and explosive population growth.

Faced with the need to expand city infrastructure, Santa Cruz made every possible effort to strengthen local management capacity, capture external and internal resources, and invest them in the city. Santa Cruz did all this through a combination of public and private interactive models that are a unique adaptation to a less-than-favorable environment for managing the city. It replaced the scenarios of confrontation between the public and the private sector as well as between local-regional and national levels of government by scenarios of negotiation. Santa Cruz adopted a pragmatic view of city development, based on the recognition that the city is built step by step by the municipality and the people working together.

It is true that Santa Cruz took advantage of its existing social capital in a stratified, disorganized, and unregulated manner. Nevertheless, its localized forms of public-private interaction established a precedent of private commitment to the city and long-term investment and thereby promoted a higher level of interaction for potential public-private partnerships under more contractualized, regulated conditions. Indeed, unregulated public monopolies frequently lead to underinvestment in public utilities and lend themselves to corruption and monopoly abuses in Latin America. The particular innovation of Santa Cruz is its creation of a climate of civil society participation in municipal affairs and neighborhood initiatives for new services. The Santa Cruz path toward strengthening and further expanding social capital sets a precedent for highly stratified cities with deeply rooted traditional families (see Escobar and Alvarez 1992).

In the final analysis, Santa Cruz's planning may not be substantially different from urban planning in other Latin American cities. What makes Santa Cruz different is the policy—sustained over time by a changing mix of public-private groups—of continuous expansion of land supply and the way planning accepted and incorporated irregular settlements. As many Latin American cities, central governments, and multilateral agencies are now finding through expensive land regularization programs, it is the city's responsibility to continuously expand the urban perimeter according to increases in land demand, even at the cost of homogeneity and urban standards. The ideal of fully equipped plots of land that comply with every urban regulation is not only an imposition of middle- and upper-class taste and expectations but the ideological source of the Latin American urban dichotomy that separates regular from irregular urban land and housing.

The particularities of the Santa Cruz case only partially restrict the potential of this case for replication in Bolivia and elsewhere. It is true that both the city and the department of Santa Cruz are relatively better equipped than other Bolivian cities and intermediate governments to claim greater independence from the central government. Part of the comparative advantages of the city and the Santa Cruz region are based on physical characteristics, such as the location of the city and the availability of fertile land and oil and gas resources. At the same time, it is also true that claims to independence and administrative self-sufficiency are partly founded on features that have been gradually constructed over the years by city governments, regional businesses, political leaders, and the communities themselves.

References

Calderón, F., and R. Laserna. 1983. *El poder de las regiones.* Cochabamba, Bolivia: Center for the Study of Economic and Social Reality.

Escobar, A., and S. E. Alvarez. 1992. *The Making of Social Movements in Latin America: Identity, Strategy and Democracy.* Boulder, Colo.: Westview Press.

Whitehead, L. 1973. "National Power and Local Power: The Case of Santa Cruz de la Sierra." *Latin American Urban Research* 3(3): 23–46.

9

Public-Private Collaboration

9-1

Partnering in Cali, Colombia, for Planning and Management

Fernando Rojas, World Bank

This study deals with two levels of government in Colombia: local, represented by the municipality of Cali, and regional, represented by the department of Valle del Cauca. Cali, the capital of the department, grew during the twentieth century as the epicenter of a region whose social, cultural, political, and economic aspects are well integrated. The city's population burgeoned between the 1930s and the 1980s (see box 9-1.1).

The department of Valle del Cauca (see box 9-1.2) includes 41 municipalities, many of which have a strong financial base, clear local identity, and distinct culture. The municipalities have preserved their regional cultural identity despite the successive waves of immigrants from other parts of the country. The department is also characterized by:

- Relatively balanced regional development, with good communications and similar standards of living in the countryside and the city
- Sustained commitment by wealthy landowners to the development of the region
- High levels of agricultural productivity and agribusiness developments, primarily in sugar, coffee, seed oils, and dairy products
- Stability of the governing class, comprising economic, political, and commercial elites, which has proclaimed itself as guardian and promoter of social and economic development.

Box 9-1.1. *Cali's Population Growth*

Cali was a small town at the beginning of the twentieth century, with a lower population and political-administrative ranking than nearby cities such as Popayán. The 1938, 1951, 1973, and 1985 population censuses illustrate the accelerated rates of urban growth, a combined result of successive waves of immigration and the natural expansion of the population. During the 1950s and 1960s, Cali achieved population growth of more than 10 percent per year, second in Latin America only to São Paulo in Brazil. In 1997, the population of the Cali municipality was estimated to be a little over two million, and that of the conurbation (including the city of Palmira) around three million.

Context for Public-Private Interaction

Over the last 40 years, the city of Cali and the department of Valle del Cauca have developed a special facility for mobilizing resources (including personnel, technology, capital, and even land) from the private sector. They exchange factors of production with private enterprise and, to a lesser extent, with the University of Valle and with the communities. The most common

---

Box 9-1.2. *The Department of Valle del Cauca*

Valle has been a pioneer department in Colombia with regard to devolving responsibilities to its municipalities. It created health districts in the 1960s and numerous satellite campuses for the regional university throughout the department. In addition to the constitution of a new free trade zone in 1995, Valle created industrial parks in 13 of its 41 municipalities, beginning with 5 municipalities in the northern and northeastern areas of the department: Cartago, Caicedonia, Rodanillo, Trujillo, and Zarzal. They were to be followed by Andalucía, Buenaventura, Buga, Cali, Guacarí, Palmira, Restrepo, Sevilla, and Vijes.

The investment funds for the construction of infrastructure (aqueducts, electric power grids, and telecommunications networks) required by these industrial parks come from the department and the respective municipalities. Departmental and municipal administrations have discussed the investment projects with private firms of various sizes within the region and with each locality to guarantee feasibility for future export projects, which will create jobs.

---

route for mobilizing and exchanging resources has been the formation of associations, partnerships, networks, or other links. This special interaction between private capital and local and regional public administration has several foundations:

- The presence of agribusiness has given landowners strong ties to the region and to the industrial and export sectors. These ties have given the most influential owners of the fertile soils of Valle del Cauca an interest in promoting the region's development.
- Private sources of capital in the region, both domestic and multinational, have established numerous precedents for the associations' redistribution of investment risks and for technological innovations.
- Above all, Cali and Valle del Cauca have been able to count on family business empires and multinational sources of capital that regard stability and regional development as guarantees of their own economic, political, and social futures. Family businesses in Valle have strong ties to the region and clearly perceive that economic growth can be achieved only by building on a foundation of social and political tranquility.

Several of these family groups have been making contributions, in funds or in other resources such as land, to obtain benefits for themselves from local and regional social investment. They have set up nongovernmental organizations (NGOs) or have become associated with the public administration to increase spending on goods and services of a social nature. These family groups have also co-administered the delivery of goods and services to make them more efficient. The main contributions from the private sector to the local and regional public sector have consisted primarily of management know-how (which includes the ability to negotiate, manage transparently, and provide services efficiently and effectively), resource mobilization and cofinancing, and coordination of varied strategies for integrated development of the region. The private sector has opened the way for a combination of strategies for promotion and industrial restructuring that decentralize productive activities, generate employment, and reduce the effects of massive immigration.

History of Public-Private Interaction

Comanagement between the public and private sectors dates back to the beginning of the twentieth century and has included numerous sectors and services, primarily benefiting persons or communities located within the city or the region. This interaction has produced some of the important landmarks in the social and economic development of the city and the department (see box 9-1.3).

Box 9-1.3. *Timeline of Public-Private Efforts in Cali and Valle del Cauca*

1920s	The Pacific Railroad was built. It united the department and opened markets for its products in other regions of the country.
1930s	The highway to the port of Buenaventura was completed. It promoted the region's exports and boosted Cali into the major urban center.
1940s	The Anchicayá Hydroelectric Power Station was built.
Late 1940s to late 1950s	Social programs were initiated to incorporate the tremendous masses of immigrants who were driven from the countryside to the city due to political violence.
1950s and 1960s	The National University's School of Agronomy and the International Center for Tropical Agriculture were inaugurated. The Cauca River, which runs through the department from north to south, was canalized. These developments encouraged agricultural progress in the region.
Late 1960s	Urban infrastructure and public spaces were expanded as the city prepared for the Pan American Games.
1970s	The Salvajina Reservoir was constructed.
1980s	The huge Aguablanca District was rehabilitated. This vast urban zone in Cali emerged irregularly and abruptly, over a period of only seven or eight years, to house a population of roughly 500,000, particularly immigrants from other parts of the country.
1990s	The region focused on increasing its competitiveness through a multifaceted strategy that included the improvement of the port of Buenaventura, the expansion of free trade zones, promotion of the Transportation and Technology Corridor, creation of the Center for Productivity and Industrial Parks, use of special laws for attracting investment (such as the Paez Law, which benefits the area immediately to the south of the department), and the creation of the Scientific Research Institute.

The association between the public and private sectors has taken many forms:

- The public and private sectors and universities engage in high-level personnel interchanges, such as the rotation of managers.
- Contracts signed between private enterprises and the municipality or the department provide new or better public services. One of the most successful cases is the public-private comanagement of the new recreational, sports, and cultural services. Also, the downsizing of the Cali Secretariat of Public Works resulted in private operation and maintenance contracts for urban infrastructure.
- Private sector staff are appointed to public enterprises' boards of directors or to management programs' boards of regents.
- Self-help programs have proliferated for citizens wishing to improve housing. Beneficiaries contribute their labor; the private sector contributes managerial input; and the public administration provides land, equipment, and personnel or creates a framework to facilitate the effort.
- Outstanding individuals from the business sector or civil society who have distinguished themselves by their civic spirit are designated "citizen mayors." These individuals identify demands and offers of the community, articulate proposals, and present initiatives for consideration by the leaders of the municipality, the department, and private organizations.

Public-Private Institutions

Joint public-private institutions (see box 9-1.4) have emerged to deal with the challenges to development, especially savings, investment, employment, and social stability. The mayor and the governor have engaged in informal dialogue and consultations with private enterprise and trade union organizations. Citizens and program beneficiaries have provided feedback through decentralized city management organizations. Other sectoral institutions in the region authorized by recent Colombian government regulations on decentralization (boards of education constituted by parents, committees of health service users, and so on) have also participated in public sector activities by providing feedback.

Beyond the sectors, the services, and the modes these partnerships cover, their common denominator is the creation of favorable conditions for increasing productivity and competitiveness. Colombia is characterized by

---

Box 9-1.4. *Examples of Joint Institutions*

The Valle Industrial Development Foundation, a public sector entity, is an example of a joint institution created by private initiative and managed with private leadership. The Foundation for Higher Education and the Carvajal Foundation are examples of private institutions whose mission constitutes common interests that transcend the interests of their founders or their members.

In the department, examples of public-private entities also include the Economic Development and Foreign Trade Authority, the Social Development Authority, and the Valle Development Institute. The new Secretariat for Economic Promotion and Competitiveness is a municipal-level example of a joint institution.

---

insecurity, violence, massive population movements, and sociopolitical instability—all of which take place within a paradoxical continuity of political structures and positive rate of economic growth. In such a country, productivity and competitiveness require confidence among the parties, continuity of public policies, strengthening of a regional identity and a sense of belonging, pacification, security, harmony, and citizen participation. Public-private partnerships are essentially mechanisms for consolidating and preserving the "peace dividend." For this reason, the common objectives of the public-private cooperation in Cali and Valle del Cauca have been to:

- Professionalize local administration so that, without a face-to-face confrontation with traditional political and bureaucratic structures, it can develop symbiotic relations with private enterprise
- Identify priority areas for social spending in the common interest and ways to provide collective social services
- Institute forms of participation that stimulate savings, investment, and a sense of belonging for the middle- and low-income sectors.

This is the context in which the two innovations described in this case study have taken place. In Cali and Valle, the public and private sectors have relied on their history of cooperation to work together for the professional development of managers and for the provision of recreation services.

Private Sector Participation in Developing Managers

Private enterprise, public and private regional universities, and the most influential decisionmakers of city and departmental public administration have an implicit agreement to share the formation of the leaders of Cali and Valle del Cauca. When the leaders trained by this informal group assume roles and responsibilities within the public sector, their main point of reference is a private enterprise approach committed to regional social and economic development. These leaders are sometimes able to overcome the rigidity and resistance of a bureaucratic structure that is predominantly self-contained or controlled by the national political parties through dependency on political patronage.

Description

The innovative approach used to recruit and train new decisionmakers creates a parallel layer of management that influences the private sector's role in development within local and regional public administration. The private sector has implicitly combined several strategies to increase the capacity of the key managerial layers in the public sector:

- Identifying a relatively small number of key positions that have to be occupied by the most competent personnel available in the region
- Training a critical mass of managerial personnel capable of maintaining, evaluating, and improving basic public services (training has concentrated on common managerial tools, especially tools oriented to promoting and evaluating social spending)[1]
- Creating and maintaining an elite cadre of leaders who can fill managerial positions in the public and private sector equally well
- Optimally utilizing the same management resources in the public and private sectors (managers are rotated through and exchanged among high-level positions in local and regional public agencies, businesses, and NGOs)

---

1. The first managerial courses offered by the University of Valle during the 1950s and 1960s took advantage of input from distinguished U.S. professors in the field of social management for competitiveness of the firms and the city as a whole. Many students in these courses later became outstanding managers in the region.

- Waging public information campaigns about local needs for social and economic development and about preparation for medium- and long-term challenges.

Enabling Factors

Above all, demand and control by the private sector constitutes an innovation by creating a parallel layer of management. Private enterprises have proposed and overseen methods of service provision and have denounced cases in which their interests are affected by costs, quality, or service coverage. Frequently, private sector officials have proposed methods for service provision or to become comanagers of services.

Common paths for professional training and employment have also enabled the innovation. The shared experiences of public and private sector managers start in school classrooms, build in the university lecture halls, and continue throughout their professional careers.

Results

The innovation has produced the following results:

- Managers in the city and region have achieved a level of professionalization beyond what the respective public administrations could have achieved on their own.
- The public and private sectors are coordinating policies, plans, and programs, including those of the principal NGOs (see box 9-1.5).
- Information and communication bases have been established to increase the efficiency of local and regional service allocation and production.
- A modern, dualistic system has been created within the public administration. The managerial cadre, which alternates between private enterprise and public administration, has promoted and partially achieved administrative reforms despite the active resistance of the traditional bureaucracy. The antagonism between these two forces has created a parallel system in the sources, selection, levels, stability, and occupational guarantees of managerial personnel, on the one hand, and the mid-level and lower-ranking personnel, on the other hand. This has led to mutual suspicion between traditional administration and the business sector in Cali and Valle del Cauca (see box 9-1.6).
- Reforms have focused on streamlining and simplifying procedures, and suppressing some of the sources of administrative corruption fed by political and bureaucratic patronage.[2] Cali and Valle have the most

---

Box 9-1.5. *Nongovernmental Organizations in the Region*

Starting in the 1960s, large nongovernmental organizations (NGOs) were created to look after problems that the local and regional governments were unable to attend to sufficiently by themselves. The Carvajal Foundation was established in 1961 and was followed by the establishment of other large NGOs deeply rooted in the private sector, such as Colgate Palmolive, Propal, FES, Goodyear, and the Entrepreneurial Foundation for the Benefit of Yumbo.

The large NGOs in the region, most of which are private, are financed by returns on the sponsoring firms' shares, employee contributions, or by banks and international agencies. Altogether, they have invested an estimated US$25 million annually in recent years. In general, these foundations work in communities, providing training and stimulating residents' savings and investments by means of counterpart funds and work or other types of in-kind contributions. Their efforts are concentrated in education, culture, recreation, health, substance abuse, youth, community development, the environment, senior citizens, low-income housing, urban development, and microenterprise development.

In Cali and Valle del Cauca, medium and small NGOs have proliferated. Their number is estimated at 1,900, which represents about 40 percent of the total NGOs in the country.

---

advanced and transparent system for monitoring budget execution and public investment in all of Colombia. The physical and financial execution of a given investment project may be followed on a day-to-day basis on computers by the officials and the interested parties. The terms for awarding a contract also appear on a publicly accessible information system. This information system has laid the groundwork for a performance- and results-based personnel information and evaluation

---

2. Cali in the mid 1990s took the most significant step made at the time in Colombia to eliminate the impediments to officials' handling of petitions and requests from citizens, and to make the officials more receptive to their "customers." The Administrative Reform of 1995 imposed the so-called positive administrative silence, under which requests from citizens are considered resolved in a positive manner if the administration makes no decision on them within 10 days. Similarly, officials now have the obligation of backing the procedures required from citizens under rules with the force of law. If such rules do not exist, citizens may demand that the bothersome and complicated procedures usually employed by the administration be abandoned.

Box 9-1.6. *Achieving Reform Through Dualism*

Over the last 20 years, Cali and Valle have attempted administrative reforms. The city, for example, unsuccessfully attempted six radical reforms in 1980 and 1986, first during the administration of Mayor Rodrigo Escobar and then during the administration of Mayor Henry Eder. These reforms were intended to promote more efficient and effective government and increase citizen participation. It was not until 1995–96, when Cali was suffering from an economic downturn, that it became possible to reach a political consensus that would allow implementation of many measures that the public managers in Cali had been attempting to promote since the end of the 1970s.

Cali and Valle overcame obstacles to reform by avoiding a head-on clash with the bureaucracy. Instead of proposing the privatization of a part of the public administration or of opting for a drastic reorganization (which would bring political opposition and conflict with the public employees' trade union), city and department officials made a pragmatic choice. They selected the most expeditious method of achieving desired reforms: placing a managerial layer over the traditional layers of bureaucracy to guarantee the influence of the private sector in public resource allocation, mobilizing the resources of civil society, and building an institutional environment favorable to productivity and competitiveness.

---

system that allows private individuals to help monitor and evaluate local officials.
- Policy continuity and the qualifications of local and regional public administration are guaranteed in a similar way to the continuity ensured by a city manager within the Anglo-Saxon administrative tradition.

Alliances for Sports, Recreational, and Cultural Services

This innovation consists of tripartite management among private enterprise, public administration, and the community to plan, finance, construct, and maintain high-capacity recreation complexes of a novel design, initially in Cali and later in every municipality in Valle.

Origins and Description

The Cali Mayor's Office surveyed the preferences of the population and found that sports, recreation, and culture ranked highest among the priorities for collective services. The mayor's office brought together private entrepreneurs to explore how they could satisfy those priorities. The entrepreneurs proposed building multi-use recreation complexes, which could hold athletic, artistic, and cultural facilities, as well as community meeting rooms.

The municipalities usually contribute the land, private enterprise manages the construction, and the community assumes responsibility for the operation and maintenance of the complexes. The land usually occupies an area of 50,000 square meters and represents 30 percent of the overall value of the contributions. Fifty percent is contributed in funds by the private sector (the Colgate Palmolive Corp., for example, has financed the construction of three complexes). The community funds the remaining 20 percent through membership or access fees and other voluntary contributions.

The institutional mode for implementing the innovation has consisted of corporations or public-private associations. The first of these corporations, the Community Recreation Corporation (Corporación para la Recreación Popular, or CRP), set out to create a recreation complex in each of Cali's 20 communes.[3] The department followed this example and established RECREAVALLE, an organization that has built a large recreation complex in each of the 41 municipalities in Valle and set a goal of the creation of 100 new complexes in villages or rural zones in the region.

Enabling Factors

The tradition of public-private interaction for innovative provision of public services prepared the way for the city and the department to research and develop endogenous methods for providing recreational and cultural services. The institutional precedents of public-private associations or partnerships inspired the search for novel institutional arrangements, free from the inflexible norms of the traditional bureaucracy.

The climate of modernization in public administration that had been developing since the end of the 1970s legitimized a renovation of the traditional administration of the department and the municipality. The sensitivity of the city's and the department's managers to transparency and accountability assisted in making new forms for collective maintenance and

---

3. Established in 1979, the corporation holds the following four basic principles, which inspire its mission and objectives: (a) recreation is a public service, but not necessarily a free one; (b) recreation integrates the family; (c) recreation is a daily and continuous activity and should therefore be close to the user; (d) recreation is everyone's responsibility (CRP 1993).

for open public accounting that were acceptable to all those interested in the success of the recreation complexes.

Results

Through the beginning of 1995, the CRP had built 26 recreational units, 4 of them open to the whole city (see box 9-1.7). Each municipality in Valle has a large recreation complex. Other departments and municipalities outside the department are following the examples of Cali and Valle.

Each neighborhood park or local recreation complex serves an area with 1,000 to 5,000 families. The facilities and their maintenance are impeccable, even compared to international standards for recreation complexes, whether public or private. As a general rule, the quality and participation are better in the complexes than in other community or municipal gathering places.

The recreation complexes are seminal to the voluntary contribution of private resources for collective goals. In fact, the complexes have become the favorite meeting place to discuss the future of the communities or the municipalities. The community agreements for operation, maintenance, or extension of the complexes constitute a foundation for coordinated action with regard to other services. For example, the small municipalities of Cerrito, Florida, Ginebra, Guacarí, and Pradera (each with around 35,000 inhabitants) mobilized public and private resources to enter into "municipal pacts in favor of infants," with the support of the department. The pacts were designed to provide early childhood education, mother-infant care, or health care advice. The complexes are also coordinated with other aspects of urban development planning, such as environmental protection.

The resources invested in the city and departmental complexes already amount to the equivalent of tens of millions of U.S. dollars, which makes

---

Box 9-1.7. *Citywide Recreation Complexes in Cali*

- Parque de la Caña (Sugarcane Park), with an area of 156,000 square meters and a capacity of 20,000 people per day
- Parque de la Salud or Parque Ecológico (Health or Ecology Park), with an area of 850,000 square meters
- Poliactivo para la Tercera Edad (Activity Park for Senior Citizens)
- Parque del Descubrimiento (Discovery Park)

them one of the most important local and regional investments over the last decade. The recreation complexes have shown not only their sustainability in terms of maintenance, but they have also begun to produce earnings that will fund their improvement and expansion.

The complexes operate as a mechanism for income redistribution, frequently by means of explicit subsidies, approved on a voluntary basis for community members. If a family does not have membership in the complex, any family member may purchase a ticket to it. Municipalities such as Guacarí and Cerrito are contemplating subsidies for children of families who cannot afford the small membership fee or the ticket.

Sustainability: Parallelism and Institutional Transition

Cali and Valle have hired managers with regional and local roots to further the cause of renovating public administration. These managers move easily among the public sector, volunteer organizations, academia, and private enterprise. This management level has gradually implemented parallelism in local management, which is clearly manifest in numerous ways:

- **Dualism in the selection, composition, and orientation of personnel for local and regional administrations.** On the one hand, the management level has as its primary reference group the corporate networks or associations within the region. On the other hand, mid-level administrative and operational personnel's reference groups are clientelistic and bureaucratic structures. The cost of this dualism is its neglect of the professionalization of mid-level personnel, which has lasted many years.
- **Dualism in the structures of departmental and local administrations**. There is both a traditional administration, generally organized around the sectoral secretariats of the governor's office or the mayor's office, and a modern administration that has just begun to take form under the recently created managerial positions at both government levels. For example, the department has created managerial positions to oversee strategic macroprojects, cultural development, and economic development and foreign trade, and the municipality has created managerial positions for sectoral management and territorial development. These positions coordinate and orient the traditional secretariats. This dualism results in duplication, confusion of jurisdictions, friction from differing management styles, and increased costs for each administration.

- **Parallelism and tense coexistence between the traditional public sector and an emerging modern public sector.** The traditional public sector generally operates strictly according to manuals of functions and as decreed in detail by the central government. The modern public sector, in contrast, is associated with the private sector; negotiates and collaborates with NGOs and communities; forms associations or joint corporations; and is governed by modern patterns of service, strategic planning, and flexibility. The modern public sector also distributes the risks and costs of innovation in the provision of local and regional public services.

Limits on Replicability

Cali's environment, although it has many special characteristics, is not exceptional in Colombia or the rest of Latin America with regard to the transformation of the large agrarian land holdings into agribusiness complexes. These complexes have formed vertical and horizontal networks with multinational enterprises to supply a relatively large national market. They have a common cause for improving their competitiveness both locally and as a defense against foreign competition.

Cali and Valle are rare in that closed or family-held corporate structures with strong ties to the region have paved the way for private interests to work toward public spending for social purposes or for investment in basic urban infrastructure. This is especially true when the firms are (a) oriented toward international competitiveness, (b) economically and politically linked to the fate of mid-size urban or semi-urban population clusters, and (c) encouraged by ideas of equity and redistribution—but also under pressure from an environment of violence and social rebellion.

Several relatively exceptional circumstances limit the applicability of the public-private interaction experiences in Cali and Valle del Cauca to other contexts and require that a careful inventory be made of the conditions for transfer or importation:

- The socioeconomic and cultural integration of Cali and Valle make the city and the region an almost inseparable unit and builds on the combined resources of the city and the province.
- Cali is a relatively large city (with nearly 2.5 million inhabitants), and the surrounding region is relatively rich in natural, infrastructure, financial, and human resources.

- Many of the other municipalities in Valle have a good tax base and access to human resources, technology, and universities. They are interconnected with good road and telecommunications networks.
- Above all, the replicability of the Cali and Valle experience presupposes the existence of an equivalent social equity or, at least, of the appropriate incentives for its gradual development.

Conclusion

The ways that Cali and Valle del Cauca produce high-level professionals and provide recreation and sports services are, in and of themselves, novel. But the results achieved are also novel: customer orientation, participatory planning coordinated between the state and civil society, application of cost-effectiveness criteria to service provision, and efficiency in allocating local and regional resources.

The context of the two innovations dealt with in this study presents serious obstacles for sustainability and extension to other sectors. First, the close association between the private sector and local and regional public administrations lends itself to the appearance of new "dole recipients" or "free riders"—private interests that could receive unwarranted benefits. The association also risks the institutionalization of new forms of corruption.

Second, permeability between the public and private sectors faces severe resistance from the bureaucratic, patronage-based organization that has characterized Colombian public administration at all levels for decades.

Thus, a confrontation arises. On the one hand, the strong participatory tradition for civil society in the city and region allowed valuable "social capital" to accrue during the second half of the twentieth century. On the other hand, the traditional way of doing politics is based on the national political parties, the central government, and the main trade union confederations that tie public spending to political-bureaucratic patronage.

Cali and Valle del Cauca have resolved this confrontation by implementing a strategic innovation worth promoting in many other Latin American cities experiencing similar confrontations. The way the administration has been managed and the behavior of its personnel have led the business sector, the university, certain NGOs, and some public managers with vision to establish—gradually, imperceptibly, and sometimes unconsciously—parallel systems for regional service delivery.

Needless to say, dualism and parallelism are not the best solutions from the administrative point of view or from the point of view of efficiency. But perhaps they are the best outlet possible for local and regional actors within a static and inflexible national context. The novelty, the precedent, and the potential impact of this innovation for other cities in Colombia and throughout Latin America may only be fully appreciated when one keeps in mind the difficult political situation.

The struggle between administrative modernization and political tradition demonstrates the urgent need to advance political reform, which is still lacking in the country and which would create a more favorable environment for public-private partnerships at the local and regional levels. This reform will have to address the electoral system, political parties, and the positive or negative signals that the executive branch and the national Congress transmit to regional and local leaders and administrative teams.

Public-private interaction has promoted efficiency by creating alliances or partnerships that adopt new, parallel institutional forms, which sometimes duplicate the structures of traditional public administration. This dualism may be seen, on the one hand, as a transitory stage toward new forms of political and public administration, based on civic institutions of association and cooperation capable of incorporating the interests of the different actors or stakeholders. On the other hand, it can also be seen as a permanent solution and relatively inefficient front for bureaucratic-clientelist structures supported by central political parties that coexist with local autonomous developments and present formidable resistance to change.

References

CRP (Corporación para la Recreación Popular, or Community Recreation Corporation). 1993. "*Un sistema masivo de recreación urbana.*" Cali, Colombia.

9-2

Privatizing Ports and Mines in Venezuelan States

Rafael de la Cruz and Arianna Legovini,
Inter-American Development Bank

República Bolivariana de Venezuela, with a population of about 21 million people, is a federal republic that consists of 22 states and 330 municipalities. In the 1990s, national-level factors promoted decentralization, while state-level factors influenced the extent to which the states accepted and privatized new responsibilities. The states undertook reform initiatives to privatize responsibilities for major infrastructure such as ports and mines. This case study describes the reform initiatives in two Venezuelan states, Carabobo and Sucre.[1]

Without any outside technical support, these states introduced transparent international privatization practices and achieved significant results (Cordero and Suárez 1992; Diaz Matalobos and Dresner 1996). They have shown that local governments may have unique abilities to implement reforms that would be too costly—in terms of coordination and negotiation—

---

1. Sources interviewed for this study include Ramón Martínez, governor of Sucre; Pedro Novera, Sucre director of planning; Jesús Noriega Rodríguez, Sucre general comptroller; Carlos Atilano, president of Puerto de Güiria; Regulo Gomez, Bidding Commission for Salt Mines; René Franco, legal council for TECNOSAL; Edith Hernandez, chief of public relations for TECNOSAL; César Peluffo, president of Sucre's chamber of commerce; Lilo Maniscalchi, vice president of Sucre's chamber of commerce; plenary session, Sucre's chamber of commerce; and Yvette León, OIKOS and Associates.

at the national level. Sucre and Carabobo's innovations in privatizing ports, mines, and other assets may have strong demonstration effects for other states and municipalities.

National-Level Context: Working Toward Decentralization

With the constitution of 1961 following the Democratic Revolution of 1958, República Bolivariana de Venezuela adopted a strongly centralized federal system as a bulwark against military subversion and the traditional power fragmentation in the provinces. The constitution concentrated all responsibilities in the center, assigning to the municipalities certain activities deemed local and assigning to the states only residual activities of an administrative nature. Similarly, the states were not granted their own sources of fiscal revenue but were expected to depend on transfers from the national government. This arrangement was reinforced by the fact that the national government, because of a secure and growing flow of revenues from the exploitation of oil resources, did not need to negotiate its fiscal base with the country's constituencies. In turn, the central government distribution of the *renta petrolera* (oil revenues) fostered the dependency mentality of provincial rent seeking.

Although this centralized system may have contributed to a certain stability of the democratic process, it also constrained a wider process of participation, representation, and accountability. During the 1980s, with the crisis of the centralist state and reduced oil revenues, civil society made urgent demands for increased representation and accountability. This gave new force to the political debate over the redefinition of intergovernmental responsibilities, which would transform the governors of the states from mere national government representatives to representatives of their own local constituencies.

The national government in 1984 created the Commission for the Reform of the State (Comision Presidencial de Reforma Estadual, or COPRE) to prepare the legal basis for the redefinition of government and to frame reforms of the states and municipalities. In 1988, the COPRE made use of Article 137 of the constitution to seek congressional approval for assigning a wider spectrum of responsibilities to the states. Congress responded by enacting the Ley sobre Elección y Remoción de los Gobernadores de Estado (Law on Electing and Removing State Governors), which sanctioned direct elections of state governors for up to two consecutive three-year terms. The first such elections took place in 1989.

The new law was reinforced in 1989 by the Ley Orgánica de Descentralización, Delimitación, y Transferencia de Competencias del Poder Público (Law on Decentralization, Limitation, and Transfer of Public Powers), which redistributed responsibilities between the national government and the states. Responsibilities were classified as "exclusive" to the states or "shared" among the national, state, and municipal levels of government (see box 9-2.1). The law established that a portion of shared responsibilities would be transferred progressively from the national to the state governments. These would require the states or the national Ministry of Interior to submit to the national Senate a proposal to transfer a service. Once the proposal was approved by the Senate, the state and the executive branch would have to enter into an agreement specifying the transfer of human and financial resources and property, and establishing mechanisms of supervision and coordination. Other shared activities, namely water, electricity, telephone, transportation, and gas, could be administered by public-private enterprises, whether national, state, or municipal. Exclusive responsibilities, however, would be automatically assumed by the state once approved by the state legislative assembly.

In addition to the existing constitutional provisions (which called for a transfer to be gradually increased from 16 to 20 percent of national revenues), the law specified new sources of revenue for the states. Concomitant with the transfer of shared functions, the national government would

---

Box 9-2.1. *State Responsibilities*

Under the 1989 Law on Decentralization, Limitation, and Transfer of Public Powers, states shared responsibilities for some activities with national and municipal governments, and had exclusive responsibilities for other activities.

Shared responsibilities: Utilities, state development, protection of families and minors, rural and indigenous populations, education, culture, sport, employment, human resource development, agriculture, industry and commerce, environment, territorial ordinance, state public works, low-income housing, consumer protection, health research, and defense.

Exclusive responsibilities: Notary services; operation and maintenance of mines, roads, highways, ports, and airports; and collection of consumption taxes not reserved for the national government.

have to transfer to the state budget the corresponding financial resources that had been previously allocated to the activity. The allocation would be adjusted yearly, proportional to the increase in national revenues. Exclusive functions were expected to be supported by self-generated revenues. Finally, the Fondo Intergubernamental para la Descentralización (Intergovernmental Decentralization Fund), financed through a portion of the value added tax, would distribute funds to the states for purposes such as new investment projects associated with the decentralization of services, modernization of state and municipal institutions, payment of obligations assumed by the state as a result of personnel transfers, and pre-investment.

Since 1989, the process of transferring responsibilities has been slow and replete with difficulties, but it has resulted in a large number of functions, mostly exclusive, being administered by the state and local governments (see box 9-2.2). Altogether, about 50 transfers had taken place as of 1995, and another 100 requests were being processed. A large proportion of states had assumed responsibility for administering roads, ports, airports, and metal and salt mines. For example, by 1995, 13 of the 22 states had assumed responsibility for roads, 9 for ports, and 10 for airports. Transfer of shared responsibilities lagged due to the intrinsically political nature of the process and its procedural complexity. Only in the area of health services did officials make some progress, transferring the function to six states. Final agreements regarding health services were drawn up in seven more states, and solicitations were being processed for another five. About half of the states signed comanagement agreements with the Venezuelan Institute of Social Security to administer the institute's health facilities.

Decentralization of services from higher to lower levels of government brings with it several immediate benefits such as the geographical closeness of the providers to the beneficiaries. This allows providers to better target their services, and beneficiaries to demand and keep providers accountable by exercising their vote. But decentralization does not ensure better management, nor does it automatically result in appropriate resources being allocated to the activity. Once services and infrastructure are transferred, these factors—managerial know-how, appropriate incentives, and resources—have to be addressed. The advantage of decentralization is that reform initiatives become more feasible at the local level (that is, they have a positive net present value), because lower expected gains are required to cover the transaction costs of their implementation.

Sustainability of the decentralization effort and good local governance will depend not only on the continued political commitment of both state

Box 9-2.2. *Timeline of Reform Initiatives in República Bolivariana de Venezuela*

1989   The national government enacts the following enabling legislation: Law on Election and Removal of Governors; Reforms to the Constitutional Law for the Municipal Regime; Law on Decentralization, Limitation, and Transfer of Public Powers.
First election of governors and mayors.

1991   Congress approves the Law on Suppressing the National Port Institute and creates the General Directorate of the Port Sector. More than 10,000 port workers throughout the country are laid off in preparation for the decentralization of ports.
The state of Carabobo assumes responsibility for Puerto Cabello and creates the Puerto Cabello Autonomous Port Institute.
The national government signs an act ceding Puerto Cabello to the state of Carabobo.
Two more states, Anzoátegui and Nueva Esparta, receive responsibility for their respective ports.

1992   Puerto Cabello generates profits for the first time in its history. The waiting time for unloading is cut to one-third of what it was, and the port begins operating 24 hours a day, 365 days a year.

1993   The state of Carabobo transfers all the facilities and land located in the port area to the Puerto Cabello Autonomous Port Institute, ceding all rights granted by the National Port Institute to the state government.
The state of Sucre enacts legislation to transfer responsibility for ports and salt mines to the state.
The National Port Authority is created.

1994   The National Port Association is created, bringing together all state port authorities.

1995   Ensal, the National Salt Mine Enterprise, is liquidated.
The state of Sucre assumes responsibility for its airports.
First salt mine privatization in República Bolivariana de Venezuela: TECNOSAL receives the first concession award to operate the Araya salt mines in Sucre.

1996   Annual production of Araya salt mines reaches 520,000 tons (up from 90,000 tons before privatization).
Puerto Cabello handles 200,000 containers (up from 36,000 containers in 1990).
The state of Sucre awards a 15-year concession to operate the International Fishing Port of Güiria.

1997   The state of Sucre begins auctioning tourism establishments.

and national governments, but also on the ability of the states to develop, in a timely manner, efficient management solutions, alternative service delivery mechanisms, and new sources of financing. Building credibility for the reform efforts and establishing a predictable environment will favor the participation of multiple actors and secure sources of finance and technical expertise. Some of the new governors of República Bolivariana de Venezuela have taken the initiative to seek innovative solutions that look at the private sector and the community as logical partners in the administration of traditionally public functions. Their capacity to attract local and international private resources is likely to strengthen growth, promote efficiency in investment decisions, and increase knowledge.

Why was the strategy for change oriented toward privatization? First, República Bolivariana de Venezuela was suffering from a long series of direct government management failures. Second, the concept of privatization of public service management had, at that time, a great deal of prestige. (In all probability, if the decentralization had occurred during the 1960s, the states would have managed the ports directly.) Governors had significant incentive to show that they could manage the port better than the national government: endorsement of their governing abilities.

These cases show that a governor who reorients a service, makes it efficient, and obtains income from it gains approval for himself and his political group. In the state of Sucre, the governor was motivated by the lack of resources to pursue decentralization, and he believed that reform could work when each party assumes due responsibility. He pioneered a far-reaching strategy for changing business as usual, capitalized on imported technical resources, generated ad hoc local resources, avoided bureaucratizing processes to keep the reforms dynamic, allowed processes to be demand-driven, and sought alliances whenever necessary.

Within this framework, it is possible to understand why the governments of Carabobo and Sucre assumed (a) a high risk of political confrontation with labor unions and the parties that supported them, (b) the costs of reorienting port activities and establishing themselves as the pioneers in a scheme of privatization of a public service, and (c) responsibility for what until then had been considered a lost cause. If a governor or a mayor makes a mistake, citizens can send a clear sign of their disapproval in the next elections. Even through the electoral system, citizen participation plays a role of fundamental importance in defining the incentives appropriate to regulate the relations between the state and society. The port decentralization experience shows that not only can the management of government services be improved under conditions of decentralization, but it also provides a clear signal of how decentralization helps reestablish the ties of confidence between electors and elected.

State-Level Context: Carabobo and Its Port

The state of Carabobo (see box 9-2.3) approved a law in August 1991 that transferred the authority over ports. A liquidation board of the National Institute of Ports (Instituto Nacional de Puertos, or INP) oversaw the dismantling and transfer of Puerto Cabello in November 1991. Contrary to expectations, the governor's office did not directly administer port operations. Instead, the administration of Puerto Cabello under state authority acquired innovative characteristics that set it apart as an example to be followed by the other states, as well as by other countries in similar conditions.[2]

Puerto Cabello is República Bolivariana de Venezuela's principal port, handling approximately 50 percent of the country's international freight. It has 11 piers organized into 26 docks, with sufficient space for future growth. Furthermore, it enjoys favorable conditions on a bay with calm and deep waters, which allows for a very deep channel that, with dredging, was expected to reach a depth of 45 feet. Table 9-2.1 provides an overview of the infrastructure of selected ports on the Caribbean.

Given its geographic position, the port of Cabello offers ease of communication with Atlantic and Pacific markets and can welcome maritime traffic and freight coming from different regions for distribution through various shipment networks. Puerto Cabello serves 14 Venezuelan states and

---

Box 9-2.3. *Profile of the State of Carabobo*

The state of Carabobo is located in northern República Bolivariana de Venezuela, with access to the Caribbean. It is 4,650 square kilometers and has a population of approximately 1.6 million people. The state's economy consists largely of manufacturing. It is estimated that more than half of the country's industrial base is located here. Carabobo also is the main producer of several agricultural products. The communications infrastructure is of good quality. The state includes Puerto Cabello (the country's most important port), an international airport, and one of the country's most developed highway networks.

---

2. The information on Puerto Cabello owes a great deal to a 1994 study carried out by Segall de Garzón and Sevilla (1994).

Table 9-2.1. *Comparative Port Infrastructure in the Caribbean*

Port	Pier length	Depth (meters)	Area (hectares)	Covered warehouses (m^2)	Gantry cranes	Computerized cargo control
Aruba	1,440	9.8	13	—	no	no
Barbados	700	9.8	—	—	—	—
Curaçao	2,500	—	—	—	1	no
La Guaira	2,557	10.2	22	120,000	no	no
Miami	3,855	11.7	243	72,000	6	yes
Ponce	1,000	10.6	8	—	—	—
Puerto Cabello	3,380	9.2	38	62,000	no	no

— Not available.
Source: Diaz and Dresner (1996).

three Colombian departments. Box 9-2.4 summarizes the situation in Puerto Cabello prior to decentralization.

State-Level Context: Sucre

Long a bastion of the center-left Acción Democrática (Democratic Action), the country's largest political party, the government of Sucre has suffered from low institutional capacity, poor implementation of its large portfolio of programs, low effectiveness, and relatively high fiscal burden. Between 1989 and 1992, the city made little progress toward decentralization due to the lack of commitment from the incumbent administration. In that period, the Legislative Assembly of Sucre passed the law for the transfer of ports, but the actual transfer did not occur until 1993. (See box 9-2.5 for an overview of Sucre.)

In the 1992 governor's campaign, the Acción Democrática candidate faced a challenge by Ramón Martínez of MAS-Convergencia, a party that had traditionally supported far left-of-center positions. In his campaign, Martínez brought together a multidisciplinary team of advisors from civil society and academia to articulate a strategy for stabilizing the state's finances and improving the targeting and effectiveness of its programs. By drawing on local resources and assembling a diverse team of advisors, Martínez developed a platform that was both realistic, in terms of assessing the limitations of public resources and capacities, and proactive, in terms of transforming the state into an attractive location for private resources and investment. His platform, "horizontal, comanaged democracy," advocated

---

Box 9-2.4. *The Situation in Puerto Cabello Prior to Decentralization*

Puerto Cabello suffered from numerous problems before decentralization:

- The unions had excessive power and, through collective bargaining contracts, imposed their will for working conditions that promoted general inefficiency among the laborers and office staff and made it impossible for the port to generate a profit.
- The port administration lacked a coherent human resources program. Personnel were very poorly trained: 52 percent had only primary education, 42 percent had not completed secondary education, and a mere 6 percent had technical training in mechanical, electrical, or basic electronic maintenance.
- None of the necessary investment had been made to modernize the port-handling technology. Port operations were carried out with the same technology used 30 years before.
- The National Institute of Ports granted concessions for 20-year terms, which promoted inefficiency.
- The rates that the concessionaires paid were calculated as a function of their gross revenue with an additional amount for movement of bulk or chemical cargo. This method of calculation was inefficient, because it required the port administration to monitor the concessionaires' revenue collection.
- The rates charged by the National Institute of Ports did not recover costs, the criteria for collection did not benefit the port, and there was no charge for the right to use the protected waters.
- The deficiencies in maintenance at the time the transfer occurred included a lack of dredging, deterioration of water pipelines and electric cables, corroded steel on the docks, damage to the maneuvering platforms, deterioration of the internal road system, aging and malfunctioning mobile equipment, and broken-down old vehicles.

---

a limited role for the state and an aggressive role for the private sector based on market principles. Proposed actions included the transfer of productive activities to the private sector, the promotion of competition, the modernization of the financial management system, and improvement in public works management.

Martínez took office in June 1993 and began work on his two-part agenda: to modernize public sector financial management and human resource

---

Box 9-2.5. *Profile of the State of Sucre*

Located in the northeastern part of the country, the state of Sucre has a population of about 820,000, only 30 percent of whom are in the labor force. Of these, only about 40 percent are in the formal sector. The low employment rate stems from the fact that more than half the population is below 18 years of age.

With República Bolivariana de Venezuela's largest fishing fleet and principal canning factories, Sucre is considered the country's fishing center. It also ranks first in the production of salt, although that activity employs only a small portion of the labor force. The large agricultural sector employs about a fourth of the work force, mainly in the production of cocoa, coffee, sugar cane, coconut, and fruit. The state is one of the poorest of the country, with lagging industrial production and an underdeveloped tourism infrastructure.

---

development and to decentralize project management. Government activities were classified into 102 self-contained projects, each managed independently. These projects ranged from social investment to establishment of a sustainable economic environment, and from the rationalization of the public sector to the promotion of private sector participation and privatization. The idea was to establish a link between budget allocation and results, while limiting administrative costs to keep investment high relative to current expenditures. To do this, it was necessary to establish budgets linked to performance targets, evaluate results, and reoptimize resource and project composition periodically. This system provided the governor with an effective mechanism for quick decisionmaking.

One issue that required attention was the management of the decentralization process. During the previous administration, only the law transferring responsibility for the state's ports had been submitted and approved by the state legislature, and the new governor felt that Sucre lagged other states in the decentralization process and was losing resources that should have been channeled to the state economy. His administration in 1993 created the Comisión para la Reforma Integral del Estado Sucre (Commission for the Reform of the State of Sucre) to help speed up this process and provide the state with the legal basis for accelerating the transfer of responsibilities from the national government. The efforts of the commission and the governor led, in the following two years, to the state Legislative Assembly's approval of the transfer of several exclusive responsibilities:

salt mines, notary public services, mineral resources, roads, and airports (Gobernación del Estado de Sucre 1994a, 1994b). As for shared responsibilities, Sucre entered into initial agreements with the national government for the transfer of health services, education, sports facilities, and the protection of minors and the elderly. Of these, only health had been transferred from the Ministry of Health and Social Assistance as of 1995. The other transfers were still awaiting Senate approval.

To ensure profitability and financial sustainability of the activities being transferred, the process of decentralization had to be complemented with a strategy for improving operating efficiency, attracting managerial know-how, and increasing investment flows. Sucre's innovators considered different solutions; namely, the traditional national government model of direct exploitation through the creation of public institutions and enterprises and the private-public partnership model with various degrees of private sector participation, including concession contracts, privatization, and direct sale of assets.

Although all activities came under state management initially, steps were quickly taken to prepare for their eventual privatization. Years of public sector mismanagement had left most activities in shambles, usually characterized by negative year-end balances, large debts that exceeded assets by many times, high administrative expenditures (particularly for personnel), poor maintenance of physical assets, and otherwise minimal capital expenditures.

Sucre's privatization plan was the product of a government with a vision and a direction, centered on the belief that a partnership with the private sector would help bring investment and growth to the state as well as efficiency to the public sector. The focus on results and the awareness of the need to reach beyond the public sector were key to making those results a reality.

Sector-Level Context: Ports

The bulk of República Bolivariana de Venezuela's international trade is shipped through seaports. Despite this, seaports prior to decentralization represented a tremendous disincentive for importers and exporters because of the fragmentation of public entities responsible for port activities, which led to a lack of coordination, duplication of efforts, and incoherent resource allocation.

The National Institute of Ports (Instituto Nacional de Puertos, or INP), which relies on the Ministry of Transportation and Communications

(Ministerio de Transportación y Communicaciones, or MTC), previously oversaw the port system (see box 9-2.6). Excessive centralization in port administration made both strategic decisionmaking and daily management ineffective, untimely, and lacking in the information needed for good administration. The INP's inability to respond to the country's regional demands and the changes in international standards for port management contributed to the growing urgency to transfer services to the states.

Box 9-2.6. *The National Institute of Ports*

The National Institute of Ports (Instituto Nacional de Puertos, or INP) was created in 1975 as an autonomous institution under the Ministry of Transportation and Communications (MTC). Its mission was to plan, build, maintain, and operate ports; equip the port terminals; provide such services as stevedoring, wharfage, storage, and reception and delivery of merchandise; and set rates with the approval of the executive branch.

The INP was a highly centralized organization whose sphere of activity included the whole country. There was little coordination and communication between the INP and other government agencies, such as the MTC and the Ministry of the Treasury, which controlled the port authorities and customs, respectively. The scarce information interchanged between the ports and the INP, the lack of autonomy in decisionmaking by the local managers, and the political interests that dominated the institute's management made the port activities very inefficient.

The INP expanded in a disorganized fashion as a result of the increase in imports during the 1970s, a period when the country's economy grew at a rapid rate due to the extraordinary level of oil revenues. The increase in imports generated tremendous congestion in all of the country's ports. The INP was unable to foresee and carry out the reforms and investments necessary to adapt to the new demands. During 1976 the average deficit in port capacity for the country was 20 percent (Sabatino Pizzolante 1992).

As a consequence of the INP's poor administration of the ports, the national government was obliged to inject large quantities of financial resources into the port system. According to MTC statistics, the INP cost the country nearly US$20 billion.

In 1991, the national government created the Law Suppressing the National Institute of Ports, which established the General Directorate of the Port Sector within the MTC. All port workers and employees were laid off, retired personnel were transferred to the MTC, and all labor debts and commitments with contractors and suppliers were canceled.

Sector-Level Context: Salt Mines

The exploitation of the salt mines, which in República Bolivariana de Venezuela dates back to colonial times, came to be considered early on as a prerogative of the national government. According to the Ley Orgánica de la Renta de Salinas (Organic Law on Revenue from Salt Mines), all revenues from the sale of salt went to the national treasury. The salt mines were administered initially by the Ministry of Finance; then transferred in 1968 to the Venezuelan Institute of Petrochemistry, the largest single consumer of salt in the country; and in turn passed on to what became the National Salt Mine Enterprise (Ensal). Ensal was acquired in 1978 by the Venezuelan Investment Fund (Fondo de Inversiones de República Bolivariana de Venezuela, or FIV), a ministry-level institution responsible for investing public assets and coordinating the national government's privatization program.

Ensal administered the salt mines in the states of Zulia, Falcón, Nueva Esparta, Anzoátegui, and Sucre, the largest being the Araya salt mines in Sucre. Although salt was one of the country's most important and strategic resources, and a fundamental input to the petrochemical industry, Ensal managed to accumulate losses year after year, and resorted repeatedly to the FIV for additional lending and capitalization to cover operational expenses. As Ensal forsook sound commercial practices in favor of politics and clientelism, administrative costs alone reached 102 percent of total revenues for 1993, due mainly to the overstaffing from Ensal's collective contract. Other mismanagement practices included unaccounted for or undersold shipments of salt to the petrochemical industry, various banking-related illegalities, unwarranted indemnification payments, and inappropriate procurement practices. The result: by 1993, liabilities of the company had increased to Bs 2 billion (about US$20 million at that time) as compared to estimated assets of less than Bs 200 million (US$2 million). According to the criteria in the national Code of Commerce, and short of massive recapitalization, the company was ready to be liquidated. In April 1994, Ensal's board agreed to the liquidation of the company, which was concluded in early 1995, with the FIV assuming its debt (see Government of Carabobo 1990 and Madrigal 1996).

Carabobo's Privatization Initiatives

Carabobo was the first state to gain responsibilities under the Venezuelan decentralization process. As early as 1990, several states requested the cession of services from the national government, but this turned out to be a long and tortuous process. In spite of the political will in República Bolivariana de Venezuela's executive branch to decentralize important sectors, some ministers and many other officials opposed the transfer of services under their charge.

This opposition moved the governors to begin to request exclusive services. Formally, all that was required was the approval of a state law. The reality turned out to be somewhat more complex. The president of the Puerto Cabello Autonomous Port Institute (Instituto de Puerto Autonomo de Puerto Cabello, or IPAPC) and some high-level government officials believed that the ports should simply be privatized. It took a great deal of political effort on the part of the Carabobo government and the Presidential Commission for State Reform, a body of the Office of the President of the Republic, to see that the law ceding port services was enforced. This cession put the credibility of the decentralization process on trial. Although decentralization had begun with the election of governors and mayors a year and a half earlier, it showed no signs of advancing the transfer of specific responsibilities to the states.

Authority over the port was finally transferred to the state of Carabobo in 1991. Previously, an interdisciplinary commission had been constituted, consisting of the INP, the MTC, and the governor's office, to study the conditions for cession. However, during the months following the transfer to Puerto Cabello, the national government transferred almost all the remaining ports to their respective states.

Carabobo had several reasons and incentives to pursue decentralization:

- The decentralization process was just beginning, and it was an excellent opportunity for Governor Enrique Salas Romer to demonstrate that the state could manage such a complex responsibility with greater success than the central government. República Bolivariana de Venezuela's system of single-candidate elections for state and local authorities, who could then be reelected, was a strong incentive for accountability to the electorate.
- The state wanted to show not only that many of the problems inherent to centralized management could be overcome, but also that the ports could be profitable and constitute an important source of income for the municipalities in which they were located and for the state of Carabobo as a whole. In the case of Puerto Cabello, the change in profitability was dramatic, going from losses of US$5 million per year prior to decentralization to earnings on the order of US$9 million during 1992.

- Local economic interest groups suffered because of the ports' poor administration. A factor that could have been important in the governor's decision to assume control over Puerto Cabello may have been a desire to develop the state's economy.

Successful innovation in managing Puerto Cabello was essentially a consequence of the decentralization process, independent of the type of strategy selected (in this case the privatization of port operations). The set of incentives mentioned previously are only possible under decentralization conditions. Under these conditions, officials are accountable to the electorate and need to show that their administration can surpass that of the central government. It was indispensable for the governor's office to assume this managerial responsibility with the goal of increasing efficiency (Government of Carabobo 1990).

Carabobo's strategy for assuming responsibility for the port had five elements:

- Limit the role of the state in regulating port services
- Create an institutional framework for port administration (for this purpose, the state of Carabobo created the IPAPC and staffed it with specialized personnel)
- Establish a free market scheme for loading, unloading, transportation, and storage operations, under which firms previously accredited by the IPAPC may freely offer their services to the ships that dock in the port
- Design a long-term investment plan to modernize the port
- Seek an alliance with municipalities through a revenue-sharing scheme (Carabobo first sought an alliance with Puerto Cabello, the municipality most affected by the port's externalities).

Given the deteriorated condition of the port, the state's successes were both surprising and substantial. It overcame multiple challenges, as described in the following section.

Personnel and the Unions

The rigidity of the collective bargaining contracts before privatization led to a series of problems. In 1990, the payroll at Puerto Cabello consisted of 75 percent active workers, 14 percent retirees, 9 percent office employees, and 2 percent others (preretirement laborers who remained on the payroll despite having no functions). The workers not only did not carry out the functions of longshoremen and stevedores in an efficient manner but also hindered work in progress and blocked the introduction of new technologies. To move their freight, ships were required to contract their own crews, even though they paid the INP for such services.

Prior to ceding the ports to the states, the INP had to determine the cost of the transfer, with particular reference to the liquidation of the labor force. The INP's liquidation plans called for laying off all port personnel (more than 10,000 people) at a cost of US$172 million for severance pay and labor liabilities. In the case of Puerto Cabello, 3,906 laborers were laid off at a cost of nearly US$74 million. The FIV paid for this (see table 9-2.2).

This transfer of resources from the central government to the states freed the ports from heavy liabilities and helped to create the conditions for profitable management, because the funds provided by the FIV did not become a part of the INP's liabilities. The FIV's contribution also left the state governments free to reorganize port activities. But in view of the amounts disbursed, it was a measure that could not be repeated for other services. Also, some argued that the states should accept the ports' and other services' financial liabilities as well as the condition that they were in at the time of decentralization.

Table 9-2.2. *Liquidation of the National Institute of Ports Labor Force*

Port	Number of workers	Indemnification (millions of Bs)	Indemnification (millions of US$)[a]
Puerto Cabello	3,906	4,228.63	74.43
La Guaira	3,331	3,173.78	55.87
Maracaibo	1,628	1,244.17	21.90
Guanta	502	531.62	9.36
Puerto Sucre	369	202.27	3.56
Guaranao	192	176.68	3.11
Carúpano	168	109.76	1.93
El Guamache	160	122.50	2.16
Caracas	13	16.32	0.29
Total	10,269	9,805.73	172.61

Note: Does not include amounts for liquidation of office employees, retirees, widows, or claims.

a. Average Exchange Rate for 1991: 56.81 Bs = US$1. The budgeted income for the central government that year was US$14,830 million.

Sources: Segall and Sevilla (1994); author's calculations.

The central government acted boldly by funding the severance pay, which represented 1.1 percent of its budgeted income for 1991. The payment seems high in proportion to other budget items. For example, during that year, salary payments for more than one million public workers amounted to US$2.8 billion. This means that each port worker collected on the average US$17,605, compared to an average annual salary of a little over US$2,100 for public employees. However, the fiscal sacrifice did save República Bolivariana de Venezuela several million dollars each year in port subsidies and put the state-level public sector in a position to obtain additional income from port services, reducing the states' dependency on transfer payments from the central government.

The central government's decision to bail out the ports by liquidating their personnel provided a solid basis for initiating state-level administration. In addition, the amount of the indemnification broke up the cohesiveness of the unions and aided in reorganizing the personnel system. This case clearly illustrates the benefits that can be garnered by cooperation among the different levels of government in the decentralization process.

The New Organizational Structure

Prior to decentralization, the dominant characteristics of port organization were a lack of coordination between the INP and the ports and an absence of local autonomy in decisionmaking, which made port activities extremely inefficient. For example, the port director's responsibilities had to be guided by the general policies established by the INP in Caracas. In practice, the director lacked the autonomy to resolve even the most mundane, day-to-day problems.

Carabolo created an autonomous institution, IPAPC, with powers to grant concessions under conditions previously authorized by the governor, as well as to set prices and conditions for service provision, and administer its own revenues. The institute has a wide margin of decisionmaking autonomy over its direction and administration, although the governor has a say in naming the highest level of port administrators. The institute is overseen by a board of directors consisting of a chairperson named by the governor and 10 principal directors, of whom 5 are named by the governor and 1 apiece by the Puerto Cabello city government, the Puerto Cabello Chamber of Commerce, the Carabobo Federation of Labor, the Puerto Cabello Shipping Association, and the port workers themselves. The board of directors approves the institute's proposed annual budget, sets the administrative and financial policies, designates and establishes the compensation package of the port director, authorizes investments, sets fees for services that the IPAPC provides directly, and assumes commitments that may not exceed US$880,250.

With regard to operational restructuring, port operations were totally privatized by granting concessions through a public bid process. Port services are now offered by private operators under competitive conditions. The contracts inherited from the foregoing administration have a 20-year term, whereas the new concessions are in effect for terms of 2 to 5 years. All contracts are subject to a yearly rate review. The concessionaires are charged a fixed rate, which allows the institute to determine its own income, free from market fluctuations, and to avoid oversight of the private firms' collection of fees, as was necessary under the former system.

With this scheme, the port operators provide, at their own liability, all services related to the ships and cargo, using their own personnel, goods, and equipment. By sharing liability with the concessionaires, the IPAPC has benefited from a reduced need for insurance coverage. The price for the concession services is agreed upon between the operator and the customer, always under competitive conditions. The institute is responsible for ensuring that concessionaires do not engage in price fixing, which is unlikely in any case because of the large number of firms.

Necessary Investments and Rate Collections

Because the port facilities were in an advanced state of deterioration due to the lack of maintenance, infrastructure improvement was one of the most important tasks of the new authorities. During the two years following decentralization, institute expenditures went exclusively to repairs to restore the port's operating conditions, such as dredging, pier defenses, water supply, sewers, and a wastewater treatment plant. The institute's financial success after 1991 made these investments possible, as reflected in its 1993 bank reserves of less than US$13,000 and a near absence of debt.

The fee schedule applied by the new administration was basically oriented to converting the port into a profitable enterprise, competitive with other ports in the area and capable of generating sufficient resources for investing in short-term infrastructure improvements. The IPAPC Board of Directors sets the prices only for the activities that remain under its jurisdiction; namely, the use of the protected waters, access channels into the port, docks, merchandise transit, the storage areas that are still under IPAPC control, and the machinery. Some officials considered rate setting as being under central government jurisdiction. However, an argument in favor of the IPAPC's position was that its administration would be inadequate if local authorities were not able to exercise broad responsibilities and over-all control of the operational process, including autonomy in rate setting.

These rates are charged in bolivars but are specified in U.S. dollars, and therefore they constitute an automatic mechanism for adjusting for infla-tion. The decision to dollarize the rates turned out to be crucial to the port's profitability, particularly during a period of successive devaluations. Other ports suffered severe negative effects, while Puerto Cabello increased its profitability.

Of the port's earnings, 25 percent goes to the state treasury for invest-ment in all of the state's municipalities and 17 percent stays in the city of Puerto Cabello. The rest, ordinary income, stays with the IPAPC to cover operating costs. This legal provision regarding Puerto Cabello has been especially important. First, it provides just compensation for the externali-ties produced by the port's activities (the streets of Puerto Cabello must bear traffic and freight loads hundreds of times greater than what would be normal for a city of its size). Second, it has allowed the new port man-agement to take over in an environment of relative political consensus in a state characterized by significant interparty rivalry.

Results

PERSONNEL. The IPAPC received responsibility for Puerto Cabello with-out either laborers or office employees, which allowed it to begin opera-tions with a completely new personnel structure that emphasized efficiency, profitability, and training (Madrigal 1996). In 1994, the IPAPC employed 140 people in fundamentally regulatory tasks. Many of these were profes-sionals or specialized personnel. For 1997, an increase to 170 employees was reported. Additionally, an average of 1,500 laborers worked in the port on the IPAPC's payroll. The IPAPC contracts the services of cooperatives and private firms for cleanup, maintenance, ship operations, and other spe-cial services.

To improve personnel training, the IPAPC remodeled and equipped an educational center; in 1993, 6,000 hours of training programs were pro-vided. The managerial staff members receive training in specific areas, at-tend conferences, and are encouraged to take courses as part of their per-formance evaluation.

PORT OPERATIONS. Coordination among port activities has improved. Twice daily, the institute's management meets to review the list of ships in the bay, channel, or docks; calculate fees according to their cargo and draft; and assign the most appropriate wharfage. Some of the results of this scheme are impressive:

- Port services, which had operated for 8-hour days prior to 1991, went to operating 24 hours a day, 365 days a year.
- In 1990, the port handled 36,000 containers. This number increased to 148,000 in 1995 and to around 200,000 in 1996. The port also handles more ships (see figure 9-2.1).
- The average waiting time dropped from 163 hours to 50 hours per ship.

Replicability and Diffusion

The decentralization of Puerto Cabello has served as a point of reference for those states that came afterward. Because this innovative experience was considered successful, it has been widely disseminated. In spite of the fact that the formal model varies from one port to the next, a majority has incorporated the privatization of operations. One state in the eastern part of the country at first decided to operate its medium port directly, but subsequently adopted the system of private enterprise concessions for port

Figure 9-2.1. *Ships Handled During 1989–95*

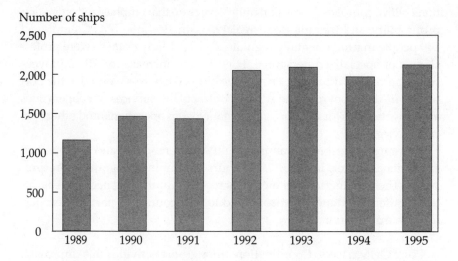

Number of ships

Source: Segall and Sevilla (1994).

activities. Even the important port of La Guaira, which is operated by the national government, has adopted a similar system, although there has been no definitive privatization of operations.

The decentralization of the ports has also led to the creation of the National Port Association, founded by an initiative of the state of Carabobo in 1994. This association coordinates the states' port activities, and it also offers training and consulting. It provides an ideal environment for horizontal transfer of experiences among the state authorities in this area.

The influence of the Puerto Cabello model has been considerable in other areas as well. The model has shown that the decentralization process is compatible with the privatization of public activities. Furthermore, it has spurred the idea that decentralization of ports can introduce incentives into their administration that enable them to compete efficiently with the model of complete privatization.

In República Bolivariana de Venezuela, Puerto Cabello has come to symbolize the right way to decentralize. This case has stimulated other governors to insist on the transfer of various responsibilities and has weakened opposition to decentralization. Since the handover of the port to the state of Carabobo, all types of exclusive and shared responsibilities have been decentralized to the states.

Sucre's Privatization Initiatives

In Sucre, the expected benefits of a privatization strategy outweighed the short-term political costs. A 1993 opinion poll in the state showed that about 75 percent of the population opposed privatization, although 86 percent favored increasing efficiency in public services through some private participation. In the face of this reluctance, Governor Ramon Martinez took his message to the streets and talked to any group that was willing to listen.

The governor targeted business associations, civic groups, academia, media, and public employees. His information campaign focused on educating the public about the principles and benefits of privatization, and about the standards of transparency and accountability he was adopting. He addressed labor fears by presenting a plan for labor and civil participation, whose main elements were the "democratization of capital," the development of an entrepreneurial culture, and the promotion of micro-enterprises to serve the sectors to be privatized. Substantial shares of the companies or activities privatized would be earmarked for workers, local businesses, and the state's population at large. This would turn employees into owners, create linkages between local and international investors, and, the governor hoped, get the population to participate more actively in the state's main economic activities. Laid-off workers and employees would be encouraged to form microenterprises, with the assurance that the privatization contracts would include requirements for their hiring. These requirements would both provide alternative employment for laid-off workers and reduce the influence of labor unions on the enterprises' management before and after privatization.

The governor and other advocates of privatization expected great and far-reaching results. First privatization would reshape the role of the state. In the case of the transfer of infrastructure to private management, the role of the government would shift from operator to regulator. Freed from operating functions, the government would be able to concentrate on sectors such as education and health. Although these sectors would not be excluded from private sector participation, they would require more complex and lengthy reform strategies to achieve it. Second, it was expected that privatization would have important fiscal impacts: it would eliminate the need for government subsidies by creating new revenues from the sale of assets, the value of the concessions, and recurrent rents on the concessioned resources. Third, it would eventually have a significant impact on the economy by (a) increasing private investment flows to the state, (b) fostering technological transfers, (c) increasing production, and (d) stimulating growth and employment. Finally, privatization would broaden share-ownership for the population at large, giving citizens a share of the profits and changing their perceptions of the private and public sectors.

Strategy and Institutional Arrangements

The areas targeted for private sector participation included the production sector (mines and agricultural land), transport infrastructure (ports, roads, and airports), public services (health, water and sanitation, and electricity), and tourism (existing facilities and development of new sites). A tailored strategy was developed for each activity, with infrastructure transferred to the state on the basis of case-specific analysis. Strategies ranged from direct sale of assets, as in the case of hotels and beach properties, to long-term concession contracts of public resources, as in the case of the salt mines, and to management contracts, as in the case of the port and airport sectors. Because direct sales of assets could be implemented quickly, they were given priority. These would be followed by the privatization or concession of productive activities that were private by nature and did not require either a regulatory framework or a major supervision effort. Monopolistic by nature, infrastructure would follow, complemented by national regulation and substantial supervision effort at the state level. The last stage of privatization would involve more complex areas, such as delivery of social services.

Breaking from the past, when concessions were awarded without an appropriate process, the governor decided that institutional arrangements would be put in place to ensure that sales and contracts would be awarded through a transparent process of international public bidding. This would include technical and financial prequalification of investors, development of criteria for evaluation of technical offers, disclosure, and other procedures.

To manage the bidding process, the governor established ad hoc commissions that would gather technically qualified members and would be supported by national consultants with wide experience in privatization, including managing the privatization program of the FIV. The commissions would be transaction specific, with a clear mandate and timetable for privatizing a particular activity. They would dissolve once the transaction was completed. This arrangement was meant to ensure that the commissions were technically valid, have focused objectives, and would not turn into costly, permanent structures. Sucre's privatization plan also included the creation of a small technical unit, the superintendent of privatization, to monitor and evaluate the resulting concession or management contracts.

The state government, however, lacked funds to pay the retainer fees for the consulting and legal firms working on the preparation of the strategies, bidding documents, and contracts. Officials tried to address this problem by starting small. Their plan was to offer a modest retainer and a larger success fee for the first privatization and hope to raise enough money to progressively finance the rest of the program. Although the sale of tourism assets was expected to proceed quickly, the first initiative to materialize was the privatization of the salt mines, followed by the privatization of one of the ports. Officials then focused on efforts to privatize additional ports, airports, and tourism establishments. Further initiatives would include roads, nonmetallic mines, electricity, and health care services.

The Privatization of the Salt Mines

The state of Sucre formally assumed responsibility for its salt mines in October 1993 with the Legislative Assembly's approval of the Ley de Régimen, Administración y Aprovechamiento de Salinas y sus Productos (Law for the Administration and Exploitation of Salt Mines and Their Products). But it was not until the end of 1994 that the state received the assets and could start exploiting the salt mines. The administrative board set up to administer the mines was not intended as a permanent structure. The decision to turn over the mines to the private sector had already been made, and the board's main function was to facilitate this transfer.

By November 1994, the governor had appointed a seven-member bidding commission, composed of representatives of the state legislative and executive branches, to create a competitive international bidding process that would lead to a concession contract for the Araya salt mines. This concession was viewed not only as a way of raising fiscal revenue for the state, but also as an engine of the state's own economic development. Attracting professional management and modern technology to increase production, efficiency, and employment would require an effort by the state to create the appropriate enabling business environment. Fomenting vertical expansion of the industry to increase the state's value added and improving participation levels of labor and the civil society would also require a careful strategy for facilitating microenterprise development and wide stock ownership programs. That the generation of fiscal revenue was not the main motivation is clear from the strategy eventually adopted, which went beyond maximizing the value of the concession to include contractual requirements addressing the impacts on indigenous populations, employment arrangements, and local social conditions.

The commission's first act was to contract for the evaluation of the Araya salt mines and the inventory of its assets to determine the base-bidding price for the offering. The FIV commissioned a similar study. The two contracted firms used different methods for evaluating the salt mines and reached widely disparate conclusions. The firm hired by the FIV evaluated fixed assets and estimated the value of the salt mines to be as low as Bs 2.7 billion (about US$16 million at the 1994 exchange rate). More appropriately, the firm hired by the state government estimated the present value of future cash flows and reached a value of Bs 3.7 billion (about US$22 million), plus or minus 10 percent depending on external conditions. On this basis, the commission set the base price at Bs 4.1 billion, or about US$24 million (Bs 3.7 billion plus 10 percent).

The commission prepared a draft concession contract with the support of consultants who had been involved in privatization at the national level. According to the terms of the contract, the concessionaire would receive a 25-year renewable concession for the exclusive right to exploit and administer the Araya salt mines, and for the production and commercialization of their raw salt. This right would have several conditions, including (a) the payment to the state government of 5 percent of the estimated yearly revenues (yearly volume of production multiplied by a reference price), (b) the transfer of a percentage of shares to the workers, (c) contractual arrangements with some newly established microenterprises (formed by laid-off workers), (d) minimum investment targets for the first three years of about US$20 million, and (e) production targets. Although the annual production of raw salt totaled about 90,000 tons in 1995, the concession contract specified a target for 120,000 tons in 1996 and 450,000 tons by 2000.

In terms of ownership, the concessionaire would purchase 90 percent of the shares and commit to sell shares equal to 10 percent of the company to the salt mine workers, and shares equal to another 10 percent to regional investors. The state government would initially keep 10 percent of the shares, most of which would later be sold in the local market. The purpose of this stipulation was to expand ownership to the state at large with the following target composition: 70 percent to the strategic investor-operator, 17 percent to local investors, 10 percent to salt mine workers, 2 percent to state residents, and the remaining 1 percent to the state.

RESULTS. The concession award process was completed in May 1995 with an offer matching the base price of about US$14 million (at the 1995 exchange rate) from TECNOSAL, a company with mixed national and international capital. This marked the first salt mine privatization ever, and it was also the only privatization in República Bolivariana de Venezuela in 1995. By starting operations in September 1995 just after the signing of the concession contract, TECNOSAL increased annual production of the Araya salt mines that year to 130,000 tons. In 1996, annual production expanded to 520,000 tons and was expected to reach 800,000 tons by 1997. This would be a ninefold increase over preprivatization levels. To put the quantities in perspective, total national demand for salt is about 400,000 tons; this means that the salt mines of Araya, which before could not equal even one-fourth of this demand, could now meet all of it and still have substantial export capability.

In addition to exceeding production targets, the privatization has been a source of job creation. In less than a year TECNOSAL created 253 new jobs, and the establishment of 24 new microenterprises servicing the industry created 310 additional jobs. Furthermore, TECNOSAL has established a number of foundations to serve the employees of the enterprise and the community at large. These include TECNOSALUD, which caters to the health needs of the employees; Pro-Desarrollo de la Península, a foundation that supports the development of the peninsula of Araya; and other foundations to support cultural and sports activities, including the reconstruction of the historic castle of Santiago León de los Caballeros.

CHALLENGES FACED. Not all expected results materialized. Two factors disrupted production, and a third favored noncompliance. The first factor was systemic to the country and was political in nature. During 1996, charges were raised through the print and electronic media, at both regional and national levels, regarding presumed fraudulent activities committed during the bidding process. These charges alleged the willful understatement of the resources of the Araya salt mines and consequent underselling of the concession. Although the allegations were investigated in depth and not corroborated by the evidence, they raised enough uncertainty on the part of the concessionaire to induce a significant delay in the implementation of its investment plans.

The second factor, of an institutional nature, was that the state government unit that was to supervise and evaluate privatization contracts, the superintendent of privatization, was not established in the period following privatization, mostly due to the lack of financial and specialized human resources. This hampered the follow-up ability of the government and provided incentives to the concessionaire to avoid compliance with some of the requirements of the contract, such as the transfer of the company shares committed to the workers. It is clear that the supervision function must be developed to ensure the sustainability and continued success of this and other privatization efforts.

These issues notwithstanding, it was expected that the Araya salt mines would continue to be profitable and positively contribute to the economic health of the region.

The Privatization of Ports

The Venezuelan ports, as previously discussed, have been characterized by poor infrastructure, abysmal levels of productivity, and low capacity utilization. As part of the new strategy of decentralization, the national government agreed to transfer administration and maintenance of the ports to the states, which in turn would agree to privatize port-operating functions. To this end, it liquidated the INP and actively promoted legislative action by the states, most of which approved the transfers in 1992 and 1993. In 1993, the national government also created the National Port Authority to regulate, monitor, and control the ports sector.

Article 2 of Sucre's Ley de Puertos del Estado Sucre (Law on Ports of the State of Sucre), approved March 16, 1992, states that the administration and maintenance of the state ports could be carried out by an administrator—either as a "public enterprise" or as "concessions to be awarded by public bidding." In the former case, a state public enterprise would be created and would enter into a contract with the state executive body specifying state financing of the port debt service, rental fee structure for the use of infrastructure by operators and end users, and supervision activities the enterprise would be expected to perform. In the latter case, the concession would be awarded for a 20-year period with similar contractual arrangements.

Whichever option the state adopted, the port administrator would be forbidden, by Article 10 of the law, to carry out directly or indirectly any of the port "operations," such as loading, unloading, and storage of goods; docking; fueling; and equipment supply. The administrator would contract independent operators, who would contribute their own resources in terms of personnel and equipment and have the freedom to price their services as long as they were sufficiently competitive. Ultimate authority to veto price increases would reside with the governor.

As opposed to, for example, the corresponding law in the state of Carabobo, the Law of Sucre left open the possibility for the private sector to both administer and operate the ports.[3] This option, although not utilized at the outset, became critical later when the decision to privatize the entire port infrastructure was made.

The administration that preceded Martínez made the initial decision to create Ports of Sucre as an autonomous public institution. Ports of Sucre assumed responsibility for the ports of Sucre, Carúpano, and Güiria and the piers of Araya, Corporiente, and Río Caribe. The institution would be responsible for port administration, including construction, maintenance, setting of user fees and rental prices, tax collection, and setting of norms. For the ports of Sucre and Carúpano, the state transferred operations to the private sector. For the International Port of Güiria, the government assumed a more ambitious strategy, aimed at transferring both administration and operations to the private sector.

Of particular interest is the International Fishing Port of Güiria. Fishing is one of the three largest industries of the northeastern region of República Bolivariana de Venezuela. This area, despite only about 14 percent utilization

---

3. The 1994 Ley Mediante la Cual el Estado Carabobo Asume la Competencia Exclusiva Sobre sus Puertos de Uso Comercial y Crea el Instituto Autónomo de Puerto Cabello (Law Through Which Carabobo State Assumes Exclusive Competency over Its Ports and Commercial Uses and Creates the Autonomous Institute of Puerto Cabello) awards responsibility for the administration of ports solely to the public sector.

of its rich fishing resources, accounts for 65 percent of national fishing production. The Port of Güiria was built by the federal government in the 1960s to support this activity and was greatly expanded in the 1970s in response to increased production. The port was incorporated in 1985 as the International Fishing Port Corporation of Güiria (Compañía Anónima Puerto Pesquero Internacional de Güiria, or CAPPIG), and it functioned as a national public company until the state of Sucre purchased 67 percent of the outstanding shares between 1994 and 1995—the balance of shares being held by the National Institute of Canals.

Four decades of mismanagement had severely affected performance, induced high staff turnover rates, and kept funds from being reinvested in the operations. Although the port had substantial capacity for freight and ship services, including dry dock, synchrolift, repair and overhaul shops, and cold storage, this capacity was largely underutilized. Furthermore, beginning in 1995, the oil industry and international trade made increased demands on the port's services. For these reasons, the state government decided to privatize the management and operation of the port, including the shipyard, cold storage, and ice manufacturing plants. CAPPIG's shareholders endorsed this decision at their meeting in May 1995, with the expectation that turning over operations to the private sector would increase both rates of utilization and installation of new capacity.

To carry out the process, CAPPIG's board of directors established a Special Privatization Commission composed of representatives from the CAPPIG, the state government, and the FIV and charged it with the planning and overall supervision of the transaction. The stated objectives of the privatization were to foster efficient port operations, ensure sufficient financial resources for repair and maintenance requirements, free the public sector from commercial and labor liabilities, promote financial self-sufficiency in port operations, generate employment, and attract investment in port infrastructure.

The commission decided to use transparent, international bidding procedures among prequalified investors. The preparation stage included the identification and evaluation of privatizable assets, a legal audit to determine property rights, and the design of the specific privatization strategy. Next, the commission began a marketing campaign and issued an invitation to prospective investors to show interest. The marketing process took longer than expected, as it required repeated distribution and publication of the invitation between October 1995 and March 1996 to finally attract the interest of one national and two international firms.

The bidding was based on a 15-year concession contract, a revenue-sharing agreement, and a base price of Bs 1.7 billion (about US$36 million). The CAPPIG would receive a growing proportion of gross revenues over the course of the contract, from 8 percent during the first five-year period to 10 and 12 percent respectively in the following two periods. The base price was to be divided between the CAPPIG's shareholders (US$15 million), an investment escrow account (US$17 million), and commercial creditors.

The technical and financial offers were opened in October 1996. Of the three interested parties, only one actually entered a final offer. The process can be deemed competitive, however, because the other two parties remained in the game until the very last minute, ensuring that the bidder would enter a bid reflective of its market valuation of the business. Duarte Vivas & Asociados was awarded the contract for an amount slightly exceeding the base price. It began operations immediately.

The initial transaction had a substantial impact on (a) the level of capitalization of port operations and (b) the financial health of the CAPPIG, which was able to repay its creditors, settle labor liabilities, and distribute dividends to its shareholders. The state government itself received about US$1 million upfront and was ensured additional recurrent revenues throughout the length of the contract.

Many of the regulatory issues require solution at the national level in order to achieve the best outcomes in terms of operations and pricing. Further progress in port privatization will require the national and regional governments to work out a national port strategy that would include a long-term vision of the sector and an appropriate institutional and regulatory framework to ensure competition and promote private sector participation. This will strengthen the already substantial prospects for sustainability.

Additional Privatization Initiatives

TOURISM. Sucre, with almost one-fourth of the nation's coast, white sand beaches, lagoons and rivers, warm waters, and historic and cultural attractions, is one of the most unexploited tourism centers of the country. Although no data on current demand exist, it was estimated in 1986 that some 156,000 tourists had flown into the state and stayed for an average stay of four days. At that level of demand, current infrastructure was insufficient to service the market effectively. Sucre had only 45 lodging establishments with a total of 1,542 rooms. Mainly as a result of past government policies that limited tourism funding to public construction and the operation of tourism centers, the remaining public hotels and beach resorts were in a state of abandonment, falling apart for lack of maintenance or rented out at nominal amounts.

From the beginning of his administration, Martínez was struck by the necessity to sell these properties to the private sector as soon as possible, create an environment conducive to private sector investment and expansion, and make Sucre competitive with the nearby tourism centers of the Caribbean. This was not an easy proposition given that the country overall has failed to generate large flows of foreign tourists.[4] Nonetheless, the governor sought to combine Sucre's privatization strategy for transport and tourism with an aggressive promotion abroad that offered incentives to international airlines and tourism operators. With efficient private sector management of the airports and the resorts, Sucre could offer incentive packages to airlines and charter companies, using their international connections with tourism operators to increase the flow of tourists.

The strategy envisioned the simultaneous sale of all 20 or so of the government's tourism establishments and the awarding of concessions for the upgrading, exploitation, and administration of two natural areas, Laguna de los Patos and Playa Colorada (Duck Lagoon and Colorado Beach), as well as the maintenance and conservation of historic monuments. To encourage international-local partnerships, a specialized firm was contracted to assist with the sales. The firm prepared contracts, audits, and property valuations to facilitate the transactions.

Several issues arose, however, that made selling public property more cumbersome than initially thought. The search for property titles led to the discovery of many complications. Although the building structures belonged to the state, the properties were located on land owned by some 12 different municipalities. In addition, a number of other institutions such as the Venezuelan Corporation of Tourism and the Ministry of Natural Resources asserted various claims and rights on the proceeds from those properties. Due to the lack of comprehensive or updated land and property registers, and the existence of various beneficiary rights, the process required not only a great deal of research into the records but also a complex orchestration of negotiations with municipal governments and national entities.

---

4. About 600,000 to 700,000 tourists traveled to República Bolivariana de Venezuela in 1996. This is approximately what Venice attracts in a single month.

To resolve the impasse, the state made municipal governments equal partners and assured them a share of the profits. In addition, beneficiary claims of national entities were formally transferred to the government of Sucre. This partnership with municipal governments is one that should characterize any reform effort at the regional level to ensure a strong democratic base as well as viability and sustainability. It is also one that requires great commitment due to the varied political affiliations and interests.

The sale process steadily advanced due to the continued commitment of the state government. The Legislative Assembly granted approval for the privatization, and a number of negotiations were carried out successfully with the municipalities and the national entities. After a three-year delay, the governor in June 1997 organized the auction of 10 separate small to medium properties with a combined base price in excess of Bs 500 million (US$1.1 million). On this first try, three of the properties sold at or above their base prices. A second date was planned for the sale of the remaining properties. Although the amounts produced by the auction may be small in an absolute sense, the spur to economic activity may turn out to be impressive.

AIRPORTS. In April 1995, with the Legislative Assembly's approval of the Ley de Aeropuertos del Estado Sucre (Law on Airports of the State of Sucre), Sucre assumed the responsibility for construction, operation, and maintenance of its regional airports, including the three main airports of Cumaná, Carúpano, and Güiria. According to the law, the state executive branch, a public enterprise, or a private concessionaire could administer and maintain the airports. In the latter case, the law specified the terms of the 10-year renewable concession as well as the rights and obligations of the two parties to the contract. The state, which had managed the airports of Sucre, began the process of transferring operation and maintenance to the private sector.

At the national level, the Ministry of Transport and Communications, through its General Sectoral Directorate for Air Transport, still retains regulatory and normative functions, including safeguarding international norms and agreements, as well as management of the International Airport of Simón Bolívar and of the nation's air traffic control system. Both the regulatory framework and the air navigation system have direct bearing on the operations of Sucre's airports. Any privatization strategy would have to take this into account.

The national government has also considered an overall airport sector reform program to (a) update the regulatory framework to conform to international standards and agreements, (b) transfer infrastructure to the private sector (in the case of the International Airport of Simón Bolívar), and (c) turn over air traffic control services to the private sector. Such a reform would make the initiative in Sucre all the more relevant and strengthen its prospects for sustainability.

The level of traffic through Sucre's airports may be too low to finance their operation. The government may need to supplement private with public financing. Indeed, the strategy for the concessioning of the airports is being developed in conjunction with several initiatives to increase the flow of passengers and tourists into the state. These include tourism development plans, plans for expanding port services to the oil industry, the creations of free trade zones, and the increase—associated with the privatization of the port—in the transport of frozen fish products through the airport of Güiria.

Replicability

The privatization experience in Sucre is the most advanced among the states in República Bolivariana de Venezuela, and its lessons come at a critically important time when a new cadre of local elected officials are feeling the pressure to find innovative solutions to managing a growing number of responsibilities. This pressure increased in the late 1990s, because the fiscal transfers from the national government, which previously covered the expenditures of the states, were becoming insufficient as a result of both the fiscal restraint at the national level and the process of decentralization, which stretched state resources across a larger number of activities. Also, most of the governors were in their first terms and needed to deliver on their campaign promises of greater efficiency and access to public services to ensure reelection.

The experience is particularly important, because Sucre's conditions are not privileged. Sucre is not one of the rich industrial states of República Bolivariana de Venezuela with abundant resources and capacity. It is one of the poorest states. As such, its accomplishments are not only all the more laudable, but also all the more replicable. Sucre's example demonstrates that much can be accomplished with a few carefully allocated resources, as long as they are well managed by various sectors in society. The Sucre experience also suggests that leadership and vision are necessary components, and that no strategy will succeed without commitment.

Diffusion and Dissemination

As local governments may have less access to information and donors' support, it is critical that an aggressive dissemination strategy be designed and sufficient outreach ensured. At the root must be a clear definition of the issues, problems, and solutions suggested by prior experiences.

Diffusion is already taking place to some extent within the state, the country, and the region. The main avenues for the flow of information and sharing of experiences are (a) with the municipalities in Sucre, through the process of negotiation and the set of agreements relating to specific assets in their territory; (b) with other states, through the regular convocation of the Association of Governors and the sharing of privatization experts; and (c) with the rest of the region, through the World Bank's regional project to support local government privatization programs. With the exception of this last effort, most diffusion activities have occurred on an informal basis, and it is difficult to assess their level of institutionalization. Because of this, the exchange of information has focused on tactics to resolve specific problems rather than overall strategies. Much must still be done to reap the benefits of the experience.

Lessons Learned

The Venezuelan experience highlights several lessons that will help in the design and implementation of successful privatization programs at the local level. It also points out areas where donors can make a substantial contribution and improve the sustainability prospects of privatization initiatives.

Lessons for Local Governments

OBTAIN COMMITMENT. Success in privatization programs demands strong commitment at the top. Although the issue of privatization may not be specific to local governments, it is of singular importance. To secure the needed changes in the legal, regulatory, and institutional frameworks, privatization programs require the active participation and support of several institutional actors, often including multiple levels of the executive and legislative branches, as well as the targeted public enterprises and the labor unions. Furthermore, the path to privatization has unanticipated obstacles that call for quick reaction times and decisions. Continuous commitment will thus be key to keeping the various parties on track and to resolving issues as they arise. This is even more important in cases such as the ones discussed in this chapter, in which national government commitment to both decentralization and privatization is not very strong.

CREATE WIDE CONSENSUS. Even at the local level, privatization initiatives cannot be sneaked in through the back door. Although, in the short run, they may affect only a small portion of the population, they tend to encounter strong political opposition. One reason for this is the existing institutions that expect to see their power base shrink as a result of privatization will condemn this type of initiative. Also, there is a lack of popular and media understanding of the dynamics and benefits of the privatization process. This lack of understanding makes the process more vulnerable to its opponents and presents an educational challenge to the reformers. It is therefore critical to preempt opposition and build a wide popular and political consensus in support of the intended initiatives.

Among the policy tools for reaching such objectives are campaigns to inform public opinion on the benefits of privatization. The effort may include speaking events in various forums (chambers of commerce, trade associations, business and community groups, schools and universities, and so on), seminars, media conferences, and radio, television, and print advertisements. Although the idea is to "sell" privatization, judgment should be used to avoid promising impossible or hard-to-reach results. Such overselling tends to backfire in the medium term, imperiling the sustainability of reform initiatives.

Another tool, particularly important at the local government level, is forming alliances with other local government leaders. Because the leaders face similar issues, they may gain from sharing experiences and even resources, and together they can create lobbying coalitions for coordinating and negotiating reform actions at the national level. In República Bolivariana de Venezuela this is done effectively through the Association of Governors.

OVERCOME INTERNAL OPPOSITION. Internal opposition arises in the institutions affected both directly and indirectly by the privatization, particularly labor unions. Long a factor in the inefficiency of public enterprises and the inflexibility of labor demand, labor unions and collective contracts are a barrier to privatization, and they reduce the efficiency gains expected from private sector management. As the strategy in Sucre's Araya salt mines shows, this problem can be solved but requires careful handling. In that case, the two main tools that broke labor's inertia were the active support of workers who organized microenterprises that would be contracted by the concessionaire and the development of ownership programs to partially compensate workers for possible loss. Of the two, the former was probably the most successful in shifting workers' perceptions of privatization.

GET THE MOST FOR YOUR MONEY. Local resources may be quite constrained, as may be the ability of local governments to obtain financing. In República Bolivariana de Venezuela, for instance, the states are constitutionally barred from financing activities through foreign debt. Privatization initiatives, however, tend to be expensive upfront and to recover costs several years later. This suggests that the implementation of privatization programs must be staggered.

To ensure that the privatization process is self-sustaining, the first stage should include the sale of all assets that require neither negotiations with other actors nor new legal, regulatory, or institutional frameworks. The early successes will generate goodwill toward the privatization and will provide funds for financing a second stage. In that second stage, the program can start focusing on privatization of productive enterprises that are competitive in nature. This may require some negotiations with labor, but again this can be accomplished without large regulatory and institutional changes. Often, in the context of local governments, even activities that require regulatory attention may be included in this stage if a national framework is already in place. The value of these activities should be more than sufficient to recover costs and finance further activities.

Up to this stage, the need for supervision and control is negligible. Once a third stage is implemented, when activities ranging from construction and operation of infrastructure to utilities and to the management of health services are transferred to the private sector, the supervisory function as well as the need to develop appropriate regulatory and institutional frameworks become imperative. This stage of privatization therefore may become much less financially rewarding and substantially more costly to implement. Coordination with national-level reforms becomes an issue, as do the timing and sequencing of national versus regional reforms. Finally, the technical capacity required at this stage increases greatly, as the supervisory team will need technical, legal, regulatory, and financial skills. At the local government level—often characterized by low technical capacity—this need may be a major obstacle.

CREATE INSTITUTIONS TO MANAGE SINGLE TRANSACTIONS. Experience in República Bolivariana de Venezuela shows that institutions created to manage privatization programs can have a short effective life. Institutional dynamics typically turn small technical groups into large bureaucratized institutions, in which the role of facilitator and promoter of transactions is soon overtaken by other concerns—namely, institutional expansion and perpetuation. The solution adopted in Sucre—creating temporary committees to implement single transactions, supported by specialized consultants—has the advantage of bringing together a sector-specific team with a very clear mandate and timeframe.[5] This does not limit the ability of the government to select people repeatedly for these posts (so as not to lose acquired experience in the management of privatization transactions), nor does it force the government to keep them on the payroll on a permanent basis. The benefit of using consultants is that it allows the state government to draw on outside accumulated experience that would be hard, if not impossible, to develop inhouse. The drawback is the capacity loss associated with the consultants' departure.

PICK A WINNING STRATEGY. No single best strategy exists for transferring operations and assets to the private sector. Each case should be analyzed on its own merits and peculiarities, and the degree of private sector participation assessed realistically. The choice of strategy must also reflect the political economy component of the process to minimize attrition with other vested interests. Options include direct sales of assets and competitive enterprises, management and concession contracts, comanagement agreements, leasing, contracting out, and private sector financing. Picking a realistic strategy will maximize the private sector's willingness to participate and save governments money and time. This is particularly the case at the local government level where, for example, utilization of large infrastructure (such as airports) may be too low to generate sufficient revenues to justify sale of that infrastructure. In those cases, management or concession contracts may be best.

Lessons for Donors

WIDEN THE CLIENT BASE. As the process of decentralization takes root in several countries, donors can build a wider array of client relationships

---

5. The governor referred to the Sucre process as privatizing privatization (*privatizar la privatización*).

with local governments that have acquired, or are in the process of acquiring, an increased number of functions and responsibilities from the national government and have become key to the success and sustainability of reform. While acknowledging national governments' sovereignty, donors can play a greater role in opening the dialogue with the different interests, providing avenues for information sharing, and building bridges between national and local counterparts. This helps donors develop an active constituency for reform, deepen technical understanding, increase the accountability of the implementing agencies, and broaden levels of donors' dialogue in the country.

DEVELOP NEW PRODUCTS. As donors diversify their client portfolio, they may need instruments for addressing client demands other than those imbedded in lending services. Direct staff provision of technical assistance, economic, financial, and sectoral analysis, and strategy development and information dissemination, may in some cases be required to help local governments get started. As for lending services, donors should focus on activities that policymakers may overlook for lack of funds or because of short political horizons.

ADDRESS SUSTAINABILITY. Donors can add greatest value in areas in which the returns are longer term, such as regulatory issues, supervision and control, and the environment. Technical and price regulation are often insufficiently addressed, creating the temptation to regulate by contract. Supervision and control are critical for ensuring the continued success of privatization initiatives, compliance with contractual conditions, and respect for competitive practices. Prior environmental assessment of privatization initiatives will help the government prevent environmental damage, instead of incurring large costs later on to contain it.

LEND CREDIBILITY. Issues of corruption and lack of transparency and accountability—rampant in the developing world—make local governments easy targets for criticism. This is particularly the case in República Bolivariana de Venezuela, a country with a strong corruption record.[6] Donors have

---

6. Transparency International, an institution monitoring corruption levels around the world, has classified República Bolivariana de Venezuela the 7th highest out of 54 target countries for corruption practices—after Nigeria, Pakistan, Kenya, Bangladesh, China, and Cameroon, and before Russia and India (Transparency International 1997).

a role to play not only in disseminating acceptable practices and requiring transparency in selection processes, but also in helping local governments build their credibility through the establishment of a consistent track record. Credibility will decrease the perceived risks on the side of investors and increase both their willingness to participate and the value of the transaction. It will also provide local governments with solid knowledge and the confidence to continue privatization efforts beyond the scope of donors' projects.

Conclusion

The path to decentralization has many obstacles. On the one end, there is the resistance from the center accustomed to controlling resources and dealing out favors; on the other, the lack of preparedness on the part of the provincial governments and the time needed to learn by doing. Success in managing public services at the local level is the very aim of decentralization. It also provides the best resistance against centripetal forces. The need for innovation to ensure success and avoid repeating the same mistakes made by the centralist governments is paramount.

The case of Puerto Cabello shows that transparent institutional arrangements, participatory port management, calls for bids to accredit firms, and specified distribution of a part of port income to the municipalities generates reliability and the conditions for good public management. In a similar manner, this case demonstrates that processes of institutional change can overcome situations of chronic corruption, inefficiency, and excessive union power. The incentives for the regional government to involve itself in decentralization, a complex and risky task, include tremendous political benefits for those who achieve success with it.

References

Cordero, Elías, and Yelitza Suárez. 1992. "La descentralización de los puertos: una responsabilidad vital en manos de los estados." In Rafael de la Cruz, ed., *Descentralización, Gobernabilidad, Democracia*. Caracas: New Society Publishers, Comission for the Reform of the State, and U.N. Development Programme.

Diaz Matalobos, Angel, and Martin Dresner. 1996. "Results from the Modernization of Caribbean Ports: The Case of Puerto Cabello." Caracas: Instituto de Estudios Superiores de Administración.

Gobernación del Estado de Sucre. 1994a. "Marco General de Acción y Plan de Privatización de Operaciones Portuarias del Estado Sucre." OIKOS Associates, Sucre.

————. 1994b. "Plan Preliminar de Privatización de Propiedades Turísticas del Estado Sucre." OIKOS Associates, Sucre.

Government of Carabobo. 1990. *Regionalización y Descentralización del Puerto de Puerto Cabello. Informe de la Comisión Técnica de la Gobernación del Estado Carabobo.* Valencia.

Madrigal, Felicia. 1996. "Puerto Cabello: Recent Improvements in Productivity and Efficiency, and New Directions." Caracas: Instituto de Estudios Superiores de Administración.

Sabatino Pizzolante, J. A. 1992. "Port Privatization in Venezuela." Working paper, Department of Marine Studies and International Transport, University of Wales, College of Cardiff.

Segall de Garzón, Blanca, and Subdelia Sevilla. 1994. *Evaluación del proceso de descentralización en el puerto de Puerto Cabello. Análisis de la gestión administrativa y financiera.* Caracas: Instituto de Estudios Superiores de Administración.

Transparency International. 1997. *Corruption Perceptions Index 1997.* Berlin.

9-3

Municipalities, Banks, and the Poor in Shelter and Infrastructure of Nicaraguan Cities

Alfredo Stein, Swedish International Development Agency

The major changes experienced by Nicaraguan society during the 1990s created opportunities for innovation in participatory development at the local level.[1] After a period of war and political polarization, the country made progress toward national reconciliation and democratization. From a collapsed, centrally managed economy with record levels of hyperinflation and the highest foreign debt in the region (700 percent of its GDP), it was transformed into a market economy with incipient growth, relative financial stability, and a significant reduction of the fiscal deficit.

In the context of severe underemployment and unemployment that occurred during this transformation, along with increasing poverty, the governments of Sweden and Nicaragua signed a cooperation agreement in July 1993 for the implementation of the Local Development Program (Programa de Desarrollo Local, or PRODEL). The two governments were interested in creating a decentralized, participatory, and sustainable program that would

---

1. This case stands somewhat apart from the others in this book, because the genesis of the Local Development Program (PRODEL) came about at least as much from outside agents as from within the local government. Still, the editors believe that the value of this case lies with the exceptionally effective, and sustained, results PRODEL has achieved with the introduction of many innovative ideas in eight Nicaraguan cities.

help mitigate the negative impacts of structural adjustment policies, especially in urban areas, and facilitate the process of pacification, national reconciliation, and democratization.

Context of PRODEL's Operations

During its 1994–97 first phase, the program operated in three mid-size cities (León, Chinandega, and Estelí) and two small ones (Somoto and Ocotal). These cities had experienced serious problems associated with rapid population growth as a result of the internal displacements caused by the civil war and the return of refugees from neighboring countries. The cities were also affected by increased levels of unemployment and underemployment, poverty, and a lack of basic services and infrastructure. During the 1998–2001 second phase, two additional mid-size cities (Matagalpa and Jinotega) and one small city (Chichigalpa) were incorporated in PRODEL.

The municipalities were slightly more urban than the average for Nicaragua but were representative of the nation's poverty. According to the 1995 national census, the population of the eight municipalities totaled about 650,000. Approximately 451,000 (around 69 percent) of their residents lived in urban areas, compared to the national average of 54.4 percent. The total population of these municipalities represented 15 percent of the country's population and 19 percent of its urban population.

An estimated 32 percent of Nicaragua's total urban population, or 758,400 people, lives below the poverty line.[2] Of this number, approximately 25 percent live in the eight cities where PRODEL operates. A significant proportion of the municipal populations—73 percent in León and Chinandega and 77 percent in Octobal, Somoto, and Estilí—consists of chronically and recent poor. Comparable levels for Managua are 55 percent and, for Nicaragua as a whole, 66 percent. These figures indicate that the area in which PRODEL operates possess higher rates of chronic and recent poor than the national average. (The comparable rate for El Salvador is 33 percent.)

In terms of unsatisfied basic necessities, the five cities involved in the first phase (except for León), rank below the national average in terms of the availability of drinking water, sanitary sewage, road repair, electric power, and waste collection services. Of the 150 neighborhoods served by PRODEL during the first phase, basic requirements were unsatisfied in 27

---

2. The poverty line defines the level of per capita monthly expenses required to buy enough food to meet a minimum daily caloric requirement. In 1993, the poverty line was approximately US$430 per year.

neighborhoods in León, 25 in Chinandega, 17 in Estelí, 10 in Ocotal , and 8 in Somoto. In October 1998, Hurricane Mitch created further problems, partially or totally destroying an estimated 10 percent of the housing stock in the eight cities. The majority of these houses were located in poor neighborhoods that lacked basic services. About 3 percent of the microenterprises also located in these areas had severe losses.

The poverty indicators help to understand the type of urban population served by PRODEL. First, major segments of the population are in the low-income bracket and lack basic services. Second, some households have income levels above the poverty line but are located in neighborhoods that are considered marginal because of the lack of one or more basic services. A third category consists of households located in the inner cities (where all the basic services may be available) but which do not have income levels sufficient to meet basic nutritional requirements. Some of these neighborhoods have mixed populations, consisting of professionals with higher levels of education living next to unskilled laborers, self-employed workers, and families employed in the informal economy.

Objectives and Strategy

Since it began operations in April 1994, PRODEL's development objective has been to improve the physical environment and the socioeconomic conditions of the poor population—especially woman and other vulnerable groups in the cities—on a sustainable basis. To achieve these goals, the Swedish International Development Cooperation Agency (SIDA), in consultation with Nicaraguan authorities, structured three investment components and a technical assistance and institutional development component. The investment components included infrastructure and community works, and housing improvements. The project also made small-scale credits available for microenterprises (see table 9-3.1 for an overview of the program).

INFRASTRUCTURE AND COMMUNITY WORKS. The program aimed to construct, expand, repair, and improve infrastructure and community works through small-scale projects of up to US$50,000. Such projects included potable water, sewage, and storm sewers systems; treatment plants; pedestrian and vehicular road systems, including sidewalks, roads, gutters, and pedestrian bypasses; public and household electrification; health centers, daycare centers, multi-use centers, schoolrooms, playgrounds, sporting facilities and sites for the collection, disposal and treatment of waste.

Table 9-3.1. *Characteristics of PRODEL's Components*

Aspect	Infrastructure	Housing	Microenterprises
Objective	Improve, expand, and maintain basic services and social equipment at the community level.	Improve the habitat conditions of individual families.	Income and employment generation in family-owned, microenterprises, especially headed by women.
Goal	Promote community participation and strengthen local governments.	Demonstrate the potential for the generation of participatory lending and housing improvement programs in the country.	Financial sustainability of the fund based on loans outside the traditional areas of activity of banks and other nonconventional lenders.
How it works	Local government with community participation defines, co-administers, executes, and maintains the projects.	A commercial bank screens, selects, and issues loans and recovers from individual families. Technical assistance provided by local government technicians. In 1999 two NGOs were incorporated in a similar scheme.	Transactions between commercial bank and individual families. In some cases, technical assistance for the creation of new microenterprises. In 1999 two NGOs were incorporated in a similar scheme.
Financial basis	Costs shared between the program, the local government, and the community.	The families repay the loans. The bank is paid a fee from the positive interest payments. NGOs operate in a similar arrangement.	Loans repaid to the bank by microenterprises, using market-based interest rates. The NGOs operate in a similar arrangement.
Type of fund	Conditional and participatory fund with an element of subsidy.	Rotating fund with long-term turnover (four years per loan).	Rotating fund with high turnover, high interest rates, and short repayment periods (six months).
Target population and users	Families of the neighborhood where the project is to be carried out.	Neighborhood families, based on ability to pay (monthly family income US$60–500).	Microenterprises, the majority of them established, with monthly family incomes between US$60–500.

Administrative responsibility	Local government is responsible and accountable to PRODEL for the funds provided.	Local government (technical assistance), the commercial bank and two NGOs (financial aspects).	Commercial bank and two NGOs (financing activity).
Implications for local development	Solutions are prioritized and negotiated between the communities and local governments.	End-user families define solutions with technical assistance from local government. The loans are given directly by the bank and the NGOs to the families. High mobilization of family resources.	Local governments establish areas of action, but the bank, NGOs, and the users of the loans establish their relationships without the intervention of local government. The result is a strengthening of the local economy.
Role of the central government	To facilitate, promote, and establish standards and procedures; strengthen local government; supervise and monitor the execution of the project; and learn lessons that can be applied in future programs.	To facilitate; establish procedures; strengthen the capability of local governments, a commercial bank, and NGOs in participatory programs; supervise; and learn lessons that can be applied in other programs and cities.	To facilitate the processes, stimulate the participation of financial intermediaries, supervise the process, and make it possible to repeat the process on a larger scale.
Requirements for success	Forum for the decentralization of responsibilities, functions, and resources from the central government to the local government and to the communities.	Clear division of functions between the financial entities and those that are providing technical assistance.	Administrative ability of the financing intermediary to work with small, short-term loans.
Sites of greatest impact	Poor and peripheral areas of small and medium cities.	Poor and peripheral areas of small and medium cities.	Poor and peripheral areas of small and medium cities.

Source: Prepared by the author on the basis of progress reports from PRODEL (1997a) and project documents for the execution of Phase I (1994) and Phase II (1997).

HOUSING IMPROVEMENTS. Small loans (between US$200 and US$1,400) were targeted to poor families who could afford to repay them. They were used to enlarge and improve houses. Projects included the construction of additional rooms, repair or replacement of roofs, repair or reinforcement of walls, construction or improvement of floors, installation of indoor plumbing, electrification, upgrades of kitchens, and the strengthening or finishing of exterior walls.

FINANCIAL ASSISTANCE TO MICROENTERPRISES. Small, short-term loans (between US$300 and US$1,500) were made to microenterprises at the neighborhood level for fixed and working capital, as well as for the creation of new microenterprises for services, trade, and manufacturing. These loans were directed in particular to microenterprises owned and operated by women.

TECHNICAL ASSISTANCE AND INSTITUTIONAL DEVELOPMENT. The program tried to strengthen the capacities of local governments, encouraging the administration and management of social investments with community participation. It also sought to encourage institutionalized financial entities to become involved in nonconventional lending programs for housing improvements and microenterprise loans to poor families.

Main Actors

A central goal of the program is to foster cooperation among the various institutions involved. Accordingly, a system of incentives and cofinancing was designed to improve participation at the local level in the decisionmaking process and in the management and contribution of resources. The goal is to ensure flexible responses to basic social problems in the neighborhoods and, at the same time, to stimulate longer-term development processes. In this sense, PRODEL supports the decentralization process by promoting citizen participation, assisting local governments, and creating a financial and institutional framework that is sustainable over the long term. Several principal entities are involved in these processes.

NICARAGUAN MUNICIPAL DEVELOPMENT INSTITUTE. The Nicaraguan Municipal Development Institute (Instituto Nicaragüense De Fomento Municipal, or INIFOM) is a central government institution that administers the funds provided by SIDA. It is responsible for the execution and supervision of the program. The INIFOM has formed a central executive unit to promote and coordinate actions at the central and local levels. Its primary interest in the program has been establishing innovative methods to promote and enhance the local government's capacities through decentralized processes. The INIFOM has used the PRODEL participation model to promote additional decentralization programs using resources from other international funding agencies.

MUNICIPAL GOVERNMENTS. Local authorities in the cities where the program operates are responsible for administering the infrastructure component and providing technical assistance to the beneficiaries of the housing improvement loans. The municipal governments are responsible for administering the funds that PRODEL transfers to them and for supervising activities at a local level. These are coordinated by a municipal commission formed in each city by representatives of the various institutions participating in the program and are chaired by the mayor. Each city has created an executive technical unit composed of personnel from the municipal government. Each municipal government signs a framework agreement with the INIFOM for the implementation of the program.

THE CONSULTATIVE COUNCIL. The eight mayors, with the executive director of the INIFOM and one representative from SIDA, form a consultative council responsible for defining the strategic guidelines and supervising the implementation of the program, as well as complying with the cooperation agreement between Sweden and Nicaragua. In addition to their interest in improving the living conditions of the population in their respective municipalities, municipal governments gain experience from managing, investing, and administering the funds for the infrastructure and community projects, and they gain a greater sense of involvement and ownership in the process of providing services.

THE BANK. A state commercial bank (Banco de Crédito Popular) is responsible for screening, approving, and disbursing the loans and supervising their correct disbursement. It is also responsible for the collection of payments for the home-improvement and microenterprise loans and for administrative, pre-judicial, and judicial arrangements for foreclosure of collateral security and guarantees. The INIFOM and the bank signed a trust fund agreement for the administration of the revolving funds. The bank offers the program additional banking services for the administration of the infrastructure components and technical assistance. The bank benefits from the program in several ways. First, it earns commissions for placing and servicing the loans, which helps it to meet its operating costs. Second, the microenterprise loans include a mandatory savings component in an account at the bank. Such accounts help increase the bank's liquidity for the promotion of its own loan programs. Third, the bank's awareness of a new segment of the market has provided it with increased opportunities for new business.

NONGOVERNMENTAL ORGANIZATIONS. PRODEL is interested in expanding the use of new financial intermediaries as a way of creating a more competitive environment in the field of nonconventional lending. In November 1998, the program turned to nonconventional financial intermediaries to allocate loans to those poor sectors of the cities where it operates that were severely affected by Hurricane Mitch. Two nongovernmental organizations (NGOs) were selected in a bidding process to handle loans for housing improvements and microenterprises. Both were interested in diversifying their portfolios and were listed among the best-performing NGOs working with microenterprises. In early 1999 they started operations in the eight cities, mainly in neighborhoods where the bank was not operating.

FAMILIES IN THE SELECTED NEIGHBORHOODS. Families participate in the selection, execution, financing, and maintenance of the infrastructure projects, and they are also the recipients of the housing and microenterprise loans. The principal benefit they derive is the improvement in their living conditions, in addition to acquiring new skills in negotiating with public and private sectors to identify solutions to their problems. The families participate either directly or via community project committees—entities established for the organization and internal representation of the neighborhoods—which are responsible for the administration, execution, and maintenance of the infrastructure and community projects. Community meetings are held to elect representatives of the local municipal commission, which the municipal government establishes for the coordination and supervision of PRODEL.

Achievements

The achievements and limitations of PRODEL's participatory model must be understood in the context of a society which for years was politically polarized and which took its first steps toward national reconciliation and reconstruction only in the early 1990s. In addition to the economic and social crisis, the program has faced changes in local and central governments.

Despite high turnover of the personnel in the institutions directly involved in the administration and execution of the components, the achievements of PRODEL were noteworthy.

Infrastructure and Community Projects Component

Between April 1994 and December 1998, the program carried out 260 infrastructure and community projects in 155 neighborhoods. These projects benefited more than 38,000 families. Total investment was US$4.4 million (an average of US$16,972 per project). Contributions from municipal governments and the beneficiary communities (in kind, cash, materials, tools, labor, administration, and supervision) totaled more than 43 percent; the balance of funding came from the program (see table 9-3.2).

In these 260 projects, the communities contributed some 132,000 days of work, both on a volunteer basis and for pay (but not from PRODEL sources), as well as material, labor, transportation, and administration. Because PRODEL concentrated the infrastructure component in the poorest neighborhoods in the five cities, it can be assumed that the majority of beneficiaries belonged to groups classified as chronically poor or recently poor.

The program far exceeded expectations by accomplishing almost twice (184 percent) of the original planned physical objectives of the infrastructure component. The reasons for this success are closely linked to the notion of community participation. Initially, the project document for the first phase established an objective of 64 projects to be completed in three years at an average cost of US$20,000 to be financed by PRODEL. As a result of the requirement for local matching funds, municipal governments decided to expand the coverage of the program to more neighborhoods to increase their impact, reduce the contribution on a per-project basis, and increase the level of community investment. The result was a greater number of lower-cost projects. Moreover, the projects mobilized a greater number of people and resources in each community and required less in the way of funds per project from the central and municipal governments.

In addition, the repayment record by families for their house improvements and microenterprise loans made it possible to refinance new loans and unnecessary to use fresh funds originally destined for these components by PRODEL. During the first phase of the program, US$1.1 million had been budgeted for financing the housing improvement loans, and US$1.2 million for the microenterprise loans, but only 50 percent of these amounts were used. It consequently became possible to reallocate funds for the financing of 57 new infrastructure projects during 1997. As a result,

Table 9-3.2. *Number of Infrastructure Projects Per City and Contributions from PRODEL, Municipal Governments, and the Communities, 1994–98*

City	Projects planned[a]	Projects executed	Execution (percent)	Programmed contributions (US$)[a]	PRODEL's contributions (US$)	Execution (percent)	Municipal contribution (US$)	Community contribution (US$)	Total (US$)
León	28	49	175	584,127	507,436	86.9	305,911	112,012	925,359
Chinandega	39	72	185	608,127	605,296	99.5	423,320	115,240	1,143,856
Estelí	31	49	158	592,127	537,574	90.8	285,526	105,735	928,835
Somoto	19	36	189	336,064	320,829	95.5	128,517	46,450	495,796
Ocotal	8	39	486	344,064	362,678	105.2	160,914	51,363	574,955
Chichigalpa	5	5	100	60,000	59,894	99.8	31,035	6,166	97,095
Matagalpa	5	5	100	70,000	48,849	69.8	40,351	11,788	100,988
Jinotega	6	5	83	70,000	67,325	96.2	47,204	31,201	145,730
Total	141	260	184	2,664,509	2,509,881	94.2	1,422,778	479,955	4,412,614
Contributions (percent)	n.a.	n.a.	n.a.	n.a.	56.9	n.a.	32.2	10.9	100

n.a. Not applicable.

Note: The PRODEL First Phase Project Document had as its objective 64 projects to be carried out in three years in five cities. The program was extended for an additional year, with an additional 46 projects and a total budgeted amount of US$2.16 million. Three more municipalities were added in 1998, bringing the amount budgeted for the eight municipalities for five years to US$2.66 million.

a. Average.

Source: Based on PRODEL (1997b, 1998b).

the planned objectives for this component during the four-year period increased to 110 projects. In all, 217 infrastructure and community work projects were carried out in the first phase and another 43 in the first year of the second phase, totaling 260 projects.

Housing Improvement and Microenterprise Loan Components

In five years, more than 4,168 loans (for US$2.7 million) were given for housing improvements, which benefited approximately the same number of families. In this component the families, in addition to repaying their loans, contributed their own resources, such as construction materials, labor, transportation, and project administration. This equated to at least 15 percent of the value of the labor, transport, and building materials (see table 9-3.3).

According to the bank's figures, about 22 percent of the families who received loans had monthly incomes between US$50 and US$100, 48 percent between US$101 and US$200, 26 percent between US$201 and US$300, and 4 percent between US$301 and US$450. Thus, 70 percent of the families targeted by PRODEL had monthly incomes of US$200 or below. At this income level, families had lacked certain basic services and lived in houses made of low-quality construction materials, but had sufficient income to make monthly payments.

The program made more than 12,451 loans for microentrepreneurs, disbursing almost US$5.5 million. This benefited approximately 2,400 families (see table 9-3.4). The loans helped create 70 new microenterprises, which employed some 210 people. This component also exceeded expectations, amounting to 117 percent of the original goals.

Women received more than 60 percent of the housing improvement loans and 70 percent of the loans for microentrepreneurs. Approximately 30 percent of the women recipients were heads of households. PRODEL and the bank actively targeted women, tailoring the program to women's priorities. Information meetings, credit analysis, and the collection of loans took place in communities where women worked and where they headed many of the households.

With more than 6,500 borrowers, the default indicators of the housing improvement and microenterprise revolving loan funds made PRODEL one of the most successful programs in the country. Cost-recovery records show that there is a real possibility that the funds will become financially sustainable. The default rate (the portfolio at risk) was manageable in both components, amounting to 18 percent for housing improvement loans and

Table 9-3.3. *Number of Housing Improvement and Microenterprise Loans and Families Benefiting Per City, 1994–98*

City	Number of loans	Total housing improvement loans	Disbursed amount (US$)[a]	Total contribution by families (US$)	Outstanding portfolio (US$)	Budgeted microenterprise loans	Total microenterprise loans[b]	Microenterprise owners benefited	Disbursed amount of loans (US$)	Outstanding portfolio (US$)
León	1,112	944	613,265	138,255	200,344	2,777	2,824	513	1,206,788	181,546
Chinandega	1,088	930	600,958	102,162	260,272	2,588	3,264	593	1,395,513	170,932
Estelí	1,120	1,029	659,734	112,155	257,065	2,500	3,532	640	1,689,578	283,271
Somoto	574	497	310,161	52,727	132,559	1,061	1,218	225	506,897	75,251
Ocotal	715	574	376,025	63,943	143,767	1,441	1,398	260	584,130	60,731
Chichigalpa	140	63	43,634	7,417	34,938	106	45	33	24,387	15,362
Matagalpa	120	64	47,777	8,122	41,824	95	73	68	36,710	26,431
Jinotega	120	67	56,896	9,672	47,016	95	97	77	55,510	31,752
Total	4,989	4,168	2,708,450	494,453	1,117,785	10,663	12,451	2,409	5,499,513	845,276

a. Estimated average loan of US$650.00.
b. It was calculated that 25 percent of the urban households have a microenterprise as their only source of income, which would mean that there are approximately 13,000 microenterprises in the five cities in which PRODEL operated during the first phase (the first five in this table). Therefore, PRODEL has reached approximately 18.5 percent of the total number of microenterprises in those five cities. The impact cannot yet be determined in the remaining three cities.
Source: PRODEL (1997c, 1999).

Table 9-3.4. *Analysis of the Financial Sustainability of PRODEL's Revolving Funds, 1995–98* (US$)

Category	1995	1996	1997	1998	Total
Seed capital[a]					
Seed capital microenterprise	414,986	0	87,000	75,084	577,070
Seed capital housing	547,767	76,044	150,000	142,780	916,591
Total seed capital (2 + 3)	962,753	76,044	237,000	217,864	1,493,661
Perceived interests microenterprise	82,289	122,813	197,709	253,977	656,788
Perceived interests housing	65,252	69,134	101,761	128,530	364,677
Total interests (6 + 7)	147,541	191,947	299,470	382,507	1,021,465
Direct costs of bank	102,448	134,598	183,004	245,591	665,641
Financial margin (8 – 9)	45,093	57,349	116,466	136,916	355,824
Provision for nonrecoverable loans	17,322	23,054	36,480	43,268	120,124
Operative profit (10 – 11)	27,771	34,295	112,818	93,648	235,700
Indirect costs PRODEL	25,000	30,000	35,000	40,000	130,000
Total Costs (9 + 11 + 13)	144,770	187,652	254,484	328,859	915,765
Sustainability indicator (8/13)	1.02	1.02	1.18	1.16	1.12[b]

a. Refers to the fresh funds from SIDA transferred by PRODEL to the bank each year for the housing and microentrepreneur revolving funds. For 1994 there are no data available.

b. Average indicator for the four years.

Source: Analysis based on PRODEL (1999).

10 percent for microenterprise loans.[3] Further, after five years of operation, the annual interest payments of the revolving fund covered the bank's direct costs, including part of the costs of PRODEL's personnel directly involved in monitoring the loan components. Thus, sustainability—measured as income generated by the portfolio divided by the commission paid to the bank, plus provision for losses on unrecoverable loans—equaled 1.16. This means that the revolving fund was able to generate a surplus of 16 percent in 1998. During four years it produced an overall profit of 12 percent (see table 9-3.4).

The results—noteworthy particularly given the economic crisis that the country experienced during PRODEL's implementation, and the administrative setbacks in 1998—indicate that this is not simply an isolated project. Rather it is a pilot with lessons to be learned that can be replicated in other Nicaraguan cities and in other countries.[4]

For these reasons, the government of Nicaragua and SIDA decided to continue financing the activities of the program for a second phase in the cities where it had been operating and to expand the program to three additional cities over a four-year period. Lessons from the PRODEL model have also started to be applied in Honduras and South Africa. The ultimate goals are to institutionalize and define a participatory model for the provision of services, equipment, housing, and income generation, which will be sustainable on a national level.

The PRODEL Community Participation Model

The PRODEL community participation model is based on the premise that families who participate in the key activities—decisionmaking processes,

---

3. An external evaluation and qualification of PRODEL's housing and microenterprise portfolio at the end of 1998 showed that only 1.5 percent of the loans with more than three payments in arrears (defined as portfolio at risk) may be unrecoverable. About 2.5 percent have been recovered through judicial procedures and 96 percent through simple administrative and follow-up procedures that the Banco de Crédito Popular has implemented.

4. The crisis and administrative setbacks are, in turn, related to the process of privatization at the Banco de Crédito Popular. This process has forced the bank to make some internal readjustments in its level of operations that has affected its personnel who are directly linked with PRODEL's operation. The second factor relates to the social and economic consequences of Hurricane Mitch that seriously affected the eight cities where PRODEL worked and some of the clients that used program loans.

administration, and execution of infrastructure and housing improvement works—increase their commitment to cofinance and maintain the projects. This fosters the sustainability of the social investments over the long term. This section describes and analyzes the process of participation in the infrastructure and housing improvement components.

Participatory Process in the Infrastructure Component

The INIFOM signs a framework agreement with the municipal governments defining the incentives, responsibilities, and contributions of each party for the execution of the different components. The INIFOM is responsible for the transfer of funds to the municipal governments under certain conditions. First, there must be community participation in the identification, execution, and maintenance of projects. Second, there must be a commitment on behalf of the municipal council to allocate resources for the execution of the infrastructure projects. Third, municipalities must provide technical assistance to those families who are entitled to a housing improvement loan, and they need to form an executing technical unit to manage the projects.

MUNICIPAL COMMISSION. At the initiative of the municipal council, a municipal commission is formed under the leadership of the mayor, with representatives of the main entities involved in the program (the INIFOM, the municipal government, Banco de Crédito Popular, and other public services institutions). Every year, based on a set of eligibility criteria established by PRODEL, the municipal commission defines and selects the action areas of the program in the city, usually according to socioeconomic data and needs assessments. The commission also provides follow-up on the physical and financial progress of the operative plan of each component.

Representatives of the communities selected are invited to attend the monthly meetings of the municipal commission, although their functions are limited. The idea is that community leaders should be given the opportunity to participate in the discussion and decisionmaking processes at the municipal level and be aware of how the areas of action are defined and selected.

MICROPLANNING WORKSHOPS. Once it has been decided to include a community as a potential participant in the program, the municipal government holds a microplanning workshop with the participation of at least 20 members of the community, of whom the majority are women. In general, the existing community organization makes the arrangements for the workshop (finding a location, sending invitations, and arranging refreshments). During the microplanning exercise, the participants (the 20 community members and technicians from the municipal government and from other government institutions) visit the community in small groups to talk with the residents and to acquire impressions about the concerns of the community. Special emphasis is placed on interviews with women and children. Then the group conducts an exercise to identify and prioritize the main problems of the community. Priorities are assigned, solutions are proposed and negotiated, and the potential project to be financed by PRODEL is identified. Project cleanup (especially trash collection) is also planned. At the end of the workshop, the representatives of the municipal government and the community organization sign an agreement summarizing the principal results of the microplanning exercise.[5]

GENERAL ASSEMBLY. The next step is organizing a general assembly of the community. This meeting includes a presentation about the results of the workshop. Technical personnel from the local government also present advances in the design of the project. They explain the procedure to execute the projects and define the project roles of both the municipal government and the community. The assembly makes decisions regarding the contributions of the community about the various activities described in the budget. This information must be annexed to the project profile presented by the municipality to PRODEL for approval.

In 1996, for example, the microplanning workshops in Somoto identified and prioritized a program to help with annual floods, which had the greatest impact on the peripheral and central communities of the city. This exercise forced the local authorities to use PRODEL's resources, municipal funds, and funds from other sources to plan a series of projects located not only in the neighborhoods in which the program was active but also in other city locations where infrastructure was needed to solve the problem. In this example, people living in the affected communities worked on the construction of a dike and a long stormwater system located several kilometers outside the program area. The experience demonstrated to the municipal government the potential of community investments and the benefits of active participation and negotiated solutions. When Hurricane Mitch

5. PRODEL has adapted the microplanning method developed by Goethert and others (1992) to the Nicaraguan context (PRODEL 1998a).

struck in 1998, several of these infrastructure works proved to be strategic assets that prevented major landslides and flooding in the city.

COMMUNITY PROJECT ADMINISTRATION COMMITTEE. The General Assembly eventually elects the Community Project Administration Committee (CPAC), consisting of seven people from the community. The specific functions of this committee are to review the budget and design prepared by the technicians from the municipal government, in particular the general characteristics regarding the location and dimensions of the project. The committee also coordinates the management of the project and administers the materials, equipment, and labor supplied both by the municipal government and by the community. The committee reports to the community about the progress of the project and the use of the funds. Finally it participates in the financial and physical audit of the project that is conducted by the municipal government and PRODEL. Likewise, the committee is required to participate in the annual evaluations of the component performed by the municipal commission.

The CPAC organizes the rest of the community for the construction of the project. Depending on the type and complexity of the project, the municipal government makes an initial proposal for organizing the work, which can be divided on a house-by-house or block-by-block basis. The social services office of the municipal government trains the committee in the management and administration of the building materials warehouse and the methods used to oversee human resources. The CPAC and the municipal technicians select the area where the materials will be stored. When the contribution is monetary, they initiate the collection among the community.

DISBURSEMENT. Once the project has been approved, PRODEL signs a specific contract with the municipal government and disburses the funds to a special account to begin the execution of the project. This contract clearly stipulates the contributions by the parties for each of the construction activities in the process. PRODEL pays up to 60 percent of the amount of the project. The rest of the money comes from community contributions (in the form of investments in materials, skilled and unskilled labor, machinery and tools, administration, and cash) and from the municipal government, and may generally not be less than 40 percent of the total cost of the project. The program will not finance the actual project unless the community is prepared to make its own contribution. Once the project starts, the CPAC controls the warehouse, materials, tools, and equipment, and it oversees the labor. Depending on the type of project, the community provides skilled and unskilled labor, which can be in the form of volunteer labor or contract labor hired by the community.

COMMUNITY PARTICIPATION IN PROJECT EXECUTION. The general procedure by which the community participates in the execution of the project depends on whether the infrastructure being built is for public or private use. In the case of private infrastructure, each family participates individually. If a school is being improved, skilled labor is hired. For the construction of sewage systems, each family excavates the section in front of their house. When gutters are built, teams are formed that work weekly. Combined teams work on projects that involve the construction of a sewage system, excavations, and manholes.

The CPAC and other members of the community participate with technical staff from the municipal government and employees of PRODEL in auditing the project. They prepare an inventory of the existing materials and tools at the warehouse (entries and withdrawals), comparing it with the purchase vouchers from the municipal government. They also keep track of the total amount of labor provided. The purpose of this activity is to increase social control over the utilization of the funds and to establish a routine and more direct procedure for the municipal government to report directly to its constituency.

EVALUATION. Members of the CPAC and other community members participate in the evaluation of the projects carried out by the municipal commission. These evaluations analyze the experience overall and the level of organization and community participation, as well as the quality of the completed project. This process can also be used to identify other requirements related to the project, resell any surplus materials, and transfer any surplus funds to the municipal accounts for use in other projects. In some of the cities, the organizational experience acquired facilitated the subsequent management and administration of other projects by the communities. The municipal governments are learning to apply the participatory methodology to other projects, which are not financed by PRODEL. Positive effects are also reflected in the processes of municipal tax collection. In Ocotal, for example, the municipal government in 1996 increased its tax collections by 30 percent. This achievement came about partly because municipal authorities directly managed their program resources. However, it also reflected the fact that the residents were prepared to pay taxes when they saw results.

Evaluation of the Participatory Process in the Infrastructure Component

The quantitative results show that with a limited amount of outside financial resources, benefits could be generated for a large number of people in marginal neighborhoods by means of the infrastructure component. In total, 38,000 families in the marginal communities benefited, and they contributed more than 155,000 days of labor. The per capita investment over five years was US$22, of which 57 percent came from outside resources and 43 percent from local resources. In terms of effectiveness, the objectives defined in the project documents for both phases have been achieved, in particular with regard to work with the poorest groups, the mobilization of local resources, and the establishment of a participatory methodology that has already been replicated in eight cities.

Key to this process has been the ability of the program to mobilize matching municipal and community funds. The purpose of introducing participatory financial and administrative procedures was to improve the efficiency and transparency in the management of funds by municipal governments, and to improve the governments' relations with communities. The community participates throughout the project cycle, from the definition of the areas of action and the identification of problems and projects to the management and administration of funds. This has created a significant capacity to target resources and to identify and plan infrastructure and urban projects.

Community Participation in the Infrastructure Component

This section presents an evaluation of the community participation in the different phases of the project cycle.

MUNICIPAL COMMISSIONS. The participation of community representatives has been more formal and relatively passive, and other members of the commission have in general made the decisions. Nevertheless, the presence of the representatives has legitimized the actions of the municipal government vis-à-vis the communities. It has also given the community representatives the opportunity to become familiar with and contribute to the process by which the municipality establishes annual operating budgets and general development work plans. Community leaders have an opportunity to become acquainted with the most important variables involved in the decisionmaking process at the local level for the provision of infrastructure and urban services.

MICROPLANNING WORKSHOPS. These workshops allow more active participation by community leaders and other members of the community. The mechanism allows participants to gain a greater understanding of their problems, potential solutions, and the types of infrastructure and community projects that can be carried out. Communities understand criteria such as the urgency of the problem, the cost of the solution, the sequence of work required, the time required for the design and execution of the construction, the technical complexity, and the contributions from each party involved. On more than one occasion, there have been serious discrepancies between the urgency assigned to a problem by the municipal government and by the community. The microplanning methodology makes it possible to create consensus so the technicians can gain a thorough understanding of the real problems facing the community and the community understands the financial and technical complexities of a project.

The microplanning workshop and its subsequent presentation at the general assembly meeting provide an opportunity for the community to earmark its contributions for the project's design, execution, and preventive maintenance. On some occasions, these contributions exceed the minimum required by the program.

The attitude of the municipal government's project manager can affect negotiations about the community contributions. If the project manager fails to clearly define the level of community involvement, residents tend to expect greater contributions from the program and the local government, rather than from the community. This problem in Nicaragua is exacerbated because, in recent years, a number of social infrastructure projects were entirely subsidized by foreign aid and did not require any active participation from beneficiaries. In some local governments, and also within the central government, this has generated the notion of a paternalistic government and the citizens as clients, resulting in a passive wait-and-see attitude in many communities.

Experience shows that family income is not an impediment to obtaining substantial financial contributions from very poor communities when projects are executed. When confronted with the blunt alternatives resulting from the scarcity of tax revenues and budget cuts, the communities have demonstrated an ability to overcome habits and traditions of paternalism without necessarily threatening their low family incomes. In the Mauricio Cajina neighborhood in Somoto, one of the poorest areas of the city (60 percent of its working age residents are unemployed), for example, low income levels did not prevent residents from participating by providing labor and making financial contributions. In four months, US$5,000 was collected through the organization of raffles, community dinners, parties, dances, and other activities. The money was used as the neighborhood's contribution for the construction of 285 meters of a sewer line, one of the key projects to prevent floods in the community.

DESIGN AND PREPARATION FOR THE EXECUTION OF THE PROJECT. Participation is intense at the level of the project committee, but not necessarily in the rest of the community. The advantage of the process is that the community leaders gain an increased understanding about the technical and financial complexities of the design of and preparation for infrastructure projects. The process is helpful as well for the technical staff, because being aware of factors that affect the population helps them overcome obstacles that are generally encountered in the introduction of public services and infrastructure in existing squatter areas, which could otherwise slow down the development of the project. Participation in the design phase is greater in the cases of schools, parks, and recreational facilities. For projects that involve the introduction or expansion of roads, electrification, and sewage and water, participation is less and the municipal technical staff must work harder to explain the aspects of the design and operation of the service. Participation in these phases means that local authorities must develop negotiating strategies to arrive at practical solutions to concrete problems that cannot be solved by the municipal government alone. This requires a willingness to empower local communities to assume certain functions. Communities must have the opportunity to participate in the decision-making process and gain some control over the administration of the resources provided by the municipal government.

PROJECT EXECUTION. This is the most delicate phase, and it requires considerable training and empowerment from the municipal government. Tensions frequently arise over the fact that the technical and financial officers from the municipal government believe that the empowerment process is an activity exclusively for social workers, and they do not want to become involved in transferring expertise to the community. On more than one occasion, this phase has also rekindled acute conflicts within the neighborhoods that affect the ability to prioritize the problems, define possible solutions, and form the project committee. On average, 3 percent of the families in each neighborhood do not want to contribute and can generate obstacles to the execution of the project. Nevertheless, this process can also produce situations of positive competition within the neighboring communities.

If a project is not quickly approved or if the municipal government is not prepared to begin physical execution, the enthusiasm of the CPAC can decline. In such a scenario, the quantity of information about the delays is important. This period of time can be used to define with greater precision the contributions to be made by the community. Ultimately, however, the community organization may turn out to be problematic if the time required by PRODEL or the municipal government is not compatible with the community's expectations. Projects that take longer to complete can result in a reduced level of participation by the families. Such projects require effective channels of promotion, communication, and understanding of the complexity of administration and community participation in established squatter areas.

PARTICIPATION IN THE EXECUTION AND ADMINISTRATION OF THE PROJECT. Broad participation makes improved control of municipal resources possible. By combining the information managed by the municipal government with the information available in the community, it becomes possible to determine how and where the resources are being used, which gives greater transparency to the management of the project by the local government vis-à-vis the community. Concerns by local governments that they may not be able to meet the objectives set in their annual construction plans can lead them to limit the participation of the community and training for the execution. Consequently, this phase requires clear strategies that minimize the conflicts between the traditional ways in which the municipal government makes decisions and administers resources. The auditing procedure, conducted in the presence of the community members, has increased the level of trust between the community and its local government.

The administration of a project with community participation also results in decreased loss and waste in the use of construction materials. This is one of the areas in which the building costs of projects carried out directly by municipal governments probably increase without community participation or under the terms of contracts with construction companies hired through public or private tender offers.

Although the costs of projects carried out with community participation are not necessarily lower, they are more realistic, and some of the resources saved can be allocated to physical extensions of the project. The cost of project supervision, if shared, is minimal. The costs of administration and supervision of projects carried out using PRODEL's methodology fluctuate between 3 percent and 5 percent of the total cost of the project. Depending on the type of project, at least one-fourth of these costs are contributed by

"We previously had an erroneous idea of what community participation was. We knew that it was a key element with a great deal of economic and human potential for municipal development, but in fact we were not providing any space in which it could take place. We are now convinced that it is essential to have community participation in all possible processes and all stages of the projects. This participation has facilitated the creation of coordinating committees and the identification of opportunities between the communities and the local government, which has been beneficial to both sides. Involving the communities has given the 'barrios' greater confidence in the management and transparency of the funds by the Municipal Government. There is now improved communication and understanding between the members of the communities and the municipal government, and a higher level of satisfaction on the part of the population with the projects which have been carried out."

—Manuel Maldonado, Mayor of Somoto

the community and the remainder by the municipal government. The low cost of project supervision is due to the fact that one or two engineers from the municipal government can supervise five projects at the same time, which can result in greater efficiency of each project.

A comparative analysis by the city of León between paving projects in the city carried out with and without community participation shows that the cost of the project carried out by a private company was 23 percent higher than the cost of the project carried out using the PRODEL methodology. The lower cost of the later project could be attributed to all the activities in which the community made intensive labor and administrative contributions. Such activities include hauling materials and other earth-moving activities, laying cobblestones, compacting pavement, cleaning, and administering and supervising the project.

Participation requires clear signals that help to establish the links between the community services introduced and the value to the individual home. This helps the families to appreciate the sense of investment made by their contribution to the community project.

The type, scale, urgency, and complexity of the project are obviously factors that the municipal governments must take into consideration in determining the participation procedures. Many times project managers are reluctant to promote participation, because they consider it a drag on the correct and timely completion of the projects. The need for compliance with the requirements of the executive technical unit, as well as continuous supervision and control of the implementation of the program, have made the municipal employees realize the variables involved in participatory projects.

The method of project approval and contracting generally employed by local governments or by state entities for works that require private tender offers can lead to significant delays in project execution. The joint execution of the project with the community involves the families in the negotiations with the central and local government entities, which helps to speed up the approval process as well as the disbursement of funds for project execution. Sometimes, the absence of reference costs means that local governments and community members will not have any criteria to determine whether the costs being described are realistic. At least in Nicaragua, unit costs are high even if the costs of the supervision remain hidden. Moreover, those who award the contract generally invite the bidder, which means that the process can be manipulated. Finally, the traditional methods of issuing calls for bids and awarding contracts entail additional costs, which can reduce the amount of money available for investment in the physical project. This does not mean that bidding and tender processes should be eliminated, but it shows that transparency in the bidding process can be greater if communities are involved.

MAINTENANCE AND OPERATION OF THE PROJECT. When the actual construction of the project has been completed, it is expected that a community structure will have been created with the ability to manage and negotiate with the municipal government. PRODEL, the municipal government, and the communities evaluate the community contribution, the organization established during the execution, the quality of the work, and any unresolved needs that are indicated in the microplanning workshop. In terms of postproject preventive maintenance, PRODEL's experience is relatively recent. Yet, it has produced important lessons that helped lead to the establishment of a national preventive maintenance fund by the Nicaraguan Social Investment Fund for the maintenance of the primary health and educational system. As in the case of PRODEL, the goal is to create a fund provided with resources, which promotes local and community contributions.

The communities participate in the payment of the water, sewage, and electric power services provided, along with additional contributions in the form of labor for the preventive maintenance of the schools, roads, health facilities, recreational facilities, and parks. The link with the nation's national health care system (Sistemas Integrales de Salud) has made possible the development of landfills for garbage collection and the cleaning of sewers, which has resulted in improved maintenance of the projects. In the second phase of PRODEL, the municipal governments and communities are contributing resources for the creation of a preventive maintenance fund before the completion of a project. One of the critical problems that has been identified in terms of the operation and maintenance of the services relates to the connection of households to the established systems, in particular when there is no financing for this process. PRODEL has established information campaigns and incentives for the municipal governments so that, with the community leaders, they can promote the process of connection by means of a home improvement loan or with the families' own resources.

The importance of community involvement can be seen in a comparative analysis of two child care centers that are operated by members of two communities in the city of Ocotal. The physical condition of the site located in the Santa Ana *barrio,* in which the community participated in the identification of the project and its construction (through labor and financial resources) was better than the center in the Nora Astorga neighborhood. In the latter, there was no community involvement in the phases of identification and execution of the project, nor was there any requirement for contributions from the community for its maintenance. In the former, there is a sense of ownership of the project, the community has made a census of the children in the neighborhood, and it has been able to negotiate agreements with the municipal government and other government institutions to provide food for the children. In the latter, little assistance is provided to children, there is no information about the number of children in the *barrio,* nor are there any agreements with the private and government institutions that financed and supported the construction of the child care center.

PARTICIPATION OF WOMEN. Measures are taken to promote the involvement of women in all phases of the infrastructure project cycle and to encourage their participation in the other two loan components. The program has dealt with the gender issue in a pragmatic manner, giving preference to projects that addressed basic needs of women, and also involving women in the process of evaluating needs, making decisions, and planning and administering projects. It also attempted to provide incentives for men to participate more in the construction of the projects, while the women had greater roles in management and administration. The methodology increased the role of women not only as physical builders of projects (some

25 percent of the unskilled laborers are women, although no progress has been made in the incorporation of skilled female workers), but also in administrative and supervisory capacities. In the microplanning workshops, the situation is particularly dramatic: more than half of those attending the meetings are women. When it comes to management and supervision, the figure climbs to 75 percent.

The Participatory Process in Housing Improvements and Microenterprise Loans

In the neighborhoods in which the housing improvement and microenterprise loan program is active, the municipal government, PRODEL's local coordinator, and the Banco de Crédito Popular loan officers prepare a joint strategy for the promotion of the loans. In the case of microenterprise loans, the loan officers from the bank visit the sites of businesses, which are generally family owned. The analysis is based strictly on the financial viability of the business in accordance with a cash flow statement, which is discussed between the bank loan officer and the owner of the microenterprise.[6] In some cases the program has promoted the creation of new microenterprises, especially for women.

In the case of housing loans, the end users participate in a series of informal meetings at community centers or schools. Representatives of the bank, the municipal government, and PRODEL explain the terms of the loans, the technical assistance that will be provided by the municipal government, and the commitments that must be assumed by the families (in terms of the use of the loan and repayment).[7] Interested families complete a preliminary application, which contains basic information on the location and condition of the home, the employment status of the potential borrower, and the socioeconomic characteristics of the other members of the family.

---

6. Loans are between US$300 and US$1,500, repayable over a maximum of six months. The annual interest rate ranges up to 36 percent, plus maintenance of value (the indexing of the local currency to the U.S. dollar), which can add an additional 12 percent. The average loan is about US$400.

7. Loans are between US$200 and US$1,200, repayable in four years at an annual interest rate of 12 percent plus an adjustment for inflation (the indexing of the local currency to the U.S. dollar), which gives an effective annual interest rate of 24 percent on the outstanding balance. The average loan is US$650 and the monthly payments vary between US$20 and US$35, depending on the financial capabilities of the families in question.

LOAN EVALUATION. The loan officers from the bank visit the family's home and conduct a preliminary credit analysis to determine the need for home improvement, the potential sources of family income, the family's borrowing capacity and financial capability, and whether a loan can be made. The purpose of this visit is to determine the maximum amount that the family can afford. The loan officer takes into consideration the family's monthly income and expenses. The analysis also looks at property ownership, the type of collateral that may be offered by the borrower (mortgage, pawns, lien, and even title to the construction materials), and the source of income. The gender of the borrower, credit history, and the type of improvement to be made, as well as the borrower's personal references (which may be provided by the neighbors), are also taken into consideration. The loan officer eventually informs the city's technical housing assistance office of the potential maximum amount that may be approved for each borrower.

A technical housing assistance office employee then inspects the house, identifying such aspects as the location of utilities on the property, potential structural problems, and the need for expansion. The purpose of the technical assistance is to help the family prioritize steps to reduce overcrowding and environmental risks. Emphasis is given to kitchen stoves close to children's bedrooms, unventilated rooms, absence of drinking water systems, sewage systems, improper disposal of wastewaters, and garbage collection. Ultimately, it is the family that decides its priorities. However, it does so in an organized manner, and the decision is subject to a weighting system applied by the technical consultant on the basis of criteria such as urgency, cost, sequence, and time required to do the improvement.

The result is the identification of the type of improvement that has the highest priority. The technical assistance orients the family toward the establishment of a plan of action for a gradual improvement of the house. The technician takes into consideration the costs that can be covered by the loan and the resources the family already has (accumulated construction materials, volunteer labor, project supervision tasks, and the money that can be used to pay for skilled labor and transport of materials).

LOAN PREPARATION AND FORMALIZATION. Once the priorities are established and the family's available resources have been analyzed, the technical consultant prepares a budget, a schedule of activities, and a brief report describing the current situation and the type of improvements that can be made. The budget also describes the activities that the loan and the family contributions can cover, and it defines possible improvements to be made in the future on the basis of the current loan. The borrower, who thereby agrees to carry out the improvement defined with the technical consultant from the municipal government, signs the budget. An additional purpose of the budget is to make it possible for the borrower to maintain some economic control over the improvement construction process, assuming that the costs in the budget are close to the real costs.

On the basis of the budget, the beneficiary proceeds to formalize the loan at the bank, providing the collateral and submitting the forms required by the bank. The bank generally issues a single check which the borrower uses to buy the materials and, in some cases, to hire labor. The invoices for the materials remain in the borrower's file at the bank. Between 5 and 10 days after the loan has been made, the bank's loan officers visit the home to verify whether the family has bought the materials and begun the construction process.

PROJECT SUPERVISION. Officials from the technical assistance department make at least one more visit to supervise the construction process and provide guidance to the borrower's family or to the laborers who are working on the project. In general, projects do not take more than 30 days. When the head of the household is a woman, the technician tries to maintain closer monitoring to assist her in the process of supervising and administering hired labor. The families participate in the construction process in different ways—by estimating the required quantities and buying the construction materials, hauling the materials to the site, mixing and laying bricks, and supervising the laborers if they themselves do not participate in the process.

One month after receiving the check, the borrower begins to repay the loan over a period of up to four years. The bank services the loan and monitors the placements and collections of the rotating fund. If the loan is not repaid and the normal administrative collection procedures have failed, legal action is taken to exercise the guarantee. Although the loans are individual, on some occasions the bank has had recourse to the community project committees to ask their assistance in collecting payments from defaulting borrowers.

Evaluation of Participation in the Housing Improvement Loan Component

The system of housing improvement loans is based on the premise that the great majority of poor families build their houses in an informal way, without any support or assistance from central and local governments or the private sector (this section is based on Morales and Herrera 1997). They usually achieve this through a long and complicated process of personal savings and mobilizing family and interfamily contributions. The program tries to create conditions so that families living in marginal squatter areas, generally not regarded as part of the loan market, can have access to resources from the institutionalized financial system. It also tries to give technical assistance in a fast and easy manner that will allow the families to accelerate their housing consolidation process. The program is based on the fact that a large part of the population in the cities where it operates owns a plot of land or is in the process of legalizing land tenure. Assistance therefore contributes to the process of self-help construction, with defined and guaranteed participation by the users in the process of the administration and construction of the home. The impact of the participation of the user families in the housing component can be appreciated on the basis of the following parameters.

The program represents a massive approach to the housing problem in the municipalities where it operates. It has created healthier environments, a reduction of overcrowding, and improvements in the standards and systems of construction in at least 4,000 houses—which represents approximately 4.5 percent of the total housing stock in the cities, and 14.5 percent of the households classified as poor.

This process increased the administrative capabilities of the local governments and communities in general, but in particular the capacity of women with regard to problems relating to their households. In 10 cases selected at random for study in the cities of Somoto, Estelí, and Chinandega, participants were asked who in the family performed the administrative tasks involved in the construction process. In five of these cases, the wife did the administrative tasks directly. In one case, the tasks of buying the materials, hiring the labor, supplying the materials, and supervising the work were shared with the husband. In the other four cases, the women participated only in the procurement of the construction materials.

The assisted self-help construction and access to credit provided a major impetus to the local economies, mobilizing more than US$2.5 million in purchases of construction materials, many of them produced locally by microenterprises (cement and clay blocks, adobe, cement tiles, and bricks) in the five cities. The housing improvement loan component has also generated indirect employment for some 270 people in the construction sector, which amounts to about 40 jobs per city in the municipalities of the first phase. Family contributions, which add 15 percent of the value of labor and transport, may represent up to 36 percent of the actual cost of each housing improvement.

The technical assistance constitutes a new service, which gives the local governments the opportunity to acquire major lessons for the definition of housing improvement and urban development policies in the country. The program has generated a base knowledge of ideas, standards, and methodologies for technical assistance to user families. Obviously, this process required a major effort by PRODEL to train technicians from local governments, as well as loan officers and other bank employees. The idea is that local government and bank officials can understand the complexities of the loan operations and manage the design, planning, and definition of solutions in a process, which involves the participation of the target population.

Some of the principal weaknesses detected in the efficiency of the program relate to the manner in which the financial and technical construction aspects must be defined simultaneously with thousands of user families. Many times, the informal introductory meetings are insufficient to explain the type of participatory work required between the technician and the end user, or for the family to understand the complexities of the financial terms of the loan. Sometimes the incorrect preparation of project plans, budgets, and schedules can affect the project. In all the cities, the site visits for supervision have been insufficient or late, sometimes resulting in actual construction errors. Nor were sufficient efforts always made to train the available labor. On some occasions, the beneficiary families did not see the link between the technical assistance and the opportunity to obtain a better quality of design and construction of the house at reasonable costs, and to repay the loan in accordance with their affordability to pay.

These are not problems only of the installed capacities of the municipal technicians and the loan promoters of the bank. They are linked to the problems of administering a portfolio of thousands of small loans and coming up with technical solutions to a large number of small and widely varied onsite improvements that are scattered over a wide geographic area and carried out individually by the families or by construction workers. The challenges of control therefore are more complex.

Nevertheless, like the infrastructure component, the housing improvement component shows that the urban housing problems faced by the urban poor are not the result of a fundamental lack of resources. Making institutionalized financing systems and technical assistance accessible to poor families stimulates the internal savings of the end users, mobilizes significant family resources, and improves the overall housing situation. The repayment levels are acceptable, in spite of the fact that the collateral provided is not of the conventional type. The financial sustainability of the rotating funds is a goal, which is within easy reach. In this sense, the multiplier impact of the borrowers on the economic and social level is undeniable.[8]

Lessons Learned, Sustainability, and Replicability

The experience gained by PRODEL has yielded important lessons regarding the potentialities and limitations of community participation and institutional and financial sustainability in social programs aimed at providing infrastructure, social equipment, housing improvement and income generation, especially for the urban poor. The results of the program suggest that community participation has been a determining factor in many kinds of community advances.

- **Improving the quality of life of the poor.** More than 38,000 poor families whose basic needs are not being met, and who represent 47 percent of the total population of the cities of León, Chinandega, Estelí, Somoto, Ocotal, Matagalpa, Jinotega, and Chichigalpa, improved the conditions in which they live. They improved their access to basic services and equipment by participating in the definition, execution, and maintenance of 260 infrastructure and community works projects, the improvement, expansion, and repair of some 4,168 houses, and the financing of some 2,400 microenterprises.
- **Targeting and focusing social investments to the poor.** The involvement of community leaders in the municipal commissions has made it possible for local governments to more accurately identify the geographical areas of the city where there are higher levels of poverty as well as requirements for infrastructure and urban services. Participatory microplanning exercises that were conducted in 150 different communities have made it easier to identify the type, amount, and scope of projects required by each neighborhood in particular. This dual mechanism of participation in the decisionmaking processes has

---

8. A thorough analysis of a sample of 15 percent of PRODEL's portfolio found no clear relation between the rate of default and the type of guarantees the families have given as collateral for their microenterprise or housing improvement loans. The preloan analysis and approval, the type of information given, the bank's follow-up, and the administrative procedures for cost recovery are more important elements than a family's collateral for an efficient administration of a portfolio such as PRODEL's.

helped to increase the efficiency and accuracy of the diagnostic measures and the proposals prepared by the municipal governments for
the design and preparation of the annual social investment plans and
the longer-term municipal development plans.

- **Making more efficient use of public resources.** To the extent that local
governments have negotiated the projects with the communities through
microplanning workshops, public investments (including those that the
central government provides via the municipal government as well as
the municipal government's own tax revenues) are more sound. The
investments reflect the priorities and preferences of the users and the
actual capacities of the municipal government in providing and financing the services. Experience shows that these preferences are not always expressed in demands for the introduction of new services, but
also for the improvement, expansion, repair, and maintenance of existing services and systems. These options have a positive impact on the
costs of the solutions and optimize the utilization of the municipal
government's scarce and insufficient resources for these types of works.

- **Improving accountability and transparency.** The participation of
beneficiary families in the different phases of the operation and management of the infrastructure and social equipment projects, including their administration and financial auditing, provides an opportunity to establish new habits of control, reporting, and joint
responsibility of local governments with the communities. It also helps
provide an improved understanding of the role of the municipal government and the real limitations of technical and financial resources
that exist to address the problems of the poor.

- **Mobilizing internal savings.** The substantive contributions by the
communities—in kind, labor, and materials—exceeded 10 percent of
the direct costs of the infrastructure and community assets projects.
In the case of housing improvements, this amount was sometimes
even greater than 15 percent. This mobilization of local and community resources also provided a positive incentive for the municipal
governments to improve the tax collection processes in response to
the program requirements to come up with local matching funds. The
resources mobilized over four years totaled US$10.5 million, of which
53 percent represented contributions from the central government with
the foreign-aid financing provided by SIDA. The remaining 47 percent represented contributions from local governments, the communities, and the user families.

- **Reducing the costs of the projects.** The evidence suggests that for a certain type and complexity of financed project, there can be a reduction by up to 20 percent in the costs of projects not exceeding a value of US$50,000. These data result from a comparison of the costs of projects with and without community participation, and are due primarily to the contributions from the beneficiary families in the administration and supervision of the project, as well as their contributions in terms of skilled and unskilled labor.
- **Increasing social and gender equity.** The experience shows that community participation can help to direct the benefits of the projects toward the poor and vulnerable sectors of society. In the case of housing improvement and microenterprise loans, the primary beneficiaries have been poor sectors with certain capacity to repay their loans. The participatory methodology employed also facilitated the incorporation of women. Some 70 percent of the participants in the decision-making and supervising processes for infrastructure and urban assets projects were women. In the case of the housing improvement loans, 60 percent of the users were women—a number that rose to 70 percent for the microenterprise loans
- **Revitalizing local economies.** In addition to making some 12,000 loans to finance 2,400 microenterprises, the informal links established between the individual participatory initiatives for the improvement of the social infrastructure and family habitat have had a positive trickle-down effect on the local economy. In the area of housing improvements, for example, the self-help construction processes have revitalized and consolidated microenterprises that are directly active in the production of local construction materials. There has also been a utilization of a greater number of skilled and unskilled workers who were unemployed in the areas where the program operates. The participants in the infrastructure projects were able to establish the economic link between the individual effort required in the construction and maintenance of the works of collective benefit and the improvement to and future value of their houses.
- **Improving national reconciliation.** The changes in attitude and contributions generated among the principal participants have made the relationship between local governments and the communities more transparent. These relations are now based on incentives and the structuring of concrete alliances founded on tangible plans and solutions, and not merely on simple social demands and false promises and

expectations. The methodology has also contributed to the transformation of a more favorable environment that facilitates communication between antagonistic groups, reduces political polarization, and coordinates positive actions for the improvement of the living conditions in the neighborhoods between groups that might appear to be politically and ideologically irreconcilable.

- **Making programs sustainable.** The system of incentives established for the contribution of national, municipal, and community resources, as well as the involvement of beneficiary families in the management and administration of the project cycle, has created a solid basis for an increased commitment and division of responsibilities between participants. This facilitates the maintenance and sustainability of projects. This commitment has positive repercussions that strengthen the link between the durability of the physical project and the performance and operation of the service. Evidence also suggests that sustainability of social programs can best be achieved when there is a clear division of labor between financial institutions and those organizations that give technical and social assistance. The fact that a bank operates at the level of the community has been a critical factor for achieving an important level of recovery. The revolving funds have rotated several times, and levels of arrears and default rates are reasonable and allow achievement of operative sustainability.

In addition, several external factors facilitated the design, organization, and implementation of the PRODEL participatory model.

- **Nonpartisan programs.** In spite of the dramatic political changes that occurred in the country, officials with the INIFOM and the local governments (regardless of their political tendencies) have created alliances and utilized methodologies that provide incentives for the participation of poor families, without any discrimination on the basis of political, ideological, or religious factors. Evidently there has always been the temptation to make use of scarce resources for partisan purposes. If rules of the game between the funding agency and the recipient government regarding funds misuse are clear, the possibility of success is greater.
- **Programs with limited resources.** Experience shows that the lack of urban services and facilities in marginal neighborhoods is not only a problem of a lack of financial resources. It also relates to methods that fail to promote the involvement of communities in the processes of

decisionmaking and administration of the most important variables involved in the management of the project cycle. It is therefore important to make available, in a combined and simultaneous manner, a series of limited resources that stimulate and provide incentives for contributions from communities. These incentives can include the introduction of urban infrastructure and facilities projects and the possibility of housing and microenterprise loans. By quantifying the real and positive contributions of participants (in terms of money, materials, and labor), the municipal governments gain an understanding of the importance of cooperating with and involving the communities. They enhance their legitimacy and mobilize real resources that give the communities greater control and decisionmaking authority over the use of the scarce tax and outside resources available to municipal governments.

- **Work with existing institutions.** In the case of PRODEL, it was important to identify and utilize the institutions at the local level that were closest to the demands and needs of the users of the services, and that could facilitate the process of community participation. The different actors were able to establish overall agreements and rules. Thus, local governments and a commercial bank (which is part of the national financial system) were able to promote different types of participatory solutions in the areas of infrastructure, improvement of the housing stock, and income generation. These activities obviously required a major effort in terms of training and the development of methodologies that made it possible for the municipal technicians to promote participation in established communities.
- **Streamlined and flexible mechanisms.** It is important to recognize that communities are made up of heterogeneous groups of people with potential beneficiaries for a series of diversified technical assistance and financial services. Participation in the introduction and upgrading of the urban infrastructure and services requires the communities to have more information and a greater understanding of the principal technical, physical, social, and financial variables that influence a construction project. At the same time, the communities must have rapid decisionmaking mechanisms and access to resources. If not, the skepticism and mistrust that usually prevails in poor communities will persist.
- **Division of functions and responsibilities.** An important factor for the development of the program is the complementary nature of activities between the administrators and other parties. PRODEL has

been able to recognize the different corporate interests, the financial feasibility of the products and services offered, and the need for an exact definition of what is expected from community participation in each component. Municipal governments try to involve communities to cofinance the projects and increase the life utility of the infrastructure and community assets. The commercial bank aims to increase the commissions it will earn from managing the portfolio of housing improvement and microenterprise loans, and to accumulate capital for the rotating funds. In fact, the effectiveness of the relationship and coordination between the participants in the program has been more effective when the sequence of the components of the program has been discussed and planned with the community and its leaders.

• **Adequate social organization of the community.** Many times in projects of this type, unrealistic expectations can be generated through community participation. Actions are based on models of community organization that have very little to do with the requirements of the construction processes. When providing infrastructure in established communities, it is important to strengthen the participation and organization of the beneficiaries by territorial divisions appropriate to the neighborhoods. It is also important to promote processes of the democratic election of representatives for each block to be able to do better technical work as a result of the administrative and physical design of the project. The different commission and committees formed must be in line with the complexity and nature of each project. When this happens, they have been effective instruments helping the program to accomplish its physical and social goals.

• **Empowerment and technical assistance to the beneficiary families.** Community participation requires efforts to provide the families with new options, capacities, and skills in different areas. These mainly relate to the identification and analysis of problems (microplanning workshops), project planning (design, scheduling, budgeting), mobilization of internal and external resources, the specialized physical execution, the administration and supervision of the projects (inventories, audits, and so on), the evaluation of projects (impact and efficiency in the use of the resources), and the maintenance of projects (cleaning campaigns, security and protection of the project constructed, and management of resources for preventive maintenance tasks).

Finally, it must be noted that in spite of its successes, PRODEL must be consolidated even further if it is to have a greater long-term impact. The first five years were used to test various hypotheses concerning schemes of participation and administration on the local level in the context of Nicaragua. The results obtained for the three components in eight different localities indicate that it is not simply a pilot project, and that community participation is a determining factor in the processes of introduction, improvement, and maintenance of urban services and facilities.

Conclusions

The encouraging results of PRODEL are due in large measure to the innovations in several interlocking systems of incentives. PRODEL, SIDA, and the participating institutions in Nicaragua acted on newly introduced incentives for the participation of communities and end users in the cofinancing, comanagement, and operation of the infrastructure projects as well as the housing improvement and microenterprise loans. The case of PRODEL is unique of those explored in this book because an external actor, SIDA, fostered and promoted the introduction of new sets of incentives. SIDA played a major role as champion and visionary in this case. The agency built upon its experience elsewhere in Latin America and Africa and with this body of knowledge sought to persuade local authorities, credit institutions, and participating community groups about the benefits of this approach.

The process of persuasion and learning required careful and patient explanation, along with demonstrations in small community experiments, to launch the innovations of participatory development more widely. In addition to its knowledge and experience, the agency offered financial assistance. Financial support made available through collaborating institutions helped to launch the process and overcome initial reluctance and doubt. After the first few years, the mechanisms of transaction and implementation became self-sustaining. PRODEL helped the bank overcome the high transaction costs of working with many beneficiaries on a small margin by developing manuals of operation and training. In a similar way, participatory microplanning exercises involved communities and families in the identification, priority setting, negotiation, and coordination of projects with local governments. Together with project committees and community working groups, PRODEL established a recognized, participatory methodology. In addition, special emphasis has been given to the involvement of women in these processes.

SIDA's recognized role as a highly professional and diligent assistance agency helped in many ways. For example, the persistence of the agency over many years both proved the concept and disseminated the results through publications and conferences. The question for future phases of PRODEL, and for future endeavors inspired by it, is whether and how the momentum put in place by PRODEL can be sustained across political administrations, particularly after cessation of the financial support offered by SIDA.

References

Goethert, Reinhard, Nabeel Hamdi, Sebastian Gray, and Andrew Sletteback. 1992. *La microplanificación: un proceso de programación y desarrollo con base en la comunidad.* Washington, D.C.: World Bank.

Morales, Ninette, and Edgard Herrera. 1997. *"Evaluación: prestación de servicios de asistencia técnica en mejoramiento habitacional en cinco Municipios."* PRODEL, Managua.

PRODEL. 1997a. *"Documento de Proyecto para la Segunda Fase de PRODEL."* PRODEL Phase Two Project Document, Nicaraguan Institute for Municipal Development, Managua.

———. 1997b. *Final Year Report.* Managua.

———. 1997c. *Program Progress Report.* Managua.

———. 1998a. *Participation and Sustainability in Social Projects: The Experience of the Local Development Program (PRODEL) in Nicaragua.* Managua.

———. 1998b. *Final Year Report.* Managua.

———. 1999. *Evaluation 1998 and Operative Plan 1999.* Managua.

Part 3

Lessons for Donors
and Policymakers

10

Challenge for Donors: Sustaining the Engine of Reform

The two articles in this chapter, prepared by two key donor agencies, the U.S. Agency for International Development and the German Technical Co-operation (better known as the GTZ), provide perspective on some of the macroeconomic conditions—decentralization processes and democratic electoral reforms—that shape the environment in which innovation takes place. Though produced simultaneously with the research and not having the benefit of its findings, both articles nevertheless touch on many policy areas covered elsewhere in this volume. For example, Mark Schneider emphasizes the importance of the electoral choicemaking process at the local level as the training ground for operating decentralized democracies. Schneider's observations reflect a conclusion in this study: that local democracy, when exercised through open elections, can attract a new breed of leader and generate a new form of pressure not seen in the region in many decades. Equally important are income sufficiency and predictability for local governments, although we note that in many of the cases described in earlier chapters, these conditions are promised in national policy, but not met. Schneider indicates five challenges facing local governments, which again are closely linked to the areas of innovation covered in this volume: transparency, participation, service delivery, financial sources of investment, and poverty alleviation.

Albrecht Stockmayer addresses the conditions of innovation and decentralization from a different angle. The author focuses on intrinsic tensions generated by divergent perspectives of local and national interests and traces many difficulties to this source; often he also describes the conditions for invention. He points to the lack of definition in policy and the challenge of making policy and implementation fit local circumstances. Meso-level organizational and institutional actors come into play here. They have both positive and negative impacts on the problem of implementing policy that has been conceived nationally and implemented at local levels in many differing circumstances. This issue is illustrated richly by the case of the Bolivian participation law. Key areas of future action include matching rules of the game to new expectations and circumstances, making use of horizontal coordination among local governments, and promoting local economic development.

Both authors stress a new and expanding role for donors to coordinate their actions, buttress local efforts, and above all to coordinate assistance locally, nationally, and internationally.

10-1

Promoting Democracy through Decentralization and Strengthening Local Governance: USAID's Approach and Experience

Mark L. Schneider, International Crisis Group, Washington, D.C.

In Mexico City, Buenos Aires, and Santiago, and in thousands of towns with names like Jiquilisco and Quetzaltenango and Patacamayo, voters now elect the men and women who govern them. Alexis de Tocqueville wrote 150 years ago after his journey through the United States, a young democracy barely five decades old, "A nation may establish a system of free government, but without the spirit of municipal institutions it cannot have the spirit of liberty" (de Tocqueville 1947). That spirit is alive and well in virtually every nation in the hemisphere. In all of the hemisphere's past romances with democratic values, the opportunity for democratic electoral choice usually has been limited to national executive and legislative contests. Local mayors and municipal councils, and even provincial or state governors, generally were appointed by the institutional executive except in historically strong federal nations such as Argentina and Brazil. Democracy never quite reached cities or states, as Spanish traditions of centralized public administration outlasted independence and national democracy.

All that has changed in the current democratic transformation of the hemisphere. Now, mayors are directly elected in 15 of the countries, and, in another dozen, they are chosen by democratically elected city councils. Equally important, they are being acknowledged as the managers of a decentralization process that is critical to a second generation of political reform essential to good governance and to the consolidation of the democratic transformation itself.

In April 1998, in an unprecedented demonstration of support for decentralization, the heads of state of the 34 democratic countries of the hemisphere pledged to strengthen their local and regional government systems of government. The Second Summit of the Americas in Santiago, Chile, was the setting for this landmark commitment. The pledge reflects not only the value of decentralization as a democracy-building tool, but also the lead role it is playing in the hemisphere's drive to build good government and modernize state institutions.

Specifically, the countries of the hemisphere committed themselves in a political declaration and a detailed plan of action covering three areas—political, administrative, and financial—that comprise any well-rounded policy of decentralization. In the political arena, each country agreed to open or strengthen mechanisms for participation by civil society organizations in subnational decisionmaking. Administratively, the countries will increase available training opportunities to improve subnational capacity and will study the possibilities for enhancing the functions of local and regional levels of government. In the financial realm, each nation will provide financing options for subnational governments to expand service delivery and promote transparency in local and regional government financial transactions. Equally important, the nations of this hemisphere agreed to share experiences and information regarding decentralization programs supported by international donor institutions.

The U.S. Agency for International Development (USAID) served as the U.S. government's lead negotiator on the subject of decentralization and local government in the multilateral negotiations that culminated in the Summit of the Americas. Throughout that process, differences among nations affected the character of the debate, but support for inclusion of this item was broad-based, strong, and unchallenged.

The landmark endorsement of democratic decentralization by the heads of state was well warranted. Since 1990, there have been more local officials elected in Latin America than in the preceding 200 years. Most countries now directly elect mayors as well as city councils. Now mayors and councils respond less to their political party's interests and much more to the independent power bases emerging from their direct ties with local citizens. Already, local elections are forcing political parties to broaden their bases, to modernize, and to turn to an up-and-coming generation of political leaders.

Greater responsibility is being assigned to local and regional governments by constitutional amendment or statutory reforms. For the first time, many subnational governments are not only carrying out their traditional duties—be they garbage collection or street cleaning—but also taking on new public services once firmly in the domain of the central government, such as water, road maintenance, police protection, environmental protection, education, and health care. So far, the examples still are limited and ad hoc. However, they demonstrate effectively the potential capacity at the local level for sound administration of public services.

We are beginning to see public-private partnerships that link communities and municipal officials to improve local government. In the past, nongovernmental organizations (NGOs) were survival mechanisms for citizens facing repression, and donors relied on them to support basic needs, rather than work with dictators. Today, they are being accepted by municipal governments as representative of public needs and as efficient delivery vehicles.

Formal networks have connected local government officials from the same province, the same country, or distant nations. Nearly every country in Latin America has created a municipal association that provides opportunities for municipal officials to interact, exchange innovations, and strengthen their local agendas. Many such organizations are lobbying hard for further decentralization, greater resources transfer, and other municipal interests. Those associations also tend to overcome partisan divisions in favor of their common destiny as municipal leaders.

At the same time, there is growing recognition that further decentralization may be essential not only for the first generation of political reforms that substituted constitutional elected civilian government for military juntas but also for the consolidation of the past decade's market-oriented economic reforms. Most institutional supporters of the market reforms are arguing that a second generation of institutional reforms must now be instituted to preserve, deepen, and extend the gains of readjustment (see IDB 1997). This second generation must introduce appropriate incentives for the efficient functioning of essential public institutions. To successfully build new institutions, central governments must now let go of some of their power, and devolve a greater measure of resources and responsibility to bring new public and private actors into the political and economic process. These new stakeholders—those who have a primary interest in the success of the new institutions—provide the political dynamic to make reform irreversible (see Graham 1998).

Consequently, decentralization must be considered a key tool for the development of democratic government and the establishment of modern institutions that can compete in a competitive world economy. Simply put, subnational reform cannot be separated from democracy-building objectives or from the formulation of second-generation institutional reforms currently underway. The commitments of the Second Summit of the Americas confirm recognition of the importance of strengthening local and subnational governments. The U.S. government and USAID, as its voice in development policy and programming, are placing increasing focus on decentralization, local and other subnational governments, and partnership with civil society as the best vehicles to achieve good governance.

In formal terms, decentralization is "the transfer or delegation of legal and political authority to plan, make decisions and manage public functions from the central government and its agencies . . . to subordinate units of government. . . ." (Rondinelli 1981, pp. 137–38). In a more practical sense, decentralization is simply a question of the transfer of power, the willingness of the central government to cede authority to lower levels of government so that they can better manage local or regional affairs. No one, neither politicians nor dictators, voluntarily agrees to relinquish power without considerable incentive, without which decentralization programs are never easily or swiftly carried out. To be successful, therefore, the pursuit of decentralization must be sustained.

Decentralization also involves three aspects. The first is the transfer of political power—the establishment of subnational units of government led by officials who have recognized political legitimacy. Periodic, open, and competitive elections are the first requirement. Subnational elections established a constituency and the basis of an official's authority, and they create the legitimacy to carry out a program of government. Political decentralization includes reforms such as the direct election of mayors, the separation of local elections from national elections, and the establishment of mechanisms for political participation.

Second, decentralization involves the transfer of real governing responsibilities. Local and regional officials must be responsible for a substantive portion of the public good. This means providing governmental functions "sufficient in number, variety, and significance to challenge the interest of both public servant and the citizen" (Martin 1967, pp. 50–51).

Finally, all the responsibilities in the world are of no use to mayors and governors if they do not also have the resources to carry out those duties. Financial power—sufficient resources, sufficient capacity to efficiently use those resources, and mechanisms of transparency and accountability to fight against corruption—are all critical to our ability to strengthen subnational government.

Why should we decentralize? The answer is that decentralization deepens democracy. It does so in three ways. First, decentralization enhances responsiveness and accountability, two related concepts that represent the essence of democracy. Responsiveness reflects the degree to which leaders are sensitive to citizen preferences, and it is what Robert Dahl has called a "key characteristic of a democracy" (Dahl 1971, p. 1). By definition, regional and local elected authorities represent territorial entities smaller than the nation as a whole. They are therefore physically closer, more attuned to, and more knowledgeable about the local needs of their constituents than the central government. Accountability is introduced, as we have seen, by elections, and it reflects the degree to which leaders must demonstrate that they are pursuing the public good (Linz 1978). With decentralization, subnational officials are held directly accountable to the community through local elections. Failed leaders are removed from office; successful ones are rewarded. Subnational government can thus serve as breeding grounds for successful, modern national leaders. In Latin America, the presidents of Argentina, El Salvador, Guatemala, and Nicaragua are former mayors of their capital cities. Colombia and Ecuador brought the former mayors of the capital cities into office. And in Peru, Mexico, and República Bolivariana de Venezuela, mayors have emerged as leading candidates for their presidencies.

Second, decentralization provides another critical ingredient of democracy: increased effectiveness. Effectiveness is "the capacity actually to implement the policies formulated, with the desired results" (Linz 1978, p. 22). Government institutions not only need to respond to their citizens, they also must efficaciously address the public's demands. The inability to be effective, however, weakens the authority of the state and the "persistence and stability" of a democratic regime (Putnam 1993, p. 22). Decentralization consists of making local (or regional) governments responsible for providing purely local services and, to the extent possible, financing them as well. Economic theorists point out that this is the most efficient way to proceed: local officials know best how to resolve local problems because they can adjust their actions to local preferences (Oates 1972). And experience demonstrates that central governments take uniform approaches to problems that often do not suit the myriad circumstances subnational governments face. The result, all too often, is gross institutional ineffectiveness.

Finally, decentralization promotes democratic socialization—the inculcation of democratic norms and values in a society, including political participation. The development of decentralized government not only allows people to observe more closely and appreciate democracy at work, it also opens new avenues for the individual to participate in the political process. John Stuart Mill argues that democracy is learned in the same way as reading, writing, and swimming—that is, not only by being told how to do it, but also by doing it. "[S]o it is only by practising popular government on a limited scale that the people will ever learn how to exercise it on a larger" (Mill 1962, pp. 200–201). With decentralization, people can become educated public citizens and receive important training in the solution of complex problems. They also do not have to traverse an immense central bureaucracy to address a community concern.

Capturing the value of decentralization requires a discussion of its three dimensions: administrative, financial, and political.

Administrative Dimension

The first dimension entails the transfer of functions or administrative responsibilities to the subnational level. In the past, many Latin American countries would have easily failed to meet this criterion.

Traditionally in Latin America, local government functions, such as street cleaning, fire protection, garbage collection, and the operation of food markets, have been basic and of entirely local import. Today, however, local governments are increasingly taking responsibility for community development, particularly projects such as building repair, infrastructure improvement, and road pavement, perhaps financed in whole or part by higher levels of government. Local governments are also being handed new functions of local concern in which higher levels of government claim significant interest, especially the delivery of primary health care, education, and participation in antipoverty programs. The result is a kind of product specialization in which each level of government provides a specific aspect of a public service, such as repair, financing, or enforcement of legal norms.

Finally, local governments are providing services in new ways. They are turning to partnerships with the private sector to deliver public services, and services are increasingly being privatized or competitively contracted out. Municipal advisory groups in several countries are required by law to include business groups. NGOs are also helping to deliver services.

In any country, however, writing a local service responsibility into the law does not necessarily mean that municipal governments are actually providing the service. Municipal systems throughout Latin America are loaded with formal responsibilities that have no relation to what local officials actually do. Even where municipal governments are taking advantage of new administrative authority, services are not necessarily being provided more effectively today than in the past. In local administration, then, we find two major challenges.

First, although reform has brought obvious improvements, the assignment of service and other functions according to level of government is often unclear. To the extent that clarity of responsibility among the levels of government can be improved, all levels will benefit. Confused or multiple jurisdiction favors the forces of tradition; the government level that has traditionally provided a service locally (such as the central government) will tend to continue to provide it, even where legal norms and efficiency considerations call for local officials to take the lead. Functions should be assigned such that public goods and services are matched with the specific populations that benefit from them. If the benefits of a public good are confined to a state or locality, the government of that state or locality should provide and pay for that good (Oates 1972). As much as possible, purely local services should be delivered locally, while services with externalities or effects that spill outside the community can be shared with higher levels of government. The one powerful caveat to that rule is that assuring equity may demand that national governments assume more jurisdiction so that some semblance of equivalence for all citizens in receiving public benefits is assured.

Second, municipal capacity is often too weak to carry out substantive new functions. General growth in municipal capacity must be a major focus. Municipal governments often lack the fiscal and managerial resources needed to meet their mandates. When this is the case, especially given the renewed expectations of newly elected local leaders in many countries, municipal legitimacy suffers. Building capacity requires, among other things, better-trained personnel, the creation or enforcement of administrative career laws to provide personnel stability, and more partnerships with the private sector.

Financial Dimension

Financing comprises the second dimension of decentralization. Although local governments have more resources than ever before, they still are far from able to meet their needs. A U.N. report notes that in the United States, Canada, and Europe more than 40 percent of all government spending takes place at the state, province, or municipal level. In most Latin American countries, however, the total is only between 10 and 20 percent, with much less for the municipalities alone (IDB 1997, pp. 196–97). Latin America's local governments remain highly dependent on revenue transfers. Transfers reduce the incentive of local officials to raise revenue locally, and transfer levels are often unpredictable from year to year, impeding local planning efforts. Raising revenue locally is always a politically difficult step for mayors and counselors, and the capacity to administer revenue collection is usually weak in any case. The efforts being made in this area will have to be much stronger if they are to hold much hope for financially strapped localities. Finding nontraditional revenue sources and carefully increasing automatic and unconditional transfers to the local level are, therefore, especially important to municipal autonomy in the region.

Local government finance, then, faces three critical challenges. First, municipal governments should at least be accorded the revenue they are legally entitled. Legally mandated revenue transfers are often more accurately viewed as ideals than as actual local income.

Second, local governments must be encouraged and given the flexibility to generate more revenue. This challenge requires the development of capable administrators and skilled specialists, as well as strong leadership initiatives involving working with the community to determine investment priorities. Municipalities must be able to demonstrate to residents that new tax money will be expended on real benefits in order to encourage the payment of taxes. Local governments also could greatly benefit from access to private capital markets. In Colombia, credit has been extended to local governments from banks and through the emission of bonds. But in the few other countries that allow municipal authorities to directly incur debt, such as Ecuador, little use is made of it.

Third, adequate institutional capacity must be in place to ensure that local resources are efficiently used. Corruption and waste must be weeded out for decentralization to sustain public credibility. Better-trained, more career-oriented personnel are required. Equally important is the strengthening of the system of independent oversight of municipal finances. The efforts of national and state comptrollers are too often weak, lacking in enforcement authority, and highly politicized.

Political Dimension

The transfer of political power is the third dimension of decentralization. Political decentralization entails the establishment of subnational units of government led by officials elected democratically, which allows the officials to take new leadership roles, and the institution of formal and informal mechanisms to promote community involvement in local decisionmaking.

LOCAL ELECTIONS. Election by popular vote is the foundation for strong representative government. It is also the best option for improving responsiveness and accountability on the part of the local executive. The separation of local elections from presidential and congressional votes prevents local candidates and issues from being submerged by national politics. Restricting voter choice for town council to candidates from one party slate or requiring voters to choose by party as opposed to the individual limits the extension of representative government. However, it offers some assurance that the mayor has a working majority on the city council and it may permit greater capacity for the mayor to make good on campaign promises. Term length and the local official's ability to run for reelection are also important factors determining the ability of local officials to respond to and address community demands.[1]

A number of these and similar reforms are being implemented by various countries in Latin America. The results must be studied and shared, further reforms encouraged, and any unplanned negative consequences avoided or rectified. Local electoral reform is not without potential drawbacks. In particular, new political authority, when coupled with additional resources and responsibilities and a lack of independent financial control, can be misused by local leaders in traditional, clientelistic fashion to build powerful, corrupt political machines. Avoiding such outcomes, particularly through the strong oversight of local spending by civil society, should be a major concern of any decentralization program. The Popular Participation Law in Bolivia established watchdog committees to monitor municipal execution of approved budgets with direct communication lines to the country's national Senate if distortions occur.

LEADERSHIP. The "skills, values, strategies, and choices of political leaders" have long figured prominently in Latin America's varied experiences with democracy (Diamond, Linz, and Lipset 1989, p. 14). Leadership at the local level is no less essential to the success of democratization. Political decentralization opens opportunities for new leaders to take the helm of local government. With direct elections, the local leader is better able to build an independent political base of support. Who runs for office is no longer as easily controlled by national political party decisions, and, because

---

1. A four-year term with the possibility of reelection at least once is probably best to allow local officials a measure of continuity and long-term planning without having to be overly concerned with electoral politics.

local governments today face greater administrative challenges and higher performance expectations, parties are increasingly pressured to select competent candidates with ties to and knowledge of the needs of their communities. For these reasons, and because the mayor's office, in rural areas as well as cities, is a post with greater substance and prestige than in the past, we are witnessing the rise of modern, innovative, and better-trained mayors and councilors. New, activist local leadership often produces major administrative renovation as mayors seek to distinguish themselves from failed practices of the past. Indigenous and other groups are playing lead roles in municipal government as never before. On all counts, democracy benefits.

As decentralization theory predicts, successful local leaders, especially of cities, are emerging on the national political scenes of their respective countries. City hall is becoming a powerful stepping stone for new leaders to reach higher office.

Equally important is the ability of political decentralization to incorporate new segments of society, particularly traditionally marginalized groups, into the democratic process. The indigenous populations of Bolivia and Guatemala especially have taken advantage of the opportunities presented by newly elected local government. Bolivia's promulgation of the 1994 Popular Participation Law created 250 new functioning municipalities, bringing the total to 311. Some 200 of these communities elected about 400 indigenous town councilors—or 25 percent of the total councilors in those communities (UNDP 1996). Bolivia's urban poor are also better represented under the new local system. In Guatemala, one-third of the mayors were indigenous as of the late 1990s.[2] The increase of indigenous participants in local government demonstrates that their absence from political participation in the past is more likely to have been a result of external obstacles and discrimination than any independent decision on the part of indigenous people.

Political decentralization, it should be noted, as yet appears to have had little impact on gender relations in local government. In a 1994 survey that captured 40 percent of the municipalities in Colombia, 92 percent of the mayors were male (World Bank 1995). In Bolivia, a mere 4 percent (12 of 311) and 8 percent (135 of 1,760) of mayors and councilors, respectively, were women (Blair 1997). Women have never headed more than a tenth of

2. This figure comes from the Guatemalan Association of Indigenous Mayors and Authorities. Some 110 out of 330 mayors identified themselves as indigenous.

the nearly 1,200 municipalities in Central America. Costa Rican, Argentine, and Chilean political parties established required levels of female participation in the 1998 elections, some by law (Jager 1997). The challenge here is to encourage new leaders, especially women, to participate in the political process, help prepare them for success through education and training programs, and highlight their progress so as to encourage further participation and new approaches in other municipalities.

CITIZEN PARTICIPATION. Community residents are physically closer to their local officials and can therefore more easily interact with municipal government. As a result, stronger local government creates greater potential for citizen input. Decentralization in Latin America has produced a series of new mechanisms for increasing public participation in the local decisionmaking process. Some are formal revisions of municipal law, others are informal procedures developed as part of local development and other programs. The following list of the mechanisms either legally instituted or increasingly utilized in recent years illustrates the strong interest in improving local political participation:

- Public budget hearings
- Mandatory publication of budget
- Town meetings
- Public council meetings
- Municipal advisory boards
- Community or council mayor-recall powers
- Participatory investment planning
- Referenda or plebiscites on issues, ordinances, and other matters
- Oversight or "vigilance" committees
- Grants of legal standing to neighborhood committees or organizations
- Public disclosure laws
- Mandates requiring citizen input
- Creation of submunicipal representative entities
- Municipal partnerships with the private sector, NGOs, andother groups in civil society.

Public-private partnerships that link communities and new local governments are beginning to emerge. As countries throughout the region consolidate their democracies, NGOs are playing a large role. NGOs are often considered by municipal governments to be more efficient service delivery systems and to better reflect public demands. Partnerships between the public sector and civil society need to be strengthened.

USAID programming has highlighted decentralization and the development of local government, because it is essential to both good governance and the consolidation of democracy (Blair 1998). Decentralizing government authority can enhance citizen participation by encouraging the public's involvement in affairs that affect them. Government can become more accountable by introducing citizen oversight and control through the electoral process. Corruption and malfeasance can be reduced by making the monitoring of local authorities easier. As the community participates in local politics, residents come to understand more fully the democratic process. Such education through experience creates a training ground for new leaders, a kind of recruitment channel that allows local leaders to rise to higher office. By according greater local autonomy, moreover, ethnic conflict can be diminished.

Local authorities are likely to be more responsive than national authorities to citizens wants and needs. Bringing authority closer to the people can empower them, or give them a greater voice and weight in local decision-making, especially in the case of groups that have traditionally been marginalized from the political process. Indeed, decentralization forces a convergence of the political demand for a service and the effective demand, or the ability to pay for it. Blair views this transfer of power to the subnational level as the approximation of a political free market in which the citizens (or buyers) make their preferences known and the local authorities (sellers) respond to them as they view necessary to remain in the business of politics.

USAID Programming Approaches: Democracy-Building through Decentralization and Local Governance

USAID programming in Latin America attempts to promote the potential of decentralization to improve democracy in all these areas. Virtually all the USAID missions have decentralization and local governance programs. Planned life of program funding in this area exceeds US$86 million, compared to US$16 million at the beginning of the 1990s. Through these programs, USAID is providing direct and intensive assistance to more than 300 municipalities. An additional 400 cities and towns are assisted indirectly through an NGO or local university. Every USAID mission is charged with promoting decentralization policy reform at the national level. Nine missions are involved in training, technical assistance, and support for national municipal associations. They also help advise on past experiences with the transfer of public services to the local level and the creation of funds for small, participatory infrastructure investments.

Dispersing Power in Society

The process of decentralization can serve to disperse power in society to different levels of government. Devolution of decisionmaking, budget and tax authority, and service delivery can profoundly alter the structure of government in states that were once highly centralized under authoritarian regimes. This can also expand the range of opportunities and mechanisms for citizens to exercise their power and influence. Whether or not local governments are more democratic than the national government, this dispersion of power in itself reduces the possibility of recurrence of authoritarianism. Several USAID activities support decentralization as a national policy.

DIRECT POLICY DIALOGUE. USAID missions and embassies have often directly engaged national political actors to encourage decentralization policies. Sometimes this has been a part of sector strategies, such as improving the quality and accessibility of education and health services, or discussing economic policy, but it always has an important political dimension.

TECHNICAL ASSISTANCE FOR POLICY REFORM. USAID provides expertise to countries considering decentralization options. This often strengthens the hand of reformers and can help quell objections from opponents. It also can speed up the process of developing legislation to enact a decentralization effort and provide analysis to sort through various options in crafting such a policy.

SUPPORT FOR MUNICIPAL ASSOCIATIONS. Support for the development of national municipal associations has emerged as the most effective strategy for promoting decentralization. This approach essentially involves organizing the natural constituency for decentralization efforts—local mayors and other local officials—and creating an internal dynamic that functions within a democratic system.

Experience shows that national municipal associations do make a difference, to varying degrees depending on the country, in the presentation of municipal government policy concerns to the central government. In some cases, associations have been important voices for change. In addition, associations promote intermunicipal efforts, in a horizontal fashion, that lead to improved service delivery. That dynamic was evidenced most clearly in the aftermath of the first post-conflict local elections in El Salvador when USAID brought new mayors from all parties to a six-week orientation in New Mexico, Argentina, and Puerto Rico. Despite the mayors' still strong partisan and ideological views, their municipal concerns produced a national mayors' association in which the demand for greater decentralization dominated their decisionmaking.

Increasing Citizen Participation

An important premise underlying USAID's approval is that local government decisionmaking processes are far more understandable and accessible to most people than national processes, and local issues have a direct impact on most people's lives. Decentralization creates greater potential for citizen input. USAID operates on both sides of this issue. First, the agency works with mayors and councilors to help them appreciate, develop, and utilize mechanisms for improving participation, transparency, and accountability. Second, USAID works with civil society to explain the operation of municipal government and encourage people to take advantage of opportunities to make their concerns known to local officials. USAID programming in support of citizen participation includes two general approaches.

TECHNICAL ASSISTANCE TO IMPROVE LOCAL TRANSPARENCY AND ACCOUNTABILITY. USAID has provided onsite technical assistance and training to local officials to improve their capacity to track and publicize the activities and finances of local governments. Some commodities, such as software packages for budgeting and accounting, may be a part of these capacity-building efforts. What distinguishes this public administration–oriented assistance is its focus on building the foundation for more transparent and accountable government and outreach to citizens.

A regional anticorruption project has begun to develop local public administration components to its training and technical assistance mechanisms. Those same concepts are becoming part of other donor and lending institution programs as well.

TECHNICAL ASSISTANCE AND FINANCIAL INCENTIVES TO DEVELOP PARTICIPATORY MECHANISMS. Almost all bilateral USAID municipal development programs are involved in efforts to increase the participation of the community in local government affairs. Several programs support onsite technical assistance to municipal governments, training of officials related to participation and transparency, and sponsoring observational trips to see citizen participation at work in other parts of the region. A number of USAID municipal development programs include capital funds for infrastructure investment that grows out of participatory decisionmaking processes—effectively serving as "carrots" for increased citizen involvement.

The El Salvador program supports *cabildos abiertos,* or town meetings, in the 18 pilot municipalities with which it works. For example, the mayor of Olocuitla convened a *cabildo* to swear in the Local Development Committee, which comprised municipal leaders representing various sectors, and to inform the community about the development committee's work. The mayor pledged to devote half of the funds the city receives from the central government to projects prioritized by the CDL. A question-and-answer period followed.

USAID's program in Bolivia in an effort to institutionalize the country's unprecedented Popular Participation Law. The program works closely with local grassroots organizations to encourage their input into the yearly municipal budget plan and assists "vigilance" committees with oversight of the operation of municipal governments.

One of the most productive efforts is the ongoing program in Paraguay, which provides a good idea of the nature of this activity. A USAID regional pilot program on decentralization and local government helped introduce the first-ever public hearing on a government budget in Paraguay. In September 1995, with the support of USAID-sponsored technical assistance, the municipality of Asuncion held the hearing on its 1996 budget. Over 400 citizens attended the four-hour meeting; some 75 proposals were delivered to the mayor for inclusion; and the hearing was widely covered by the press and regarded as a major success as an innovation in both citizen participation and government accountability. Within two weeks, other Paraguayan municipalities had announced that they too were going to initiate the process of public hearings on their budgets. The following year, the municipality of Asuncion increased from one to four the number of public hearings held during the budget approval process. These meetings were convened at neighborhood locations to facilitate public access. To help institutionalize the hearing concept and to legitimize the right of the citizenry of Asuncion to make requests of their local officials, a special section was added to the 1997 budget that, for the first time, listed all citizen requests and the corresponding action taken, whether positive or negative, by the municipal administration.

A second major initiative in Asuncion, also supported by the regional project, involved the passage by the municipal council of the "sunshine" ordinance. The ordinance guarantees that any citizen of the municipality has open access to all the municipality's records, except for private personnel documents. It ensures an unprecedented degree of press access to information. The law was subsequently expanded by amending the municipal ordinance to require that substantial background data be routinely provided on the Internet for all municipal financial transactions in excess of US$25,000, so that the country's citizens, public and private organizations, and news media would have immediate access to such information.

Clearly, then, the promotion of decentralization through the democracy lens can lead to major innovations. The sunshine law and amendments to it can only assist the development of a more informed citizenry and participatory society. The difficult challenge of these pro-participation efforts, however, is to make them stick. They must become sustainable. USAID missions typically work with a group of pilot municipalities and, as we have seen, local officials appreciate the political benefits to be derived from incorporating citizen concerns into policy decisions. What remains to be seen is the extent to which the use of these mechanisms is maintained and even extended to new municipalities once outside encouragement and financial support ceases. The key is to establish the right incentives for local leaders, and to get them to understand through their own experience the political benefits of community involvement in local decisionmaking.

Improved Government Responsiveness

Another premise of USAID is that local government service provision must be improved. Again, its efforts are democracy-focused. The combination of administrative decentralization of national ministries, shift of political power to the local level, and transfer of resources and legal authority to municipal governments is making the municipal government the center of action for the community. Cities and towns are becoming the first recourse of citizens looking for government to address their demands. Recognizing that participation is of little use if local governments cannot effectively respond, USAID programs are aiming to improve the capacity of local governments to provide basic services and address needs.

USAID's training and technical assistance to targeted municipal governments is focused on improving the ability of local governments to carry out their primary functions and deliver critical services. Six country programs have created a grant fund for basic infrastructure projects that are developed with input from civil society. Programs in Bolivia and El Salvador are increasingly shifting their focus on improvements in education, health care, and environment services to the same municipalities receiving democracy-oriented technical assistance.

As always, the results of these activities are difficult to measure. But there has been clear improvement in local public services in a number of countries that have been assisted by USAID support. For example, five town councils in Nicaragua received USAID training to improve community services and revenue generation for local projects. Progress was evident in each case, which was at least in part attributable to program efforts. In Matagalpa City, for example, revenue increased 30 percent, costs were cut 20 percent, and garbage collection was expanded.

In Paraguay, USAID's "Sustainable Cities" activity helped bring municipalities together to create viable options for the management of solid waste disposal—with the involvement of local communities and technical assistance provided by an NGO. Also in Paraguay, USAID is working with the Ministry of Health on the ministry's plan to implement a new law that decentralizes the provision of basic health services. Local government authorities and community representatives in pilot municipalities receive training in the administration of these services.

If decentralization in Latin America is to be strengthened, five major, related challenges must be faced. The first is enhancing transparency and responsiveness. Citizens have a right to know how their money is being spent, how decisions are made, who made them, and why. Democracy requires a critical flow of information. In Bolivia, one of the innovations of the Popular Participation Law is the creation of watchdog committees (*comites de vigilancia*), whose task is to monitor local governments. They have the ability to send their reports directly to the national Senate if they feel the government has diverted funds or failed to fulfill its commitments in the locally approved budget. USAID has helped monitor the success of this process, and such innovative experiments need to be initiated in other countries.

The second is increasing citizen participation. Active citizen participation in local affairs is one of the linchpins of effective democratic government. Citizens must demand good government for government to be good. Centuries-old traditions of paternalistic politics must be broken down.

Recognizing that civic participation traditionally has been quite weak, Latin American countries have adopted a variety of mechanisms as part of their decentralization programs to enhance the public's role. Colombian and Venezuelan municipalities are obligated to hold town meetings (*cabildos*); Bolivian vigilance committees can file complaints against their local officials that can lead to a suspension of the delivery of national funds; Chile, Honduras, and Costa Rica require the establishment of community advisory councils; Chilean localities can convene plebiscites; Nicaragua has mandated open budget hearings; and Honduran municipalities increasingly convene them—and these are just a few examples. Changing political culture is a slow and difficult process of socialization, but programs to achieve that objective are being pursued in Peru to broaden citizen participation, and in Paraguay and Haiti to increase local government responsiveness and accountability.

The changing political landscape being shaped by decentralization and democracy offers new opportunities and presents challenges to women in the Americas. Driven by a concern for safe neighborhoods, the education and health of their children, and local employment opportunities, many women are already accustomed to interaction with government—an interface that all too often is frustrating and unfruitful. Democratization and decentralization offer the promise of empowerment by bringing this level of interaction closer to the voter, male or female. Consequently, women may have increased potential to influence government decisionmaking in areas of direct relevance to their greatest concerns.

Women also have increased opportunities to become politically active. We are witnessing throughout the Americas women who are entering into political service through participation in their local governments, either as mayors, council members, or other elected positions. The beginnings have been modest. Well under 10 percent of mayors in Latin America are women. But there are promising indications. Already, women who first served as local officials have become members of Congress or have emerged as candidates or potential candidates to higher levels of public office. More has to be done to incorporate women and minorities, both as equal constituents as well as political activists.

The third challenge is to increase subnational government effectiveness. Again, the success or failure of democracy at any level is determined by whether it delivers the basic services of government. Localities and regions need training support, because the great majority of small and medium municipalities, especially those in rural areas, have never attracted sufficient, well-trained personnel. Many mayors and councilors, and even governors and regional legislators, are insufficiently trained and lack the managerial skills to operate a government effectively. In Paraguay, public officials at the national level number 96,000, while there are only 4,000 local officials—3,200 of them in Asuncion. The growth of responsibility and resources has created a great demand for skilled managers. A cadre of trained professionals in local government can be built only if new laws are adopted assuring depoliticized and merit-based hiring and career standards.

The fourth is providing resources. Although local governments have more resources than ever before, they still are far from able to meet their new responsibilities or citizen needs. Municipalities in El Salvador receive only 3 percent of national revenues, for example, and Honduran local leaders 1.5 percent, although Honduran law mandates 5 percent. Peruvian and Mexican localities receive 4 percent, although Mexico also transfers 16 percent of revenues to the states.

If the trend in resources is slow, it is at least favorable. Local government need stronger financial support, yet they also have to spend those resources wisely, honestly and transparently.

The final challenge is enlisting local government in bringing people out of poverty. The chief difference between poverty today and poverty in the past is that it now takes place with new democratic governments in office. People must see the benefits of democracy in their daily lives. And they must see themselves as benefiting from the state modernization that is crucial to regional progress and economic integration. The role of local government, in concert with the private sector, must be to help increase productivity through effective public investment. Decentralization has given local leaders in many countries a direct role in community development. In Chile, local governments are responsible for collecting poverty data for key social programs and for preserving local infrastructure in health and education. They also are vital to ensuring the adequacy of the local physical infrastructure such as roads, irrigation systems, and communications facilities that attract businesses and create jobs.

When contrasted with the complete absence of active, elected, responsive local government in many Latin American countries just a generation ago, one realizes that these five challenges—which in many ways comprise the essence of stronger decentralization and deeper democracy in the hemisphere—clearly are within our grasp. The stage is set. The hemisphere is in the midst of an era of reform that includes decentralization. The huge importance of sound local government to achieving the summit commitments is being recognized. Will local government continue to progress and contribute to democratic development, a lessening of poverty, and the creation of dynamic, market-oriented economies? Will local reform lay the groundwork for further decentralization? If the five challenges are met, the answers will be clear and compelling. If political will wavers, the force of inertia is likely to see power retained at the center, less responsiveness to local needs, and a threat to this new era of democracy. That is why the stakes are high and why USAID is dedicating a rising share of its resources to local government, community partnerships, and decentralization.

References

Blair, Harry. 1997. "Democratic Local Governance in Bolivia: A CDIE Assessment." Draft report of the Center for Development Information and Evaluation, U.S. Agency for International Development, Washington, D.C.

————. 1998. "Spreading Power to the Periphery: A USAID Assessment of Democratic Local Governance." Draft report, Washington, D.C.

Dahl, Robert J. 1971. *Polyarchy: Participation and Opposition.* New Haven, Conn.: Yale University Press.

de Tocqueville, Alexis. 1947. *Democracy in America.* Henry Steele Commager, ed. New York: Oxford University Press.

Diamond, Larry, Juan J. Linz, and Seymour Martin Lipset, eds. 1989. *Democracy in Developing Countries.* Vol. 4: *Latin America.* Boulder, Colo.: Lynne Rienner Publishers.

Graham, Carol. 1998. *Private Markets for Public Goods: Raising the Stakes in Economic Reform.* Washington, D.C.: Brookings Institution Press.

IDB (Inter-American Development Bank). 1997. *Economic and Social Development Progress Report.* Washington, D.C.

Jager, Harry. 1997. "Decentralization Status in Central America: Policy Suggestions." A report to the U.S. Agency for International Development, Regional Urban Development Office, Guatemala City.

Linz, Juan J. 1978. *Crisis, Breakdown, and Reequilibration.* Baltimore, Md.: Johns Hopkins University Press.

Martin, Roscoe C. 1967. *Grassroots.* New York: Harper & Row.

Mill, John Stuart. 1962. *Essays on Politics and Culture.* Gertrude Himmelfarb, ed. Garden City, N.Y.: Doubleday and Company.

Oates, Wallace E. 1972. *Fiscal Federalism.* New York: Harcourt Brace Jovanovich.

Putnam, Robert. 1993. *Making Democracy Work: Civic Traditions in Modern Italy.* Princeton, N.J.: Princeton University Press.

Rondinelli, Dennis A. 1981. "Government Decentralization in Comparative Perspective: Theory and Practice in Developing Countries." *International Review of Administrative Sciences* 47(2): 133–145.

UNDP (United Nations Development Programme). 1996. "Local Governance." Report of the U.N. Global Forum on Innovative Policies and Practices in Local Governance, Sept. 23–27, Gothenburg, Sweden.

World Bank. 1995. *Local Government Capacity in Colombia: Beyond Technical Assistance.* World Bank Country Study. Washington, D.C.

10-2

Policy Choices and Institutional Dynamics of Decentralization: Operational Implications for Technical Cooperation

Albrecht Stockmayer, GTZ

Analyzing the institutional dynamics of policy alternatives in the public sector appears has been a cornerstone of recent work on decentralization in Latin America (see in particular the section, "Institutional Dynamics: Policy and Operational Implications" in Campbell, Fuhr, and Eid 1995, p. 9).[1] Such an approach is not only reasonable, but it also appears to be a necessity given that reform programs throughout the region are embedded in political processes that are potential targets for program support and development.

Institutional dynamics is also of particular relevance to technical cooperation organizations, such as the German Technical Cooperation (Deutsche Gesellschaft für Technische Zusammenarbeit, or GTZ), that need to take a broader look at public sector reform in order to design a contribution to ongoing change processes that is both institutionally sustainable and politically feasible.

GTZ has been a strong supporter of the approach to decentralization and innovation in the present research project. Likewise, GTZ is concerned with the four sectors of innovations and policy recommendations in

---

1. This chapter is a slightly revised and edited version of a paper presented at the World Bank's Round Table on Decentralization in Latin-America, held in Washington, D.C., April 16–17, 1997.

subnational government: financial and human resources, local participation in public policymaking, service provision, and private sector development. Yet, given the GTZ's experiences, I should add another key "sector"—the political and administrative management of the decentralization reform process. The overall policy process, once propagated as the standard objective that forms a part of all structural adjustment programs, is much more complex than getting the prices right.[2]

This subject has gained additional importance, because reform programs, such as decentralization and the strengthening of subnational government, need to be conceived and implemented at a time when the powers and resources of central governments in the developing world have considerably weakened. This is true not only for Latin America, but also for many other countries where the power of the central government to design and implement complex policy reforms has eroded.

A number of factors have contributed to the weakening of central governments:

- Central states have lost their incentive-setting monopolies because of globalization.
- National governments, facing fiscal problems, have little bargaining power.
- Centralized democracies are becoming less effective compared with networks of organizations at the local level whose members cannot be easily co-opted by the national elite.
- Local organizations are becoming more popular as they win legitimacy through local action programs.

In addition, a new political configuration is building support for decentralization. Although conservatives and progressives used to be divided over the benefits of decentralization, there now seems to be a much broader consensus for it. Both those on the right who champion a lean state and those on the left who want equity ensured at the local level seemingly converge in the new vision of a decentralized state responding to the needs of a local civil society. Add to this a newly found confidence of private investors at the local level, as well as the widely held perception that a

---

2. The GTZ agrees with the definition of successful decentralization as "an iterative process which leads to new, self-sustaining subnational institutional arrangements which provide new incentive structures for public and private actors to engage in long-term goals of economic and social development" (Campbell, Fuhr, and Eid 1995, p. 5). For a similar definition, see Stockmayer (1990, 1996).

central state is economically ineffective and politically dominated by dictators, and the new paradigm appears even more promising.

The following sections will briefly review and analyze somewhat typical situations that the GTZ encountered in its roughly 60 development projects that help fund local government and decentralization reforms over a decade and a half. [3] They will also explore new avenues for technical assistance. The goals are to ensure that we fulfill our mandate as a development institution more effectively and to review options for more effective cooperation with other donors working in the same area.

Technical cooperation projects that promote decentralization have a mixed record. But because decentralization is very attractive as a structural reform, it has been embraced in almost regular intervals with technical cooperation often used to improve the chances for success.

There are two sets of objectives for supporting decentralization reform. First, decentralization, especially in concert with local democratic reform, is considered an end in itself. The objective is to create an environment in accordance with the principle of political and administrative subsidiarity. Second, decentralization can also be considered an instrument to ensure sustainability of other political and social reforms. Understanding this distinction is important in order to both determine the indicators for successful decentralization and define the dimensions of a decentralization program.

As a result of proposals by the Development Assistance Committee working group on participatory development and good governance, decentralization has been categorized among the key elements for sustainable development because of its importance in effective, accountable, and democratic governance. "While not themselves the subject of suggested numerical indicators, we reaffirm our conviction that these *qualitative aspects of development* are essential to the attainment of the more measurable goals we have suggested." (OECD-DAC 1996b, p. 2; italics added). The presence of qualitative elements can ensure that main societal objectives, such as economic well being, social development and environmental sustainability, can be better pursued and gain significance and sustainability.

> Decentralization would, consequently, be part of a number of a these key elements, such as a sound policy framework encouraging stable, growing economies; investment in social development; enhanced participation of all people, and notably of women, in economic and

---

3. GTZ's experiences in supporting decentralization relate mainly to the Andean and Central American countries.

political life, and the reduction of social inequalities; good governance and public management, democratic accountability, the protection of human rights and the rule of law; sustainable environmental practices; [and] addressing root causes of potential conflict. (OECD-DAC 1996b, p. 3).

Progress in decentralization would in these cases be measured against the underlying objectives of social, environmental, and economic development. But, regardless of the final objective, it appears that the *process* of decentralization, in terms of its obstacles and chances for success, presents very common features.

This chapter supports the notion—also made by Campbell, Fuhr, and Eid (1995)—that one of the key ingredients for effective decentralization is the presence of effective intermediate-level (or meso-level) institutions. In view of the general framework conditions and the nature of the decentralization process, special emphasis should consequently be given to measures that support these organizations (Eid 1994; González and Jaramillo 1996). The organizations, regardless of whether they are considered an additional level of government or, alternatively, deconcentrated offices or regional ministerial departments oriented toward the local level, can play a crucial rule in keeping the decentralization process alive. By the same token, they may also help those affected by this process in recognizing their roles as stakeholders.

As a complementary measure, we strongly suggest donor coordination as an instrument that is as important as the highly demanding and complex reform programs needed to tackle decentralization. Donor coordination would help reduce the additional burden placed on reform managers caused by the wide array of programs inspired by domestic donor practice, rather than by developing country demands.

Two phases stand out when it comes to defining the hurdles for decentralization: the initiation phase and the start-up phase of decentralized decisionmaking. They present an assortment of characteristics—some related to each other and some quite different—with regard to the decentralization process.

The First Steps of Reform: Widely Differing Bases and Expectations as Obstacles to Implementation

Top-Down Policymaking. The concepts that are guiding decentralization reforms were not developed in a participatory way. Rather they were the result of an exercise in authoritarian thinking. Only in very few cases, such as when the reform was part of a constitutional reform process, did institutions and the general public have a say in its design. When the drafting of the Bolivian "Basic Law" for decentralization began, the task was entrusted to a group of no more than eight experts. A massive information campaign eventually informed the population of the intentions and contents of the bill. Although the bill was eventually approved, key institutions and organized parts of civil society were left out of the process. Ownership of the process remained with the authors and their principals.

FRAGILE REFORM COALITIONS. Those interested in reforms may have varying motivations and expectations. The motivations may be based on some secondary effects of decentralization. Although some of the results are welcomed, it is not necessarily the reform, as such, that is the aim. Instead, decentralization may represent a way of pursuing overall political goals, such as enlarging the power base of the executive, granting wider discretion to an agency, or ensuring a captive market. Thus a decentralization reform process may be abandoned at any time once a more convincing instrument emerges that furthers such initial political goals.

OPEN-ENDED REFORMS. Decentralization has rarely been defined comprehensively as an ultimate goal within public sector reform. Neither has there been any clearly defined implementation path at the outset. The costs and benefits of each step of reform, therefore, cannot be measured and controlled as part of an overall strategy, let alone compared with alternative costs of competing schemes. If the costs and benefits (and their timing) cannot be determined in advance, and the process is subject to permanent bargaining, the reform necessarily will face many obstacles. Monitoring and policy evaluation systems are hard to come by, and their introduction would be a reform in itself, adding more of an administrative burden but contributing to the decentralization process.

DIFFERENT ACTORS. Decentralization, especially if it is a government-led reform program, cuts across numerous sectors and requires the participation of many authorities. Before the first implementation steps are finished, those who are expected to play a leading role and those likely to be affected by it need to be drawn into the process. In reality, however, most such programs are "owned" by few, and possibly unrelated, actors. For instance, the reform may be the political priority of one minister or undersecretary. Other colleagues will be tempted to follow—not for reasons related to reform, but rather because of peer pressure, or pressures building up from below. Others actors may prefer watching from the wings. (In this respect, typical nonmembers of the reform team are the departments of finance and civil service and the more powerful sector ministries, such as public works, education, and health.) Alternatively, actors will come up with a competing reform scheme to neutralize their opponents. In any event, everybody has a preferred decentralization scheme and wishes to see it prevail over others.

POWER SHARING. In some reforms, observers and actors agree upfront to a systemic change but are unable to fully effectuate it. For instance, new revenue-sharing schemes or automatic transfers of fiscal resources have sometimes been undercut by autonomous funds for subnational development. If investment funds remain firmly within the central purview, decisions to favor autonomous local investment and budgeting will have diminished impact.

SELF-FULFILLING, LOCAL-LEVEL PROBLEMS. A program of gradual reform without a clear strategy often conceals the problems that have to be tackled at the central level. This effectively creates a basis for an early opt-out due to self-fulfilling administrative problems at the local level. It seems rational to make transfers of powers and resources contingent on an adequate level of installed local management capacity. The reform program in this case may outline the powers and resources to be eventually transferred. But the time and the modalities of such a transfer may vary according to a later determination. This determination, however, is effectively left to the "ceding" authority, because it possesses all the required information and the personnel capable of handling it.

The case of República Bolivariana de Venezuela is very interesting in this respect. The transfer of nonexclusive powers was negotiated with resource transfers eventually depending on the result of the negotiation.[4] This type of bargaining is bound to relegate the institutional and political dynamics of decentralization to a secondary role, leaving the central administrators to decide on central elements of the process. In addition, it would be objectively difficult to judge future performance of local authorities according to standards external to the local level.

---

4. For a description and analysis of Venezuelan decentralization, see Knoop (1994).

Implementation: Obstacles to the Reform Process

The difficulties in starting a decentralization process often persist during implementation. Some of these obstacles are due to conceptual shortcomings. But many obstacles simply slow down the process or change its direction. Experience from our assistance projects reveals four major barriers to effective implementation.

Expertise Is Lacking at the Local and Central Levels. Decentralization problems are caused either internally at the local level or externally at the central level and, in either case, often result from lack of expertise. Internal obstacles include, first, the possibility that essential administrative capacity at the local level may be weak. Second, local staff may use the new opportunities to pursue private interests, because a common direction and a sense of ownership of the reform have not yet developed at the local level. Third, elected council-members may spend far more time accommodating the expectations of their electorate than focusing on the decentralization process.

However, many of the reasons for reform congestion at the local level are external and can only be addressed at the central level. First, resources flow haphazardly, if at all, and often just for routine activities and not for investment expenditure. Expectations relating to new physical infrastructure are, consequently, disappointed. Second, rules and regulations for decentralized levels of government and public administration are at best incomplete; at other times they are incomprehensible to the local level or even lacking altogether. At any rate they cannot be applied. Third, staff at reform agencies, however motivated, may be inexperienced or arrogant. Frequently, they are of little or no help in helping to start the local authority.

Sequencing Is Key. Decentralization reforms need high upfront investments in leadership and resources. For the process to get started and develop its own dynamic, a shock treatment appears to be warranted. An example would be the decision to transfer substantial resources to newly autonomous entities, such as required in a 1985 Colombian law. Such a shock approach notwithstanding, further progress in the decentralization process would need some type of sequencing, because management capacity will not be sufficiently developed to accommodate new policies and absorb them at the local level.

Sequencing, however, also represents a latent risk for the process for two reasons. First, most decisions relating to sequencing—with related power and resource ramifications—reflect short-term considerations of those governmental departments most affected or most supportive of decentralization. Their decisions, consequently, do not include broader requirements for the reform process to be sustained soundly. Second, sequencing opens the reform to the changing balance of power between various stakeholders and affected institutions. It subjects the reform to frequent renegotiation. Decentralization may thus bog down in constant rounds of negotiations, eventually leading to instability and loss of direction.

POLITICAL PARTIES OR OTHER ORGANIZATIONS FOR REPRESENTATIVE DECISIONMAKING HAVE NOT BEEN ESTABLISHED. Once a local executive has been elected and assumed office, there are still serious medium-term obstacles to an effective functioning of local autonomy. In cases in which either traditional relationships prevail (such as established relations of personal trust and loyalty) or short-term political considerations between the executive and the citizens are overriding factors in local government decisions, significant parts of the population are likely to be left outside the political space of local government. In addition, local problems needing new approaches and more complex coalitions between stakeholders would be left unaddressed. In short, there is a risk that autonomous public decisionmaking reproduces exclusively preexisting relations of personal, economic, and social power. The mobilizing effect of local autonomy is jeopardized if no political sphere will correspond to the newly created decisionmaking structures and patterns.

TECHNICAL ASSISTANCE PROJECTS COULD HELP IMPROVE DECENTRALIZATION REFORMS. Such programs could also be useful for mediation and conflict resolution between old and new actors. Unfortunately, existing services often are not supportive, as they have never been demand driven. When the Colombia Ministry of Finance and Public Credit decided to reorganize its tax department, for example, it ended up with a considerable number of trained public accountants who would not fit into the newly designed general directorate. The resulting directorate for financial support activities was expected to lend a hand to the municipalities and their newly elected mayors to sort out their financial problems. For obvious reasons, most of these public accountants lacked an understanding of their new sectors and were therefore of little help.

A wide array of factors could improve the likelihood of success in implementing decentralization reforms. They include intermediate levels of government as engines of reform and two complementary areas for stimulating and supporting the decentralization process.[5] The first relates to the role of the local civil society; the second to the local economy.

The Intermediate Level as Key Ingredient

In the 1960s and 1970s new intermediate-level institutions were created in many countries in Latin America. At that time, decisionmakers hoped to spread the benefits of their national programs to all corners of their countries. These institutions, however, never lived up to expectations. They were either mirror images of national institutions, or they were inefficient because they were unable to create a self-sustaining local space.

For example, the history of decentralization of Bolivia (see Galindo and Medina 1996) includes many attempts to introduce intermediate-level organizations, beginning with the victory of the Federalists in the civil war that ended in 1900. The attempts never came to fruition. Considerations related to national unity, or problems of consolidating political or personal power, prevented these ideas from being realized. Such attempts were abandoned as soon as their very supporters rose to power.

As a result, the potential role of intermediate-level institutions needs to be evaluated in terms of the particular features of ongoing decentralization processes. The following points need to be kept in mind:

- **Decentralization is a gradual and incremental process.** It cannot be successfully managed by the national level, or according to nationally prescribed patterns, because its success depends on the active and informed participation of the local level.
- **Decentralization has to reconcile local conditions with national rules.** Appropriate solutions have to take into account both the particularities of local governments and certain national standards that act as guideposts during reforms.
- **Decentralization is an issue of structural relations.** The number of levels with autonomy and the type and number of public tasks that are devolved to the local level have to be adapted to the visible results that are expected and realistically feasible in a given local context. Public tasks must be of a certain dimension and nature in order to stimulate political interest and help build legitimacy among the constituencies.

---

5. See González and Jaramillo (1996) for a more complete summary of the various patterns of the intermediate level in Latin America.

- **Decentralization is a community issue.** The discussion needs to include local-level civil society leaders and representatives of other relevant bodies who have to lend their support to new alternatives for policymaking and service delivery in the face of incapacitated and deconcentrated central government administration.

In current practice, however, the principle of a unitary and indivisible state power, and the interest of identical reform patterns nationwide, prevent intermediate institutions from exercising an appropriate margin of discretion.

Coherent Policy between Deconcentration and Decentralization

Deconcentration and decentralization for many reasons have traditionally been considered mutually exclusive. Deconcentration as administrative decentralization was thought to be a mere instrument for more effective central administration and government, while democratic decentralization, as an aim in itself, enjoyed broad support, also from the donor community.

Experience has shown, however, that both policy options may have to be pursued jointly. Some illustrations can underline this point. First, on the macro level, local autonomy and national integration are two objectives that depend on each other's success. Local autonomy may lead to separatism, and national integration may lead to a sterile order that has no productive lien with local developmental forces. Second, decentralization as a complex and long-term reform exercise depends for its survival on an appropriate incentive structure. It has to be developed in accordance with the progress achieved, but it also needs supervision in order to keep incentives intact, thereby invigorating the reform process and ensuring the monitoring of costs and benefits.

Third, the reform process thrives on norms and plans conceived and organized from the top. But it cannot succeed unless these norms are put into daily local practice that, eventually, may differ so much that they put into question the validity of central reform norms. Hence, decentralization as a reform process cannot function under decisionmaking processes, especially at the local or regional level, that answer to different sets of criteria. A type of consensual decisionmaking that is sometimes seen between various levels of government is an example of successful decentralized practice.

Fourth, the use of new laws seems most appropriate to guide reforms and transport reform values and concepts, yet discretionary space is sometimes needed at the local level to accommodate local circumstances and obstacles of reform. Although the contents of the law may be permeated by the central reform concepts, the central agencies need to ensure their validity and relevancy for the local level.

This joint strategy encompassing elements of decentralization and deconcentration, however, may not be politically viable because of popular demands or because of a very low capacity at the national level to introduce politically and socially complex reform projects.

Changing Balances of Power, Rules of the Game, and Monitoring

Decentralization is a process with many actors, many interests, and many patterns of behavior and activities. To participate effectively in this process, groups and institutions must be guided by some basic rules that permit them to both engage in the process and forgo immediate rewards for later gains. Such rules, in order to ensure proper functioning (and to ensure that those joining the reform at a later stage have the same understanding), would need constant monitoring. Rules that are applied and enforced by mutual conviction, in fact, can foster a transparent reform process, help accommodate new stakeholders, and align their efforts. Monitoring and control may later be required at the local level as well in order to ensure that certain national obligations are met. But they are of equal importance during the reform process itself, often in a contradictory manner.[6]

Again, intermediate institutions may play a strategic role in designing and exercising monitoring and control functions. But such institutions suffer from deficits of central state action, and they informally impose their will on municipal authorities.

Intermunicipal Cooperation to Increase Capacity for Decisionmaking

An alternative to creating implementation capacity at the local level is institutionalized intermunicipal cooperation (Rojas 1994). First, intermunicipal

---

6. For example, consider Blair (1978): "In rural development the contemporary version of the center-periphery conflict lies in the area of supervision. There must be control from the top, yet there must also be flexibility at the bottom, and the two needs are fundamentally contradictory: Finding the right mix of supervision and autonomy is probably the most difficult bureaucratic problem there is in the whole field of rural development (p. 72)." One can argue that supervision and flexibility are contradictory. But the mix is obviously an essential ingredient for the reform process.

cooperation can provide, on a provisional basis, capacities necessary to assume the administration of newly transferred powers. Cooperation with neighboring municipalities would allow officials to (a) sustain and increase the legitimacy that comes with the successful provision of new services to local constituencies, and (b) improve productive self-organization at the local level. Second, intermunicipal cooperation can play a useful role on a more permanent base as well, and not only where economies of scale require solutions outside the realm of a local authority.

Whenever local authorities prefer to fulfill own tasks in a larger context, joint ventures can be beneficial. But such joint action requires certain preconditions:

- The legitimacy of elected local officials has to be clearly established.
- Decisionmaking authority on powers and resources (such as limits that apply to individual executives) has to apply to the joint venture.
- Officials must have relations with the next higher level, or the project runs the risk of establishing a new administrative level or changing relations with established levels.

In contrast to such options, most countries demonstrate a dispersion of responsibility, accountability, and therefore trust between centrally accredited service providers or autonomous authorities that execute public tasks without being directly accountable to a specific local constituency.

Political Support for Local Protagonists and Participation as a National Objective of Reform

One obvious source of support for decentralization reform could be those groups that were previously excluded from direct access to decisionmaking or from participating in institutions on the local level. The challenge for any decentralization reform, consequently, is to turn this part of the population into active citizens and owners of decentralization reform.

A number of entities can be deployed to help engage such groups:

- **Districts and other submunicipal structures.** These can be turned into participatory channels for local policymaking. In most cases such structures are weak and need to be strengthened, or they do not exist at all and need to be built gradually.
- **Local associations.** These have a broad range of objectives and may be dedicated to specific issues or user groups. Their priorities need to be brought into the municipal arena.

- **Locally based networks.** Networks, particularly those including economic actors, can take a more proactive role in shaping the public space of the municipality.

A good example of mobilizing a local civil society is related to the Ley de Participación Popular (Law of Popular Participation) in Bolivia. The law provides a role for so-called *organizaciones territoriales de base,* a generic term for associations with very different reasons for being. These organizations are expected to act as focal points for indigenous groups, neighborhood associations, and the like (see Mercado 1996, pp. 43–44) and assist them in articulating priorities within the reform process of their municipalities, the lowest level of the formal public sector in Bolivia.

How these groups can be incorporated eventually into local decision-making, and what institutional links may work to accelerate this process, are matters of local consideration. Although these groups are necessary for a robust and lively civil society, the local executive may not welcome such activities. But the rules and incentive structures of the reform as applied by the intermediary level should limit such reactions.

In the absence of such participatory structures, newly acquired autonomy cannot ensure a direct and immediate response to local preferences. The central state, in such a case, would have devolved power into a vacuum.

Promoting Local Economic Activity

Introducing more specifically economic and social considerations into the debate on decentralization is a relatively recent phenomenon. Two developments seem to have prompted it. The first is the emergence of programs to mitigate the social costs of adjustment policies. Social Investment Funds, for example, often used local private voluntary organizations and nongovernmental organizations as conduits for transferring funds to their target groups. The second is the work of broader interests to mobilize economic networking at the local level. Both developments made the promotion of the local economy and local jobs an obvious task for newly elected mayors and, more generally, for elected bodies at subnational levels. The types of local programs are, of course, very different from former centrally led economic programs. At the local level, the main thrust is to support emerging networks of small and medium enterprises and other private actors by way of improving—often only marginally—framework conditions for their activities.

Improving conditions for economic activities is a powerful and very effective means to build a basis for legitimate local action (Fuhr 1993). For local citizens this is an area in which private interests of local economic actors and public interests coincide and depend on each other. Contrary to the central level, such relations in the local context can be made transparent and comprehensible. Creating a favorable environment for economic actors and, at the same time, understanding local government's responsibilities to put people to work are local tasks whose links are open to the public eye. It is therefore not only advantageous for the local level to take up this challenge, but local government may actually be forced by its constituency to act in an area that has been all but abandoned by the central level.

Designing workable and understandable programs to promote local economic activities, indeed, requires knowledge and skills that may not be easily available. But pressures on the local executive to attract investment, put investment funds to use, and meet the expectations of the economically active local citizenry may make the addressing of this task inevitable.

In contrast to such optimistic scenarios is the traditional, two-tiered local society in many Latin American countries. As a replica of the central level, a local economic society determines the use of local resources, while the local civil society is called upon during election periods.

Donor Cooperation on Governance

Demanding more donor coordination is, of course, nothing new in the area of decentralization (see Fuhr 1994, p. 169). But whenever coordination effectively took place, it was due more to individual efforts of a group of like-minded people than to a general and abstract regulation or agreement. And such agreements covered mostly isolated sectors of a country's strategy for development cooperation.

Numerous attempts have been made to coordinate donor efforts, as epitomized by consultative meetings, roundtable discussions, and the like. They all produced little, resulting in the transferring of coordination responsibilities to the national governments—where they nominally belonged, but where they have not been successfully assumed. Having done this, donors felt free to pursue their individual concepts and strategies, thereby adding to the coordination tasks of national governments. Furthermore, they did little to promote the continuity required to bring programs and projects to fruition.

The picture became even more somber once development cooperation started to operate in areas where even a common definition of goals and activities was difficult to come by. In these softer areas of development cooperation, it was not uncommon for different cooperation regimes, mostly for internal organizational reasons, to follow different tracks in the very same sector. A case in point is the apparent division of a decentralization issue into a rural and an urban branch.

Donors have made efforts to reach some type of consensus or coherent behavior. For example, the Organisation for Economic Co-operation and Development-Development Assistance Committee Working Group on Participatory Development and Good Governance appointed donors acting as coordinators for decentralization activities in a given country. This effort, while it may have lacked focus and practicality in some areas, had three distinguishing features concerning decentralization. First, it was directed toward a combination of strategies, such as decentralization and democracy as well as human rights and public sector management. Second, it provided for (or required) networking between administratively unrelated projects—that is, it dealt with decentralization in specific sectors (such as public health or agriculture) as a principle of territorial administration and as a goal for newly created and legitimized local authorities. Third, it brought nongovernmental organizations into the coordinating dialogue, something that is easier to pursue for bilateral donors than for international cooperative institutions.

The overall process, according to the working group, is to be guided by an appointed lead donor. Its objective is to help governments better manage the governance process. The apparent discrepancy, a process initiated from the outside to strengthen internal ownership, points to the specific goals that may be reached if the instrument is carefully applied (OECD-DAC 1996a). The new coordination effort may present a unique opportunity to:

- Leave behind the very general and abstract level of coordination hitherto prevailing for roundtables and formally constituted consultative groups
- Observe closely the specifics of intragovernmental processes and the opportunities and limits of government-civil society interaction in order to be able to better relate to these processes
- Focus on specific subject matters that can serve as testing grounds for better governance and more participatory development (thereby combining sectoral aims, such as the provision of social or physical infrastructure, with the cross-sectoral demands for participatory development and good governance)
- Make the link between the international governance process and public domestic governance transparent and thereby eventually manageable.

Whether such opportunities can and will be seized, and whether they will be dealt with more successfully than previous coordination issues, depends to a large extent on the approach of the lead donors and the participating donors in pilot countries. If these opportunities are seized, the vital nexus between national and international governance can be made a future area of common concern and improvement.

A first step in this direction may be the establishment of a common system and instruments of appraisal-assessment, preparation-design, and control and evaluation of activities relating to participatory development and good governance issues (OECD-DAC 1996b, paragraphs 8 and 11–14). To the extent that these coordination activities are seriously pursued, donors will likely identify bottlenecks of particular importance to the process and direct attention to factors that are essential for the success of development cooperation in soft areas.

Despite such more sophisticated schemes, the standard terms of reference for coordination exercises in the area of decentralization remain largely unaffected. These terms include, first, the development of programs instead of hitherto prevailing, mostly short-term projects, thus allowing donors to avoid the cumbersome task of inserting such projects into a coherent decentralization reform policy of national governments. The second term is the elaboration of new instruments enhancing ownership. Such instruments can help governments improve their technical and political management of reform processes at all levels. One such measure, for example, could temporarily provide concessionary finance for autonomous entities, helping them to start operating even before the deadline for financial transfers (as part of a possibly very complicated national equalization scheme). Third, they include designs for dual track approaches. These would consist of programs that support decentralization as well as local infrastructure investment and, at the same time, encourage local accountability, technical effectiveness, or economic feasibility.[7]

References

Blair, Harry. 1978. "Rural Development, Class Structure and Bureaucracy in Bangladesh." *World Development* 6(1): 65–82.

Campbell, Tim, Harald Fuhr, and Florence Eid. 1995. *"Decentralization in LAC: Best Practice and Policy Lessons—Initiating Memorandum."* Washington, D.C.: World Bank.

---

7. For example, the case of Ecuador in Fuhr (1994).

Eid, Florence. 1994. "Institutional Development and the Meso Level of Government." Unpublished paper, World Bank, Washington, D.C.

Fuhr, Harald. 1993. "Mobilizing Local Resources in Latin America: Decentralisation, Institutional Reforms and Small-Scale Enterprises." In Brigitte Späth, ed., *Small Firms and Development in Latin America: The Role of the Institutional Environment, Human Resources and Industrial Relations*. Geneva: International Labour Organization/International Institute of Labour Studies.

―――. 1994."Municipal Institutional Strengthening and Donor Coordination: Experiences from Ecuador." In Paul Collins and Peter Blunt, eds., *Institution Building in Developing Countries*. Special issue, *Public Administration and Development* 14(2): 169–86.

Galindo, Mario, and Fernando Medina. 1996. *Descentralización Fiscal in Bolivia*. Serie Política Fiscal 72. Santiago: La Comisión Económica para América Latina.

González, Edgar, and Iván Jaramillo. 1996. *El nivel intermedio en el arreglo institucional– diagnóstico y perspectivas en el ambito Latinoamericano*. Serie Política Fiscal 86. Santiago: La Comisión Económica para América Latina.

Knoop, Joachim. 1994. *Descentralización fiscal en Venezuela*. Serie Política Fiscal 60. Santiago: La Comisión Económica para América Latina.

Mercado, Rodolfo. 1996."*Dezentralisierung und Participación Popular*." *Lateinamerika Analysen-Daten-Dokumentation 39*. Hamburg: German Overseas Institute.

OECD-DAC (Organisation for Economic Co-operation and Development-Development Assistance Committee). 1996a. *Shaping the 21st Century: The Contribution of Development Co-operation*. Paris.

―――. 1996b. *Participatory Development and Good Governance*. Paris.

Rojas, Fernando. 1994. "Strengthening Local Management Capacity through Municipal Associations." Unpublished paper, Bogotá.

Stockmayer, Albrecht. 1990. "Aspects of the Decentralization Process in Indonesia." Technical Report. German Technical Cooperation (GTZ): Eschborn.

―――. 1996. "Making Subsidiarity Work, 10 Years of GTZ Support for Democratic Decentralization Programs." Paper presented at the Organisation for Economic Coooperation and Development-Development Assistance Committee, Sept. 5–6, 1996, Paris.

11

Conclusions and Policy Lessons

Tim Campbell, World Bank
Harald Fuhr, University of Potsdam

This book has helped us gain insights into the dynamics of subnational institutional change in Latin America over the past decade. The case studies focused on propitious initial conditions for reform. We also know about actors of change and their interests in reform. But such progress may be fragile and can even prove insufficient unless policymakers better understand how such innovations can be made to move from first attempts or maiden voyages of single innovations to sustained sequences of change that produce reform at the local level. We need to better understand how such innovations eventually get locked into their local environment and become institutionalized. Given the recent—and renewed—focus of international donor agencies on sustained urban development, knowledge about the motivation and dynamics of reform at the subnational level can help to better define roles for national and subnational governments as well as for donors.

Conceptual Approach to Institutional Change

The authors have found it productive to make use of several new streams of thought to inform the urban policy dialogue about subnational development. Since the early 1990s, literature on the "new institutional economics" and, more generally, on political economy, has highlighted the importance of incentives for change and the need to reflect subnational policymaking within a framework that stresses both vertical and horizontal sets of incentives.[1]

Vertical incentive structures refer to defined rules for intergovernmental relationships. Horizontal incentive structures refer to defined rules between local governments, their citizens, organized local groups, and the local private sector. Both sets of incentives are products of underlying sociopolitical processes. Such rules, in order to be credible, accepted, and sustainable, need to be agreed upon by major stakeholders. Both sets of incentives may stimulate better results from decentralization and better performance of local governments. Yet sustainability of local innovation and reform, and improvements in the overall capability and effectiveness of the local public sector, are likely to occur only if there is better synergy, at least over time. For example, swift local decentralization without due consideration of these intertwined incentive structures (or worse, without one of these two sets) could produce unbalanced and ineffective relationships, weakening the capacity of organized groups or the private sector to hold public institutions and decisionmakers accountable. Above all, politics and processes are key to understanding and, eventually, managing decentralization effectively.

In line with these ideas, the following discussion and concluding remarks will, first, reflect what has happened within the public sectors of our country cases at the macro level during the 1990s. The arguments in this section go somewhat beyond the narrower boundaries of our empirical cases, drawing on complementary literature on the subject. Second, the discussion will review the micro level factors that contributed to effective reform and sustained institutional change at the local level. It is important to stress that neither micro nor macro factors *alone* can explain how subnational innovations and reform became such prominent features during the 1990s and maintained momentum well toward the end of the decade. Rather, it is the combined effect of the two in a given period.

The Bigger Picture: Reviewing Macro Factors for Subnational Innovations

As discussed in chapter 2, Latin American countries changed dramatically during the 1990s. Most countries faced a multifaceted challenge—rearranging their public sectors and moving to both democratic political systems

---

1. This latter idea was first developed in Work Bank (1997, chapter 7). On intergovernmental fiscal relationships, see World Bank (1999, chapter 5), and on related "subsidiarity," see Simon, Stockmayer, and Fuhr (1993).

and market-driven economies. This altered the context for subnational policymakers enormously. Once part of largely clientelist political systems with party machines ensuring strong top-down rule, local decisionmakers were among the first to shift to more participatory policymaking with strong demands to introduce democracy at the local levels. Local decisionmakers were also embedded in an economic system that favored state-led development and rent seeking.

THE DISINCENTIVES OF STRONG TOP-DOWN RULE. Véliz (1965, 1980) explained in detail the long history of political centralism in Latin America and the obstacles to the creation of more pluralistic and "modern" societies. Later, authors in the area of political economy, some employing the notions of rent seeking to explain behaviors, added further economic evidence to his observations. In a nutshell, they argued that, first, Latin America in the 1980s was highly centralized, both politically and economically. The region had high barriers of entry both to the political system and to the economy—in fact, both systems reinforced and depended on each other. Second, Latin American political features, such as authoritarianism, patronage, populism, and corporatism, corresponded strongly with economic development based on "rents" extracted either from the primary sectors or from state-led, oligopolistic manufacturing and services organizations.[2] Third, elites from both the private and the public sectors, united at least in their attempts to shield themselves from domestic and foreign competition, simply divided up their countries' resources and channeled them down through a mesh of clientelist relationships. The result, the authors argue, is societies with strong top-down rule with corresponding sets of vertical incentives.

The well-described features of the local sector in the region—organizational inefficiency and low institutional performance in municipalities—have to be analyzed within this vertical pattern of development. The cases of Mexico, Ecuador, and República Bolivariana de Venezuela are quite illustrative in this respect. Given the nations' impressive oil resources, and macroeconomic and financial policies with incentives for quick spending, most budget transfers became highly discretionary allocations to subnational governments that were mostly guided by clear-cut partisan considerations

---

2. Latin America's oligopolistic land tenure is another perfect example of such barriers to entry for the majority of peasants. On styles of clientelism and corporatism, see the contributions in Malloy (1977); on economic policymaking and its underlying causes, see, for example, the contributions in Dornbusch and Edwards (1991), as well as those in Larraín and Selowski (1991).

and political favoritism. Such structures clearly set up the incentives for overall local development, encouraging both national and local decision-makers to become engaged in politically determined bargaining processes and clientelistic rent allocation in a search for either political support or selective political integration. The same system, consequently, set strong disincentives for any kind of horizontal efforts to mobilize resources at the local level and to manage scarce resources effectively.[3]

Similarly, intergovernmental fiscal relations often allowed highly discretionary allocations and mechanisms in many countries, such as special funding, which motivated spending and rising deficits at all levels of government instead of imposing fiscal discipline or maintaining budgetary control. Not only would such measures of fiscal discipline have led to various kinds of popular protest at the local level; the system simply provided little incentive—that is, no reward—to behave with fiscal soundness or to improve the tax base to finance better municipal services. Some mayors and municipal council members tended to avoid major reforms in their municipalities in order to maintain party support and assure their own careers. And because municipal laws at that time—for instance, in Colombia—did not provide for reelection, there was little stimulus, other than intrinsic motivation, for municipal leaders to become committed to issues of development within their jurisdictions (Ecuador's mayors are an example). As a result, local administrative performance was invariably poor, with local administrations, one might say, "failing successfully." In a nutshell, there were few incentives for policymakers to become overly interested in local governance and support innovations prior to the mid 1980s.

INTERTWINED ECONOMIC AND POLITICAL REFORMS. The scenario changed dramatically with the advent of decentralization, democratization, and economic reform. Pressures for effective political liberalization and democracy on the one hand, and economic liberalization and strengthening market forces on the other hand, led to a collapse of the traditional structures and to a new role of the state in Latin America. Campbell (2003) has stressed

---

3. Clearly, one needs to add some other factors that affect subnational economies and politics, such as geography and ethnicity. We have chosen to focus on the specific set of incentives and disincentives guiding intergovernmental relationships, similar to the contributions in Burki, Perry, and Dillinger (1999, chapters 2 and 3), and in Burki and Perry (2000, chapter 2). Recent work by Giugale and Webb (2000, chapters 3–5), on intergovernmental reform in Mexico stresses precisely these macro dimensions.

the importance of political power shifts during the "quiet revolution" with electoral reform and the move to local democracy.[4] Grassroots organizations helped usher in such change, providing alternative channels for those articulating various choices (see Reilly 1994). All the case studies in this volume, in essence, reaffirm the positive repercussions of stronger citizen participation. Policymakers played strong roles in some cases (República Bolivariana de Venezuela and Mendoza); nongovernmental organizations (NGOs) or even international organizations played important roles in others (Nicaragua and Tijuana). In each case, the result was public sector reform. But in order for these reforms to become a broader phenomenon, change was needed in the larger political system—and this would eventually provide room to maneuver at the local level and incentives for local action and innovation.

The opening of the political and electoral system in Colombia, for example, reversed a long tradition of centralism. A new government changed direction, transferring social service delivery to the local level and opening up the rigid political appointment system to local electoral choice (with the goal of addressing the country's critical security problems). Similarly, in República Bolivariana de Venezuela and other countries in South America, active local governments have changed the responsiveness of local administration and the quality of services provided, often dramatically. Bottom-up pressure toward participation (smartly used by local governments, as we have seen) and a keen central government interest in regaining legitimacy and stabilizing the countries politically through a series of decentralization policies met at a crucial point. These two trends complemented and reinforced each other.

But decentralization and democratization were only part of the picture. Economic reform helped to decompose the bases of centralized, bureaucratic, and rent-seeking states and open up new paths for subnational development. The fiscal crises of the Latin American states led to stabilization and adjustment policies and, eventually, to a series of reforms that did away with the traditional mechanisms of financing local government. These reforms included a thorough overhaul of intergovernmental fiscal relationships, which aimed to regain transparency, predictability, and fairness of transfers as well as to establish new revenue and expenditure authorities. Although the implementation was far from satisfactory and, at times,

---

4. See also Blair (2000) with a cross-country study on the same participation-accountability nexus.

suffered from opportunistic behavior of subnational governments (see, for example, Burki, Perry, and Dillinger 1999, chapter 3), such reforms have, in many cases, provided new resources and incentives for policymakers to engage more actively in subnational development. The private sector, which underwent important development beginning in the late 1980s, provided another push for public sector reforms at all levels. Cumulative political and economic reforms thus provided new incentives to act—and innovate— in municipal, provincial, regional, and state governments.

INTERNATIONALIZATION AND GLOBALIZATION. The introduction of economic reform broke up another monopoly—that of access by local actors to international information, markets, and technology. While Latin American nation-states and their governments largely dominated external relations for decades, trade liberalization and privatization helped private sectors and citizens gain access to international high technology and services and, incrementally, to modern tools for information. Openness to trade, in fact, was accompanied by openness to ideas and modern communication, which spread quickly by fax and later over the Internet. Such openness, in addition, has encouraged subnational governments to get prepared for, and attract, new investment. This has coincided with strategies of modern transnational businesses to seek "region states" for their strategic investments.[5] In essence, local private sectors and citizens were able to examine reforms in other countries and constructively press their governments to adopt desirable policies and improve services accordingly (Fuhr 2001). Although these scenarios are optimistic, they are supporting factors and need to be dealt with carefully case by case. They assisted to some extent in the privatization of ports in República Bolivariana de Venezuela and the referendum of Tijuana, and they clearly played an important role in Curitiba's (and Paraná's) successful economic development.

Two groups of international actors become important in this setting. First, bilateral and multilateral aid agencies, by vigorously supporting political

---

5. Ohmae (1993), for example, points out that globally operating corporations no longer select their locations solely based on country-specific criteria. Instead, they increasingly consider particular conditions within subnational units and regions. As Kanter (1995, p. 154) argues, education and continued training of the work force, sound local administration, and reliable public-private sector partnerships at the subnational level become key criteria for many of today's foreign investments, thus encouraging in a certain way the development of "region states" (Ohmae 1993).

and economic liberalization through the provision of new concepts and resources, gave decisionmakers incentives to embark on reforms. Second, the new openness in Latin America boosted networking among subnational stakeholders and actors concerned in local politics.

In most of our case studies, sustained reform depended on decisive public relation efforts with the outside world, demonstrating good practices to other countries of the region and overseas. Decisionmakers began to link themselves to international NGO constituencies that helped them to manage reforms and gain support within their own environment. During the 1990s, the International Union of Local Authorities' activities and regional mayors conferences helped spread the merits of local reform and good practice in local governance (with Porto Alegre, Brazil, assuming a prominent role in this respect). This provided new incentives for others to follow suit and innovate.

The Smaller Picture: Reviewing Micro Factors
For Subnational Innovations

All the cases documented in this book are idiosyncratic in terms of the conditions and circumstances of their creation. But they also share a variety of features, or at least a family resemblance, in three specific phases of the cycle of innovations: origins, launch, and dissemination (Campbell 1996). Table 11.1 summarizes this information for five of the cases. Except where noted, the generalizations made here hold for all cases documented in this study.

LEADERSHIP IS KEY. As observed in related literature (for example, Hopkins 1994; Leeuw, Rist, and Sonnichsen 1994), a champion or visionary is found behind virtually every innovation.The Latin American cases are no exception. A champion—whether an author, entrepreneur, or leader—is able to read what is possible at a given moment, understand what the public wants, and visualize a new way of doing things. Above all, the champion is able to convert this vision into reality.

Leadership is crucial to innovation. It is hard to imagine the successful beginnings, let alone positive outcomes, of the innovations documented in this book without the driving force of leadership. Local leaders such as Tasso Geraisati and Ciro Gomes in Ceara, Hector Osuna in Tijuana, Jaime Lerner in Curitiba, and Octavio Bordón in Mendoza played the role of provocateur, challenging and inspiring citizens to see how a venture might be formulated. Leaders are on the lookout for good ideas, and they find or invent ways to offset the risks of failure. More than a few of the innovations described in this book were actually adaptations of experiences observed

Table 11-1. *Features of Selected Urban Innovations, Latin America and the Caribbean*

Feature	Mendoza	Curitiba
Context of origins	Political renewal; cholera	Congestion; oil crisis
Conceptual model	Previous program (*ahorros previos*— prior savings)	Buses as underground railways
Who acted	Governor	Mayors
Outside help	None	Help in later phases
Preconditions	Prior experience; political leadership	Urban plan, wide streets; commitment to sustain land use
Launch	Small, contained pilot	Single axis, large re-designed buses
Evolution	Limited expansion of basic concept	Extensive elaboration of basic concept
Next steps	Longer-term credits; market finance; bigger projects	Electrification of bus-ways, wider use in Brazil
Dissemination	Limited impact on other provinces; municipal governments alert to it	Moderate; many Brazilian and Latin American cities have adopted pieces
Replication	Good potential	Good potential; but not fully realized (need for land-use controls and dedicated lanes)

Source: Authors.

elsewhere; for instance, the referendum and betterment levy introduced in Tijuana drew inspiration from local governments in the neighboring state of California in the United States.

Dedicated leaders and champions have existed in the last two centuries in Latin America, but mostly at a national level. Given the macro picture

Tijuana	Cali	Manizales
Floods; opposition government	Historical identity	Decentralization restored democracy
Betterment levy	Company town	French institute
Mayor	Mayors; private sector	Mayors
Hired consultants	No	Outsiders recruited
Cadastre records; spending reform	History of commitment; decentralization of authority	Electoral and municipal reforms created need for professionalization
Full-blown program	Revolving management in parks and planning	Founding of institute
Revised to smaller programs, different forms of participation	Gradual elaboration and extensive application	Elaboration and integration with career plan and pay
Borrow and implement	Tighter linkages with regional and national development schemes	Integrate with hiring criteria and career; application to other public authorities
Via municipal associations	Ideas spreading to other cities in Colombia	Contributed to reform in other cities
Good potential (for referendum and communications)	Possible for selected applications	Good potential

mentioned in the previous section, the opportunities for local decision-makers to become local heroes were limited, because there were few economic or political rewards for becoming overly active and interested in an agenda of local change. In these cases, elected local leaders acted in an environment of larger imperatives, such as the Argentine political reform that was felt in Mendoza in the early 1990s, or the wave of political renewal in Colombia that affected Manizales, or the local floods in Tijuana. Even the fuel crisis of the 1980s helped give the Curitiba transport system extra momentum.

As indicated in half of the case studies, a supporting environment of economic and political reform, or a crisis of the central state—fiscal, natural, or political—is key for providing a powerful impetus to political, business, and societal leaders to embark on local reforms jointly with local constituencies. Hence, it seems to be leadership plus a conducive macro environment that provides a new set of incentives and triggers reform, rather than leadership alone as often stressed in the literature. To be sure, local leaders in many cases were interested in advancing their political careers to the national level. In some cases this might even have been their most important objective. But, unlike the situation that existed before the mid 1980s, they were able to take advantage of an environment of power sharing and democratization to prove their abilities in a local context and enjoy the spotlight before moving up. Engaging in local politics now has rewards.[6] And, once such local structures were shown to work (in Mendoza and Curitiba, for example), professional staff and civil servants became motivated to innovate creatively as well.

LEARNING FROM OTHERS AND NETWORKING. The study revealed that mayors learn from each other more than from any other single source. They may get ideas from afar (such as through the Internet and by going to conferences), from printed works, or from interacting with technical experts. But assistance from independent, foreign, or external sources, although sometimes important as a means to ensure the legitimacy of a new venture, usually follows consultation with other elected leaders.[7] Furthermore, the seminars held in conjunction with the study revealed—for instance in Porto Alegre's participatory budgeting and Mendoza's neighborhood infrastructure, as well as in an El Salvadoran education program—that leaders learn better from oral rather than written communications, and best from each other. Mayors tend to be doers, not academics, and they can go far with

---

6. In terms of the political motivation of leaders, one might add that, in a specific point of time, intrinsic motivation for change and innovation (as derived from the person's own values) and extrinsic motivation (prompted by the outside world) go hand in hand, creating a more robust momentum for change.

7. This pattern is analyzed similarly in the literature; see, for example, the contributions in Clark (1994) and in Leeuw, Rist, and Sonnichsen (1994).

visually demonstrable examples. Some experiences also show that mayors are especially effective as retransmitters of ideas. The rapidly expanding computer technology of the 1990s greatly supported such mechanisms of horizontal communication (Fuhr 2001). Interestingly, such developments resemble features of the late 1950s when Latin American peasant movements and political protests similarly benefited from better communications—in that case, the introduction of transistor radios.

LONG-TERM COMMITMENT AND TRUST. Local government leaders must be able to convincingly articulate commitment to sustain public trust. This is particularly difficult in Latin America, where short mayoral administrations are the rule. Often, continuity in trust is achieved through periodic doses of direct contact with neighborhoods participating in a project. The length of such direct contact varied in the cases presented in this book. Jaime Lerner of Curitiba sustained a consistent vision during three non-sequential terms as mayor and then during his time as governor—a span of more than 20 years. Officials in Cali have the longest track record of direct contact with residents participating in projects, dating to the 1920s. Tijuana accomplished a great deal in only six years. In other cases (such as Curitiba, Mendoza, and Ceará), mayors and governors were able to pass on their initiatives to former colleagues, thereby maintaining momentum in state and municipal reform.

CRITICAL ROLE OF THE MIDDLE CLASS. In Cali, Ceará, Curitiba, Manizales, and Mendoza, strong middle-class involvement proved to be an important ingredient in reform experiments, and it helped trigger innovations. The middle class played a dual role: leaders came from middle-class backgrounds and the reforms were carried forward by middle-class interests at the local level. In Mendoza, for example, even though one of the innovations was aimed primarily at the poor, the comparatively advanced socio-economic composition of the area helped push development of the city and province ahead of other comparable subnational governments. The success of leaders from this particular social strata was obviously facilitated by the reemergence of the middle class during democratization and the turn toward deregulation and liberalization.[8]

---

8. See Huntington (1991, pp. 66–68) and the contributions in Diamond and others (1997, vol. 1), in particular, Adan Przeworski and others on "The Middle Classes and Democratization."

The point to stress here is that, much as was the case with Latin American peasant movements, the better-off constituencies have been the ones to advocate successfully for reform agendas and mobilize local populations (Fuhr 1986). Leaders reflected the middle-class interests in economic and political integration, formed new alliances within local environments, and expected political support from the middle class to advance their political careers. Recent subnational reforms and innovations may thus have been somewhat hidden, but were, at least in part, middle-class endeavors.

APPLICATION OF MODELS TO THE LOCAL CONTEXT. Each innovation has some sort of a model—a precedent, a nearby example, or a visually concrete scheme—as a starting point. But innovators also need high-quality, up-to-date information about their immediate environment to see the connection between an inspirational idea and local circumstances. For example, land use and cadastre information were decisive in both Curitiba and Tijuana. This suggests that cities can provide the basic building blocks of innovation by maintaining basic data.

Scale and Launch: Simple Beginning, Gradual Elaboration

The origin of complex, multigenerational experiences, like the first-time innovations reported in these cases, tends to be simple. Usually the innovation begins with a single step that is clearly visible and has broad public support. No experience is more illustrative in this respect than in Curitiba, where a fundamental concept—controlling automobile use and giving buses some of the speed and volume of underground railways—was extended in a dozen directions over a 15-year period. From today's perspective, the innovations in Curitiba appear complex and impossible to replicate. But they began with a single conceptual change, based on the premise that the city could control automobile use by controlling land use. Many cities already know this premise is true but cannot yet find a way to get started.

Where this pattern of small and simple first was broken, the innovation faltered. This is illustrated by Tijuana's Urban Action Program (*Plan de Activación Urbana*, or PAU), which had a wide scope. Although errors in tactics and design may have contributed, the downfall of the PAU was not due to a bad idea or poor execution. Rather, the problem is that large undertakings create more institutional friction and are more vulnerable to outside forces, like the monetary and fiscal crises that swept Mexico and overturned the PAU.

The scale of operations is critical, especially for neighborhood works. The small scale of the Mendoza infrastructure program, which was implemented block-by-block, helping 200 to 300 families at a time, facilitated sustained personal contact between program officials and leaders and hence made legitimacy easier to achieve. This type of small-scale implementation was also seen in Nicaragua's PRODEL program, as well as in Conchalí and in Tijuana's Manos program. Small-scale works accommodate, and sometimes even foster, a sense of partnership between neighborhood residents and program officials. Increasing the face-to-face contact between neighbors engaged in a project tends to heighten mutual responsibility, and this, in turn, is key to managing the risks for community members who undertake credit obligations. Finally, small projects yield results faster.

The cases also suggest that launching in a harbor—that is, protecting new ventures from political and social reactions—helps foster success. In Mendoza, the harbor proved to be an office in a provincial ministry; in Manizales, a small-scale training program supported the innovation; and in Valledupar and Conchalí, local infrastructure programs were started in only a few neighborhoods.[9]

Dissemination and Sustained Efforts to Reform

SOCIAL ORGANIZATIONS AS BUILDING BLOCKS. A corollary to the aspects of a strong middle class, simplicity, and protection in innovative start-ups is that basic social building blocks are needed at the local level to advance common purposes. In addition to effective partisan politics and political alliances, the reforms in Mendoza and Manizales, and also in Valledupar, Conchalí, and Porto Alegre, relied on the organizational strengthening of grassroots, often single-purpose, organizations that were gradually mobilized to move beyond the objectives of their founding. Grassroots interests have been moving forces behind participatory innovations, and in many cases they become the organizing principle around which community efforts are mobilized.[10] The community organizations in Mendoza typically

---

9. Other cases, like El Salvador's education program (included in the original sample of case studies), expanded very quickly, building on a basic innovation piloted in a few rural districts. See Meza (1997) and Government of El Salvador (1997).

10. Evidence from our case studies indicates that within such grassroots organizations, the middle class, again, plays important roles in leadership, conceptual development, and financial support.

involved 200 to 300 families living in a contiguous neighborhood, but they also involved as few as 5 families and as many as 4,000. Alliances between governments and grassroots organizations, and appropriate arrangements to deal with complexity, were found in Conchalí, Tijuana, and Porto Alegre.

COMMUNICATIONS AND PUBLIC MARKETING. A common factor in the innovations was the use by local leaders of various public communication devices to define the ideas, give them an identity, reduce uncertainties raised by the opposition, and persuade the public and other political leaders that the innovations were worthwhile. Private firms understand the value of advertising and consumer awareness in marketing products, but public agencies generally do not, except in electoral campaigns. The successful cases in this study are made conspicuous by the quality of publicity generated to win over the public. Too often, public officials are not cognizant of the quality of their message and are unaware of ways to improve communications with the public. Local leaders, like donors, are rarely willing to pay what seem to be the high costs of strengthening this critical communications linkage between support of reforms and their execution.

PARTNERSHIPS AND SOCIAL PROCESSES. Participatory arrangements were needed not only to launch and implement reforms, but also for sustainability. Our cases demonstrate that local governments often face enormous challenges in ensuring that reforms are carried on by subsequent governments. Even without a change of administrations, policymakers embarking on reform often face a disillusionment, a staged slowdown, or a serious backlash after initial success. Curitiba's Lerner, for example, faced serious opposition before and after the opening of the first pedestrian mall. Sometimes there is even a reversal, with reforms fully abandoned. For instance, the assumption of responsibility for primary education in the state of Lara in República Bolivariana de Venezuela, which might have been a case study of innovation, in fact collapsed after one year under pressure from teachers' unions over wage demands.

Many factors can bring about the partial or total collapse of local innovations, such as bad management (overreaching) at the top, low professional capacity of local governments to deal with new procedures,and ambitious local leaders who want to advance their careers instead of focusing on local development. Sometimes local leaders are unable to change the contextual circumstances in which they find themselves. Local decisionmakers and staff genuinely interested in maintaining reforms should avoid fast-moving "fireworks"—that is, a series of spectacular and rapid changes implemented within such a short period of time. Such an approach diminishes the chances for sustainability. Instead, innovations require timely and gradual steps, including an agreement on, and phased introduction of, new rules guiding local policymaking and local governance and, of course, the successful replacement of previous patterns of governance. The introduction of budgetary changes in Mendoza illustrates the importance of this slow and steady approach. Only if the initial stage is completed effectively do innovations seem to get locked in and become a part of the regular procedures of subnational administrations.

Although more analytical work needs to be done in this area, our case studies reveal the many delicate processes affecting innovation. Unlike traditional organization sociology and management sciences, institutionalization seems to depend on political and personal dynamics, and on the incentives that spark the impetus for change, rather than merely on consulting expertise, a new technology, or development finance. As the case of Mendoza demonstrates quite clearly, administrative innovations need to be embedded effectively within a proper administrative environment, and a rule change within one sector (budgeting by results) requires—to a certain extent—rule changes in other sectors (flexible human resource management). The social foundations and sociopolitical processes mentioned earlier help both to kick start and maintain subnational reforms, some of which have been explored in the analysis of policy change and policy implementation at the national level.[11]

Local institutionalization, as is the case with institutionalization generally, is, to a large extent, a sociopolitical process in which new rules are formulated by stakeholders and actors—some of which are new as well. Such new rules may lead in time to new institutional arrangements at the subnational level and, eventually, to new subnational institutions. What is most important is how such rules are made and who participates in the rulemaking practice. Our cases illustrate the wide variety of modalities for the effective inclusion of stakeholders. It seems clear that the more participatory and inclusive the design of participatory processes, the more likely the new rules will be accepted by participating actors, and the better the chances for repeated interactions.

---

11. See the broader literature on the political dimensions of managing economic policy reform, beginning with studies such as Nelson and Waterbury (1989) and Haggard and Webb (1994), and the literature on policy implementation in less developed countries, in particular Grindle and Thomas (1991) and Grindle (1999).

Citizen orientation and participation are thus not goals in themselves, nor is partnering with private sectors. Rather, these factors are instrumental to success. They are costly, and they require time, talent, and consensus on all sides of the bargaining table. The support for participatory arrangements, however, is key not only for sustainability of local innovations, but for effective and long-term institutional development. Partnering with the poor was vital for the provision of low-cost social infrastructure in Mendoza, as was partnering with small businesses for innovations in local transport and infrastructure development in Curitiba and Cali. The support of both citizens and the private sector is required for changing the rules of the game on a sustained basis.

Employing a stronger actor-centered institutional analysis has helped explain these developments and, by extension, sheds light on innovations in local governments in Latin America (Mayntz and Scharpf 1995; Scharpf 1997). As our analysis has shown, innovations beginning in the mid 1980s were part of a broader public sector change in the countries studied. Furthermore, the innovations emerged from a dual set of new political and economic incentives at the macro and micro levels. Our analysis has stressed the importance of local sociopolitical processes in innovations and institutional reform, and thus highlighted new options for local governments to foster such processes. The study also helps to open a debate on the proper role of international assistance, and on appropriate instruments to assist in the innovation and reform of local government. Shifting the arena for public sector reform to the local level will help fill a gap in the drive for better governance and management in Latin America.

References

Blair, Harry. 2000. "Participation and Accountability at the Periphery. Democratic Local Governance in Six Countries." *World Development* 28(1): 21–39.

Burki, Shahid Javed, and Guillermo Perry, eds. 2000. *Annual World Bank Conference on Development in Latin America and the Caribbean 1999. Decentralization and Accountability of the Public Sector.* Washington, D.C.: World Bank.

Burki, Shahid Javed, Guillermo Perry, and William Dillinger. 1999. *Beyond the Center; Decentralizing the State.* Washington, D.C.: World Bank.

Campbell, Tim. 1996. "Innovation and Risk Taking: The Engine of Reform in LAC." World Bank Discussion Paper 357, Washington, D.C.

———. 2003. *The Quiet Revolution.* Pittsburgh, Pa.: University of Pittsburgh Press.

Clark, Terry N., ed. 1994. *Urban Innovation: Creative Strategies for Turbulent Times.* London: Sage Publications.

Dornbusch, Rüdiger, and Sebastian Edwards, eds. 1991. *The Macroeconomics of Populism in Latin America.* Chicago, Ill.: University of Chicago Press.

Diamond, Larry, M. F. Plattner, Yun-han Chu, and Hung-mao Tien, eds. 1997. *Consolidating the Third Wave Democracies* (2 vols.) Baltimore, Md.: Johns Hopkins University Press.

Fuhr, Harald. 1986. "The State, Cooperatives and Peasants' Participation in Peru." *Land Reform, Land Settlement and Cooperatives* (1)2: 1–18.

———. 2001. "Constructive Pressures and Incentives to Reform: Globalization and Its Impacts on Public Sector Performance and Governance in Developing Countries." In David Hulme and Charles Polidano, eds., *Governance Reform in Developing Countries.* Special edition of *Public Management Review* (3)3: 419–43.

Giugale, Marcelo M., and Steven B. Webb, eds. 2000. *Achievements and Challenges of Fiscal Decentralization. Lessons from Mexico.* Washington, D.C.: World Bank.

Government of El Salvador. 1997. *EDUCO. A Learning and Teaching Experiment.* San Salvador: Ministry of Education.

Grindle, Merilee S. 1999. "In Quest of the Political: The Political Economy of Development Policy Making." Center for International Development Working Paper 17, Harvard University, Cambridge, Mass.

Grindle, Merilee S., and John W. Thomas. 1991. *Public Choices and Policy Change. The Political Economy of Reform in Developing Countries.* Baltimore, Md.: The Johns Hopkins University Press.

Haggard, Stephan, and Steven B. Webb. 1994. *Voting for Reform. Democracy, Political Liberalization, and Economic Adjustment.* Washington, D.C.: World Bank.

Hopkins, Elwood. 1994. "The Life Cycle of Urban Innovations," vol I. Urban Management Program Working Paper Series. World Bank, Washington, D.C.

Kanter, Rosabeth Moss. 1995. "Thriving Locally in the Global Economy." *Harvard Business Review* (September–October): 151–60.

Larraín, Felipe, and Marcelo Selowski, eds. 1991. *The Public Sector and the Latin American Crisis.* San Francisco, Calif.: ICS Press.

Leeuw, Frans, Ray Rist, and Richard Sonnichsen, eds. 1994. *Can Governments Learn? Comparative Perspectives on Evaluation and Organizational Learning.* New Brunswick, N.J.: Transaction Publishers.

Malloy, James M., ed. 1977. *Authoritarianism and Corporatism in Latin America.* Pittsburgh, Pa.: University of Pittsburgh Press.

Mayntz, Renate, and Fritz W. Scharpf. 1995. *"Der Ansatz des akteurzentrierten Institutionalismus."* In Renate Mayntz and Fritz W. Scharpf, eds., *Gesellschaftliche Selbstregelung und politische Steuerung.* Frankfurt am Main: Campus.

Meza, Darlyn. 1997. *Descentralización educativa, organización y manejo de las escuelas a nivel local. El caso de El Salvador.* Washington, D.C.: World Bank/Latin America and the Caribbean Human and Social Development Group.

Nelson, Joan M., and John Waterbury. 1989. *Fragile Coalitions: The Politics of Economic Adjustment*. Washington, D.C.: Overseas Development Council.

Ohmae, Kenichi. 1993. "The Rise of the Region State." *Foreign Affairs* 72(2): 78–87.

Reilly, Charles. 1994. *Nuevas Politicas Urbanas. Las ONG y los gobiernos municipales en la democratización latinoamericana*. Washington, D.C.: Inter-American Foundation.

Scharpf, Fritz W. 1997. *Games Real Actors Play: Actor-Centered Institutionalism in Policy Research. Theoretical Lenses on Public Policy*. Boulder, Colo: Westview Press.

Simon, Klaus, Albrecht Stockmayer, and Harald Fuhr, eds. 1993. *Subsidiarität in der Entwicklungszusammenarbeit.: Dezentralisierung und Verwaltungsreformen zwischen Strukturanpassung und Selbsthilfe*. Baden-Baden, Germany: Nomos Verlagsgesellschaft.

Véliz, Claudio. 1980. *The Centralist Tradition of Latin America*. Princeton, N.J.: Princeton University Press.

Véliz, Claudio, ed. 1965. *Obstacles to Change in Latin America*. London: Oxford University Press.

World Bank. 1997. *The State in a Changing World. World Development Report 1997*. New York: Oxford University Press.

———. 1999. *Entering the 21st Century. World Development Report 1999–2000*. New York: Oxford University Press.